MASCULINE AND FEMININE

GENDER ROLES
OVER THE LIFE CYCLE

MASCULINE AND FEMININE

GENDER ROLES OVER THE LIFE CYCLE

SECOND EDITION

Marie Richmond-Abbott
Eastern Michigan University

McGraw-Hill, Inc.

New York   St. Louis   San Francisco   Auckland   Bogotá   Caracas
Lisbon   London   Madrid   Mexico   Milan   Montreal   New Delhi
Paris   San Juan   Singapore   Sydney   Tokyo   Toronto

Masculine and Feminine: Gender Roles over the Life Cycle

1 2 3 4 5 6 7 8 9 0 DOC DOC 9 0 9 8 7 6 5 4 3 2 1

ISBN 0-07-052357-6

This book was set in Palatino by The Clarinda Company.
The editors were Phillip A. Butcher and Sylvia Shepard;
the production supervisor was Louise Karam.
The cover was designed by Wanda Siedlecka.
The photo editor was Debra P. Hershkowitz.
Project supervision was done by The Total Book.
R. R. Donnelley & Sons Company was printer and binder.

Library of Congress Cataloging-in-Publication Data

Richmond-Abbott, Marie.
    Masculine and feminine: gender roles over the life cycle / Marie
Richmond-Abbott.—2nd ed.
        p.   cm.
    Includes bibliographical references and index.
    ISBN 0-07-052357-6
    1. Sex role.   2. Life cycle, Human.   I. Title.
HQ1075.R52   1992
305.3—dc20   91-16340

About the Author

MARIE RICHMOND-ABBOTT is a professor of sociology and women's studies at Eastern Michigan University, where she teaches courses in gender roles
and family. Her degrees are from Florida State, the University of Miami, and
Duke University. Her publications include books on immigration, adaptation,
and family structure among Cubans in the United States and an edited book
dealing with the American woman. Recent articles have dealt with gender-
role attitudes and behavior in single-parent families and gender roles as they
affect life-satisfaction and happiness among the elderly. She is married and
has two children.

For Hank, Kim, and Charlie—for the second time

Contents

Preface

When I wrote this book, I wanted to do three things that were not being done in gender-role textbooks. The first was to attempt a more equal balance in discussions of masculine- and feminine-stereotyped roles in this society. The second was to present a life cycle perspective of gender roles and show how gender-role socialization continues while gender-role prescriptions change in adult years. The third was to include material on certain groups whose gender roles deviate somewhat from the American cultural norm. I believed that these groups, such as single-parent families, remarried families, and black families, could tell us a great deal about changing roles and the possibilities and probabilities for different kinds of behavior in the future.

While writing the second edition, I realized that the intervening years had changed my focus but that my problems remained the same in many ways. Today there are many gender-role textbooks on the market, and many of them include material on men. I found it very difficult when I wrote the first edition to find quality material about men's roles. The original literature was largely anecdotal, and I had to search through the literature on sports, health, aging, and other areas to find relevant information. While there is more information today, I still do not find the hard base of research that one sees in studies about women's roles. In this edition as well, I have found the material on men localized and sparse, not covering all areas. It is still difficult to discuss the male role in some areas because it is the dominant or normative role. It is difficult to discuss variations from the dominant norm and not just restate what most people already know about cultural stereotypes.

My problems in the second area were different. There is a wealth of information about adult socialization; the problem is sorting through the mounds of data to find what is relevant. In most cases little has changed: Details have been added to the life cycle picture, but the basic framework remains the same.

The objective of including information about various groups that might be in the vanguard of change was in many ways more difficult than before. While there was new information on gay couples, single parents, and the aged, there was very little new research on working-class families and black families.

I had a fourth objective in writing this second edition. In the years since the first edition, I have become more convinced about the overriding importance of institutions which perpetuate stereotypes and control gender-role behavior. While this book still emphasizes socialization over the life cycle, I wanted to show that societies initiate and perpetuate the kinds of socialization they want. Socialization is only a reflection of the larger society. What does it serve women, for example, to be socialized to be achievement-oriented and competitive if they are kept out of sports, academia, and rewarding occupations? Does it help men to learn to express their emotions and to be nurturant if the corporate world continues to punish that kind of behavior? I want to emphasize that societal values and institutions give us the kind of gender roles we have and that the institutions of society must change if we are to socialize our children in a different manner. Obviously, institutions are established and perpetuated by those who have power. This second edition therefore deals in more detail with the issues of power and control.

Writing a book that attempts to describe the roles of men and women in our culture has other problems. As a woman, it is tempting for me to emphasize the problems of stereotypical women's roles over those of men and to push for change that will help women. I have tried to be evenhanded, but I am aware that I have not succeeded. I can only restate to the reader what I say to my gender-role classes: "To be profemale does not mean that one is anti-male." Male-dominated institutions have been my source of information about stereotypes and control of behavior that inhibit the choices of both men and women.

As I wrote this edition, I was aware of another problem that had not been obvious to me a few years earlier: Androgyny may not be a solution to our gender-role problems even in the realm of socialization. For a longer discussion of the issue of androgyny, I refer the reader to Chapter 1. Here I would simply like to say that I hope we can move beyond a state where "masculine and feminine elements are present, accepted and accessible within the individual" to a point where "it suggests a spectrum upon which human beings choose their place without regard to propriety or custom [or their sex]." I hope we can move to a point where all kinds of characteristics will be equally valued and the words "masculine" and "feminine" will have no function when one is referring to traits or behavior.

Obviously, a prerequisite for this is that there cannot be male-dominated or female-dominated institutions but that human values will predominate and all persons will have equal access to high status and positions of power regardless of biological sex. This is obviously an ideal state and not one which is easily attained. To get to this point there will have to be simultaneous changes in socialization, values, and institutions.

One of the major tasks of this book is to document the assertion that traditional gender roles are limiting to human potential and that androgyny or some form of transcendence of gender roles is a healthier and more productive state for the individual and the culture. To that end I have tried to explain the reasons why we are socialized into traditional roles and examine our institutions so that we can see the sources of our oppression.

Chapter 1 introduces the concept of gender roles and examines some of the assumptions about such roles. It also looks at how gender roles combine with biological sex, status, and power. I have attempted to show that cultural roles are deeply embedded in our cultural history and reinforced by societal institutions. Chapter 2 discusses the historical and cross-cultural roots of the different status accorded to each gender. Chapter 3 examines controversial questions about physical differences and similarities between the genders, with an emphasis on the paucity of differences and the extent of similarity. Chapters 4 and 5 trace the mechanisms by which children are socialized into traditional roles: parents' expectations and behavior, toys and play, books, media, and school. Chapters 6 and 7 describe the adolescent years with their emphasis on establishing a mature individual identity and the convenient but limiting definition of such an identity that traditional roles give the adolescent. I have tried to point out in these chapters the difficulty young people have in deviating from traditional roles; it is difficult for them to establish an identity approved by parents, peers, and the culture, much less to risk charting the unknown territory of self-knowledge and different behavior.

The last section describes various institutions that shape our behaviors with their norms and sanctions. Chapter 8 discusses the American family and how this institution encourages certain gender roles with stereotypes such as "provider" and "child raiser." This chapter also looks at how power relationships and roles have changed in recent years. Chapter 9 discusses current family variations. As we look at dual-career families, single-parent families, homosexual families, black families, working-class families, and the like, we see different definitions of gender roles. These families may be the vanguard of gender-role change in this country. Chapter 10 looks at how religion, science, and medicine shape our norms and control our behaviors. Chapters 11 and 12 describe how the economic and political institutions of our country have reinforced traditional gender roles and examine the changes taking place in institutional structures. Chapter 13 examines the possibilities for moving beyond traditional gender roles in the future.

As I wrote this manuscript, I became more aware of the interconnection between individual socialization and behavior, the constraints of societal institutions, and the pervasive power of cultural values. I am convinced that initiating change in one area without initiating changes in all three is of little use. Since writing the first edition, I have also become a little cynical. As I have delved more into stratification and power issues, I have come to realize how difficult change will be.

At the same time, I am even more convinced of the need to initiate such change, to move beyond stereotyped gender roles as we have known them. If we can free ourselves from the behavior and social roles assigned to us because of biological sex, we will have greatly increased the possibility that each person will be able to realize his or her individual potential.

McGraw-Hill and the author would like to thank the following reviewers for their many helpful comments and suggestions: Jacqueline Boles, Georgia State University; Pat Keith, Iowa State University; Barbara Risman, North Carolina State University; and Joan Spade, Lehigh University.

Marie Richmond-Abbott

MASCULINE AND FEMININE

GENDER ROLES
OVER THE LIFE CYCLE

Part I

PERSPECTIVES ON GENDER

Chapter 1

Looking at Gender: An Introduction—Sex Roles, Gender Roles, and Power

. . . but this is fixt
As are the roots of earth and base of all;
Man for the field and woman for the hearth;
Man for the sword and for the needle she;
Man with the head and woman with the heart;
Man to command and woman to obey;
All else confusion. . . .

                —TENNYSON, "THE PRINCESS"

People have long been preoccupied with what it means to be male and what it means to be female. In all cultures, including ours, being a man or a woman is not limited to one's biological sex. Being a man means that one is also likely to be "masculine," and being a woman means that one is also likely to be "feminine." Thus, not only do we have a gender or sex (male or female), we also have a gender role (masculine or feminine). Emotions and occupations tend to be characterized as masculine or feminine. We may act in certain ways because we have been socialized to be feminine; others may expect a certain type of behavior from us because we are male and thus are supposedly masculine.

Almost everyone is concerned about fitting into the model of masculinity or femininity that the culture mandates. We may also be aware that ideas about what is masculine or feminine go far beyond the effects of individual socialization. These ideas may determine not only what work each sex does but also who runs the major institutions in society. If you think about the most important officials in the country and the people who make the most money, what do you notice? Most of these persons are men. We may wonder, then, why and how sex and gender roles seem to be influential in getting positions of power and being successful. However, before we look at how people become masculine or feminine and how this influences their chances in life, we must define what we mean by sex role and gender role and examine their linkages to power in this society.

THE LINKAGE OF SEX ROLES AND GENDER ROLES

Although the terms **"sex roles"** and **"gender roles"** are often used interchangeably, there is an important difference between them. The term "sex roles" has come to mean behaviors determined by biological sex, such as menstruation, erection, and seminal ejaculation. The term "gender roles" has come to mean entirely socially created expectations of masculine and feminine behavior. These expectations are initiated and perpetuated by the institutions and values of a particular society. Thus, bearing and nursing children may be a feminine sex role, but raising children is a gender role. The people who raise children and the things that are done with them are defined by a particular culture and the power structure in that culture.

While the sexes are far more similar than different, early research on male and female characteristics tended to concentrate on biological differences between the sexes. These differences were seen as proof that the sexes have different and supposedly unchangeable functions; for example, women bear children, and so they have to raise them. Early research often argued that physical differences reveal that women have great biological limitations and a similarly limited role in life. Even a writer such as Herbert Spencer argued in 1879 that because women bear children, they have little energy left over for intellectual achievement and their education should be restricted so that they do not become fatigued. In 1968, Broverman and his colleagues argued that hormones affect the cognitive activity of women so that they can easily learn simple, repetitive tasks but have difficulty with more complex, creative endeavors. As late as 1977, claims were made that women's hormonal functioning affects their emotional stability and makes them unfit for high economic positions or political office. Jeane Kirkpatrick's appointment as the U.S. representative to the United Nations was resisted by some White House staffers because of her "feminine temperament."[1]

Later researchers recognized that most differences between the sexes are based on the differential **socialization** of men and women. This gender-role model tried to specify the ways in which males and females are socialized to be what is considered masculine or feminine in a particular culture. However, this model was limited because it did not emphasize that gender-role socialization is only a reflection of the larger society. It did not focus on how societies initiate and perpetuate the kinds of socialization they want. The gender-role model implied that one can change the socialization of men and women and thus solve all the problems of inequality and difference. However, changing socialization would probably not change the basic inequalities in a culture. How does it serve women, for example, to be socialized to be achievement-oriented and competitive if they are kept out of sports, academia, and other rewarding occupations? Does learning to express their emotions and be nurturant help men if the corporate world continues to punish that kind of behavior?

THE LINKAGE OF GENDER ROLES AND POWER

A different model of gender roles attempts to emphasize the extent to which gender relations are based on **power.** It incorporates ideas about how stratification has led to more power for men and "how historically derived definitions of masculinity and femininity reproduce those power relations."[2] In other words, because men have had power and have dominated social institutions, masculine traits and occupations have been more valued and "masculinity" has become a collection of traits that lead to success. If men are socialized to be masculine, they will have traits (independence, aggressiveness, and competitiveness) that make them successful and keep males in positions of power. If women are socialized to be feminine (passive and dependent), it will be difficult for them to achieve power and change institutions and the value structure.

THE CONTENT OF GENDER ROLES

While the specific content of gender roles is defined differently in every culture, gender roles usually contain certain general characteristics. These characteristics include the expectation of certain personality traits (women are nurturant and dependent; men are assertive and independent), **social roles** (men are fathers and breadwinners; women are wives and mothers), and **social positions** or occupations (men are soldiers and politicians; women are nurses and volunteers).

Gender is often attached to these social roles and social positions in different ways according to time and the particular society. In the early United States, secretaries and nurses were almost always male. In other cultures, even roles such as that of the husband may be part of the feminine gender role. Among the Dahomeans of Africa, wealthy women can fulfill the position of husband, supporting a wife and, with the help of a male acquaintance, having and raising children with her.[3]

In our culture, women may be considered better at such jobs as elementary school teacher and social worker because these jobs involve the kind of nurturing and sensitivity that are associated with femininity. Men may be considered better engineers and doctors because they are thought to be more logical and rational. Yet in China most engineers are women, and they are supposed to be better at the job than men, and in the Soviet Union most doctors and dentists are women.

Stereotypes

Thus, there are certain culturally defined expectations of the traits and behaviors of males and females. The biological factor of *sex* (maleness or femaleness) is used to construct a social category of *gender* (masculinity or femininity).[4] The cultural expectations associated with gender are often expressed as gender-role stereotypes. **Stereotypes** are oversimplified descriptions of a group of people. Gender-role stereotypes thus are beliefs that men possess certain traits and should do certain things and that women possess other traits and should do other things. You may not believe that you or many people you know are actually like these cultural stereotypes. However, the stereotypes are still very important because many people *do* believe in them and base their behavior on them.

In fact, there is a surprising amount of agreement in our heterogeneous culture on gender-role stereotypes. A number of studies done in the 1960s and 1970s support the belief that people in the United States agree about sex-role stereotypes. Broverman and his colleagues did studies in 1968 and 1970 on 1,000 males and females and found a great deal of agreement about the differing characteristics of men and women. Even though the men and women in the sample varied in terms of age, religion, educational level, and marital status, they agreed on the characteristics possessed by masculine men and feminine women.

Gender Roles Seen in Terms of Opposites

These studies confirmed that masculine and feminine gender roles are often perceived in terms of opposites. If a man is considered to be independent, for example, a woman is seen as dependent.[5] The sexes were described in opposite ways whether the respondents listed their own beliefs about male and female traits or checked these traits on a list that was given to them.

However, studies done to see which traits men and women actually do possess do *not* show a pattern of opposites.[6] In reality, men and women overlap in regard to many characteristics. For example, some men and some women are competitive, and some men and some women are nurturant. There is also a great deal of variation within each sex in terms of the degree to which a trait is evidenced. Some women may be highly emotional, and other women may not be so at all; some men may be very assertive, and other men may not be assertive at all. A good way to picture this variation in each sex and the overlapping between the sexes is to use a model of overlapping curves (Figure 1).

People tend to think that the traits associated with men—masculinity—and the traits associated with women—femininity—are negatively correlated. That is, if you are high on the number of masculine traits you possess, you will be

Figure 1

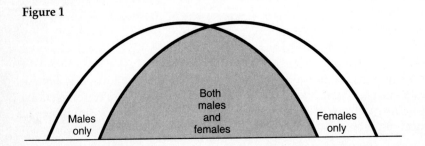

Males only | Both males and females | Females only

low on your number of feminine traits and vice versa. However, this is not true. A person can be high on both masculine and feminine traits (and thus be considered "androgynous"), low on both masculine and feminine traits ("undifferentiated"), or high on one and low on the other ("masculine" or "feminine").

Stereotypes may also vary in accordance with perceptions of a person's major role in life. Thus, traits are attributed differently to a woman according to whether she is seen as a nurturant wife and mother, an independent career woman, an athlete, or a sex object. Similar types for men include the business-man, athletic man, blue-collar working man, and macho man.

Masculine Gender Roles and Stereotypes Evaluated More Positively

When the respondents in a study evaluate whether traits are good or bad, the traits attributed to men are usually seen more positively than are those attributed to women. Very few of the characteristics attributed to women are seen positively; these are the traits clustered around warmth and nurturance. Not only do male traits seem to be more highly valued in our culture, but when mental health professionals were asked to describe the characteristics of a mentally healthy adult, their descriptions were remarkably similar to the traits used to describe a man.[7] While some recent studies have shown no dif-ference in the way people evaluate masculine and feminine traits,[8] the traits attributed to men are still more likely to be associated with prestige and occu-pational success.

What a Catch-22 (dilemma) for women. To live up to the stereotype of being feminine, women must possess traits that are valued less by society and are unlikely to lead to success and that may be seen as less mentally healthy. In fact, having stereotypical traits may actually make women less mentally healthy.[9] It is hard to conceive of a mentally healthy adult who is passive, dependent, and illogical—traits frequently associated with women.

Stereotypes as Real and Ideal

Are stereotypes only ideals, or are they really related to behavior? While there has been disagreement in research findings in this regard, the consensus seems to be that those who feel strongly about a particular trait will try to act in accordance with it.[10] Thus, a woman may try to be nurturant because she feels that women *should* be nurturant. A bright girl may play down her intel-lectual capacities and emphasize her domestic skills if she believes that a man likes traditional women. Studies have shown that women interviewing for jobs may try to fit in with an interviewer's expectations. If they believe that he values traditional women, they will dress in a more feminine manner and wear jewelry and makeup.[11]

Thus, stereotypes may come to be prescriptions, or ideals. They may iden-tify an aspect of behavior, exaggerate it, and overgeneralize it. For example, men are seen as aggressive although we know that not all men are aggressive and that many women are as aggressive as some men are. However, the idea of being aggressive has been incorporated into the idea of being masculine. The stereotypes thus comes to define what *should* be as well as what is. They become self-fulfilling prophecies as people strive to achieve the ideal held up by the culture.

Many problems arise when stereotypes are seen as ideals for behavior. The traits involved may not match a person's real inclinations or characteristics. Some of these traits are also dysfunctional. High degrees of aggression and competitiveness may lead to stress and heart disease or violence in men; passivity and dependence may leave women unable to support themselves in a crisis. If a person cannot live up to an ideal or norm, that person may also feel guilt or experience low self-esteem. As few people *can* live up to the stereotype of masculinity or femininity, this is a serious problem. Few women feel they are really beautiful; even glamorous entertainers feel they are not attractive enough. There is not enough room at the top for many men to feel that they are truly successful and have made it. The great majority of men and women probably have secret doubts and fears about not living up to certain parts of the masculine or feminine stereotype, although they may hide these doubts from all but a few intimates.

It is also difficult for many people to know what to do to live up to the stereotype of masculinity or femininity because these stereotypes are inconsistent and change. There may indeed be several stereotype clusters that are pertinent for a particular person, and some of the traits in them may be mutually exclusive. As was noted above, there are different stereotypes for working-class men and middle-class men. While a man may be able to choose between these two rather easily depending on his situation, what about a woman who has to choose between living up to the traits expected of the ideal mother and those expected of the ideal career woman?

Stereotypes Differ by Class, Race, and Ethnic Background

Another inconsistency in stereotypes is that they vary among classes, races, and ethnic groups. For example, Franklin points out that in many instances structural barriers keep black men from assuming the provider-protector role. High unemployment, a changing economic structure, discrimination by white-dominated unions, and other factors have made it very difficult for black men to be providers. In the same way, Franklin points out, it has been difficult for black men to assume a protector role when they are a minority protecting their families against a majority. This means that the black stereotype of masculinity is likely to emphasize other ways of being masculine: physical strength, dominance, and being "cool."[12] For black women, economic variables also mean a stereotype different from that which is operative for white women. Most black women are not free to choose either the homemaker or the independent career woman stereotype. Black women are expected to be strong, assertive, independent, and able to take care of themselves and their families financially, yet they are also expected to be nurturant, sensitive, and attractive. There is no room in the black female stereotype for passivity and dependence.

Franklin emphasizes the interaction of race with class. He asserts that the black masculine role and the white masculine role are the two dominant American male stereotypes. He believes that with certain specific cultural additions, men who are Hispanic-American, Asian-American, and the like will assume the white or black role stereotype, depending on socioeconomic variables.[13]

Stereotypes Are Changing

As we look at the inconsistency in gender-role stereotypes, we see that gender roles are changing. Pleck distinguishes between the traditional male role (characterized by an emphasis on physical strength, strong male bonding, lack of emotional expression and self-revelation, expectation of dominance over women, and belief in a sexual double standard) and the modern male role (which includes economic achievement, intellectual and interpersonal skills, heterosexual tenderness, and emotional intimacy). He also points out that the distinctions between these two roles parallel to some degree the distinctions between the working-class and middle-class stereotypes for men and show how the society is moving toward a more middle-class, service orientation[14] (Figure 2).

Many problems are associated with the coexistence of older and newer stereotypes. At the same time that these new roles have emerged, many old expectations have persisted in some form. Komarovsky discovered that college men often want to date bright and capable women but expect these women to subordinate their careers and become housewives and mothers after marriage.[15]

A study in the mid-1980s looked at college students' perceptions of ideal female, ideal male, and self-portrayal sex roles. Women described an androgynous model for themselves and their ideal. However, men described an androgynous model for their ideal self but sex-typed portrayals for their ideal

Figure 2

Traditional Male	New Male
Physical strength and aggression	Economic achievement Intelligence Interpersonal skills
Not emotionally sensitive or self-revealing	Emotionally sensitive and self-expressive with women
Anger is acceptable	
Prefers company of men	
Strong male bonds but no intimacy	Prefers company of women Heterosexual relationships as a source of support
Marriage as necessity, not romantic	Romantic marriage
Domination of women	Equal relationships
Sexual double standard	Less of a double standard
Good girl/bad girl	Women seen more as individuals

SOURCE: Joseph Pleck, *The Myth of Masculinity* (Cambridge, Mass.: MIT Press, 1981): 131–134.

male and ideal female.[16] This study seems to show that women are able without stigma to incorporate masculine behavior in their repertoire more easily than men are able to incorporate feminine behavior in theirs. It also suggests confiicts for both men and women. While women's ideal male is similar to men's self-portrayal, the men did not feel they were living up to their own ideals. Among the women who were consistent in describing androgynous ideals and selves, there was still the problem of contending with men whose ideal female was traditional. For both sexes, then, there are confiicts between the ideal male and female and the realities of traits and behavior.

Androgyny

We used the word "**androgyny**" in the previous paragraph, and while it was defined briefly in the preface, we need to look in more detail at what it means. Carolyn Heilbrun in *Toward a Recognition of Androgyny* tells us that "androgyny is an ancient word taken from the Greek andro (male) and gyn (female) and defines a condition under which the characteristics of the sexes and the human impulses expressed by men and women are not rigidly assigned."[17] The duality of the nature of the individual has been recognized since the time of the Greek Pythagorean myth of creation, in which people sought their other halves to reunite in mating and find a sense of wholeness. Almost all religions include beliefs about dualities that represent masculine and feminine characteristics as they are defined in this culture and that must unite to form a whole person.[18]

Originally, in studies of gender-role stereotypes in this culture, masculinity and femininity were thought of as separate ends or poles of a single long line. Thus, perfect masculinity was at one end of the line and perfect femininity was at the other end. By this definition, if you were perfectly masculine, you had no feminine traits, and if you were perfectly feminine, you had no masculine traits.[19]

However, some researchers argued that masculinity and femininity are not polar opposites but instead are independent measures; attributes considered masculine are found in feminine girls, and less masculine boys have more of some masculine attributes than do boys who look more masculine. These researchers believed that there are really two lines, one representing masculinity and the other representing femininity, and that a person can be low on one and high on the other, low on both, or high on both.[20] Sandra Bem, who did some of the pioneering work in the measurement of androgyny, developed the Bem Sex Role Inventory, in which a person's androgyny is measured by the difference between that person's masculinity and femininity scores. A large difference (high femininity and low masculinity or high masculinity and low femininity) means that a person is sex-typed. A small difference in a person with two high scores means that that person is androgynous; a small difference in a person with two low scores means that that person is **undifferentiated.** Bem found and other experiments confirmed that only people who are high in both femininity and masculinity have the range of fiexible responses to situations that characterize the androgynous person.[21] Thus, **androgyny** came to be defined as being able to call forth elements of both masculinity and femininity and thus being relatively high in measurements of both.

Unfortunately, the Bem Sex Role Inventory and other measures did not really solve the problem of measuring masculinity and femininity. As you can imagine, these stereotypes not only are changeable but contain subsets of other things. Some researchers believe that they are really only measures of instrumental and expressive personality traits rather than gender roles.[22] There is also the question of whether people report certain traits because it is socially desirable to do so. For example, a woman may say she is nurturant because she knows she is expected to be so. There is, in addition, the question of whether measures of traits really measure behavior.

When we speak of androgyny, then, we must realize that we are not speaking of a clear-cut measurable entity in terms of either personality traits or behavior in an individual. It is a loose structural concept. Definitions of androgyny differ in the degree of masculine and feminine traits needed to consider someone androgynous and in whether a person can be considered androgynous if these traits are theoretically possessed but not evidenced in behavior. Judith Laws asserts that androgyny is a "state in which feminine and masculine elements are present, accepted and accessible within the individual."[23] Bem says, "It is possible for the person to be both instrumental and expressive, both agentic and communal depending upon the situation."[24] As Heilbrun put it almost three decades ago, androgyny

> suggests a spirit of reconciliation between the sexes; it suggests, further, a full range of experience open to individuals who may, as women be aggressive, as men tender; it suggests a spectrum upon which human beings choose their places without regard to propriety or custom.[25]

Others have said that the "androgynous individual [is one] who identifies with both desirable masculine and desirable feminine characteristics and is freed from . . . gender role limitations and is able to more comfortably engage in both `masculine' and `feminine' behavior across a variety of social situations."[26] Furthermore, "the concept of androgyny denotes a person who is fiexible, socially competent, able to respond to shifting situational demands, and more complete and actualized in developing and maximizing personal potential."[27] Androgynous persons seem to be higher than sex-typed ones in self-esteem, creativity, and psychological adjustment.[28]

However, we will see in later chapters that androgyny may not be the best of what we are looking for in human behavior. People may want to explore the option of completely transcending gender roles.

THE SEX/GENDER SYSTEM

One of the reasons we are concerned about stereotypes is that they not only operate on an interpersonal level but also are embedded in the structure of society. Stereotypes permeate all the institutions of society: family, religion, the educational system, the economic system, and the political system.

In fact, stereotypes often persist for so long because they help the society or its dominant groups get what they need or want. As an example, our economic system "needs" dedicated workers who are willing to work long hours and be competitive and aggressive. It is no accident that the masculine stereotype in our culture emphasizes the breadwinner role and assertive behavior. Later in this book we will look at how stereotypes are encouraged and even enforced by some of the institutions in this society.

The Sex/Gender System and Stratification

Whenever people are considered different, it is also likely that they will be differentially valued. We call this differential ranking or valuing **stratification.** As we have seen, in almost every culture about which we have information the traits and roles associated with men and the social positions that men hold are seen as more valuable then those encompassed by the feminine gender role. In our culture, even very young children seem to be aware of this ranking. Most studies show that both boys and girls prefer the male role. Boys would not want to be a girl, but many girls say they would happily trade places with a boy.[29]

We also have seen that some mental health professionals associate masculine traits with better mental health. Nielsen has suggested that many measures show that masculinity and males rank higher than do femininity and females. He argues that the rewards associated with social positions fall into four general categories: material rewards such as money, prestige, formal or informal power, and psychological gratification.[30] In almost all cases, material rewards, prestige, and formal power are higher for the social positions associated with men; women's status sources are more informal and indirect, although they may include more psychological gratification.

Stratification and Power

The traits in the male role are associated not only with success but with power. The active person directs the passive one; the independent person subdues the dependent one. Power has been defined as the "process whereby individuals or groups gain or maintain the capacity to impose their will upon others, to have their way recurrently, despite implicit or explicit opposition, through invoking or threatening punishment as well as offering or withholding rewards."[31]

The dominant group—the one with power—controls the institutions of society and can make laws, set economic policy, and determine educational policy in a way that keep less powerful groups from getting resources. Lipman-Blumen points out that once power has been firmly established, one hardly has to use punishments and rewards. The control of social and economic resources is sufficient to make the less powerful fall into line. This use of institutions or formal power is called *macromanipulation.*[32] For example, although women got the vote seventy years ago in this country, there are laws that control their access to certain jobs, and there have been laws that have kept them from controlling their fertility and thus have effectively kept them in the home. The less dominant groups often use *micromanipulation* such as interpersonal skill and charm to offset the control of the powerful; they do not have the control of resources necessary to use macromanipulation.

Power relationships are often part of the stratification system and are usually taken for granted by both the powerful and the powerless. Lipman-Blumen states that women who live with men, essentially segregated from other nonrelated women, are prevented from recognizing the sources of their powerlessness. They are also socialized by the prevailing stereotypes to adopt traits which keep them from being powerful, and they accept the domination of the powerful because they believe that the people in this group are more capable and have women's best interests at heart.[33]

Power and Powerlessness for Both Sexes

It is true that the gender-role stereotypes that have been perpetuated give men power and have until recently left women with only micromanipulation to use in gaining their ends. However, while the stereotypes confine women, they also have many disadvantages for men. In *Why Men Are the Way They Are*, Warren Farrell describes female powerlessness as being divorced and having two children, no child support, and no job experience. He gives a parallel example of male powerlessness stemming from stereotypes as a man being in the hospital with a coronary bypass operation caused by the stress of working two jobs to support children his former wife won't let him see.[34] He points out that ironically, male powerlessness often derives from the definition of masculinity. To be a success, a man may spend his life chained to the office; to be cool, he may suppress his feelings and miss out on important human relationships. Farrell asks the question, Is power money, influence, and status, or is it the ability to control your own life? If it is the latter, rigid stereotypes mean that no one truly has power.

We would like to suggest that the truth lies somewhere between the view that men have all the power and the view that they are victims and powerless, too. It is obvious that men have had and continue to benefit from the power of occupying certain positions and associated social roles. However, they have paid a price in terms of their often rigid adherence to the prescriptions of the male gender role. Women obviously have gained in some ways by not having the responsibilities of power (not being drafted, for example) but have suffered much more from being powerless.

In the next few chapters, we will develop a historical perspective on power and then look at the biological differences and similarities between the sexes. At that point, we will be ready to examine how tradition, socialization, and biological sex interact to form gender roles. We will explore how each sex learns its gender-role stereotypes—how men learn to be masculine and how women learn to be feminine—according to the dictates of our culture. We will see how difficult it is for anyone to escape the omnipresent messages about gender roles.

ESSAY QUESTIONS

1. Differentiate between the terms "sex roles" and "gender roles" as they are currently used. Why do feminists think this distinction is important?
2. How are gender roles linked to power, and how do they reproduce the power advantage of men in a patriarchy?
3. Discuss the characteristics of stereotypes involving men and women in this culture, for example, that masculinity and femininity are seen to be negatively correlated or vary with perceptions of a person's occupation.
4. Are stereotypes real or ideal?
5. Discuss some of the sources of inconsistencies in masculine and feminine stereotypes.
6. Define androgyny. How is it conceptualized in terms of measurement? Describe how one can determine an androgynous score on the Bem Sex Role Inventory.
7. What is meant by the sex/gender system?
8. Define macromanipulation and micromanipulation as used by Jean Lipman-Blumen and discuss how they are used by each sex.

EXERCISES

1. Make up a list of personality traits and behaviors, classify them as either masculine or feminine, and explain why. You can do the same for all manner of things (musical instruments, drinks, and the like).
2. Do a lifeline and discuss what you plan to be after school. Will you get married and have children? If so, when? Who will stay home with the children? Who will do the housework? If one of you has to relocate for a job, will the other go? What criteria will you use to decide?
3. Keep a log for one week and notice the roles you see men and women performing.
   a. At the service station, who is working?
   b. At the restaurant, who are the cooks and who are the servers?
   c. At the department store, who sells the stereos and who sells small-ticket items?
   d. At the elementary school or at the university, who are the teachers and who are the administrators?
   e. As you watch television, who are the heads of government?

---

*To the teacher: These exercises and those in the next chapter are appropriate for almost any of the chapters and could be used at the beginning of a semester and then again at the end of a term. They are meant to be general and thought-provoking about the stereotypes and different statuses of men and women in our society.

NOTES

1. Cynthia Fuchs Epstein, *Deceptive Distinctions: Sex, Gender and the Social Order* (New Haven: Yale University Press, 1988).
2. Michael Kimmel, *Changing Men: New Directions in Research on Men and Masculinity* (Beverly Hills, Calif.: Sage, 1987), p. 13.
3. Joyce Nielsen, *Sex in Society: Perspectives on Stratification* (Belmont, Calif.: Wadsworth, 1978), p. 5.
4. Clare M. Renzetti and Daniel J. Curran, *Women, Men and Society* (Boston: Allyn & Bacon, 1989).
5. P. Rosenkrantz, S. Vogel, H. Bee, and D. Broverman, "Sex-Role Stereotypes and Self-Concepts in College Students," *Journal of Consulting and Clinical Psychology* 32 (1968):287–295.
6. K. Deaux and L. Lewis, "Structure of Gender Stereotypes: Interrelationships among Components and Gender Label," *Journal of Personality and Social Psychology* 43 (1984):996–1004.
7. H. C. Foushee, R. L. Helmreich, and J. T. Spence, "Implicit Theories of Masculinity and Femininity: Dualistic or Bipolar?" *Psychology of Women Quarterly* 3 (1979):259–269.
8. C. M. Noseworthy and A. J. Lott, "The Cognitive Organization of Gender-Stereotypic Categories," *Personality and Social Psychology Bulletin* 10 (1984):474–481.
9. E. S. Bassoff and G. Glass, "The Relationship between Sex Roles and Mental Health: A Meta-Analysis of 26 Studies," *The Counseling Psychologist* 10, no. 4 (1984):105–111.
10. M. P. Zanna and S. J. Pack, "On the Self-Fulfilling Nature of Apparent Sex Differences in Behavior," *Journal of Experimental Social Psychology* 11 (1975):583–591.
11. C. L. Von Baeyer, D. L. Sherk, and M. P. Zanna, "Impression Management in the Job Interview: When the Female Applicant Meets the Male (Chauvinist) Interviewer," *Personality and Social Psychology Bulletin* 7 (1981):177–185.
12. Richard Majors, "Cool Pose: The Proud Signature of Black Survival," in Michael S. Kimmel and Michael A. Messner, eds., *Men's Lives* (New York: Macmillan, 1989), pp. 83–87.
13. Clyde W. Franklin II, *The Changing Definition of Masculinity* (New York: Plenum, 1984); Hope Landrine, "Race × Class Stereotypes of Women," *Sex Roles* 13, no. 1 (1985):65–75.
14. Joseph Pleck, *The Myth of Masculinity* (Cambridge, Mass.: MIT Press, 1981).
15. Mirra Komarovsky, "Cultural Contradictions and Sex Roles: The Masculine Case," *American Journal of Sociology* (January 1973):873–884.
16. Dena Scher, "Sex-Role Contradictions: Self-Perceptions and Ideal Perceptions," *Sex Roles* 10, no. 7/8 (1984):235–242.
17. As quoted in M. C. Taylor and J. A. Hall, "Psychological Androgyny: Theories, Methods and Conclusions," *Psychological Bulletin* 92 (1982):347–366.
18. C. G. Jung, "Anima and Animus," in *Two Essays on Analytical Psychology: Collected Works of C. G. Jung,* vol. 7 (New York: Ballinger Foundation, 1953), pp. 186–209.
19. Epstein, *op. cit.*
20. Noel Jenkins and Karen Vroegh, "Contemporary Concepts of Masculinity and Femininity," *Psychological Reports* 25 (1969):679–697.
21. Sandra Bem, "Sex-Role Adaptability: One Consequence of Psychological Androgyny," *Journal of Personality and Social Psychology* 31 (1975):634–643.

22. Taylor and Hall, *op. cit.;* K. Deaux, "From Individual Differences to Social Categories: Analysis of a Decade's Research on Gender," *American Psychologist* 39 (1984):105–116.
23. Judith Laws, *The Second X* (New York: Elsevier, 1979).
24. Bem, *op. cit.*
25. Carolyn Heilbrun, *Toward a Recognition of Androgyny* (New York: Knopf, 1964).
26. Warren Jones, Ellen Chernovitz, and Robert Hansson, "The Enigma of Androgyny: Differential Implications for Males and Females," *Journal of Consulting and Clinical Psychology* 46, no.2 (1978):298–313.
27. Bem, *op. cit.*
28. Taylor and Hall, *op. cit.;* B. E. Whitley, Jr., "Sex-Role Orientation and Self-Esteem: A Critical Meta-Analytic Review," *Journal of Personality and Social Psychology* 44 (1983):765–778; B. E. Whitley, Jr., "Sex-Role Orientation and Psychological Well-Being: Two Meta-Analyses," *Sex Roles* 12 (1984):207–225.
29. G. E. Inoff, C. F. Halverson, Jr., and K. A. Pizzagati, "The Infiuence of Sex-Role Stereotypes on Children's Self and Peer-Attributions," *Sex Roles* 9 (1983):1205–1222.
30. Nielsen, *op. cit.*
31. Jean Lipman-Blumen, *Gender Roles and Power* (Englewood Cliffs, N.J.: Prentice-Hall, 1984), p. 6.
32. *Ibid.*
33. *Ibid.*
34. Warren Farrell, *Why Men Are the Way They Are* (New York: Random House, 1983), p. xvii.

Chapter 2

Status Differences between the Sexes: Where Did It All Begin?

When we look at American culture today, we can see vast differences in power and prestige between the sexes. Women still make around two-thirds of what men make, and few women are top corporate executives or wield political power. Such differences in power and prestige seem to have existed since the beginning of recorded history in all human societies about which we have information.

Why is there such a difference in the status of men and women across cultures? When and why did these differences begin? The obvious physical differences between the sexes are certainly not sufficient to account for the tremendous differences in power, prestige, and opportunity that have developed between men and women. Although men on the average have larger and more muscular bodies than women do, this does not necessarily mean that men should gain power, especially in societies that do not depend heavily on physical strength. Nor should having and caring for young children push women into the inferior status that is theirs in almost every culture. What is defined as appropriate for men and women in terms of labor and behavioral characteristics varies from culture to culture, yet in almost every society it is the men who make the rules, control the economic system, and define the rituals and the ideology. This ability of men to control the laws and institutions of society, combined with men's superior status, is known as *patriarchy*.[1]

How did masculine and feminine gender roles get started, and how did the masculine role come to have more prestige? Many authors have been tempted to say that because this kind of stratification has existed for so long and is so widespread, it must be "natural" and therefore is the way things should be. However, biological and social evidence, as well as information from more recent history, indicates that this difference in power is not at all natural. Nor is this a difference that would be fruitful to continue in the future. While men have had prestige and power, they have also suffered crippling stress and high death rates; women have had unfulfilled opportunities and depression. A culture needs healthy, creative people of both sexes contributing to the

19

building of society. We need to examine the history and nature of the power differences between women and men in order to understand our past and plan a better future.

THE ORIGIN OF MALE DOMINANCE: SEVERAL POSSIBLE EXPLANATIONS

Early Humankind: Work, Roles, and Power

Most theorists agree that the different status of men and women is based on the division of labor among early human beings and the elaboration of a stratification system based on that division. Biologists and anthropologists who have studied primates and early humankind agree about the general facts of evolution and the division of labor but disagree in their emphasis on and interpretation of these facts.

It is generally believed by sociobiologists that one of the primary events in the evolution of human social bonds was the loss of estrous, or seasonal sexuality, in the female. Many anthropologists believe that as human women became sexually receptive year-round, men were more likely to stay in their vicinity and with their children and thus form a bond with them.[2] The fact that humans developed bipedal locomotion and walked upright is also considered important. The upright posture not only freed hands for tool development and use but also may have led to increasing interaction among early hominids. In primates, the seasonal sexuality of females is usually announced by a pink swelling in the genital region, which alerts males to the fact that a female will be sexually receptive. With upright posture, no physical sign of sexual receptivity could be seen, and so women may have had to develop social signs to show their interest in mating. There were, however, probably no long-term pair associations other than mother and child among very early hominids, although the reproductive unit was the fundamental core of short-term social association.[3] Anthropologists hypothesize that as climate changes brought on droughts and protective forests receded, small familylike units joined their forces in hunting bands so that they could protect one another and share food. Gradually there was a division of labor in this food finding: Males did more of the far-ranging hunting, and females—who were literally held down by clinging infants—did more of the gathering close to home.[4]

Biological Explanations

Biological theories stress the importance of biological characteristics in dividing labor among early humans and the fact that this division of labor led to stratification and male dominance. These theories emphasize the suitability of men for hunting—the fact that they were larger, stronger, faster, and more mobile. They emphasize that the male hormone androgen was likely to produce aggressive behavior that made men daring and competitive hunters. At the same time, it was difficult for women to hunt because they needed to carry, nurse, and watch children.

Social and Cultural Theories

Social theorists emphasize that this division of labor was not inevitable although it might have been functional for early humans. Judith Brown, an anthropologist, points out that there are women seal hunters among the Copper Eskimos and women reindeer herders among the Tungus.[5] When male hunters were killed in the Ojibwa tribe, women were trained as hunters.[6] Social theorists acknowledge, however, that hunting was difficult for women. Such work is potentially dangerous, requires intense concentration, and is not easily interrupted to care for a child.

While certain anthropologists, such as Zuckerman, emphasize the role of "man the hunter,"[7] others (Tanner and Zhilman) emphasize the role of "woman the gatherer" and point out that women must have provided 50 to 90 percent of the food.[8] They also stress the importance of the female in developing human culture and suggest that she not only originated significant social signs but also developed tools to gather and carry food and a sling to carry a baby when she no longer had fur to which the baby could cling. They suggest that the female chose the more social, cooperative males with whom to mate and by her choice determined which genes would be passed on.

Friedl postulates that men did not gain prestige by virtue of hunting and providing daily food but because they had a surplus to distribute after a kill. It is not the amount of food that seems to be the major differentiating factor in developing power for one sex; rather, it is the control over a valued product and particularly over a surplus. She theorizes that through the distribution of food, men developed a system of bonds and alliances that women did not have a chance to form.

While this dominance based on the distribution of the valued result of the hunt exists only among hunting and gathering societies, Friedl believes that the same basic dominance occurs among shifting agriculturalists because the men have a monopoly on the clearing of land. Men clear the land not only because they are physically stronger but because new land often borders on the territories of other people so that warfare is possible. She says that men, by virtue of their control over warfare and land, "are more deeply involved than women in economic and political alliances which are extradomestic and which require for their maintenance the distribution and exchange of goods and services. Thus, by monopolizing the resources by which they can establish extrafamilial bonds, men develop power."[9]

Another popular writer, Lionel Tiger, goes much further than Friedl in proposing that men's power developed from their hunting tasks. In *Men in Groups*, Tiger proposes that the men who did the hunting developed a complex series of rituals and signs that constituted their early bonds. He believes that these bonds carried over into other kinds of male enterprises, such as politics, and that men are thus better suited to these fields because they recognize certain signs from one another. According to Tiger, one of these signs is sexual activity and the rituals surrounding it. Thus, sexual relationships with women and dominance over them become an important part of the culture. If women needed protection from predators, they had to submit and be lower in the dominance scale.[10]

Tiger's theory has been discredited by scholars. While most anthropologists admit that male dominance hierarchies protected females and established sexual relationships with them, the concept of male bonding has found little support. It is difficult to believe that men, more than women, have a particular series of rituals, signs, and signals or that these supposedly ancient signs and signals have carried over into modern activities and made males better suited to dominate in prestigious areas. However, Tiger's book must be discussed because it remains popular. Many people still seek a justification for contemporary sex stratification by talking about male bonding.

These theories do not explain why women did not develop the same bonds (if, indeed, any were developed) or why value was attached to defense and hunting but not to gathering and reproduction. Sanday tried to answer the question of why, despite the fact that women provide most of the food, they have lower status. She suggests that in this kind of situation, men are busy with defense and thus women are dependent on men in a dangerous environment; conversely, if women provide the daily food, men are free to accumulate surpluses and gain monetary rewards. Thus, Sanday suggests that control over surplus goods or the need for defense may give the group that provides these factors more power.[11]

Other anthropologists have proposed that male activities were probably more elaborated and rewarded because they were public and showy[12] and were associated with "civilization" or "culture."[13] Women were seen as being associated with nature. As humankind moved toward a mastery of nature, admiration of the natural declined. Men who manipulated nature by doing things such as irrigating and fertilizing saw themselves as dominating nature, and the cultural was considered to be superior to the natural.

Thus, women became identified with the natural, domestic, and private or family side of life, while men were identified with the cultural, technological, and public sphere. The value placed on the cultural and public part of life was greater, and an ideology developed that gave authority and value to the roles and activities of men.[14] This sounds like a logical approach to explain prevailing male authority, yet Ortner and others have been criticized because the split between nature and culture cannot be found in many kinship societies.[15]

Sanday, like Friedl, believes that with the coming of more technologically advanced societies, the power of women declined markedly. While one might expect women to have gained power when physical strength was not needed as much, the development of technology usually favored men. It was men who gained access to technological advances and were called upon to do the heavy work connected with technological society, such as mining and steel work. This was particularly true when traditional societies were colonized by more developed nations. For example, when the Dutch opened gold mines in South Africa, African men got jobs that gave them cash and power. In other cases the role of women in planting and raising crops was ignored, and new seed, plows, and fertilizer were given to the men, who then raised surpluses that gave them power. Thus, men worked for cash or controlled the production of exchange crops, and women were left to raise food for the family and do household chores. In the process, leadership roles changed as well. In the village or tribe, women could inherit rank or property and wield a great deal of influence. In the new urban centers, men consolidated their public power and took over leadership roles.[16]

Engels carried the idea that men gain power in a technological society one step further. He stated that with the development of technological skill, men could produce surpluses, and these surpluses became established as individual private property. Men wished to pass the surplus on to their heirs and make sure that only their blood relatives could inherit it. Restrictions on women increased as men attempted to limit sexual access to their wives so that they could be sure the children their wives bore were their own. Thus, according to Engels, private property was the root cause of sexual discrimination.[17]

A Word about Formal and Informal Power

Many of the theories we have looked at have been criticized because they do not consider the extent of informal female power that countered formal sources of authority. We have seen that formal authority or legitimate power lies with men in almost every society. However, women may have a great deal of informal power. Indeed, in their own realm or through manipulation of various sorts, they can exert a great deal of influence, although legitimate public power is reserved for men.

As societies developed and changed, women could use formal power only if they inherited it or moved into the male realm of activity. The difference between a woman getting power through inheritance and a man achieving power on his own is important and is related to public and private spheres. Because the private sphere or family is considered woman's place, female power that comes through family inheritance is considered legitimate. In a contemporary example, widows of deceased congressmen are sometimes elected to Congress, although they would be unlikely to achieve that position on their own.

OTHER INFLUENCES

Religious Ideology

Religious ideology reflected and justified the higher status of men. We can see the codification of this higher status in the writings of organized religion. The Book of Genesis sets forth the Judeo-Christian tradition that is the bulwark of

Jewish and Christian beliefs about sex differences. Eve is depicted as being made by God from Adam's rib and is thus seen as an appendage to be used for his pleasure. Eve is further devalued when she is seen as the cause of humankind's original sin. She tempts Adam to eat from the forbidden "fruit of knowledge," and they are subsequently expelled by God from the Garden of Eden for disobedience. Eve is not seen as inherently evil. The serpent—a thinly veiled allusion to the Devil—tempts her originally, and so she is seen as weak and foolish, the unwitting instrument of man's downfall. There is also a sexual allusion in the "eating of the fruit of knowledge," so that Eve is also seen as a sexual temptress.*

These differing views of men and women are elaborated in later writings by the early church fathers. The scriptures emphasized the link between sexuality and sin and showed men who were made in the image of God the Father as the ultimate authorities in all matters. An example is Paul's letter to the Corinthians:

> For a man indeed ought not to cover his head, forasmuch as he is the image and glory of God; but the woman is the glory of man. For the man is not of the woman; but the woman of the man. Neither was the man created for the woman; but the woman for the man. (1 Corinthians 11:7–9)[18]

This was interpreted to mean that women were not only inferior but also to be disdained, particularly because of their link with sexuality and evil. Women were presumed to have an insatiable sexual nature and to tempt men from their spiritual duty as Eve had tempted Adam in the Garden of Eden.

Another version of Genesis and other gospels that were kinder to women were suppressed or lost during early Christian times, and the version of scripture that persisted justified male dominance. We will look in more detail later at the religious institutions that controlled stereotypes concerning the proper traits and behavior for men and women. However, we must emphasize here that early Judeo-Christian doctrine underlined the idea that women are sinful, secondary, and inferior beings who should submit to men. As Christianity spread across Europe, the words of Saint Paul justified the curtailment of women's legal rights and set a pattern for women's subordinate position in the following historical periods.

Women in the Middle Ages and Beyond

Women's rights were severely limited in the legal codes of the Middle Ages, although some noblewomen managed to exert control over land and gain limited political power. During the Renaissance, although wealthy women received more of an education, aristocratic women who had run large estates and exercised political influence lost a great deal of their power as the nation-

---

*There are two versions of Genesis. For elaboration, see the discussion in Chapter 10.

states consolidated. The fourteenth century onward also marked the declining status of working women.

In some ways women had more freedom in the sixteenth and seventeenth centuries, as they did not always have to take care of young children. Many children were wet-nursed and later apprenticed outside the home. As fathers worked in and near the home, they took responsibility for a large part of child rearing and the job training of their children. The father was supposed to take over basic child training once the child reached an educable age. However, seventeenth-century women worked hard: They tended animals, produced and marketed food, made clothes, and participated in their artisan husbands' work. Widowed women could run their own businesses, and many women took over the family business when their husbands were away at war. Bloch says of this era, "Women were measured against essentially the same standards as men and were judged worthy of a position on the ladder, although one rung beneath men."[19]

However, in the eighteenth and nineteenth centuries, the pendulum swung back and the work of women was devalued again. In the 1800s, the industrial revolution had a great effect on work and gender roles. As surplus production for cash was taken out of the home and centered in factories, it was also taken out of women's control, and women lost power. Domestic work other than surplus production for cash was seen as having little value, and while many women and children worked in mines and factories during the early days of the industrial revolution, they gained no power. They had little say about the long hours, the terrible working conditions, and the low pay they received; their wages were so low that they had nothing left with which to trade or build up reserves.[20]

With growing industrialization, many middle-class women withdrew entirely from the paid labor force. By the middle of the 1800s most middle-class women did not work outside the home. The focus of their domestic work changed from economic production to child rearing. As fathers left the home for business enterprises outside, wet nurses and servants went out of fashion; because children were seldom apprenticed outside the family, mothers became the principal child raisers.[21]

Changing Stereotypes

At the same time, the ideal of romantic love developed and the new "leisure class" of women was idealized as pure and asexual. In the middle class it was reasoned that if women were not producers, they had to be frail and delicate. The idealized body was sought by lacing women into tight corsets and having them wear high-heeled shoes. The image of women as frail and fainting was probably reasonably accurate with tightly laced "stays" cutting off their breath. This fragile image was not connected to the earth mother image of past women but represented a new image of an asexual Madonna or Virgin Mary figure. Her counterpart, the temptress Eve, was found in the numerous prostitutes who flourished during the Victorian period.

In a total reversal of viewpoint, the wanton women of the past came to be seen as a force for good who would control the base impulses of men. Women were viewed as the enforcers of moral and religious standards. As they could participate in public life through churches and the arts (although women were seen as supporters of art and not as creative artists), they turned their attention to these areas while men moved into the secular, competitive economic realm.[22] The spheres of men and women were seen as separate and distinct, as were the sexual nature and personality traits attributed to each sex. This perception of distinct spheres continued into the first part of the twentieth century. It was not until after 1940 that married women moved slowly back into the world of paid employment. Later still, men began to share family responsibilities so that ideas about the particular nature of each sex were reopened for debate.

WOMEN AND MEN IN THE UNITED STATES

So far we have looked at the Western cultural tradition that has influenced our attitude toward the different positions of men and women. We shall now look specifically at men and women in the United States. While many of the European attitudes toward women carried over into this country, certain elements specific to the colonies and the frontier led to differing attitudes toward men and women and their interactions.

American culture defined male and female gender roles in a way that emphasized the particular historical background of the new nation. Most other cultures had encouraged a certain blending of the traits of the sexes when masculine and feminine roles were defined. While this varied by historical period, men were often allowed large measures of cooperation, displays of emotion, participation in art and dance, and participation in the care of young children. They were encouraged to be creative and literary as well as courageous and skilled.

As the difficulties of settling a frontier helped shape the American value system, different masculine traits received emphasis in the American definition of the masculine gender role. In the new country, practicality and rationality took precedence over intellectual endeavor; the intellectual was put to the task of invention and obtaining immediate useful results. In general, the rough-and-ready new culture celebrated the man who had the physical skills for survival and did not think much of the man who was interested in the arts. It was believed that the refinements of dance, literature, and painting could be left to the care of women, who supposedly did not have hard work to do. In addition, in a new country where every man theoretically had the opportunity to succeed, competition came to be emphasized. Cooperation was a virtue to be extolled only in countries where extended kinship ties and group structure were maintained by cooperative cement. In the United States men stood on their own. Nuclear families were predominant, and such families might be separated from friends and neighbors by many miles. It is no wonder that the new country extolled independence, self-reliance, and achievement as the primary components of the masculine gender role. The ideal man was competitive, practical, successful, and individualistic. There was little room in the stereotype for a man who was sensitive, contemplative, or intellectual.[23]

The French writer de Tocqueville, who visited the United States in 1831, pointed out the uniqueness of this value system. He also showed that these values did not apply to women. While frontier women were expected to be able to take over men's concerns when necessary, the ideal woman was valued for a set of characteristics very different from those desired in men. The woman was to be the support system for the man and was expected to be cooperative, oriented toward people, and concerned with nurturance and peacemaking. She was to be sensitive and uphold moral and religious truths. Her main concerns in life were supposed to be her husband and family.[24]

Women in colonial America and on the frontier were viewed as intellectually inferior to men but were not regarded with overt hostility. However, they had few legal advantages and carried some of the taint of the temptress Eve in spite of looser laws about courting. There was a definite limit on how far they could get from their "place" if their work was not actually needed. Women who showed more ability than "feminine" weakness would allow were often accused of being witches, and witchcraft trials resulted in the death of a number of these women.

People such as Benjamin Franklin and Mary Wollenstonecraft attempted to modify this view of women, but their efforts had little success; formal structures of power remained under the control of men. As industrialization reached the United States in the nineteenth century, women's power decreased even further. Women's "finer nature" was emphasized, but this could not make up for the loss of power in the productive and public realm.

As time progressed, this finer nature was also defined to include a lack of interest in sex, and so women were again confined to the "Virgin Mary" role. A well-known doctor of the time, William Sanger, spelled out the tremendous difficulty too much sexual desire could bring to a woman. He stated, "The full force of sexual desire is seldom known to a virtuous women, . . . and [evil could only result if] a mutual appetite equally felt by both [occurred] ."[25] Once a woman had enjoyed sex, he said, she would enter into a bottomless pit of sexuality from which she was likely to emerge promiscuous and turn to prostitution.[26] Although feminists resisted this view and even pressed for birth control information, Sanger's beliefs were commonly held.

We thus find dualistic views of women and their sexuality. On the one hand, women were seen as pure, nurturing, and asexual mothers; on the other hand, the threat from their sexuality was always present and they could become a source of evil and temptation. In economic, productive areas, women lost many of their functions, and if they did work or produced outside the home, it was seen as an extension of their basic role as wife and mother.

While traditional religion and scientific thought modified the view of woman as inferior morally and physically, women in early America were not considered equal by any stretch of the imagination.

The Persistence of Patriarchy

The differences in power and prestige between the sexes that started so long ago have carried over, with few changes, into the modern United States. Women still have little power in the productive realm; various ideologies and beliefs about their nature limit their attempts to join men in the public sphere. Changes are taking place, particularly as women leave the home and enter the public economy, but beliefs about women's proper role and the old ideologies and taboos remain.

Men continue to dominate economic and political life, and their contributions are more highly valued. Why has patriarchy persisted? The dominant group controls the institutions of society and can make laws, economic policy, and educational policy that consolidate their power. In this culture, the traits associated with the male gender role are more likely to lead to success, reinforcing the status of the dominant group. Both women and men are socialized to accept the prevailing stereotypes, and only recently have women challenged the established patriarchy.

Let us now look at biological similarities and differences between the sexes to see if biology can shed any light on gender differences in power and prestige.

ESSAY QUESTIONS

1. How do anthropologists account for the division of labor between early male and female human beings?
2. Friedl differs from other anthropologists in saying that men did not gain prestige just by bringing in food for sustenance. To what does she attribute the greater prestige of men?
3. How does the fact that human beings learned to master nature (by developing irrigation and the like) relate to the prestige levels of men and women?
4. Discuss the likelihood of women gaining or losing prestige in more technologically advanced societies.
5. Why did Engels believe that the development of private property hurt the prestige of women?
6. In what ways did early Judeo-Christian ideology influence the views of the nature and thus the status of men and women?
7. How did the development of a leisure class influence views about women and their sexuality?
8. What unique contributions did the American colonial and frontier expe-

rience make to the stereotype of what is ideally masculine in the United States?

EXERCISES

1. Make up a list of adjectives that describe a man and ones that describe a woman. Then rank the adjectives in terms of traits you believe are desirable. Do the adjectives describing men or the ones describing women have higher rankings?
2. If you awakened tomorrow and discovered that you were the opposite sex, how would your life be different in terms of work and status? How would you feel about these differences?
3. Try to imagine that everything you have ever read in your life uses only female pronouns: "she," "her" (meaning both girls and boys, women and men). Imagine that most of the voices on the radio and most of the faces on television are women's and that when important events are covered, you see only female faces. Imagine that you spend your life dealing almost entirely with female professionals: doctors, lawyers, judges, and police officers. You might prefer to deal with men, but they are not in these jobs. Imagine that almost all the politicians are female and that you have only one male senator in Washington. Imagine that there is a female President and that people are saying it will be a very long time before there is a male one (a male has never been President). You are a man. How do you feel?

NOTES

1. Claire M. Renzetti and Daniel J. Curran, *Women, Men and Society: The Sociology of Gender* (Boston: Allyn & Bacon, 1989), p. 12.
2. Sherwood Washburn, quoted in Donna Haraway, "Animal Sociology and a Natural Economy of the Body Politic," *Signs* 4 (1979):37–60.
3. J. Collier, Z. Rosaldo, and S. Yanagisako, "Is There a Family?" in B. Thorne and M. Yalom, eds., *Rethinking the Family: Some Feminist Questions* (New York: Longman, 1982), pp. 25–39.
4. Sally Zuckerman, quoted in Haraway, *op. cit.*, p. 43.
5. Judith K. Brown, "A Note on the Division of Labor by Sex," *American Anthropologist* 72 (1980):1074.
6. Ernestine Friedl, "Society and Sex Roles," *Human Nature* (April 1978):63–75.
7. Zuckerman, *op. cit.*
8. Nancy Tanner and Adrienne Zhilman, "Women in Evolution: Innovation and Selection in Human Origins," *Signs* 1 (1976):31; Adrienne Zhilman, "Women in Evolution: Subsistence and Social Organization among Early Hominids," *Signs* 1 (1976):4–20; Rosalind Coward, *Patriarchial Precedents* (London: Routledge & Kegan Paul, 1983).

9. Friedl, *op. cit.*, pp. 63–75.

10. Lionel Tiger, *Men in Groups* (New York: Vintage, 1969).

11. Peggy Sanday, *Female Power and Male Dominance* (Cambridge, Mass.: Cambridge University Press, 1981), pp. 94–95, 105.

12. Michelle Z. Rosaldo, "The Use and Abuse of Anthropology: Reflections on Feminism and Cross-Cultural Understanding," *Signs* 5 (1980):384–417.

13. Sherry Ortner, "Is Female to Male as Nature Is to Culture?" in Michelle Z. Rosaldo and Louise Lamphere, eds., *Women, Culture & Society* (Stanford, Calif.: Stanford University Press, 1974), pp. 172–173; Ortner, "Theory in Anthropology Since the Sixties," *Comparative Studies in Society and History* 26 (1984):126–166.

14. Ortner, *op. cit.*

15. E. B. Leacock and J. Nash, "Ideology of Sex: Archetypes and Stereotypes," *Annals of the New York Academy of Science* 285 (1977): 1123–1129.

16. Sanday, *op. cit.*, pp. 58–68; Roslyn Dauber and Melinda Cain, eds., *Women and Technological Change in Developing Contries* (Boulder, Colo.: Westview, 1981).

17. Friedrich Engels, *The Origin of the Family, Private Property and the State* (1884; reprint ed., New York: International Publishers, 1942).

18. Virgil Elizondo and Norbert Greinacher, *Women in a Men's Church* (New York: Seabury, 1980), p. 5.

19. Ruth Bloch, "Untangling the Roots of Modern Sex Roles: A Survey of Four Centuries of Change," *Signs* 4 (1978):245.

20. Rosemary Reuter, *New Woman, New Earth: Sexist Ideologies and Human Liberation* (New York: Seabury, 1975), pp. 196–204.

21. Bloch, *op. cit.*, p. 251.

22. Renee Hirschon, "Introduction: Property, Power and Gender Relations," in R. Hirschon, ed., *Women and Property/Women as Property* (London: Croon Helm, 1984), pp. 1–22; Coward, *op. cit.*; Swasti Miller, *Common Fate: Common Bond; Women in the Global Economy* (London: Pluto, 1986).

23. Alexis de Tocqueville, *Democracy in America*, 2d ed., 1953.

24. *Ibid.*

25. William Sanger, *A History of Prostitution* (New York: Harper, 1958), quoted in Vern Bullough and Bonnie Bullough, *The Subordinate Sex* (Baltimore, Md.: Penguin, 1974), pp. 297–299.

26. *Ibid.*

Chapter 3

Heredity, Environment, or Both? Similarities and Differences between the Sexes

Here and in Chapters 4 and 5 we shall analyze the similarities and differences between the sexes in regard to traits, abilities, and behavior. Such an analysis must deal with questions about whether and how much a trait or behavior is physically determined and what role socialization and cultural expectations play in defining and obtaining certain behaviors. Socialization and cultural influence will be discussed in Chapters 4 and 5. In this chapter, we emphasize the physical nature of the similarities and differences between the sexes.

PROBLEMS OF DISCUSSING PHYSICAL SEX CHARACTERISTICS

Discussing physical similarities and differences between the sexes is fraught with difficulty because in the past these differences were often used to justify discrimination against women. As we saw in Chapter 2, biological differences were taken as proof that the sexes have different and supposedly unchangeable functions; for example, women bore the children, and so they had to raise them.

Not only was past research used to justify discrimination against women (and minorities), but because the research was done primarily by men, it emphasized traits connected with the male role, such as aggressiveness and competitiveness. These characteristics are also valued by the American culture and, not coincidentally, are possessed by more men than women. As fewer women were seen to have these societally valued characteristics, woman's nature was portrayed as different and inferior.

Few of the positive characteristics which were connected with women's roles and few areas in which women excelled were studied. When they were studied, "female characteristics" such as nurturance and compassion were used to justify women's having a separate "sphere" of activity (home and hearth) and being a support group for male society.[1]

Because of this bias, it is not surprising that feminists are concerned about discussions of sex differences. As Jeanne Gullahorn put it, "Our conceptions of sex differences are so deeply ingrained in the culture that preconceptions are hard to shift . . . particularly because many stereotypes involve implicit assumptions about biological determinants and about the implications of biological factors."[2]

In addition, there are problems in the methodology and reporting of sex-difference research. These studies usually concentrate on finding a sex difference; those which find no difference or find differences that vary from what is expected are not likely to be published or widely circulated. In most of these studies, the differences are highly overstated and the great overlap in traits and abilities between the sexes is not emphasized. Often the difference in a trait or ability accounted for by sex is quite small, sometimes less than 1 percent. In very few studies is sex a variable that accounts for more than 5 to 10 percent of the difference in a trait.[3] In some studies the samples are very large, and so average differences are likely to be statistically significant even when the actual differences are very small.

Another problem is that many studies dealing with brain development or hormone function have been done on animal populations, with the results then generalized to humans. However, it is not valid to apply results from animal studies to the different biological structure of humans.

Researchers have also overemphasized biological causation and neglected the influence of social events and psychological states on physical functioning; an example would be the impact of cultural expectations on female biological experiences such as menstruation and childbirth. Although the effects of socialization on gender roles have received more emphasis recently, the interaction between biology and cultural expectations has not received enough attention outside feminist sociology.[4]

Thousands of studies dealing with sex differences are assessed in Eleanor Maccoby and Carol Jacklin's encyclopedic review, *The Psychology of Sex Differences*.[5] The authors performed a tremendous service by collecting and systematizing the research on sex differences, but even this monumental task has been criticized. Maccoby and Jacklin point out that negative findings (studies that reveal no sex difference) are likely to be underrepresented. Block has criticized their rationale for including some studies. All studies dealing with a given area (such as verbal ability) were considered to have equal weight and their results were averaged, but there is a wide variation in the sampling size and methodology of these studies. One-third of the studies had sample sizes of sixty or less, and 20 percent had sample sizes of forty or less—too few people to generate valid results that can be generalized to a larger population.[6] Many of the studies used measures that did not seem to measure what they were supposed to or could not be duplicated by later researchers. There was also an overemphasis on younger age groupings in which measurement of differences may be difficult to achieve; 75 percent of the studies reported in the book were done on children age 12 or younger.[7]

Interpretation of the results of sex-difference studies is often biased in other ways as well. While Maccoby and Jacklin were very careful in their work, interpretation of results has often been slanted by other researchers. Kimball points out that "girls' greater verbal ability is not usually interpreted as enabling them to qualify for high positions in fields such as politics, law, and academics . . . yet their supposed lack of math ability theoretically makes them unfit for careers in engineering or the sciences."[8]

In sum, great difficulties are involved in finding worthwhile research about sex similarities and differences and in reporting the results in an accurate and unbiased manner. One must be aware that there is far more similarity than difference between the sexes and that far more variation exists in traits within one sex than can be found between the sexes. One must also remember that biology predisposes but does not predetermine the functions of human beings. People tend to convert description into prescription and say, "That's the way it *should* be." However, we know that biological differences cannot account for the variation in gender roles across cultures and at different times in the same culture. With these cautions in mind, let us look at the physical makeup of men and women.

GENDER AND HEREDITY

We are used to defining gender roles as masculine and feminine, and we think of ourselves and others as fitting clearly into one of the classifications, male or female. However, the definition of sex is not so simple. We may be talking about biological sex (the physical characteristics we inherit), our definition of self (the inner understanding that we are male or female), other people's definition of us, or "gender role" (the behavior we exhibit, feminine, masculine, or a combination of the two). All these facets of gender may be the same. A person may have female body characteristics, think of herself as female, and exhibit what our culture calls feminine behavior. However, these aspects of gender may vary and cause confusion or difficulty.

Hoyenga and Hoyenga describe eight definitions of gender; five of them deal with physically inherited aspects of sex, and three with culturally determined gender roles.[9] Table 1 displays these definitions.

Chromosomal sex refers to the kinds of chromosomes a person inherits. In normal males, the sex chromosomes are XY; in normal females, XX. Gonadal sex refers to the type of internal sex glands or sex hormones (substances secreted by the gonads) present in a person's body. Hormonal sex usually is the same before and after birth, but sometimes variations occur. Hormones produced by the gonads when a fetus is still in the uterus determine whether the internal and external sex organs will be male or female.

Usually the type of rearing a child receives is determined by the child's external sexual organs. Parents raise a child as the sex they believe it to be,

Table 1   Eight Definitions of Sex and Gender

Type of Definition	Males	Females
Chromosomal sex	XY	XX
Gonadal sex	Testes	Ovaries
Hormonal sex	Mostly androgens	Mostly estrogens and progestins
Sex of internal sexual accessory organs	Prostate glands, ejaculatory ducts, vas deferens, and seminal vesicles	Uterus and Fallopian tubes
Sex of external genitals	Penis and scrotal sacs	Clitoris, labia, and vagina
Gender of rearing	"It's a boy!"	"It's a girl!"
Gender identity	X Male __ Female	__Male X Female
Gender role	Masculine behavior	Feminine behavior

SOURCE: Katherine B. Hoyenga and Kermit Hoyenga, *The Question of Sex Differences* (Boston: Little, Brown, 1979), Table 1a, p. 5.

male or female, and teach it masculine or feminine behaviors. From this socialization probably comes gender identity, an identification not only with biological sex but with the behaviors usually expected of men or women. Gender identity usually is determined directly from physical characteristics and/or the gender of rearing. Thus, the words "sex" and "gender" may have many meanings. They may denote strictly physical characteristics, the feelings we have about ourselves, or the perception others have of us. They may also mean gender role, or appropriate behavior. When people say of someone, "He is a real man!" they do not mean that the person is physically a male but that he exhibits culturally appropriate masculine behavior.

Let us look at how sex and gender are determined in our culture and at some of the conflicts that may occur between the various aspects or definitions of sex and gender. The abnormalities in one part of sex, usually chromosomes or hormones, may cause confusion in the gender of rearing and gender identity. When sex or gender is confused, people may be born with external genital structures that are ambiguous (hermaphrodites); sometimes they have a gender identity that is different from that of their biological sex (transsexuals). A transsexual often feels that he is a woman when he has the body of a man or vice versa.[10]

Chromosomal Sex

When an embryo is conceived in the form of a fertilized egg cell, the ovum and the sperm each contribute twenty-three chromosomes, which align in twenty-three pairs in the egg. One pair of chromosomes determines the sex of the fetus. The ovum always contributes an X chromosome, and the sperm contributes either an X or a Y chromosome. The Y chromosome determines the sex of the fetus. No matter how many X chromosomes are present, the fetus will be male if a Y chromosome is also present. Recent research has proposed that one can determine the sex of a fetus by the timing of fertilization. The andosperm, which contains the father's Y chromosome, is faster but does not endure as long as the gynosperm, which contains the father's X chromosome. Therefore, if one wants to have a girl, fertilization should occur slightly before ovulation so that the father's hardier X chromosome will survive to fertilize the ovum and produce an XX (female) combination of chromosomes. If one wants a boy, fertilization should occur when ovulation has already taken place and the egg is ready, as the Y chromosomes will get to the ovum faster and be more likely to produce an XY (male) combination.

The X chromosome is larger and contains more genetic material than does the Y chromosome. If some genetic material is lost in the process of fertilization, the fetus will survive with only an X chromosome (X ———, an abnormality known as Turner's syndrome). However, a fetus cannot survive with only a Y chromosome.

The hardy, dominant X chromosome also seems to carry useful traits. Ashley Montague has reported that women have a greater resistance to illness and disease than men do. He lists fifty-nine ailments that occur more frequently in men than in women and only twenty-nine that occur more frequently in women than in men.[11] Other researchers speculate that there are factors on the X chromosome that protect against specific diseases or increase resistance to various kinds of degeneration.[12]

However, characteristics such as hemophilia, color blindness, and possibly the ability to handle concepts involving three-dimensional space seem to result from recessive genes carried on particular X chromosomes ("recessive X chromosomes"). These traits do not show up in women with two normal X chromosomes (that is, chromosomes without the particular characteristic) or in women with one normal and one recessive chromosome. The normal X chromosome without the recessive trait is dominant and cancels out the recessive characteristic on the recessive X chromosome. These traits show up in men, however, because the Y chromosome carries only sparse genetic material and is not strong enough to produce this canceling effect. The traits also show up in women with two recessive X chromosomes. Thus, women may carry a trait such as color blindness but are not likely to exhibit it (they would need two recessive X chromosomes to do so); however, their sons will demonstrate the trait if they get a recessive X chromosome from the mother plus a Y from the father.

Chromosomal abnormalities in which genetic material is lost or duplicated are rare, but they do exist. People who possess these abnormalities show the effect that chromosomes and their resulting hormones have on traits such as body build, intelligence, and even behavior. One of these abnormalities is Turner's syndrome (X ———), in which only one X chromosome is present in the fetus. People with Turner's syndrome look female but tend to be very short and may have physical deformities and performance deficits. They are almost always infertile and, without estrogen therapy from adolescence onward, do not exhibit secondary sex characteristics such as developing breasts. These women do not have the normal amounts of any of the three major types of sex hormones. Thus, they show that the second X chromosome is not necessary for female genitalia but is necessary for having children.

People with Klinefelter's syndrome are males born with extra X chromosomes (XXY or even XXXY). They are male in appearance because they have the Y chromosome, but the influence of the multiple X chromosomes overwhelms the Y chromosome. Although these people are male in chromosomes, they are somewhat female in appearance, may show breast enlargement, and have small penises and little body hair. They have low levels of testosterone (the major male hormone) and frequently exhibit mental retardation. They may also have difficulties in social adjustment and are more likely to be found in institutions than is the typical XY male.[13]

A male who has the XYY chromosome pattern (an extra Y chromosome) is characterized by being unusually tall and having subnormal intelligence. It has been thought that such men exhibit high levels of impulsive aggression and have criminal tendencies. The belief about criminal tendencies has led to sensational but inaccurate reports. Some studies have shown that XYY males are more prevalent in prison populations than can be accounted for by chance. One study surveyed thirty-five instances of XYY males in mental and penal institutions and concluded that the incidence of XYY males in these institutions was approximately twenty times what could be caused by chance.[14] However, other studies have disputed the belief that these men exhibit excessively aggressive behavior. A review of the actual crimes committed by XYY men shows that they did not commit crimes any more violent than those of the other inmates. Some researchers suspect that, as in the case of men with Klinefelter's syndrome, these men are overrepresented in prison populations because of their lower intelligence and difficulty adjusting to normal social patterns. They may commit slightly more minor crimes because of their social behavior pattern and may get arrested more often than are men with normal intelligence.[15] The great majority of XYY men, however, lead normal lives among the general population.[16]

Hormones and Their Interaction with Chromosomes

Chromosomes determine the sex of a fetus largely through their ability to form the testes or ovaries that produce the sex hormones. These internal sexual organs are usually formed between the sixth and tenth weeks of fetal development and later secrete an enzyme that helps synthesize the appropriate hormones. Both men and women possess some of all the sex hormones. However, the primary hormones for men are androgens, particularly testosterone; for women, the primary hormones are estrogen and progesterone. The development of a female fetus does not seem to require any specific hormones.[17] The fetus will differentiate as a female unless the Y chromosome and a sufficient amount of androgen are present; if they are, it will differentiate as a male.

Sex Hormones and Development

During fetal development, sex hormones can enter the brain and affect areas such as the hypothalamus, which later determines the development of the brain and the connections among its parts. Most of the evidence for the effect of sex hormones on the brain has come from animal studies. It is believed that the critical period for humans occurs from the third week to the eighth week of fetal development, as studies show a high concentration of hormones in the amniotic fluid of human fetuses during that time.[18] The influence of these sex hormones may result in some small differences between the brains of men and women.[19] These differences are referred to as brain dimorphism.

One of the hormonal abnormalities that may occur during the critical period is the androgenital syndrome. Female fetuses with this syndrome produce an abnormally high amount of androgen. This imbalance can lead to a masculinization of their external genitals even though they have normally functioning ovaries and internal female sex organs. If treated with hormones after birth, they will go through normal pubertal and menstrual cycles and later will be able to conceive and deliver babies normally.[20] Some researchers have examined whether the behavior of these girls differs from "typical female behavior" in childhood. In one Buffalo research sample of seventeen girls who had the syndrome and were compared with their normal sisters, 59 percent of the androgenital girls were identified by themselves and others as tomboys all during childhood.[21] These girls preferred boy's clothes, toys, and play; they had little or no interest in playing with dolls and showed reduced maternalism and a lack of concern about having children. This pattern was not true of their unaffected sisters. However, these girls had been treated with continuous doses of cortisone, a potent drug that can affect behavior. In addition, the surgical correction undergone by these girls for their genital abnormalities might have produced physical or psychological trauma. Also, the mothers of the androgenital girls were aware of the problem and might have treated them differently. Finally, the study relied on self-reports of the individuals and reports from their families. Thus, we are not certain to what degree physical factors or environment was operating.

In another study, female fetuses who were masculinized by artificial progestins (which have properties similar to those of androgen) given to their mothers to maintain pregnancies later exhibited behavior similar to that of androgenital girls. They were reported to be more competitive, self-assertive, independent, and self-reliant than average girls their age, and they preferred male playmates and male clothes. There is again the question of environment. The parents may well have treated the girls differently because their genitals were somewhat masculine. However, a study that compared only females whose genitals were not masculinized found the same kinds of behavior.[22] Males who had the androgenital syndrome or were exposed to artificial progestins as fetuses seem to have accentuated masculine behavior: They show even greater interest in sports and athletics than most boys do and are more independent and self-assured than are other males of the same age.

One study examined the effect of hormones on cognitive abilities by sampling umbilical cord blood from fetuses and then following up and testing the young children for different abilities. In this study, lower levels of prenatal androgens were associated with lower spatial ability in girls but not in boys. Other studies have not found an association between hormone levels and abilities.[23]

Androgen insensitivity can occur in a male (XY) fetus whose body cells are insensitive to androgen. The male internal organs and external genitals do not develop in response to the androgen produced by the testes. There are no internal female organs either, but in the absence of androgen, the external genitals differentiate as female genitals, with a vagina and a clitoris. These men later develop normal-sized breasts and look like normal females, but they are infertile. When raised as females, they are quite "feminine" in certain typical intellectual patterns (good verbal ability).[24]

Thus, although the possibility of a hormonal influence is intriguing, we cannot be certain that hormones played a role in the "different" behavior of the androgenital girls or the other groups studied. It is also possible that androgen has an effect on factors relating to behavior, such as an increased level of activity and an increased expenditure of energy, but not on more complex behaviors. There is some indication that high levels of certain prenatal hormones are associated with spatial abilities, but the evidence is inconclusive.

In addition, we do not have enough information about sex hormones to know with certainty which ones, if any, act in particular situations. The picture is even more unclear because it is known that, at least in rats, hormones are converted into one another (androgens undergo transformation into estrogens at the cellular level in the brain). We also know that low levels of hormones may be present in humans or animals when their primary source—the ovaries or testes—has been removed.

Gender Identity and Gender of Rearing

Gender identity, or the sex a person thinks he or she is, may differ from the physical manifestations of sex. Gender identity is often the focus of the heredity-versus-environment controversy. Money and Earhardt, along with others who have done extensive research in this area, firmly believe that psychosexual identity, or gender identity, is a learned factor. It is a matter of the sex assigned to a child and how that child is reared. In studies of the relative influence of chromosomes, hormones, physical appearance, and the manner in which a child is reared, the sex of rearing is almost always found to be the primary factor. Even when the external genitals contradicted the sex of rearing, Money and Earhardt reported that twenty-three of twenty-five patients believed themselves to be the sex which they were reared.

Money believes that children acquire a gender identity from the age of 6 months to 3 or 4 years. It is difficult after age 2 years, he states, to change a child's primary orientation without severe emotional trauma and permanent damage.[25]

In support of Money and Earhardt's assertion, several dramatic instances have been reported in which sex reassignment took place after a decision about indeterminate sex or after an accident. These instances show how important the influence of those around us can be. In one case, the parents of 7-month-old twin boys had their sons circumcised by means of electrocautery. The current used on one of the twins was too strong, and his penis was burned off flush to the abdominal wall. The parents agonized over what to do and decided to sex-reassign the damaged boy so that he would not have to compete with his normal brother. The child was reassigned as a female at 17 months of age and was given a new name, new clothing, hair ribbons, and feminine toys. The parents and all other people interacting with the child made every attempt to treat her as a girl. By age 5 the little girl was helping her mother around the house, exhibited motherly behavior toward her twin brother, and had asked for a dollhouse and doll carriage for Christmas. However, the little girl still exhibited a high activity level and a great deal of dominance behavior.

In a similar case, a genetically normal boy was born with a very small penis, and his parents decided to reassign him as a girl. A new name, new clothes, new toys, and different behavior by the parents and older brother followed. The girl imitated her mother but still showed signs of dominant behavior and seemed to be louder, more aggressive, and more energetic than other girls her age.[26]

Even in the case of gender identity, one cannot be certain that environment is operating in the absence of physical influences. Some evidence exists that hormones, especially in the fetal stage, help determine the sex in which one feels comfortable. In 1972, two villages in the Dominican Republic were discovered where some of the males had an enzyme deficiency. They could not metabolize testosterone properly, so that at birth their genitals looked female. These boy babies were thought to be girls and were raised as girls in the household; they did chores, baby-sat, and stayed close to their mothers. At puberty, however, they metabolized testosterone normally, and so their testes descended, their clitorides grew into penises, their voices deepened, and their muscles developed.

The conflict between hormones and rearing has left two of the eighteen hermaphrodites who were studied confused. One knows he is a male physically but feels and dresses like a woman. The other, who also feels like a female, married a man and wants a sex-change operation. In these cases we see the influence of sex rearing. However, the remaining sixteen people who had been raised as girls have assumed male identities.[27]

What do these cases tell us? How could the "girls" have changed gender identity so easily? One critique states that the children might have had enlarged clitorides which made them and their families question their sexual identities at birth, especially in a town where gender changes were known to occur.[28] However, Imperato-McGinley, the author of the original study, said that she had studied older people who had not known about the disease, and in rare cases in other countries, people also converted to the identity and behavior of the other sex without a problem.

Another question that might be raised is whether the male role was decidedly preferable in Dominican society. Some have claimed that this is likely to have been the case and that the "girls" who found themselves "boys" at age 12 might have been pleased to give up the restrictive nature of the Latin woman's role. It would have been difficult to continue in that role anyway, as they now had the bodies of men.[29]

Hampson has suggested that there may be some "imprinting" of sexual identity on the brain during the critical period of fetal development. This imprinting, or predisposition to feel or behave in a certain way, may develop later, possibly under the influence of other hormones. However, Hampson clearly believes in the importance of sex rearing and says that although there may be some imprinting of sexual identity during critical periods of fetal development, "psychologic sex . . . appears to be learned . . . we can [postulate] a concept of psychosexual neutrality in humans at birth."[30]

How can we reconcile the roles of fetal hormonal imprinting, later parental action, and environment in determining gender identity? For the moment, there is no firm evidence for the degree of importance of any of these factors. Although proponents of gender of rearing seem to have more evidence on their side, the Dominican example reminds us that the gender of rearing does not always determine gender identity.

Physical Characteristics of Infant Boys and Girls

The physical characteristics of males and females are clearly evoked by sex hormones. Aside from their different genitalia, boy and girl babies are extremely similar in characteristics such as height, weight, and general behavior. However, some minor differences may later become accentuated by interaction with the environment. The hormone androgen facilitates the synthesis of proteins from amino acids, aiding the development of muscle and bone in males. At birth the average male infant exceeds the average female baby by 2 percent in height and 5 percent in weight, although he has less body fat from birth onward. Male infants also have a consistently higher average basal metabolism after age 2 years. This is partially accounted for by the greater bone and muscle mass. As one might expect, they also tend to develop larger hearts and lungs and have a lower resting heart rate.[31] The male infant grows faster before birth and for about seven months after birth.

The development of the internal organs occurs more rapidly in the average girl baby. After age 8 months girls grow faster than boys, and they reach the limits of their growth an average of one to two years sooner. They also reach puberty about two years earlier than boys do. In the infant girl, estrogens, which are activated at puberty, help reduce serum cholesterol and provide protection against heart attacks, although they encourage tissue deposits of fat, with girls at all ages having more body fat than boys do.[32]

Infant boys on the average seem to have greater use of the large muscles, whereas most infant girls have a more developed use of the fine muscles and show more manual dexterity immediately after birth. Female infants on the average spend more time smiling reflexively, mouthing rhythmically, and moving the mouth toward objects.[33] There is usually no difference in activity level during the first year of life; afterward, when differences exist, boys are usually found to be more active. In one study, male infants were awake more often than females, displayed considerably more facial grimacing, and engaged in more low-intensity movement. In this study, the experimenters did not know the sex of the infants they were watching, eliminating an important source of bias.[34]

In other areas the sexes do not seem to have well-established differences. Where differences do occur, it appears that heredity has interacted with environment.

Other Physical Characteristics: The Sexes and the Senses

People have always believed that boy and girl babies differ in their use of sight, hearing, smell, taste, and touch as well as in the physical characteristics described above. Maccoby and Jacklin tried to make sense of the many contradictory studies and findings and concluded that boy and girl infants are much more similar in the use of the senses than had been believed.

Hearing.   It was originally believed that newborn females respond to auditory stimulation more intensely than newborn males do. It was also believed that such auditory stimulation as speaking softly can be used to reinforce or reward other behavior in girls. However, Maccoby and Jacklin's review of the relevant research does not support this belief. Although girl infants respond slightly more when some measures of response to sound are used, this occurs only during a very limited age span.[35] We do not know why these beliefs developed. Perhaps because girl babies use the small muscles around their mouths more than boys do and give reflex "smiles," parents think their daughters are responding to them. Parents seem to react to the belief that their daughters hear them better, as they talk more to infant girls than to infant boys.

While infant sex differences in hearing cannot be established, such differences do exist at older ages. Adult women in our culture seem to have a higher sensitivity to sound than men do. They appear to hear better in the higher ranges but are less tolerant of loud noises. At 85 decibels and above, any sound is twice as loud to a woman as it is to a man. Women are also less tolerant of repetitive sounds. Thus, there seem to be some differences between men and women in their responses to sound, but these differences are not readily apparent in infants.[36]

Vision.   No consistent difference has been found between newborn males and females in regard to vision. However, there are slight differences between the sexes among adults. Adult men on the average are reported to have better visual acuity from age 18 to age 70, and men are supposed to have better day-light vision while women have better night vision.[37]

Touch.   Newborn boy and girl babies seem to be equally sensitive to touch. If soothed with a blanket or soft fabric, both sexes quiet equally well. Neither sex shows any real differences in touch sensitivity when meters are used to measure their skin responses. In older adults, however, there does seem to be a statistical difference in that women are more sensitive to touch. In one experiment, women reported greater sensitivity to pressure than men did, but the discrimination differed according to body part.[38]

Smell.   Most studies have found little differences in the sense of smell among newborn babies.[39] However, several studies of adults have shown differences between men and women in regard to sensitivity to odors, with women showing more sensitivity to musk and various urinary smells. While some of this response may be learned (woman wear perfume), there is evidence that changes in estrogen levels are associated with sensitivity to smell. The difference in sensitivity appears only after puberty and may decline after menopause.[40]

Taste.   The female seems to have more of a sweet tooth than does the male. Girl babies increase their sucking rate for sweet solutions, while boy babies do not. Sex hormones also seem to directly affect preference for food, possibly through the mediating factor of blood sugar levels. In the premenstrual period, women often report an increased urge for carbohydrates and sweets. Men, in contrast, generally seem to prefer more sour and bitter tastes, such as quinine.[41]

Thus, infant boys and girls are remarkably similar in their use of at least four of the senses. We are not sure why sensory differences appear in adults—whether those differences are biologically based, are socially learned, or develop through a combination of the two.

THE SEXES AND THE BRAIN

There is evidence that the organization of men's and women's brains is slightly different. It is believed that this difference in organization stems from the circulation of prenatal hormones because some individuals (such as androgen-insensitive men) have a brain organization that is similar to that of a woman. However, it is not certain whether this different organization is developed by birth or is activated by hormones at puberty or later. Factors other than sex hormones may influence such organization. In any case, this organization may influence language and related motor skills as well as certain spatial skills. We will look at this difference—brain dimorphism—in more detail when we discuss language and spatial abilities.

Let us examine some of the similarities and differences in older boys and girls and in men and women. Studies of similarities and differences between the sexes often concentrate on cognitive abilities and behavior.

Possible Differences in Cognitive Abilities

Verbal Ability.   Almost all the research on verbal ability agrees that the average girl exceeds the average boy in verbal ability after about age 10 or 11 and scores higher on both simple verbal skills and higher-level tasks, including vocabulary, listening, speaking ability, comprehension of difficult material, creative writing, fluency, and spelling.[42] However, the average differences between the sexes are small. Many of the studies have used large samples to establish a statistically significant difference; on the average, girls score only about 5 percent higher then boys.[43]

Research differs on whether this verbal advantage develops in early childhood. Maccoby and Jacklin surveyed more than a hundred recent studies and found almost no difference between male and female infants in terms of verbal ability, although females develop this ability sooner.[44] Girls acquire phonemes (the basic speech sounds out of which mature language is built) before boys do and, according to rigorous studies, talk sooner than boys do.[45] Girls also lead in developing more complex speech constructions such as the passive voice, reflexives, and subordinate clauses.[46] Some research has indicated that girls talk more than boys and outscore boys on word fluency tests,[47] although this research is dated. Girls seem to articulate more clearly than boys do and have many fewer speech disorders. Boys have more speech defects, including stuttering, and more boys than girls have difficulty learning to read.[48] Girls outperform boys on measures of verbal comprehension and reasoning, and there is some evidence that language plays a greater part in girls' intellectual development.[49] Data from two longitudinal investigations indicate that female infants' scores on various language measures correlate substantially with their subsequent scores on general intelligence measures at ages 3 to 26.[50] As no such relationship has been observed in males, these findings suggest that linguistic skills may be more important in females' than in males' thinking, problem solving, and general intellectual ability.

Girls score higher than boys on the verbal parts of the Scholastic Aptitude Test (SAT) and the Graduate Record Exam (GRE). On the verbal portion of the GRE, a recent mean for women was 503, while for men it was 493. Although the difference is small, it is significant at the 0.001 level of probability. Beginning in the 1950s, an attempt was made to balance the content of these tests, particularly the SAT, by including items in which men might be more interested in the hope that the scores would then be more balanced between the sexes. However, no attempt was made to balance the even larger difference between the scores of men and women on the mathematical part of the SAT.[51]

A more recent reanalysis of some of the studies used by Maccoby and Jacklin shows that the difference in verbal ability may be as little as 1 percent.[52] Fausto-Sterling points out that in their original work, Maccoby and Jacklin emphasized studies that showed verbal superiority by women but could easily have emphasized studies that showed no difference at all.[53]

Cultural expectations about abilities also seem to play an important part in the development of verbal skills. Johnson reports that girls score higher than boys in reading skills in the United States and Canada but that boys outscore girls in reading skills in England and Nigeria. In the latter nations, teachers say they expect boys to be better readers.[54]

Mathematical Ability.   Boys and girls do equally well in mathematics in the early years; when differences are found, girls outperform boys. However, beginning at about age 13, boys seem to increase their mathematical performance more than girls do. The difference between the average girl and the average boy is small and depends greatly on (1) whether the number of math courses taken is accounted for and (2) the general attitude that math is a male domain.

When older boys and girls are compared without controlling for the number of mathematics courses taken, males do far better than females on measures of performance. However, some of these studies may be based on questionable measures or assumptions. Large differences in mathematical ability were reported in Benbow and Stanley's 1980 study. They used the SAT and gave this instrument, which measures achievement among high school seniors, to a group of highly talented seventh- and eighth-graders. The authors reasoned that the younger children would show potential math ability by their scores. Boys and girls did equally well on the verbal test, but boys scored far better on the math test. To this point the boys and girls had taken the same courses in high school, and both scored well on the tests even when they did not like math. Because of these results, Benbow and Stanley concluded that "sex differences in achievement in mathematics result from superior male mathematical ability, which may in turn be related to greater male ability in spatial tasks."[55] Their conclusions were published in *Science,* excerpted in *The New York Times,* and given a great deal of publicity.

In a critique of this study, Fausto-Sterling points out that (1) the results were based on a test designed to measure achievement and not aptitude and (2) attitudes about sex roles may be equally important. She reports that in the research fewer talented girls than boys enrolled in accelerated classes, and those who did enroll said they found the classes dull.[56] She also suggests that Benbow and Stanley overemphasized inborn factors as a strong cause of sex differences.

Other studies show that the number of math courses taken greatly influences performance. The National Assessment of Educational Progress (NAEP) mathematics study done in the spring of 1978 found a significant sex difference in terms of enrollment in and completion of elective advanced math courses such as trigonometry, precalculus, and calculus. The College Entrance

Examination Board reported in 1978 that approximately 63 percent of college-bound men but only 43 percent of college-bound women had taken four or more years of high school mathematics.[57] Wise, Steele, and MacDonald did a longitudinal study of 400,000 high school students in 1979 to determine differences when the effect of taking math courses was controlled. They found no difference between ninth-grade boys and girls who had had similar amounts of math at that grade level, but three years later the boys and girls differed significantly. Boys' gains on the test were twice those of the girls in the three-year period. However, when the number of math courses was held constant, sex differences in ability disappeared.[58] In other research, when the number of math courses was controlled, the differences in ability between boys and girls were very small, with boys exceeding girls by only 5 percent, a matter of two test items.[59] Girls seem to take fewer courses than boys because they (1) have lower confidence in learning math, (2) see less usefulness for math, and (3) have lower visual-spatial ability.[60]

Whether mathematics is considered a male domain also influences test scores. Fennema and Sherman studied 1,000 boys and girls who were ninth- to twelfth-graders at four different public high schools in Wisconsin. In two of the schools boys and girls performed equally well on tests of math and spatial ability, but at the other two schools the boys performed about 5 percent better than the girls did in math. In the two schools where sex-related differences appeared, there were significant differences in parent and teacher attitudes toward math as a male domain.[61] Other studies confirmed that both boys and girls saw math as a male domain.[62]

Fausto-Sterling says, "In fact, if all of the variables affecting math performance were taken into account, less than 2 percent of the achievement difference remained unaccounted for and might, therefore, be considered by some to represent `pure' sex differences (although they too might disappear if earlier childhood experiences were factored in)."[63]

The significance of general background in the ability to do math can be seen in some of the other results of the NAEP in the spring of 1978. Significant sex differences were found among samples of 13-year-olds and 17-year-olds on some of the subjects in the mathematics achievement assessment. At age 13, boys scored higher on the practical application subtest but girls scored higher on the computation subtest. No sex difference was found on the computation test for 17-year-olds, but boys continued to outperform girls on the applications subtest.[64]

Thus, there are many questions about the small (5 percent) difference usually found between boys and girls in mathematical ability after puberty. Several studies have found that achievement test items are biased in favor of boys in terms of content or sex-appropriateness and that bias causes differential achievement on such tests. The learning and application of mathematical skills outside of school may also be greater among boys than girls, and boys are likely to improve their achievement scores by taking advanced mathematics classes.[65] When girls take advanced math classes, they improve their scores rapidly.[66]

Visual-Spatial Ability.   One of the differences in ability between the sexes that Maccoby and Jacklin believed they established was the slight superiority of men in regard to visual-spatial ability. It has been hypothesized that one reason males may have an edge in advanced mathematics courses is that some of these courses, such as geometry and trigonometry, rely on three-dimensional spatial concepts. Actually, three types of visual-spatial ability have been identified, and in only one are strong sex differences seen. This type involves the ability to rotate objects mentally in space, an ability that is sometimes called for on intelligence tests and in engineering.[67] In most visual-spatial tests, men show a slight superiority or there is no difference between the sexes.[68] However, the degree of training in skill-related areas is not held constant in most tests, and so it is difficult to know the true degree of difference between males and females in terms of the ability to visualize space. Studies of the performance of first-grade children on tests involving embedded figures and blocks show small sex differences when the children have not practiced the tasks. With practice, the girls improve their scores much more than boys do.[69] Among older students taking drafting courses, the girls soon catch up with the boys in visual-spatial skills.[70]

Boy often learn to handle three-dimensional spatial concepts early in childhood. They have toys that are large and can be manipulated, such as erector sets and building tools, and they deal with movement through space when they use sports equipment. In school courses, boys may continue this kind of experience as they put things together in shop. Children who are allowed more independence, have varied experiences, and have less verbal interaction are also more likely to develop strong spatial skills. These criteria dovetail much more with the childhood experiences of boys than with those of girls. Girls who are independent and tomboyish tend to have higher spatial skills than does the average girl.[71] Differences in spatial ability seem to be decreasing as girls engage in sports and other activities previously reserved for boys.[72]

Whether the cultural environment demands such skills also seems to be important. Berry has compared the ability of the Eskimos, the Scots, and the Temme people of Sierra Leone in this regard. In the Eskimo culture, where spatial skills are needed for survival in a snow-covered environment, no differences between the sexes are found in this area. Where there is little need for these skills (as in the Temme culture) or where there are distinct male and female role separations (as in urban-industrial society), differences exist in the skill displayed by men and women, with men showing general superiority. The encouragement of responsibility, self-assertion, and general curiosity in a child also seems to be related to field independence or spatial skills, whereas the repression of aggression and a stress on discipline and conformity seem to be related to a lack of this ability.[73]

Intelligence, Creativity, and Styles of Analytic Behavior

As noted above, no difference exists between the sexes in regard to overall intelligence and analytic ability. Whether one defines males or females as more analytic or more creative depends on the kind of test used. While men excel in visual-spatial restructuring, women excel in verbal problem-solving tasks. There is no evidence that women are better at overlearned rote tasks and that men do better in creative analytical situations.

Are girls less rational or logical than boys? We often hear that women are not logical, yet neither sex seems to have an advantage in terms of reasoning or concept mastery. Only in tests that require the use of mathematical processes do men seem to have an edge in reasoning. In creativity tests measuring the "ability to produce unique and novel ideas," girls seem to show a slight superiority to boys from age 7 on.[74]

BIOLOGICAL THEORIES EXPLAINING SEX-DIFFERENTIATED COGNITIVE ABILITIES

At this point we need to take a look at the theories that have been proposed to explain the slight sex-linked difference between men and women in cognitive abilities. Only recently has it been recognized how great a role the environment plays in determining cognitive strengths and weaknesses. Previously and to some extent even today, researchers have been intrigued by biological explanations for the small differences in cognitive abilities between the sexes.

In 1961, one theory proposed that mathematical and spatial abilities are carried on recessive genes; as with hemophilia, women can carry the recessive trait or ability but are not as likely as men to evidence it.[75] Other researchers suggested that math and spatial ability genes exist in everyone but have to be activated by male hormones, as in the case of baldness.[76] In 1974 Broverman proposed that women and men have different and opposite cognitive styles. In the automated style, a person can do well on practiced or learned tasks such as typing. The other style, called cognitive restriction, requires the inhibition of automatic responses to familiar stimuli in order to respond to something new. Broverman and his colleagues theorized that all sex hormones aid an automated style of cognition but that women do better on automated as opposed to creative tasks because estrogen is a more potent hormone.[77] None of these theories were proved by subsequent research, although a great deal of stereotyping has been based on them.

A study done in 1976 was designed to test hormone levels and performance on visual-spatial and verbal tasks.[78] While the researcher did not measure hormone levels directly, she compared the degree of secondary sex development in thirty-five men and fifty women with their performance on both types of tasks. She compared each subject at ages 13, 16, and 18. There was no relationship between performance and secondary sex characteristics among the subjects at the younger ages, but at age 18 she noted that males who had highly masculine secondary sex characteristics (deep voices and body hair) had high verbal fluency and poor spatial ability. Among females the results showed that highly developed secondary sex characteristics were related to poor spatial ability but not to verbal ability.[79] Thus, if one assumes that levels of hormones are consistent with developed secondary sex characteristics, there may be some support for the idea that high levels of hormones inhibit spatial ability.

The interesting part of the Peterson study is the finding that men with supposedly high levels of testosterone are also limited in spatial ability but excel in verbal ability in a pattern similar to that of women with high levels of estrogen. Other research has confirmed that men with high mathematical ability frequently do not appear to have the masculine body build that may be linked with high levels of testosterone.[80]

We saw above that high levels of prenatal hormones, especially androgens, may have an effect on women's spatial abilities. A study completed in 1988 links women's skills to adult estrogen levels. The researchers, Doreen Kimura and Elizabeth Hampson of the University of Western Ontario, had 150 women perform a variety of tests designed to measure cognitive and motor skills at different phases of the menstrual cycle—when estrogen levels were high and when they were low. The women did better at spatial tasks when their estrogen levels were low and better at verbal tasks and fine motor skills when the levels were high. Kimura postulates that these results reflect the findings of recent research suggesting that estrogen generally enhances the function of the left hemisphere of the brain. Other recent studies have linked androgen to spatial abilities in men but not in women.[81]

Sex Hormones and Brain Development

Many theories concerning the development of male and female brains rely on the fact that the human brain has a right hemisphere and a left hemisphere, each of which processes information in a slightly different fashion. In nearly all right-handed people and in about two-thirds of left-handers, the right hemisphere specializes in spatial or nonlinguistic operations and "gestalts," or total pictures, when processing information. The left hemisphere specializes in logical, analytic analysis of information, with verbal labeling, details, and time variables. The similarity of the different hemispheric modes of processing information to the slightly different verbal and spatial skills of women and men has led researchers to hypothesize that gender, through the medium of hormones, is related to slightly different development of the hemispheres of the brain between the sexes.

There is general agreement that the two hemispheres are not specialized at birth and that specialization and subsequent transfer of information occur later.[82] Some people believe that such specialization is complete by age 5,[83] and others believe that it is not complete until adolescence. Some believe that the age of maturation (puberty) affects the degree of specialization and the use of subsequent verbal and spatial skills.[84]

Marylou Reid of the University of Massachusetts has used tests of neurological performance to determine verbal and spatial abilities in boys and girls 5 and 8 years old. Right-handed girls developed the left hemisphere more quickly than the right and moved ahead in verbal skills. Right-handed boys developed the right hemisphere more quickly than the left and advanced in spatial abilities. However, in left-handers the reverse was true. The maturation pattern was the same: Girls developed the left hemisphere more quickly, but their spatial skills developed first. Boys developed the right hemisphere more quickly, but their verbal skills developed first. However, other studies do not show this particular pattern. There is also no strong evidence that brain specialization patterns predict verbal ability.[85]

One study attempted to relate hemispheric specialization and the cognitive abilities of boys and girls directly to the rate of body maturation. Waber found that the late maturers in both sexes were better at spatial tasks than were the early-maturing children of the same sex; no relationship existed between verbal skill and time of maturation. She hypothesized that the difference in spatial ability is related to the degree of specialization of the brain hemisphere and that late maturers have a higher degree of specialization. In diotic listening tasks designed to measure whether one or both hemispheres were functioning, she found that late maturers were more specialized than early maturers. Boys are more likely to be late maturers and thus have greater specialization of function in their brain hemispheres. However, she found no sex differences among children who were early or late in maturation.[86] In other words, if some girls were late in maturating, they were also more likely to be specialized in hemispheric functioning and to have cognitive skills similar to those found in boys. A more recent study has confirmed that the age of maturation is related to spatial ability, but other research has not found this relationship.[87]

The theory that the brain processes information in slightly different ways in men and women is connected to the idea of *brain lateralization*, that is, the ability of the brain to transfer information from one side to the other. In normal people the two hemispheres are connected by a structure called the corpus callosum. Messages received in one hemisphere can be transferred to the other to aid in the processing of information. Occasionally, as a treatment for extreme epilepsy, the corpus callosum is surgically cut. In people treated this way, messages cannot be sent from one hemisphere to the other. We have learned a great deal about the specialization of each hemisphere of the brain from such people and from others with specific hemispheric damage.

Almost all this research finds that women transfer more information from one side of the brain to the other than men do.[88] One experiment tested 200 right-handed boys and girls between the ages of 6 and 14 and found that the girls did equally well in recognizing spatial objects with both hands, while the boys did significantly better with the left hand. (The right side of the brain operates the left side of the body, and vice versa.)[89] Studies of Braille learning indicate that girls have more bilateral representation of spatial processing than do boys.[90] There are also higher correlations between verbal and spatial performances in females than in males.[91]

The proposed reasons for this greater transfer of information by women vary. One possible physical reason for such transfer is that the corpus callosum (particularly in the posterior lobes of the brain) is twice as big in women as it is in men. Some research also has pointed to such kinds of transferring. In one study of accident victims, only men showed specific verbal deficits after left-hemisphere damage or specific spatial deficits after right-sided damage to the brain. Women showed less severe losses in verbal and spatial skills no matter which side of the brain was damaged. It was thus hypothesized that a woman's spatial and verbal abilities are more likely to be duplicated on both sides of her brain, while a right-handed man is more likely to have the speech center on the left and the spatial skills on the right.[92]

However, extensive longitudinal research by Kimura has shown that women's verbal skills are on the left hemisphere but are located in only a few areas while the areas controlling men's verbal skills are more widespread. In accidents, it is more likely that men will lose some of the area that controls their skills.[93]

Some theories suggest that dual processing of information does not necessarily occur in women. These theories postulate that women may simply develop a preference for a left-brained verbal approach and use linguistic strategies to solve spatial problems. However, most recent research gives more credence to differences in brain specialization between males and females.[94]

Kimura summarizes the findings by saying that "it is probably true that hormones organize the brain early in life and also true that we see typically distinct patterns of brain organization in adult men and women for speech and motor function. But the fact of menstrual cycle fluctuations in abilities must mean that current hormonal environments also have an influence."[95] She cautions, however, that sex is only one of several predictors of brain organization. Another is hand preference, and the research of Richard Harshman suggests that intelligence level also is related to brain organization and that both factors interact with each other.

Another researcher cautions us further: "One must not overlook perhaps the most obvious conclusion, which is that basic patterns of male and female brain asymmetry seem to be more similar than they are different."[96]

We have looked at some biological factors that may influence cognitive activities, but it is important to remember that cultural factors are even more important. The toys used by boys and girls, the expectations of parents and teachers, the chance to practice a skill, and the stereotyping of a domain as masculine or feminine are extremely important factors in determining whether abilities develop and evidence themselves.

Are There Behavioral Differences?

Aggression.   It is frequently asserted that the one sex difference that has been established involves aggression. However, it is difficult to characterize aggression as a sex difference because even defining aggression presents a problem. Aggression can be physical, verbal, or ritualized, as in football. Even when the definition is limited to physical aggression, it is difficult to differentiate rough-and-tumble play from aggressive acts. This problem of definition affects any determination of sex differences or similarities in regard to aggression. Boys may be more likely to engage in physically active behavior and thus are more likely to be defined as aggressive. Aggression also varies in accordance with what a culture defines as aggressive and with whether one includes ritualized aggression. The degree of behavior defined as aggressive is almost certain to vary according to whether a particular culture rewards aggression for one gender or the other and according to specific situations.[97]

In spite of these problems, Maccoby and Jacklin claim that with the exception of maternal aggressiveness in defense of young, the male of all species is on the average more likely to engage in almost every kind of aggressive behavior. They believe that this is found in all human societies for which evidence is available and that differences in aggression are often seen early in life, when there has been little chance for differential socialization. At least in animals, aggressive behavior seems to be related to levels of sex hormones, and the degree of aggressive behavior can be changed by altering the level of these hormones. Many researchers concur with Maccoby and Jacklin that there is a sex difference in regard to aggression in all species, including humans; that this difference is particularly influenced by prenatal sex hormones and by sex hormones at puberty; and that the male of each species tends to be more aggressive under more conditions than the female.[98]

Research on hormone levels and aggressiveness in humans has been limited. Frequently, hormone levels are inferred by the degree of secondary sex characteristics rather than measured directly. In studies where these levels have been measured, a particular environment may have influenced aggressiveness. For example, studies on prisoners found no connection between hormone levels and verbal aggressiveness or fighting behavior in prison, yet prisoners with higher androgen levels had committed more violent crimes during adolescence.[99] In studies such as this, aggressiveness might have been influenced by the environment, and such studies lack control groups for comparison.

It is also difficult to control for the influence of a particular cultural environment. Although Maccoby and Jacklin claim that differences in aggression are found in children too young to be exposed to socialization pressures,[100] this claim has been disputed. Fausto-Sterling points out that in studies of children up to age 5, half the studies showed no sex-related differences, and that the observers knew the sex of the children and were looking for specific behavior. In addition, it is difficult to take into account particular cultural influences.[101] In this culture, boys are more likely to be reinforced for aggressive behavior and thus are more likely to show it as adults. Aggression is also defined as congruent with the masculine gender role; thus, males are more likely to evidence aggression rather than suppress it as females are apt to do.[102]

Dominance and Competition.   Dominance and competition are two other social behaviors that have been linked to aggression. While dominance can stem from aggression, there are many kinds of dominance. For example, one can dominate by means of greater skill or through manipulation. Maccoby and

Jacklin report that while there are no significant sex differences in dominance, dominance seems to be more of an issue in boys' groups and boys make more attempts to dominate each other. However, because younger children usually play in sex-segregated groups, boys make fewer attempts to dominate girls. Maccoby and Jacklin report that in adult groups, formal leadership tends to go to males at the beginning of any interaction but that as the relationship continues, influence becomes more nearly equal between the sexes. Thus, it is questionable whether any legitimate difference in dominance exists between the sexes. The differences that appear seem to be highly influenced by cultural norms.[103]

There is mixed evidence about sex differences in the area of competition. Some studies show boys to be more competitive, but many studies show the sexes to be similar in competitive level. Boys seem to need a stimulus to compete, but when aroused, they sustain a higher level of competition than girls do. Girls seem to care less about competition but try hard when put into a competitive situation. Some studies have postulated that girls avoid competitive situations because they do not want to disrupt social relationships, but this hypothesis has received only mixed support.[104] Much of the observed difference in competitiveness may be due to social roles. Traditionally, in our culture boys have been expected to compete; this competition is part of the masculine gender role and self-image. Girls, in contrast, have not until recently been urged to engage in much competition and have not received rewards for competing.[105] With the growing popularity of sports for women and as women enter more varied occupations, the picture may change.

Achievement Orientation and Self-Esteem

Women seem to have as great a motivation to achieve as men do and to be as persistent in achieving their goals. However, the goals that motivate achievement may differ between the sexes. To some degree, women may be more interested in goals that relate to social interaction, and the basis for women's self-esteem also seems to lie in different areas. Women are more likely to feel good about interpersonal skills than about concrete achievements. Affective factors such as the atmosphere in an academic program are also more likely to influence women's achievements.[106]

Although some studies show women's general self-esteem to be as high as that of men, others do not.[107] Some evidence shows that women do not feel as good as men do about their specific abilities. They do not expect to do as well as men on problem-solving tasks in spite of past success. They rate masculine qualities higher than those they consider feminine, and they rate work believed to be done by men as better than work believed to be done by women.[108] Some research has reported that from age 18 to age 26 females studied longitudinally lost self-confidence, while males at the same age developed a greater sense of competence. When women fail, they are more likely to blame it on lack of ability, while men blame their failures on lack of motivation or bad luck. Men who succeed believe they have done so by virtue of their own abilities, and women who succeed often believe they have been lucky. Women are more likely to be victims of the "impostor syndrome," in which they believe that even if they achieve higher levels of success, their abilities are not adequate.[109]

Fear, Timidity, and Anxiety.   Researchers do not usually find that girls are any more fearful than boys; however, girls are more willing to admit to having fear and anxiety. Some researchers have suggested that this greater willingness to admit to fear leads to an avoidance of situations in which fear is conquered. A girl who stands at the top of a ski slope and says she is afraid to go down may never try the slope and conquer her fear; a boy who cannot admit his fear and must go down the slope to preserve his self-image may find that the fearful situation is not so bad. Boys and girls both report that boys are more exploratory and assertive than girls are.[110] Girls have also been reported to be more eager to receive social approval. The evidence supporting this hypothesis is mixed, although girls score higher on measures of social desirability and compliance to adults.[111]

Nurturance and Maternal Behavior.   It is not known whether the ability to nurture and care for young infants is an area where inheritance and instinct play a dominant role or whether nurturing behavior is primarily learned. With the recent changes in sex roles and the controversy about whether men are able to care for children as well as women do, research on maternal behavior is particularly important.

No evidence exists for a maternal instinct of any sort, although hormones may play a role in stimulating maternal behavior (at least in animals), as may critical periods of interaction with a newborn.[112] Recent studies of human infants and their mothers and fathers seem to show that the bonds between a mother and father and their child are strongest when the parents can hold the child and care for it immediately after birth.[113] However, most researchers believe that the response to infants is learned rather than instinctive, because not all mothers exhibit maternal behavior even when they are in constant contact with their infants after birth. History has recorded many cases of mothers killing unwanted babies, and child abuse has occurred frequently.

Researchers also believe that nurturing is learned because men may exhibit this behavior. While male rats are often initially cannibalistic, they frequently develop nurturing behavior if given successive litters of baby rats to care for. Although little research has been done on the nurturing potential of human fathers, men who care for infants seem to establish the same close bonds with them that women do, and many men seem willing to exhibit nurturing feelings if they can do so without public disapproval. In one experiment on androgyny, men who did not define themselves as "macho" were quite willing to play with a small kitten or a baby; in fact, they played more with the kitten or baby than did women who defined themselves as "stereotypically feminine."[114]

The fact that maternal, nurturing behavior is probably learned can also be inferred from cross-cultural studies. Such behavior is not usually found in very young children of either sex, and when it does occur, it does not differ by sex. In one cross-cultural study that compared children in Kenya, India, Okinawa, the Philippines, and Mexico, no difference was seen in nurturing behavior among 3- to 6-year-olds. Among 7- to 11-year-olds, however, the girls offered more help to younger children and gave them more emotional support.[115] In the Veroff study of a national sample of American women, many women mentioned nurturance as a desirable feminine trait that they would like in their personalities.[116]

Sociability.   Little evidence supports the contention that girls are more sociable than boys. At early ages, girls have no more preference than boys do for being with people or for toys that represent faces or people. Girls are also more likely at slightly older ages to play in smaller groups than are boys, and their friendships seem to be based on more intimacy than those of most boys, although they are equally likely to exclude strangers from their groups.[117]

Some researchers have found that girls seem to be more empathetic than boys and seem to be able to interpret nonverbal cues and discern emotions more accurately.[118] In her androgyny studies on college-aged women, Bem found that women who accepted beliefs concerning traditional female roles were more likely to be able to decode feelings in others.[119] Perhaps because of the social stereotype that women are empathetic and more social, traditional women believe that knowledge of and sympathy for the feelings of others are what they "ought" to have and thus are more tuned in to obtaining these feelings.

Some of the "myth of sociability" may lie in how much emotion is shown. Girls learn to suppress their negative emotions more than boys do, and so they seem more sociable. After age 18 months, boys show more anger than girls because girls decrease the number and intensity of their outbursts. Boys may be allowed to express more anger and frustration because their parents see this as evidence of spirit and strength, while girls are taught to suppress anger and act in sociable ways. However, when we look at willingness to help others, there are no consistent sex differences.[120]

SOME CROSS-CULTURAL DIFFERENCES IN BEHAVIOR

To underscore the fact that culture is the predominant force in determining behavior, let us look at three cultures in which the behavior of the sexes differs markedly from that in our society.

A classic example of how cultures can influence behavior through their definitions of what is masculine and feminine is given in Margaret Mead's *Sex and Temperament in Three Primitive Societies.*[121] Her description of three "primitive" cultures in New Guinea shows how their concept of the ideal sex role differs drastically from ours. Among the Arapesh, both men and women are raised to be nurturant. The dominant ethic of the culture is to "grow" things, including young human beings. The responsibility for growing is shared between men and women. While the women do more of the actual child care, the men are expected to be nurturing and maternal-paternal in nature. Even before a child is born, the father is thought to be participating in the growth of the fetus by contributing his sperm to the mother's blood, and he participates in pre- and postbirth rituals. Neither sex is supposed to demonstrate aggression, competition, or even assertive behavior. The ideal is cooperation and peace. The role of the authority figure is repugnant, but the Arapesh have ways of selecting leaders and training them to be more aggressive. The role of the leader is not envied; in fact, his contemporaries pity him for having to be assertive and display asocial traits.

This is a tribe where both sexes follow norms for behavior that would be called "feminine" in the United States. Those who are not passive, cooperative, and nurturant are considered abnormal, and they are outcasts as surely as are those in our culture who do not adopt the appropriate sex role.

At the opposite extreme is the culture of the Mudugamor, in which both sexes exhibit in an exaggerated way the kinds of characteristics we might call masculine. Both men and women are expected to be violent, competitive, jealous, aggressive, and sexual and to enjoy display, action, and fighting. The culture is structured to evoke these characteristics. Mother, daughter, and cowives are pitted against one another for the attention of the father in an incestuous family structure. Sexual jealousy establishes a pattern of distrust which is continued through imagined insult and severe fighting. In this culture, competition to display one's status and material goods is rampant and aggression is common. Until fairly recently, the Mudugamor were cannibalistic.

The third culture, the Tchambuli, does show differences between the sexes, but it is the reverse of what we would expect to find in our culture. It is the women who take care of the most important economic affairs and are considered rational, practical, and good providers. They have control of the important property in spite of patrilineal institutions. They also are considered to be the gender with the stronger sex drive.

In contrast, Tchambuli men are considered weak, inefficient, and even childish. They are very much concerned with personal ornamentation and sit by the hour in "club houses," primping and gossiping and giggling. They are known for their artistic ability, sensitivity, nervousness, emotional dependence, and petty jealousy. Of course, much as in our culture, all the behaviors prescribed are ideals that are not necessarily lived up to in fact.

We can see that physical predispositions toward behavior seem to be overcome by cultural training. Margaret Mead, a student of human nature and cultures for over forty years, says, "Many, if not all, of the personality traits which we have called masculine or feminine are as lightly linked to sex as are the clothing, the manners, and the form of head-dress that a society at a given period assigns to either sex . . . the evidence is overwhelming in favor of the strength of social conditioning."[122]

Many of the differences that have been attributed to men and women are nothing more than well-established social myths. In other cases, some differences may exist in personality traits or in abilities of one kind or another, but the differences seem to be based almost completely on social learning. Only in the cases of aggression, verbal ability, and mathematical and visual-spatial abilities is there a consensus that some differences exist between the sexes, but even here the differences are "average" differences and are very small. Similarities between the sexes are much greater than differences, and when a difference is found, it is largely based on what society expects and rewards. The society also gives greater opportunities for one sex or the other to learn and practice certain abilities. In all cases, the part played by socializing agents—parents, cultural reinforcers, and social institutions—is of the utmost importance in shaping behavior.

ESSAY QUESTIONS

1. Identify the aspects of gender presented in the first part of this chapter and discuss each one.
2. Describe some chromosomal and hormonal abnormalities that may affect sexual identity.
3. What is the opinion of most researchers about hormonal imprinting and later behavior? What part do they believe environment plays? Use the case of the girl/boys in the Dominican Republic as an example.
4. Discuss the nature of gender identification and explain how it relates to gender of rearing. Use as examples the children discussed in the chapter who, because of an accident or indeterminate sex, had a switch in sexual identity.
5. Compare and contrast the physical characteristics of infant boys and girls. Be very specific. Be sure to include a comparison of how they differ in regard to the five senses.
6. Discuss the research that has been conducted on differences in verbal and spatial abilities between men and women. Be sure to include research on brain lateralization and studies to determine if and when this occurs.
7. Discuss what we know about hormones and aggressiveness. In the case of aggressiveness, why do researchers believe that there may be an inborn tendency for males to be more aggressive whereas they do not believe that inborn tendencies shape other behavior?
8. Discuss why or why not researchers believe that there is a maternal "instinct."
9. What cautions should be used in looking at research on male and female differences and similarities?
10. How do the three tribes discussed by Margaret Mead in *Sex and Temperament* show that male and female gender roles are learned?

EXERCISES

1. Have you ever noticed what you believe to be hormonal cycles in your-self or your friends? When did they occur and why?
2. Discuss whether you believe that all men are inherently more aggressive than all women. If you believe they are, what are the implications for society? If you do not believe they are, what are the implications?
3. List some stereotypes in our culture that deal with verbal and mathematical abilities between men and women (for example, that women can't balance their checkbooks). Are there equal numbers of positive and negative stereotypes for each sex? Discuss.
4. What examples in your experience would make you think that verbal and mathematical abilities differ between men and women? What examples would make you think that there is little difference, if any?

NOTES

1. Anne Fausto-Sterling, *Myths of Gender: Biological Theories about Women and Men* (New York: Basic Books, 1985), Chap. 1.
2. Jeanne E. Gullahorn, "Sex-Related Behaviors: Historical and Psychological Perspectives," in E. Donelson and J. E. Gullahorn, eds., *Women: A Psychological Perspective* (New York: Wiley, 1977), p. 1.
3. Meridith M. Kimball, "A Critique of Biological Theories of Sex Differences" (unpublished paper); Fausto-Sterling, *op. cit.*
4. Joan C. Chrisler, "Age, Gender Role Orientation and Attitudes toward Menstruation," *Psychological Reports* 63 (1988):827–834.
5. Eleanor Maccoby and Carol Jacklin, *The Psychology of Sex Differences* (Stanford, Calif.: Stanford University Press, 1974), pp. 169–177.
6. Fausto-Sterling, *op. cit.*, pp. 39–40.
7. *Ibid.*
8. Connie I. Stark-Adamec and Meredith Kimball. "Science Free from Sexism: A Psychologist's Guide to the Conduct of Nonsexist Research," *Canadian Psychology* 25 (1984):23–34.
9. Katherine B. Hoyenga and Kermit Hoyenga, *The Question of Sex Differences* (Boston: Little, Brown, 1979).
10. Michael W. Ross, Lesley Rogers, and Helen McCulloch, "Stigma, Sex and Society: A New Look at Gender Differentiation and Sexual Variation," *Journal of Homosexuality* 3 (1978):315–330.
11. Ashley Montague, *The Natural Superiority of Women* (London: Macmillan, 1968).
12. Jarrick F. Lissey, "Sex Differences in Longevity," in Hugo G. Biegel, ed., *Advances in Sex Research*, 2d ed. (New York: Harper & Row, 1984), p. 156.
13. Fausto-Sterling, *op. cit.*, pp. 77–84.
14. Bruce Bender and Daniel Berch, "Sex Chromosome Abnormalities: Studies of Genetic Influences on Behavior," *Integrative Psychiatry* 5 (1987):176–178.
15. Alice Theilgaard, "Aggression and XYY Personality," *International Journal of Law and Psychiatry* 6 (1983):413–421.
16. H. A. Witkin et al., "Criminality in XYY and XXY Men," *Science* (1983):547–555.

17. Hoyenga and Hoyenga, *op. cit.*, p. 112.

18. *Ibid.*

19. Doreen Kimura, "Are Men's and Women's Brains Really Different?" *Canadian Psychology* 28 (1987):135–147.

20. Hoyenga and Hoyenga, *op. cit.*

21. Anne A. Earhardt and Heino Meyer-Behlburg, "Prenatal Sex Hormones and the Developing Brain: Effects on Psycho-Sexual Differentiation and Cognitive Functions," *Annual Progress in Child Psychology and Child Development* (1980):177–191.

22. J. M. Reinish, "How Prenatal Exposure of Human Fetuses to Synthetic Progestin and Estrogen Affects Personality," *Nature* 266 (1977):561–562; Earhardt and Meyer-Behlburg, *op. cit.*

23. Carol N. Jacklin, "Neonatal Sex-Steroid Hormones and Cognitive Abilities at Six Years," *Developmental Psychobiology* 21 (1988):567–574; Ruth Doell and Helen E. Longino, "Sex Hormones and Human Behavior: A Critique of the Lineal Model," *Journal of Homosexuality* 15 (1988):55–78.

24. Kerrin Christiansen and Ranier Knussmann, "Sex Hormones and Cognitive Functioning in Men," *Neuropsychobiololgy* 18 (1987):27–36.

25. John Money and Anke Earhardt, *Man and Woman, Boy and Girl* (Baltimore: Johns Hopkins University Press, 1972).

26. *Ibid.*, pp. 123–125.

27. J. Imperato-McGinley, L. Guerrero, and T. Gautier, "Steroid 5 Alpha Reductase Deficiency in Man: An Inherited Form of Male Pseudohermaphrodites," *Science* 186 (1974):1213–1224; J. Imperato-McGinley, L. Guerrero, and T. Gautier, "Androgens and the Evolution of Male Gender Identity among Male Psuedohermaphrodites with a 5 Alpha Reductase Deficiency," *New England Journal of Medicine* 300, no. 22 (1979):1233–1237.

28. Gilbert Herbt, "Mistaken Gender: 5-Alpha Reductase Hermaphroditism and Biological Reductionism in Sexual Identity Reconsidered," *American Anthropologist* 92 (1990): 433–446.

29. Imperato-McGinley, quoted in Anne Fausto-Sterling, "Hormones at the Helm, Part 1" (unpublished draft chapter), 1983, p. 28.

30. J. Hampson, quoted in Bernard Rosenberg and Brian Sutton-Smith, eds., *Sex and Identity* (New York: Holt, Rinehart & Winston, 1972), p. 27.

31. Earhardt and Meyer-Bahlburg, *op. cit.*

32. *Ibid.*

33. *Ibid.*

34. Doell and Longino, *op. cit.*

35. Maccoby and Jacklin, *op. cit.*, pp. 17–38.

36. Diane McGuiness and Karl Pribram, "The Origins of Sensory Bias in the Development of Gender Differences in Perception and Cognition," in Morton Bortner, ed., *Cognitive Growth and Development: Essays in Honor of Herbert G. Birch* (New York: Brunner/Maxwell, 1979).

37. *Ibid.*

38. Hoyenga and Hoyenga, *op. cit.*, pp. 323–327.

39. Maccoby and Jacklin, *op. cit.*, pp. 17–38.

40. Hoyenga and Hoyenga, *op. cit.*, p. 324.

41. Maccoby and Jacklin, 1974, *op. cit.*, pp. 17–38; see also Fausto-Sterling, 1985, *op. cit.*, pp. 25–35.

42. Fausto-Sterling, *op. cit.*, pp. 26–29.

43. *Ibid.*
44. Maccoby and Jacklin, *op. cit.*, pp. 76–85; A. C. Petersen, L. Crockett, and M. H. Tobin-Richards, "Sex Differences," in H. E. Mitzel, ed., *Encyclopedia of Education Research,* 5th ed. (New York: Free Press, 1982), pp. 1178–1186.
45. F. F. Schacter, "Do Girls Talk Earlier? Mean Length of Utterance in Toddlers," *Development Psychology* 14 (1978):388–392.
46. Anne C. Petersen and Michele A. Wittig, "Sex-Related Differences in Cognitive Functioning: An Overview," in M. A. Wittig and A. Peterson, eds., *Sex Related Differences in Cognitive Function: Developmental Issues* (New York: Academic Press, 1979).
47. Janet S. Hyde, "How Large Are Cognitive Differences? A Metaanalysis Using Omega and 'd,' " *American Psychologist* 36 (1981):892–901.
48. Robert Plomin and Terryl Foch, "Sex Differences and Individual Differences," *Child Development* 52 (1981):383–385.
49. *Ibid.*
50. *Ibid.*
51. Hoyenga and Hoyenga, *op. cit.*, p. 238.
52. Fausto-Sterling, *op. cit.*, p. 29.
53. *Ibid.*, p. 20.
54. Anat Ninio, "The Effects of Cultural Background, Sex and Parenthood on Beliefs about the Timetable of Cognitive Development in Infancy," *Merrill-Palmer Quarterly* 34 (1989):369–388.
55. C. P. Benbow and J. C. Stanley, "Sex Differences in Mathematical Ability: Fact or Artifact?" *Science* 210 (1980):1261–1264; "Are Boys Better at Math?" *New York Times* (December 7, 1980):57; Anne Fausto-Sterling, "Hormones at the Helm, Part 2" (unpublished draft chapter), p. 65; Anne Fausto-Sterling, *Myths of Gender: Biological Theories about Women and Men* (New York: Basic Books, 1985).
56. Fausto-Sterling, "Hormones at the Helm," *op. cit.*
57. Lynn H. Fox, *The Problem of Women and Mathematics* (report to the Ford Foundation, March 1980), p. 13.
58. Wise, Steele, and MacDonald as reported in Fox, *ibid.*, p. 10.
59. S. F. Chipman, L. R. Brush, and D. M. Wilson, eds., *Women and Mathematics: Balancing the Equation* (Hillsdale, N.J.: Lawrence Erlbaum, 1985).
60. J. Eccles (Parsons), "Expectancies, Values and Academic Behaviors" in J. T. Spence, ed., *Achievement and Achievement Motivation: Psychological and Sociological Approaches* (San Francisco: Freeman, 1983), pp. 75–146
61. J. A. Sherman, "Mathematics, the Critical Filter: A Look at Some Residues," *Psychology of Women Quarterly* 6 (1982):428–444.
62. S. L. Boswell, "The Influence of Sex-Role Stereotyping on Women's Attitudes and Achievement in Mathematics," in Chipman et al., *op. cit.*, pp. 175–197.
63. Fausto-Sterling, *op. cit.*, p. 68.
64. *Ibid.*
65. Fausto-Sterling, *op. cit.*, pp. 56–59.
66. Fox, *op. cit.*
67. M. C. Linn and A. C. Petersen, "Emergence and Characterization of Gender Differences in Spatial Ability: A Meta-Analysis" (paper presented at the meeting of the American Psychological Association, Anaheim, 1983).
68. N. Wattenawaha and M. A. Clements, "Qualitative Aspects of Sex-Related Differences in Performances on Pencil-and-Paper Spatial Questions, Grades 7–9," *Journal of Educational Psychology* 74 (1982):878–887.

69. R. Rosenthal and D. B. Rubin, "Further Meta-Analytic Procedures for Assessing Cognitive Gender Differences," *Journal of Educational Psychology* 74 (1982): 708–712.

70. J. M. Connor and L. A. Serbin, "Visual-Spatial Skill: Is It Important for Mathematics? Can It Be Taught?" in Chipman, Brush, and Wilson, *op. cit.,* pp. 151–174; S. Keves, "Sex Differences in Cognitive Abilities and Sex-Role Stereotypes in Hong Kong Chinese Adolescents," *Sex Roles* (1983):853–870.

71. N. Newcombe, M. M. Bandura, and D. G. Taylor, "Sex Differences in Spatial Ability and Spatial Activities," *Sex Roles* 9 (1983):377–386; Jane L. Pearson and Lucy R. Ferguson, "Gender Differences in Patterns of Spatial Ability, Environmental Cognition and Math and English Achievement in Late Adolescence," *Adolescence* 24 (1989):421–431.

72. B. J. Becker and L. N. Hedges, "Meta-Analysis of Cognitive Gender Differences: A Comment on an Analysis by Rosenthal and Rubin," *Journal of Educational Psychology* 76 (1984):583–587; Diane F. Halpern, "The Disappearance of Cognitive Gender Differences: What You See Depends on Where You Look," *American Psychologist* 44 (1989):1156–1158.

73. J. W. Berry, "Ecological and Cultural Factors in Spatial Perception Development," *Canadian Journal of Behavioral Science* 3 (1971):324–326; Ninio, *op. cit.*

74. Fausto-Sterling, 1985, *op. cit.,* pp. 56–59.

75. J. Stafford, "Sex Differences in Spatial Visualization as Evidence of Sex-linked Inheritance," *Perceptual and Motor Skills* 13 (1961):428.

76. D. R. Bock and D. Kowalkowski, "Further Evidence of Sex-Linked Major-Gene Influence on Human Spatial Visualizing Ability," *American Journal of Human Genetics* 25 (1973):1–14.

77. D. M. Broverman, E. L. Klaiber, Y. Kobayashi, and W. Vogel, "Roles of Activation and Inhibition in Sex Differences in Cognitive Abilities," *Psychological Review* 71 (1974):23–50.

78. *Ibid.*

79. A. C. Peterson, "Physical Androgyny and Cognitive Functioning in Adolescence," *Developmental Psychology* 12 (1976):524–533.

80. *Ibid.*

81. R. Weiss, "Women's Skills Linked to Estrogen Levels," *Science News* (Nov. 26, 1988):341 (discussing new findings by Doreen Kimura and Elizabeth Hampson).

82. Christiansen and Knussmann, *op. cit.;* Donna Kimura, "Sex Differences in Cerebral Organization for Speech and Praxic Functions," *Canadian Journal of Psychology* 37 (1983):19–35.

83. Hoyenga and Hoyenga, *op. cit.*

84. M. Hines and C. Shipley, "Prenatal Exposure to Diethylstilbestrol (DES) and the Development of Sexually Dimorphic Cognitive Abilities and Cerebral Lateralization," *Developmental Psychology* 20 (1984):81–94.

85. J. Levy and M. Reid, "Variations in Writing Posture and Cerebral Organization," *Science* 200 (1976):1291–1296; Fausto-Sterling, 1985, *op. cit.*

86. Deborah P. Waber, Madeline Mann, James Merola, and Patricia Moylan, "Physical Maturation Rate and Cognitive Performance in Early Adolescence: A Longitudinal Examination," *Developmental Psychology* 21 (1985):666–681.

87. J. McGlone, "Sex Differences in Human Brain Asymmetry: A Critical Survey," *The Brain and Behavioral Sciences* 34 (1980):3215–3263; K. Santhakumari, George Kurin, and N. K. Sharma, "Cognition in Women," *Psycho-Lingua* 18 (1988):59–66.

88. M. P. Bryden, "Sex-Related Differences in Perceptual Asymmetry" (paper presented at the meeting of the American Psychological Association, Anaheim, 1983); Peterson andWittig, *op. cit.*

89. Richard Harshman, Elizabeth Hampson, and Sheri Berenbaum, "Individual Differences in Cognitive Abilities and Brain Organization; I. Sex and Handedness Differences in Ability," *Canadian Journal of Psychology* 31 (1983):144–192.

90. McGlone, *op. cit.*, p. 226.

91. J. Sherman, *Sex Related Cognitive Differences: An Essay on Theory and Evidence* (Springfield, Ill.: Thomas, 1978).

92. *Ibid.*

93. Doreen Kimura, "Are Men's and Women's Brains Really Different?" *Canadian Psychology* 28 (1987):135–147.

94. David C. Geary, "A Model for Representing Gender Differences in the Pattern of Cognitive Abilities," *American Psychologist* 44 (1989):1155–1156.

95. Kimura, *op. cit.*

96. M. Hines, "Prenatal Gonadal Hormones and Sex Differences in Human Behavior," *Psychological Bulletin* 92 (1982):56–80.

97. Fausto-Sterling, 1985, *op. cit.*, pp. 123–154.

98. Eleanor E. Maccoby and Carol N. Jacklin, "Sex Differences in Aggression: A Rejoinder and Reprise," *Child Development* 5, no. 1 (1980):964–980.

99. Theilgaard, *op. cit.*

100. Maccoby and Jacklin, 1974, *op. cit.*

101. Fausto-Sterling, 1985, *op. cit.*, pp. 23–54.

102. I. Fagot and R. Hagan, "Aggression in Toddlers: Responses to the Assertive Acts of Boys and Girls," *Sex Roles* 12 (1985):341–351.

103. S. W. Alagna, "Sex-Role Identity, Peer Evaluation of Competition and the Responses of Women and Men in a Competitive Situation," *Journal of Personality and Social Psychology* 43 (1982):546–554.

104. F. Geis and J. Walstedt Jennings, "Are Women Invisible as Leaders?" *Sex Roles* 9 (1983):1035–1049.

105. Alagna, *op. cit.*

106. Lynn H. Fox, Linda Brody, and Diane Tobin, eds., *Women and the Mathematical Mystique* (Baltimore: John Hopkins University Press, 1980), pp. 179–191.

107. Jeanne Mellinger and Carol J. Erdwine, "Personality Correlates of Age and Life Roles in Adult Women," *Psychology of Women Quarterly* 9 (1985):503–514.

108. A. S. Goldberg, and S. Sheflett, "Goals of Male and Female College Students: Do Traditional Sex Roles Still Exist?" *Sex Roles* 7 (1981):1213–1222.

109. P. R. Clina, *The Imposter Syndrome: Overcoming the Fear That Haunts Your Success* (Atlanta: McGregor, 1985).

110. L. R. Brody, "Sex and Age Variations in the Quality and Intensity of Children's Emotional Attributions to Hypothetical Situations," *Sex Roles* 11 (1984):51–59.

111. Fausto-Sterling, 1985, *op. cit.*, pp. 123–154.

112. Earhardt and Meyer-Behlburg, *op. cit.*

113. Janet L. Hopson, "Boys Will Be Boys. . . ./Girls Will Be. . . ." *Psychology Today* 21 (1987):60–69.

114. Sandra Bem, "Probing the Promise of Androgyny," in A. Kaplan and J. Beam, eds., *Beyond Sex Role Stereotypes: Readings Toward a Psychology of Androgyny* (Boston: Little, Brown), pp. 47–62.

115. Beatrice Whiting, *Six Cultures: Studies of Child-Rearing* (New York: Wiley, 1963).

116. J. Veroff, C. Depner, R. Kulka, and E. Douvan, "Comparison of American Motives: 1957 vs. 1976," *Journal of Personality and Social Psychology* 39 (1980):1249–1262.
117. Maccoby and Jacklin, 1974, *op. cit.*, pp. 91–105.
118. M. Hoffman, "Sex Differences in Empathy and Related Behaviors," *Psychological Review* 84 (1987):712–722.
119. Bem, *op. cit.*
120. Maccoby and Jacklin, 1974, *op. cit.*, p. 180.
121. Margaret Mead, *Sex and Temperament in Three Primitive Societies* (New York: Dell, 1963).
122. Margaret Mead, quoted in Janet S. Chavitz, *Masculine, Feminine or Human?* 2d ed. (Itasca, Ill.: Peacock, 1970), p. 260.

Part II

SOCIALIZATION

Chapter 4

Early Socialization into Gender Roles

The infant years are crucial in the development of patterns of personality and behavior. These years are also critical in the establishment of beliefs about appropriate masculine and feminine behavior. Learning gender-role norms and behavior is a complex process. Infants, toddlers, and young children are socialized into, or taught, appropriate gender-role beliefs and actions in many ways. Language provides subtle but constant messages. Other means of socialization, such as toys, games, television, and books, convey much more direct messages about appropriate masculine and feminine behavior. Parents and the school contribute both subtle and overt messages about the correct way to act as a boy or girl.

The combined force of these sources of beliefs and behavior is very strong. A young child has no previous knowledge to bring to bear in evaluating what he or she hears and sees; the tendency, therefore, is to accept the values that are set forth. Until recently there was little questioning of the masculine or feminine behavior a child learns in the formative years. Indeed, few people were aware of the extent to which children *are* socialized into male and female roles during this period. However, it is crucial to be aware of the values a child learns. Thus, in this chapter and Chapter 5 we shall examine in detail the major influences on the gender-role socialization of children.

PARENTS AND CHILDREN

Parents are the earliest and probably the major influence in the gender-role socialization of young children. The emotional content of parents' interactions with their children gives their input great significance. How and why do parents consciously or unconsciously influence the gender-role beliefs and behavior their children develop?

Is There a Preference for Boys?

In the 1970s, researchers documented the fact that Americans clearly prefer male children, especially as firstborns.[1] However, in more recent studies women in the United States do not express a preference for either sex, although American men still prefer to have a male child.[2] In other cultures, the preference for boys remains strong. In China, where the government has encouraged a policy of having one child per family, boy babies are so strongly preferred that in some rural areas infant girls may be killed. If parents have a preference for one sex, it may affect their expectations of the behavior of boys and girls. Children may also be aware of their parents' preference, although there is no direct evidence of this awareness.

Parents' Expectations of Children

Parents often have different expectations for the sexes. In a hospital study of thirty pairs of new parents, fifteen with boys and fifteen with girls, the parents were asked to describe the characteristics of their infants. In some cases the parents had not even held the newborn but had only looked at her or him behind the nursery glass. They tended to describe their children according to the typical stereotypes of the culture; the fathers in particular described their children in these terms. Boy babies were described as firmer, larger-featured, more alert, and stronger. Girls were described as more delicate, more fine-featured, softer, and smaller.[3]

Apparently these stereotyped beliefs about infants are merely extensions of beliefs parents generally hold about boys and girls. Parents describe boys as rough at play, noisy, able to defend themselves, physically active, competitive, and fond of mechanical things. Girls are described as more likely to be helpful around the house, neat, clean, quiet, reserved, sensitive to the feelings of others, well mannered, and easily upset and frightened.

There seem to be some differences in sex stereotyping between fathers and mothers. In several studies, fathers stereotyped more than mothers did. In addition, the fathers of boys stereotyped the most, and the mothers of both boys and girls were more traditional than were the mothers of girls. In general, parents seemed to specify more traditional traits for their sons than for their daughters. Boys who interacted more with their fathers and girls who interacted more with both parents showed greater gender-role stereotyping.[4] The fact that 4- and 5-year-old children of feminist parents were more free of gender-role stereotypes seems to confirm that parents influence the gender-role beliefs of their children even at this early age.[5]

Another study showed that it is not only parents who are willing to attribute sex-typed characteristics to newborn infants. In other research, kindergarten children were introduced to a 4-month-old baby boy. Some of the children saw the infant dressed as a boy and called John, while others saw him dressed as a girl and called Laura. After playing with the baby for five minutes, the children were asked to rate the infant on scales that described it as big or little, cuddly or not cuddly, noisy or quiet, and so on. Most of the children rated the baby as cuddly and friendly whichever sex they saw. On the other adjective pairs, however, they differentiated according to the sex they thought the baby to be. As a boy the baby was described as big, tough, and fussy, and as a girl the baby was pictured as little, cheerful, and gentle. Neither sex stereotyped more than did the other.[6] But if at age 5 years children have distinct ideas of what babies will be like, it is not surprising that parents have strong feeling about the gender characteristics of their infants.

Parents' Treatment of Boys and Girls

Parents are also more likely to treat male and female infants and children in ways consistent with how they view the sexes. In general, fathers are reported to roughhouse with boys and to be more gentle with girls.[7] Parents also openly encourage sex-stereotyped behavior in their children. In a study that points to early differences in treatment, mothers of young babies were asked to play with a 6-month-old child. Two female infants and two male infants appeared equally often as actor babies, sometimes dressed as their own sex and sometimes as the other sex. In the mother-baby play period, the toy the mothers chose for the infant varied with the perceived sex. Boy babies were verbally encouraged to engage in large-muscle motor activities such as crawling more than girls were, and the mothers responded more to the boys' activities.[8]

As infants become toddlers, parental interaction with them continues to be sex-differentiated. In certain studies, both parents emphasized achievement for boys and urged them to control their emotions. Both parents characterized their relationship to their daughters as having more warmth and physical closeness. They believed the daughters were more truthful and showed a reluctance to punish them. They discouraged rough-and-tumble play for girls and doll play for boys.[9] They were more likely to let boys be independent. Differential treatment was particularly apparent in the areas of aggressiveness and dependence. They listened more to girls, especially girls who asked for help, and attended more to boys' attempts at assertiveness.[10] Parents responded more to girls when the girls were gentle or talked softly. The children soon learned to use the style of behavior which got more attention. When observed again eleven months later, the little girls were more talkative and the little boys were more aggressive.[11]

Another important study showed that mothers talk in different ways to little boys, questioning and teaching them more. Even parents who deliberately attempted to avoid treating the sexes differently still showed some differential treatment of boys and girls.[12]

One classic study seems to show that dependence is encouraged in girls and independence is encouraged in boys. In this study of independence, Goldberg and Lewis studied the willingness of very young children to be independent of their mothers. A mother and her toddler were placed in a room marked off in squares. The mother sat in one corner, and the researchers kept track of how far the baby wandered from the mother and how often it returned for reassurance. At one point a barrier was placed between the mother and the baby, and the baby was left to find a way around it. Girl babies stayed closer to their mothers and returned more often for reassurance.

They were also more upset by the barrier and tended to hold on to it and cry rather than actively seek a way around it.[13]

In other cases, parents may consciously teach their children gender-role stereotypes. Boys may be told that "big boys don't cry," and fathers may refrain from hugs and intimate physical contact with their sons as they get older. Girls may be asked to be neater or told to be nice to relatives.[14]

Fathers are especially likely to discourage feminine behavior in boys. Maccoby and Jacklin quote a man who represents the strong feelings fathers often have about finding feminine behavior in boys. When asked if he would be disturbed by indications of femininity in his son, he said, "Yes I would be, very, very much. Terrifically disturbed—couldn't tell you the extent of my disturbance. I can't bear female characteristics in a man. I abhor them."[15] Conversely, fathers are likely to encourage and enjoy feminine and coy behavior in their daughters. Goodenough reports that half the fathers in her study described their daughters as "soft, cuddly, and loving," saying, "She cuddles and flatters in subtle ways. I notice her coyness and flirting. . . ."[16] Fathers obviously like feminine-typed behavior and reinforce their daughters when they exhibit it.

As children get older, their parents may also attempt to teach them "sex-appropriate" skills. A father may throw a ball to his son, and a mother may teach her daughter how to sew or bake cookies. While some cross-sex behavior may be taught—for example, a boy is taught to cook or a girl to fish—it is unlikely that it is stressed unless the father is looking for a substitute son in his daughter or the mother is looking for a substitute daughter in her son. (Interestingly, some women who rose into the managerial ranks in the 1950s and 1960s were only children and had been treated by their fathers like boys, taken hunting and taught to shoot.)[17]

Parents may also teach stereotypes by the way they assign household chores. A national study in 1989 showed that men and older persons were more likely to assign chores on a traditional basis, with girls doing dishes and boys taking out the garbage, for example. Yet among the almost 4,000 adults surveyed about eight chores they assigned, 70 to 90 percent made some non-traditional assignments.[18]

Parents as Models for Children

Children learn from their parents by seeing what their parents do. Nothing may be said directly, but children pick up many important messages by watching. If the mother always does the cooking and grocery shopping, the implication is that this is women's work. If the father is always the one to climb on the roof to clean the gutters, children soon learn that this is a man's job. It is significant that in households where the mother works outside the home, the children have less stereotyped gender-role perceptions.[19] This modeling of gender-role stereotypes by parents can be very subtle. The author has visited one home where both the mother and the father work outside the home and share the housework; however, their daughter has picked up the idea that men are better drivers because the father always drives the car in the evening.

Thus, parents engage in actions that for a number of reasons influence their children's gender roles. Parents may be stimulated by a boy or girl baby to behave in a specific way, may have special expectations of boys and girls that cause differential treatment, may consciously or unconsciously attempt to teach a child appropriate gender-role behavior, or may model gender-role behavior for a child to imitate. Parental action has a strong influence and when combined with the other influences makes childhood a crucial period in forming gender roles.

TOYS

Toys also influence a growing child. Young children learn to differentiate at an early age between toys appropriate for boys and those appropriate for girls. The media play a major role in stimulating a child's desire for certain kinds of toys; parents also play a role by the toys they give their children.

When children are very young, both boys and girls receive many of the same kinds of toys. The very young may receive a stuffed animal, rings that stack on a pole, blocks, or a pull toy. Even at a very early age, however, some of the toys are likely to be designed to be sex-appropriate. Thus, a girl may get a doll and a boy may get a truck. A study of 20-month-old children showed that they already knew the appropriate toys for their sex and preferred to play with them. This is not surprising when one considers the influence of the media. Another study showed that toys sex-stereotyped for boys (vehicles and sports equipment) were almost always shown with pictures of boys in advertisements, in catalogs, and on toy packages; the reverse was true for girls' toys.[20] Parents add to this stereotyping. While children may initiate play with a sex-typed toy, parents, especially fathers, reinforce this behavior.[21] Salespersons of toys also lead purchasers to toys that are sex-stereotyped.[22] Children soon get the message: While parents purchase 70 percent of the toys, the children usually request gender-stereotyped toys.[23] Boys requested and received more vehicles than did girls, while girls requested and received more domestic items than did boys.[24]

Many researchers have suggested that toys have important implications for cognitive and social development in boys and girls.[25] One study showed that children who play frequently with dolls may receive more opportunities to learn and practice language than children who use other toys do.[26] These toys also have implications for the activity levels and learning of the children who use them. One study pointed out that boys and girls are significantly more active when playing with stereotypically masculine toys.[27]

Boys are also far more likely than girls to get sports equipment such as bats, balls, basketballs, footballs, and hockey sticks and are encouraged to use them. The sports equipment given to girls is different and often includes a jump rope or skates. In one study, parents said that a baseball glove and sim-

ilar items would be appropriate toys for either sex, but they only gave their children toys appropriate for that sex.[28] Thus, different kinds of equipment encourage more active play and more team play among boys than among girls.

Girls are more likely to get passive toys, such as dish sets, clothes, and coloring books. They may get toy ovens, irons, and sewing machines. The more elaborate models of these toy household appliances actually work, and so girls can start ironing and baking at an early age. Many of these toys are realistic representations of the things that girls may do later in life. Girls may also get dollhouses in which they can move the furniture and play house. Their dolls frequently can be handled like real babies: fed, diapered, and even bathed.

Boys are more likely to get toys that encourage creativity and manipulation: chemistry sets, erector sets, toy trains, and tool chests.[29] Boys are also more likely to get mobile toys, action toys (such as a gun or a bow and arrow), and sports equipment. The toys that boys get are often connected with action and exciting occupations, such as being a cowboy, a policeman, or an astronaut. For the most part, however, these toys do not represent occupations likely to be entered by most young men. Seldom does a boy get a toy briefcase and a bunch of papers to shuffle in an imitation of an adult's likely role.

Boys seldom get dolls after they are 2 or 3 years old. Although a young boy may want to cling to the comfort of a stuffed animal, dolls and stuffed animals are considered babyish or sissy for him. By contrast, a girl may continue to have stuffed animals on her bed through the college years. Male dolls do exist (one catalog shows about 68 male dolls in contrast to 356 female ones),[30] but they are justified in terms of supermasculinity or activity. A little boy can choose a GI Joe with a kung fu grip that can chop a board at the pressing of a button or an Action Jackson with a rescue rig. These dolls emphasize action, and the accessories include scuba outfits, mountain-climbing equipment, and spaceships.

The contrast with girls' dolls is striking. After their baby dolls, slightly older girls often get Barbie dolls and their counterparts. These dolls are supposed to be models of the appropriate feminine body and activities for older girls. What do the girls receive as an appropriate model? The Barbie doll, with its unrealistically big breasts and long slender legs, is made to be dressed up in expensive and elaborate outfits, complete with a wig and high heels. Barbie has an escort, Ken, who is also a clotheshorse. Barbie's little sister, Skipper, may express the ultimate idea of how to grow up in a hurry. In one version of the Skipper doll, a child can rotate Skipper's arm and she will grow breasts and develop a thinner waist—truly a model of how to become a desirable sex object. None of the Barbie, Ken, and Skipper accessories emphasize action or competence.

Even unisex equipment, such as bicycles, is differentiated in style, price, and use between boys and girls. Boys' equipment is usually more expensive, intricate, and sturdy. It is also different in kind and intent. A boy will get hockey skates, and a girl will get figure skates. The subtle message is not lost: Boys skate fast and play rough games, whereas girls do graceful figure eights. As children get older, their presents tend to converge somewhat and both sexes get more clothes, records, and books.

Both sexes are thus limited in the range of interests and activities they are encouraged to explore through toy use. Boys may learn that the world of men is a place of excitement and toughness. Conversely, girls learn by implication that they are expected to do housework even if they plan on having a career as well and also learn that they are expected to be attractive but passive.

GAMES

The gender-role messages implied in girls' and boys' toys may be further emphasized in the games they play. Young boys play more fantasy roles than girls do and imitate exciting, creative people. Boys may play cowboys and

Indians or cops and robbers, but girls often imitate their future household roles by playing house or taking care of dolls.

Boys and girls also learn to relate in different ways to their playmates. Girls are more likely to play in smaller groups. They may play jacks or jump rope in twos and threes. They are also likely to play in a more unstructured way. The rules to their games are minimal. The emphasis is on cooperation and taking turns, not necessarily on winning.[31] Even some of the competitive sports girls engage in, such as horseback riding, skating, and swimming, put more emphasis on individual than team competition. Lever, in a study of the nature of boys' and girls' play, showed that only 47 percent of girls' activities are competitive, compared with 65 percent of boys' activities. Even if we eliminate team sports for both sexes, only 30 percent of girls' activities are competitively structured, compared with 54 percent of boys' activities. Girls are also more likely to join affiliative groups like the Girl Scouts in the course of their play.[32]

In contrast, boys are more likely to play in larger groups and often on teams where performance is related to the role of the whole group. Boys are also more likely to engage in games of greater complexity, with rules and strategy. They learn to combine competition and cooperation and to play with children they may not like so that there will be the required number of players for the game. In *Games Mother Never Taught You*, Betty Harragan points out that many of the lessons learned on the playground stand a boy in good stead when he is later working his way through the corporate world. He learns to "play his position," "not to talk back to the coach," and to "play by the rules and . . . be a team player."[33]

One of the striking aspects of boys' play is the pressure to be good or to win. A boy who learns skateboarding must equal or surpass the others on the street in the number of tricks he can perform. If he plays hockey, shoots baskets, or throws a baseball, he must do it well enough to be chosen for neighborhood and school teams. While we have mentioned cooperation in these team sports, competition is also encouraged. Boys learn early that they must be tough and willing to play in spite of injury or difficult conditions. Even when they engage in affiliative activities, competition and toughness are emphasized.

Thus, gender-appropriate traits are reinforced by the nature of the games children play. Boys learn to be competitive and to achieve at all costs even if such a style is not their natural inclination. Girls learn to be more affiliative and often suppress their competitive desires. Both sexes are limited by the gender stereotypes they learn.

CLOTHING

Clothing is another subtle influence on gender-role behavior. Even clothes for infants are differentiated. I recently tried to buy a gift for a baby shower, looking for something that would be appropriate for either a boy or a girl.

Even knit crawler sets were pink and had lace or were bright-colored and had baseball motifs. Gender-neutral clothes were almost impossible to find even for children of this age. This differentiation in infant clothing is important because people treat children differently according to the sex they think the children are.

Today little girls are much more commonly seen wearing the jeans, shirts, and sneakers that active boys have worn for so long. However, it is still not unusual to see girls wearing dresses and slick-soled shoes in both preschool and elementary school. One can observe the same children dressed in that fashion day after day. Often these little girls are unable to run, climb, and be truly active, at least if they are going to obey the injunction to be modest and "not let your panties show." Even for a girl in slacks there may be disadvantages. In contrast to boys' clothes, girls' slacks are often made without pockets. Young girls must carry a comb and tissues in their hands or begin to carry a purse.

As girls get older and enter junior high school, other styles of dress inhibit their movement. Even in junior high school, girls often wear high heels and hose or uncomfortable pointed-toed shoes. They may also begin to wash, blow-dry, and curl their hair every day and to wear makeup. If a purse was not carried before, it now becomes necessary, as makeup and other elements of a good appearance must be portable. The clothes worn are often uncomfortable and unhealthful and inhibit active motion, yet they are "the style," and girls and women who do not wear the appropriate feminine dress may be reproved. In late elementary school, a girl starts spending more time and money on her appearance. Girls of 10 or 11 frequently have their ears pierced and start acquiring earrings and other jewelry. They may spend time curling their hair—and later bleaching it—and applying makeup. They may worry about the length of their fingernails or how their hair will look if they engage in volleyball or swimming.

Many girls and women spend a great deal of time and money attempting to improve their appearance, and their interest in and desire to engage in more active pastimes may thus be limited. The author knows several girls who gave up the swimming team in high school because of the problem of doing their hair between swim practice and the next class. While boys are certainly interested in their appearance and spend considerable time picking out clothes and washing and blow-drying their hair, the emphasis is not as extreme. The young male seems to gain approval from what he does, while the young female often tries to gain approval from how she looks.

Some changes have occurred. The emphasis on clothes and appearance has been recognized by some people as artificial, and the natural look that started in the 1960s has persisted to some degree. Women have access to more comfortable styles of clothing, although they may not choose to wear them. Where changes have been made, many men seem to have taken on women's styles rather than the reverse. We now see men wearing pants without pockets, carrying purses, and blow-drying their razor-cut hair. However, although some convergence toward a unisex mode in clothing has occurred, there is still differentiation. Both sexes are also still learning to wear clothing that is uncomfortable and inhibiting. While women suffer in high heels and hose, men suffer in ties and three-piece suits. Both sexes learn that on many occasions it is important to dress "appropriately" for their sex, whatever the discomfort.

Thus, some of the early actions of parents as well as the way they dress their children, the toys they give them, and the games the children are encouraged to play place subtle pressure on the children to behave in gender-appropriate ways. Even parents who want to avoid pushing their children into gender-stereotyped behavior may unconsciously pass on subtle messages about appropriate actions.

SOME RACIAL AND ETHNIC VARIATIONS

Much of what was said above applies to all children, but there are some differences by race and ethnic group. Black boys and girls seem to be more independent and self-reliant than white children are.[34] Older girls in the black family almost always have child-care and home-care responsibilities. In addition, black boys may be pressured to be strong and unemotional. Athletic ability, strength, and being cool as well as a certain degree of "street savvy" are seen as necessary.[35]

Nonetheless, black children seem to be raised to be less stereotyped. They are more likely to see models of gender roles that are not so highly differentiated. Black women have traditionally worked outside the home and have developed independence and assertiveness as well as being nurturant. Black men have often been more nurturant and expressive than their white counterparts.[36]

SOME THEORIES OF GENDER-ROLE LEARNING

Let us look at some of the theories that have described how a child comes to use certain **sex-role** behaviors. At some point in the interaction among a child, significant others, and the environment, the child decides what sex he or she actually is (that is, establishes a sexual identity) and then begins to practice behavior the culture says is appropriate for that sex. Each of the theories about this phenomenon emphasizes different stages in acquiring the behavior and different reasons for its acquisition. The controversy over heredity versus environment, biology versus cultural conditioning, is exemplified in some of the more popular theories.

Freudian Theory

Freudian theory proposes that "anatomy is destiny."[37] Freud believed that each infant goes through a series of physical and psychosexual stages that follow in a definite sequence and are based on physical growth. These stages are linked to the child's level of mental and social development and to his or her feelings about parents.

In the oral stage, which lasts from birth to about age 1 year, the child is largely an instinctual being and the *id*—the primitive and impulsive part of the mind—is in control. The child derives pleasure and information largely by putting things into his or her mouth.

The anal stage begins from age 1 to 3 years, and the child is concerned with the other end of her or his anatomy. This is when parents try to institute toilet training, the first necessity for the child to take control over id impulses. As the child begins to gain some control, a new section of the mind, the *ego*—the rational, conscious mind—begins to develop. With the development of the ego, the child may reason that if she goes to her appropriate potty chair, her mother will be pleased with her, she won't get a scolding, and she may even get a reward. Therefore, the child begins to operate through reason and not just through impulse. During these first two stages, both male and female children identify with their mothers. They see them as sex and love objects and imitate some of their actions.

The phallic (genital or Oedipal) stage follows from about age 3 to age 7, and the sexes begin to differ in development. During this stage, both boys and girls become aware of their genitals and their similarity to or difference from the mother and father. The little boy is still very close to the mother, but according to Freud, he begins to see the father as a rival for her affections. This scares him, as his father is big and powerful, and he develops an Oedipus complex. He is in love with the mother and afraid of the father. He may also have a sister whom he sees without a penis, and he fears that he will be castrated if he competes with his father. He resolves this fear by identifying with the father and recognizing his own similarity to this strong male. In this way he feels secure. He is no longer afraid of the father, he can love the mother, and he can turn to other women later and obtain their love as his father has obtained the love of his mother.

A little girl goes through this genital stage in a different way, according to Freud. She sees that boys have penises and blames her mother for not getting her one (penis envy). She may transfer her love to the father and be very angry with the mother for a while. In time, she realizes her own similarity to the mother and replaces her wish for a penis with a desire to have a child. She begins to identify with the mother partly out of fear of the mother's jealousy but also out of recognition of similarities to her.

Thus, according to Freud, both sexes identify with the same-sex parent and acquire some of that parent's personality characteristics. The two sexes then enter a period of **latency** in which they sublimate sexual urges in activities such as collecting frogs or string. Then, at puberty, the stage of adolescence begins and each sex becomes attracted to the opposite one, firming up sexual identity and gender roles.[38]

There are many problems with Freud's theory. We have not discussed some of its more "far out" parts because they are not directly relevant to gender roles. Three problems are directly relevant to our concerns: (1) Freud's insistence that two parents must be present if the child is to go through the stages correctly and develop appropriate sexual identity and gender-role behavior, (2) his view of women, and (3) his idea of fixed stages of development.

First, children develop firm sexual identities in the many single-parent families found today.[39] Second, Freud's view of women as inferior men who wish they had a penis also seems to be erroneous and probably reflects only women's envy of the masculine gender role. While young boys and girls both rate their own sex-appropriate roles as being more fun, older girls are more willing to say they wish they were a boy. Cross-cultural evidence also shows that some men envy women's childbearing capacities and that there may be a "womb envy" that Freud has not touched on. Third, Freud's view of biological stages as fixed and unchangeable is open to question. In one study, children were given figures of boys and girls and men and women cut into three pieces each. The children were told to assemble the four figures of man, woman, boy, and girl from the twelve pieces given to them. As long as the figures were dressed in sex-appropriate clothes, the children made few mistakes. However, when the figures were undressed, 88 percent of the 3-year-olds made an error. Thus, children may reach different stages of awareness about their bodies at different times.[40] Freud's theory has been important in developing our ideas about children's stages of development and the later behavior of adults, but it does not take into account important differences in families, environments, and cultures.

Social Learning Theory

Mischel, Bandura, and Walters have developed a theory of learning sexual identity and gender-role behavior known as **social learning theory**. In this theory, imitation and reward and punishment for correct and incorrect behavior play very important roles. The young child is told that he is a boy or she is a girl and is treated in ways the parents think are appropriate for that sex. A father may come home from work and say, "How's my big boy tonight?" and toss the infant son into the air. Conversely, he may come home and say, "How's my sweet little girl?" to his infant daughter while tickling her under the chin and saying, "Come on, now, give Daddy a smile." The child thus learns to think of himself or herself as a boy or a girl. He or she then identifies others who are similarly called boys and girls and notes how they are alike. Usually, these noted similarities in sex characteristics are obvious external things such as "girls have longer hair than boys" and "boys are bigger than girls." Children also notice that boys and girls are treated differently and are expected to behave differently.

A young child learns the behaviors of both sexes by means of such observation but is much more likely to imitate the behavior of his or her own sex. Thus, a little girl may be more likely to dress up high heels in imitation of her mother, but she could, if pushed, imitate her father by puffing on a cigar.

The child imitates not only because the behavior is associated with the appropriate sex but because she or he is reinforced or rewarded for displaying sex-appropriate behavior. Thus, a little girl who dresses up in her mother's high heels may be told that she is "cute and quite a little female," but a little boy who tries the same thing is not likely to get approval. He may even be told that "boys don't do that" and be ordered to "go outside and play."

Thus, by others' reactions to their behavior, by seeing how others are treated, and by imitating the behavior of older models, children learn sexually appropriate behavior. They learn to generalize this behavior to other situations as well. They do not have to experience the behavior personally to know whether it is appropriate for their own sex: A young boy knows that it is not appropriate for a man to dress in women's clothes and walk down the street even though women may wear the equivalent of men's clothes in public. Children also learn that reinforcement for the behavior is determined by the content of the situation. A boy may be teased for sewing or cooking at home, but it is all right for him to sew a patch on a tent or cook over a camp fire.

As children are responded to in terms of their sex and as they learn to act in gender-appropriate ways, they develop sex identities as boys or girls. Thus, according to this theory, children acquire sex-stereotyped behavior before they acquire sex identities.

Parents are the primary models for young children and the primary reinforcers of sex-appropriate behavior. Models who are the most imitated are nurturant, but they are also seen as successful. The strong influence of parents can be seen dramatically in children who have had sex-reassignment surgery: The parents' behavior toward such children clearly influences the children's subsequent identification as the other sex. Peers are also strong reinforcers of appropriate gender-role behavior. In one experiment, the behavior of nursery school children was analyzed and divided into "male-stereotyped" and "female-stereotyped" behavior. Researchers then looked at teachers and peers to see how much sex-appropriate behavior was reinforced. The teachers actually preferred more feminine behaviors and rewarded them more in both sexes, but the peer groups almost always rewarded sex-appropriate behaviors. The one boy who exhibited some feminine behavior had fewer playmates and was criticized more than was any other boy.[41]

There are some specific problems with social learning theory, in particular, the insistence on models being present, the imitation of the same sex, and the use of reward and punishment as learning mechanisms. Children do not necessarily resemble their same-sex parents. Girls imitate both parents more than boys do. Some sex differences persist in spite of a lack of reinforcement or even in the face of punishment. Boys are consistently punished more for aggressive acts than girls are, but they continue to exhibit more aggressiveness, whereas girls do not necessarily learn to be more aggressive in this situation. Of course, boys are also rewarded subtly for aggressive behavior, but this theory does not emphasize reward systems such as peer approval or a personal feeling of what is right. The theory emphasizes specific, tangible rewards, although it is clear that other kinds of rewards are just as important.

Boys in one experiment would not change their toy preference to dolls in spite of a reward system.[42] Nevertheless, the idea of modeling and reward is obviously important, and the theory has had a great impact.

Other Developmental Theories

Other theorists have talked about how differences in early childhood experiences lead to a different cognitive organization and different ways of seeing moral issues. Many developmental theorists have seen women as inferior to men in terms of moral development. As Freud tied the formation of the superego (conscience) to castration anxiety, he believed that women can never have as strong a superego as men do. He stated that "for women the level of what is ethically normal is different from what it is in men" and that "women show less sense of justice than men, that they are . . . more often influenced in their judgments by feelings of affection or hostility.[43]

Kohlberg believes that individuals move through stages of moral development as they grow older, progressing from concern only with individual or self issues to higher levels which include adult reasoning. Level 3 involves a concern with maintaining trust and a bond with other people. At this level, one is concerned with others' interests and tries to be a "good" person. Level 4 "is a move to a societal level of thought, where moral issues are considered in terms of a system of law or justice that must be maintained for the good of society."[44] While a person has both levels of thought, level 4 appears later than level 3, and in this sense a person who uses level 4 considerations is more mature in moral reasoning. (An example of level 4 might be the presumption that an accused person is considered innocent until proved guilty. This is a general principle rather than something that applies in every case.) Kohlberg believes that women seldom reach level 4 of moral development and usually operate primarily at level 3. Jean Piaget, the child development theorist and educator, said, "The most superficial observation is sufficient to show that in the main the legal sense is far less developed in little girls than in boys."[45]

In 1982, Carol Gilligan published a reexamination of these points of view entitled *In a Different Voice: Psychological Theory and Women's Development*. Gilligan expands Nancy Chodorow's writings about the masculine bias of psychoanalytic theory and argues that women are *not* fixed at an immature level of moral reasoning but develop their moral sense along a different path. She points out that women are raised to identify with the primary caretaker, the mother, and thus experience a strong bonding relationship that is the model for others in their lives. They are, of course, later trained to nurture and care for others as well. Men, conversely, find an identity in separation from their first primary relationship and thus have more difficulty in establishing attachments later in life.[46] Because women are "bound into a network of intimate interpersonal ties . . . they are more compassionate, more concerned lest they fail to respond to others' needs, and made more anxious by the threat of separation from their loved ones."[47] They therefore respond to moral dilemmas in a way different from that of men, who may be willing to sacrifice individuals for a larger societal or abstract principle.

Gilligan also agrees with Eric Erickson that because women do not have to separate from their mothers to form an identity, they may develop intimacy before they develop identity.[48] (Boys reverse the process, with separation from mother leading to identity and, later, the ability to become intimate with others.) However, Gilligan disagrees with Erickson's belief that finding an individual identity is a higher form of personality development and argues against using a male standard as the norm for what is mature or good.

While Chodorow and Gilligan's approach to the way in which the sexes learn particular kinds of gender-role behavior makes us aware of developmental differences, we must insist upon factual proof of this theory. Their ideas may resonate as true to many women, but Gilligan's critics point out that she bases her findings on only a small, female sample.[49] Other studies show that while men are more likely to be interested in abstractions than in relationships, they are equally likely to be altruistic and show helping behavior to those who need it.[50]

However, Gilligan's statements about women judging themselves in terms of relationships and intimacy rather than by an abstract male standard has a number of implications for things we will look at in this book. For example, we have seen that boys and girls play in different ways, with girls tuned into small-group relationships and cooperation and boys concerned more with large-group situations organized in accordance with abstract rules. Boys and girls have different views in adolescence about what being a good friend means, women are more likely to value relationships in their work lives and intimacy in their marriages, and even in politics, women's concern for social issues and peace makes itself felt in the "gender gap."

Cognitive Development Theory

In a widely accepted theory of learning gender identity, Kohlberg proposes that **gender identity** and gender-role behavior are acquired in stages. These stages are consecutive like the ones Freud proposed, but they are mental rather than physical. They are based on Piaget's stages of cognitive development and the readiness of the child's mind to handle certain concepts. According to this theory, at the stage when the child's mind is ready to handle a concept, the acquisition of certain kinds of information and behavior takes place without external reinforcement being necessary.[51]

While the stages of Kohlberg's theory are consecutive, they may depend on intelligence and physical maturation. At the appropriate stage, the child must, however, also have the necessary experience—or information—to learn.

For example, a very young child may call everything that is warm, fuzzy, and small "kitty." Later the child learns to differentiate "puppy," "kitty," and "squirrel." In a similar way, a young child may differentiate between men and women on the basis of external cues such as long hair, wearing lipstick, and wearing a skirt or behavior such as cooking dinner and feeding the baby. Even when the differentiation is finer and the child recognizes genital differences, he or she may not believe they are permanent.

At one family gathering at which the author was present, a 5-year-old boy had just been told by his parents that boys have penises and girls do not and that this is the way a person can tell one from the other. He went around the room of fully clothed adults and tested his new knowledge by pointing to each one in turn and saying, "You are a boy, so you have a penis; you are a girl in a skirt, so you don't have one." He waited until each person gave the answer that told him he was right, and when he had made the full circuit of the room, he walked off satisfied. Later, the mother confessed that he was still not sure about the permanence of these characteristics. He had told her that afternoon, "When you grow up, you can be a boy and ride a bicycle like Daddy."

The stages in cognitive development theory roughly correspond to the age of the child, although children differ in their progress through each stage. From about birth to age 3 the child differentiates the sexes according to external cues or differences in observed behavior such as cooking and mowing the lawn.

At about age 3 the child begins to label himself or herself as a particular sex. In keeping with a strong sense of self, this is seen as good. Thus, at this stage one's own sex and its activities are preferred because the self is valued. When asked why he liked a particular baby-sitter, one boy replied, "Why, because he's a boy, of course!"[52] Thus, a boy might also say, "I'm a boy; therefore, I want to do boy things, play with boy toys." Discrimination has taken place so that children are indeed able to tell what toys are appropriate for them to play with, although they may not be sure what toys are appropriate for the opposite sex. However, in this stage, from age 3 to age 4 or so, the child does not yet realize that gender cannot be changed. He can label himself as a boy and still say he's going to grow up to be a mommy.

In the period from about age 4 to age 6 children acquire the knowledge that gender cannot be changed. They achieve this knowledge at about the same time they learn certain facts about the constancy of objects—for example, that one can't change a quantity of water by pouring it from one container to another or that a kite doesn't shrink when it gets farther away.

Stereotypes and behavior derived from stereotypes become very important at this stage. Children want to imitate adults who are like themselves and who also are seem to be powerful and competent. After about age 8 children stop imitating adults in general and model themselves only after persons whose skills or other characteristics they see as relevant to their own competence. According to Kohlberg, sex typing does not increase much after this age.[53] Thus, according to this theory, the child learns his or her own gender identity at the proper time and then engages in appropriate sex-role behavior because it is "right and good." Models provide clues to this appropriate behavior, but rewards come mainly from the child knowing that he or she is doing the right thing.

Most of Kohlberg's work has been done on boys, but the implications for girls are disheartening. A girl who wants to value her own gender but also wants to associate with a powerful model who has prestige is going to have difficulty finding one. Many same-sex models will not have this power or prestige; those who do may not display the "appropriate" behavior for women. Thus, the girl is left in a double bind. If she accepts the female stereotype, she does not have power; if she does not accept it, she is not doing sex-appropriate things. Either choice is disturbing. Hoyenga and Hoyenga describe a 4-year-old girl whose mother was a doctor and who still insisted that only boys become doctors.[54]

This conflict shows up in girls' attitude toward their own sex at this stage. Children of both sexes say that fathers are bigger and stronger than mothers and that they have more social power. Girls like their own sex less often than boys do. At age 5, although both sexes are sex-stereotyped, girls show less of a preference for their own gender role.[55] They frequently cite boys' activities as being more fun and exciting, and quite a few say they would like to be a boy.

However, cognitive development theory has several positive aspects which the other theories do not. While it is based on consecutive stages of development, these stages can vary from child to child according to physical development and IQ. These ideas about how a child develops sexual identity are also consistent with single-parent homes, because in this theory the father is not the only model for boys.

In addition, some current research about sex typing and parental identification seems to support cognitive development theory. Research has shown that sex typing is positively associated with father identification in both boys and girls, which Kohlberg would have expected as he emphasized the modeling of a competent, powerful model. Masculinity in boys is also associated with a nurturant, warm father figure. Neither girls nor boys identify with a passive father, and behavior shows an increasing similarity to that of the dominant parent as the children grow older.[56]

Gender Schema Theory

However, as Sandra Bem points out, cognitive development theory does not answer the question of why children begin to categorize primarily on the basis of sex rather than on the basis of other categories. In our culture sex is probably the most obvious distinction between persons that children perceive, but in other cultures factors such as caste and spirituality are at least as important.[57]

Gender schema theory as proposed by Bem states that the child learns society's definitions of what it is to be male and what it is to be female and that this is the organizing perspective for the child in learning other information. Bem believes there are two reasons why these sex-linked associations become a natural way to organize new information: They include areas of life such as reproduction, labor, and personality in a linkage of associations, and gender has a broad functional significance. Therefore, children use this gender schema or cognitive organization as a way to assimilate new information. In the process, many things become gender-associated or gender-typed.

Children learn that certain things are parts of the definition of masculinity and femininity. Boys learn that to be masculine includes the prescription to be strong. Girls learn that to be feminine includes the prescription to be nurturant. Children want to do things appropriate for their sex, and a child chooses "from among the many possible dimensions of human personality only that subset defined as applicable to his or her own sex and thereby eligible for organizing the diverse contents of the self-concept." Children also learn to evaluate their adequacy as persons against this gender schema: "The gender schema is a standard or guide and self-esteem becomes its hostage."[58] Children are compelled to regulate their behavior to conform to what they believe is appropriate for their sex. The original cultural beliefs become a self-fulfilling prophecy.

Bem points out that research supports gender schema theory and shows that those who are the most sex-typed are the most likely to assimilate new information in terms of sex differences. They are also more likely to respond to situations in terms of what they consider appropriate sex-typed behavior and to describe themselves in terms of sex-typed characteristics. This seems to be almost an automatic response rather than an evaluative process. Bem says that "when deciding whether a particular attribute is or is not self-descriptive, sex-typed individuals do not bother to go through a time-consuming process of recruiting behavior evidence from memory and judging whether the evidence warrants an affirmative answer. . . . Rather, sex-typed individuals 'look up' the attribute in the gender schema. If the attribute is sex in-appropriate, they quickly say no." They are slow to admit that they have a sex-inappropriate trait.[59]

From the point of view of gender schema theory, gender is the primary cognitive way to organize new information because cultures have allowed a dichotomy between male and female to influence almost every aspect of experience. Bem believes that the gender schema probably stems from the importance of reproduction but points out that cultures have elaborated gender difference to the point where almost everything (toys, clothing, occupations, and even language) varies according to sex. She believes that if cultures limited their gender arrangements to biological functions alone, children would be much less likely to become sex-typed.[60]

SUMMARY

We can see by examining theories about gender identity that we are still looking for explanations of how heredity, early childhood development, other forms of socialization, and social structure shape gender roles. Certainly the environment that shapes gender roles is not just the one provided by the immediate family. It includes the values developed and reinforced by many cultural institutions. For example, early messages about appropriate masculine and feminine behavior that are derived from childhood games and toys are strengthened and reinforced in the playing fields of the elementary school. Language provides children with other subtle messages, and the masculine and feminine stereotypes are repeated and reemphasized in books, on television, and at school. We will look at the specific influences of language, the media, and educational institutions in Chapter 5.

ESSAY QUESTIONS

1. Many people say that sex stereotyping begins in the cradle. What evidence can you cite to support that statement?
2. In what ways do parents model gender-role stereotypes for their children, and how do they directly teach the children what they believe to be sex-appropriate behavior?
3. How do the toys given to little girls and little boys differ after about 2 years of age? What implications does this have for the activities of boys and girls?
4. In what way are the different toys given to boys and girls realistic or unrealistic representations of their future occupational roles?
5. How do the games played by little boys differ from those played by little girls in terms of structure and number of players?
6. What does Betty Harragan mean in *Games Mother Never Taught You* when she says that the games boys and girls play affect their future attitudes and behavior in the work world? In terms of what you know about Gilligan's ideas, would you say that women could change their success ratio in the occupational world if they changed their type of play in childhood? Would they be likely to do so?
7. Compare and contrast social learning theory and cognitive development theory in terms of the use of modeling and reward and punishment. From what source do the rewards come in each theory?
8. If you were to pick a theory to describe the learning of gender roles in single-parent families, which theory would you choose and why?
9. How are Kohlberg and Gilligan similar and different in their descriptions of men's and women's moral development? Do you believe that women and men take different paths in developing intimacy and identity? Is this inevitable?
10. How does Sandra Bem's gender schema theory relate to what you know about children's toy and play preferences?

EXERCISES

1. Make a list with two columns headed "Baby Girls" and "Baby Boys." List things you have heard or believe about the characteristics of each in the appropriate column. Discuss where you have heard or learned each belief. Do you think the belief is accurate?

2. Discuss any evidence you have from your own experience (watching your parents, an older sister with a baby, and so on) that parents treat boys and girls differently. Do you think your parents treated you differently from your sisters or brothers? If so, do you think this affected your masculine or feminine behavior?

3. How do you feel about parents teaching their children appropriate masculine or feminine behavior? What do you think would happen if they didn't? (Would the children learn such behaviors anyway? Would they be less sex-stereotyped?)

4. Pretend you are going to visit an old college friend whom you haven't seen in six years and who now has a child 4 years old. You do not remember the sex of the child and are embarrassed to ask. You want to bring a nice present for the child. What can you pick that would be appropriate for either sex? Try to list at least ten possibilities.

5. Imagine that you are a parent who wants to raise your child in a nonsexist way but that you do not want to make the child unhappy by having him or her teased by friends. What toys could you give a fifth- or sixth-grader that would be nonsexist and yet acceptable to the child's peer group?

6. Pretend that you are a girl going to a job interview and that you want to be appropriately dressed. Would you be willing to wear slacks rather than a skirt? Why or why not?

7. If you are a girl, have you ever rebelled against wearing hose and high heels to a dressy occasion? Do you think women should give up wearing hose and high heels? Why or why not?

8. Do you remember your parents exhibiting any behavior that was an unconscious modeling of gender roles (such as your mother sliding over to let your father drive the car when she picked him up)?

NOTES

1. R. Steinbacher and F. D. Gilroy, "Preference for Sex of Child among Primiparous Women," *Journal of Psychology* 119 (1985):541–547.
2. Max Hammer and James McFerran, "Preference for Sex of Child: A Research Update," *Individual Psychology* (December 1988):486–492.
3. J. Rubin, F. Provenzano, and Z. Luria, "The Eye of the Beholder: Parents' Views of Sex of Newborns," *American Journal of Orthopsychiatry* 44 (1974):512–519.
4. Gary D. Levy, "Relations among Aspects of Children's Social Environments, Gender Schematization, Gender Role Knowledge and Flexibility," *Sex Roles* 21 (1989):803–811.
5. *Ibid.*
6. Caroline Smith and Barbara Lloyd, "Maternal Behavior and Perceived Sex of Infant: Revisited," *Child Development* 49 (1978):1263–1265; Marilyn Stern and Katherine Karraker, "Sex Stereotyping of Infants: A Review of Gender Labeling Studies," *Sex Roles* 20, no. 3 (1989):501–511.

7. K. McDonald and R. D. Parke, "Parent-Child Physical Play: The Effects of Sex and Age on Children and Parents," *Sex Roles* 15 (1986):367–378.

8. Smith and Lloyd, *op. cit.*

9. McDonald and Parke, *op. cit.;* Hildy Ross and Heather Taylor, "Do Boys Prefer Daddy or His Physical Style of Play?" *Sex Roles* 20, no. 1/2 (1989):23–31.

10. Beverly Fagot, Richard Hagan, Mary Leinbach, and Sandra Kronsberg, "Differential Reactions to Assertive and Communicative Acts of Toddler Boys and Girls," *Child Development* 56 (1985):1499–1505.

11. *Ibid.*

12. N. Weitzman, B. Birns, and R. Friend, "Traditional and Nontraditional Mothers' Communication with Their Daughters and Sons," *Child Development* 56 (1985):894–896.

13. S. Goldberg and M. Lewis, "Play Behavior in the Year-Old Infant: Early Sex Differences," *Child Development* 40 (1969):21–31.

14. *Ibid.*

15. Eleanor Maccoby and Carol Jacklin, *The Psychology of Sex Differences* (Stanford, Calif.: Stanford University Press, 1974), p. 329.

16. E. W. Goodenough, "Interest in Persons as an Aspect of Sex Differences in the Early Years," *Genetic Psychology Monographs* 55 (1957):287–323

17. Margaret Hennig and Anne Jardim, *The Managerial Woman* (Garden City, N.Y.: Anchor/Doubleday, 1977).

18. Pat N. Lackey, "Adults' Attitudes about Assignments of Household Chores to Male and Female Children," *Sex Roles* 20, no. 5/6 (1989):271–280.

19. Linda A. Jackson, Nicholas Ialongo, and Gary Stollak, "Parental Correlates of Gender Role: The Relations between Parents' Masculinity, Femininity and Child-Rearing Behaviors and Their Children's Gender Roles," *Journal of Social and Clinical Psychology* 4, no. 2 (1986):204–222.

20. Lori Schwartz, "Sex Stereotyping in Children's Toy Advertisements," *Sex Roles* 12 no. 1/2 (1985):157–164.

21. P. O. Peretti and T. M. Sydney, "Parental Toy Stereotyping and Its Effects on Child Toy Preference and Sex-Role Typing," *Social Behavior and Personality* 12 (1985):213–216.

22. Nancy Kutner and Richard M. Levinson, "The Toy Salesperson: A Potential Gatekeeper for Change in Sex-Role Definitions" (paper presented at the annual meeting of the American Sociological Association, New York, August 1976); L. A. Schwartz and W. T. Markham, "Sex Stereotyping in Children's Toy Advertisements," *Sex Roles* 12 (1985):157–170.

23. C. Robinson and J. T. Morris, "The Gender-Stereotyped Nature of Christmas Toys Received by 36-, 48- and 60-Month Old Children: A Comparison between Nonrequested and Requested Toys," *Sex Roles* 15 (1987):21–32.

24. Marilyn Bradbard, "Sex Differences in Adults' Gifts and Children's Toy Requests at Christmas," *Psychological Reports* 56, no. 3 (1985):969–970.

25. Cynthia I. Miller, "Qualitative Differences among Gender-Stereotyped Toys: Implications for Cognitive and Social Development in Girls and Boys," *Sex Roles* 16, no. 9/10 (1987):473–487.

26. Marion O'Brien, "Parent's Speech to Toddlers: The Effect of Play Context," *Journal of Child Language:* 14, no. 2 (1987):269–299; Dyanne M. Tracy, "Toys, Spatial Ability and Science and Mathematics Achievement: Are They Related?" *Sex Roles* 17 (1987):115–136.

27. Marion O'Brien, "Activity Level and Sex-Stereotyped Toy Choices in Toddler Boys and Girls," *Journal of Genetic Psychology* 146, no. 4 (1985):527–533.
28. Marie Richmond-Abbott, "Sex Role Attitudes and Behaviors of Mothers and Children in Divorced, Single-Parent Families," *Journal of Divorce* 8 (1984):61–81.
29. Greta Fein, David Johnson, Nancy Kosson, Linda Stork, and Lisa Wasserman, "Sex Stereotypes and Preferences in the Toy Choices of 20-Month-Old Boys and Girls," *Developmental Psychology* 11 (1975):527–528.
30. Schwartz, *op. cit.*
31. Sheila Fling and Martin Mansovitz, "Sex Typing in Nursery School Children's Play Interests," *Developmental Psychology* 7 (1982):146–152.
32. Janet Lever, "Sex Differences in the Complexity of Children's Play and Games," *American Sociological Review* 43 (1978):471–483; C. I. Miller, *op. cit.*
33. Betty Harragan, *Games Mother Never Taught You* (New York: Warner, 1977).
34. J. R. Bardwell, S. W. Cochran, and S. Walker, "Relationship of Parental Education, Race and Gender to Sex-Role Stereotyping in Five-Year-Old Kindergartners," *Sex Roles* 15 (1986):275–281.
35. Janice Hale-Benson, *Black Children: Their Roots, Culture, and Learning Styles* (Baltimore: Johns Hopkins University Press, 1987).
36. Bardwell, Cochran, and Walker, *op. cit.*
37. Calvin Hall, *A Primer of Freudian Psychology* (New York: World, 1954).
38. *Ibid.*
39. David Lynn, *The Father: His Role in Child Development* (Monterey, Calif.: Brooks/Cole, 1974).
40. Katherine H. Hoyenga and Kermit Hoyenga, *The Question of Sex Differences* (Boston: Little, Brown, 1979), p. 182.
41. Walter Mischel, "A Social Learning View of Sex Differences in Behavior," in Maccoby and Jacklin, *op. cit.*, pp. 56–81.
42. D. Bruce Carter and Gary D. Levy, "Cognitive Aspects of Early Sex-Role Development: The Influence of Gender Schemas on Preschoolers' Memories and Preferences for Sex-Typed Toys and Activities," *Child Development* 59 (1988): 782–792.
43. Sigmund Freud, quoted in Carole Gilligan, *In Another Voice: Psychological Theory and Women's Development* (Cambridge, Mass.: Harvard University Press, 1982), p. 7.
44. Catherine G. Grenno and Eleanor E. Maccoby, "How Different Is a Different Voice," in "On `A Different Voice': An Interdisciplinary Forum," *Signs* (Winter 1986):305–335.
45. Jean Piaget, *The Moral Judgement of The Child* (New York: Free Press, 1965), p. 77.
46. Carol Gilligan, *In a Different Voice: Psychological Theory and Women's Development* (Cambridge, Mass.: Harvard University Press, 1983).
47. Grenno and Maccoby, *op. cit.*, p. 312.
48. Eric Erickson, *Young Man Luther* (New York: Norton, 1958).
49. Linda K. Kerber, "Some Cautionary Works for Historians," in "On `In a Different Voice,'" *op. cit.*, p. 306; Zella Luria, "A Methodological Critique," in "On `A Different Voice,'" *op. cit.*, p. 317.
50. Grenno and Maccoby, *op. cit.*, p. 313.
51. L. Kohlberg, "A Cognitive-Developmental Analysis of Children's Sex Role Concepts and Attitudes," in Maccoby and Jacklin, *op. cit.*
52. *Ibid.*
53. *Ibid.*
54. Hoyenga and Hoyenga, *op. cit.*, p. 189.

55. P. H. Mussen, "Early Sex-Role Development," in D. A. Goslin, ed., *Handbook of Socialization Theory and Research* (Chicago: Rand McNally, 1969), pp. 707–720; Mavis Hetherington, "A Developmental Study of the Effects of Sex of the Dominant Parent on Sex-Role Preference, Identification, and Imitation in Children," *Journal of Personality and Social Psychology* 2 (1965):188–194.
56. Kohlberg, *op. cit.*
57. Sandra Bem, "Gender Schema Theory and Its Implications for Child Development: Raising Gender Aschematic Children in a Gender Schematic Society," *Signs* 8, no. 4 (1983):598–616.
58. *Ibid.*, p. 605.
59. *Ibid.*, p. 607.
60. *Ibid.*, pp. 609–611.

Chapter 5

Early Socialization into Sex Roles: Language, Media, and the Schools

Some of the most pervasive and influential messages about sex-appropriate behavior are given to children in language and in the gender-role behavior portrayed in books and on television and reinforced in school. Language and the institutions that produce the media and educate children in the United States reflect American cultural values regarding sex-appropriate behavior.

LANGUAGE

The following quote from Thomas Mann's *The Magic Mountain* illustrates the importance of language in social interaction.

> Conversation is the bonding agent between ourselves and society. It enables us to reaffirm our own existence. Speech is civilization itself . . . it is silence which isolates.[1]

Language is a subtle but extremely important aspect of gender socialization. It is the lens through which we see the culture; it may set limits on our thoughts and our ability to describe things. In the languages of some cultures there is no past or future tense; this lack imposes limits on expressing one's imagination. In other languages there is no word for "I"; there is only the tribal "we." You can imagine how difficult it is to develop a self-identity without the word "I."

In our culture, the sexes are conceived of as distinct and separate. We will see that different adjectives are used for men and for women and that different occupations, behaviors, and even ways of standing and sitting are designated as masculine or feminine. Adjectives or implied meanings of words shape how we feel about men and women. When people are defined in this fashion and learn the definitions of self at a very young age, they come to believe the definitions and act in accordance with the labels.[2]

It is even easier to believe in labels and definitions that are inherent in language because the meanings are very subtle and one is not always conscious of the stereotyping that is taking place. Language is always with us, and so we are continually exposed to its influence. Communication does not always have to be verbal; it can include facial expressions and gestures as well as general body posture and the use of space.

Sexism in Language

Sexism is perpetuated in language in many ways. Women are frequently excluded totally from language or are assumed to be part of the male sex. As an example, until very recently in the state of Michigan, feminine pronouns were absent from the first two readers used in the first grade. The excuse was that the word "she" does not appear high enough on word lists. Therefore, if "he" and "it" are talked about more in print, they must continue to be talked about first, and so a cycle of females being ignored is perpetuated.[3] Women also learn that they are part of mankind (shortened to "man"), are part of the "brotherhood of man," and have been freed to enjoy "liberty," "equality," and "fraternity." However, studies show that people do not think of human beings when they hear the word "mankind"; they think of men (males).[4]

Women also learn that important and exciting jobs are referred to by masculine terms such "fireman" and "policeman." While progress has been made toward more neutral terms such as "fire fighter" and "police officer," many occupations are still defined in masculine terms. Doctors, dentists, and pilots are almost always referred to as "he," while nurses, dental technicians, and elementary school teachers are referred to as "she." Certain occupational titles are differentiated for women and carry an inferior implication, such as "poetess" (not quite a poet?) and "authoress."

Another area where achievements or honors are defined in masculine terms is educational degrees. One gets a bachelor of science or a master of arts degree. The thought of a spinster of arts seems absurd because the word "spinster" carries more negative loadings than does the word "bachelor."

The implication, or connotation, of certain words is as important as the actual meaning, or denotation. Language differentiates between the sexes both obviously and more subtly by means of such implication. For example, the term "bachelor" implies a carefree, sociable playboy; the term "spinster," however, implies a withered old crone although its original meaning was simply "a woman who spins." The title "master" implies dominance or power, as in "the master of his trade." However, the parallel word for women, "mistress," now implies being dominated by a man and giving him sexual favors, although it originally referred to the person who ran a household. In like manner, "gentleman" has positive implications of high social status or at least of being mannerly, while its counterpart, "lady," can be used much more freely. Someone may yell out, "Hey, lady!" One may also use "lady" in the context of "ladies of the night," or prostitutes.[5] Other pairs of titles or words are not as obviously differentiated, but the masculine version usually carries a more positive connotation. Compare "patron" and "matron" or "wizard" and "witch," for example.

The verbs and adjectives applied to men and women may also show a difference in terms of positive or negative implications. Women are trivialized or looked at negatively. They chatter or engage in "girl talk" (which is assumed to be inconsequential talk), while men "discuss" or simply "talk." She "nags" while he "reminds," she "bitches" while he "complains," and she is "picky" while he is "careful."[6] The worst insults for a man are those inferring that he has feminine characteristics. Thus, he can be called a "sissy" (diminutive of "sister") or be told he "swings a bat like a girl." Other insults tie a man to his mother and insult him by questioning her sexual character. Someone with whom a person is extremely angry is often referred to as a "son of a bitch." People have probably forgotten the original meaning of the term, but the demeaning implication and the tie to a female relative are still there.

Many terms that refer to both men and women have sexual meanings, although there are more negative sexual terms referring to women. Thus, men become "studs" or "jocks" and women become "broads," "dogs," or "chicks." The terms applied to men imply more power and success, while those applied to women imply promiscuity or being dominated. Why is the term "promiscuous" applied only to women even though its literal meaning pertains to either sex? While it may seem picky to complain about being called an animal such as a "dog" or a "chick," the following excerpt shows the cumulative effect of such characterizations:

> In her youth she is a "chick" and then she gets married and feels "cooped up" and goes to "hen parties" and "cackles" with her women friends. Then she has her "brood" and begins to "henpeck" her husband. Finally, she turns into an "old biddy."[7]

Women are referred to by their sex even when sex is not relevant to the subject at hand. Compare the following statements and decide which one you would be likely to see in a newspaper headline: "Widow opens real estate office"; "Grandfather runs for office." Women are also referred to by their relationship to men. A woman is "Ed's widow," although it would be rare for a man to be referred to as "Vera's widower." Women are known as "Miss" or "Mrs." according to their marital status, although the term "Ms." is much more common today; one cannot differentiate a single from a married man by the title "Mr." It is also difficult to recognize a woman's title when she is part of a married couple. We can say Dr. and Mrs. Jones, but it seems awkward to say Mr. and Dr. Smith. A woman may become "the senator's wife" or "the first lady." If a husband and wife are described together, it is likely that he will be described in terms of what he does and she will be described in terms of what she is physically: "Ralph is a brilliant young lawyer, and he has a beautiful blond wife."[8]

Finally, behavior can be inferred from style of language. Men are often described in the active voice—"He romanced her"; "He took her in marriage"—while women are described in the passive voice—"She was romanced by him"; "She was given to him in marriage." We learn subtle messages from this language style.[9]

Styles of Speech

In addition to differentiation through language, men and women differ in their styles of speech and in what they talk about. Men tend to talk about external things and use straight, factual communication. In particular, they talk about sex, sports, politics, work, and other men. They talk louder, employ stronger statements, and press their arguments on the listener.

Women are more likely to talk about feelings and people. They tend to talk about their physical and psychological states and say that they are cold, tired, hungry, or feeling good or bad. Their talk is more polite and indirect. They use qualifiers to keep from imposing their beliefs on others, as in the statement "It's sort of cold in here." Each sex finds the other's style of speech uncomfortable. Men see women's speech as consisting of illogical recitals of feelings, and women see men's speech as wearing and competitive.

Women use qualifiers that make their speech more polite but may make it less forceful. These qualifiers include phrases such as "I guess that," "I could be wrong, but," "I guess this is silly, but," and "Don't you think we should?" While a woman may be trying to soften what she is saying so that it is not offensive or imposed on anyone, the qualifiers may give her statements an unsure or apologetic air.[10]

Although the results of studies vary, there is some indication that women use tag questions. A tag question is something that is added at the end of a regular statement. While there are legitimate uses for tag questions, such as in starting conversations ("It's fun here, isn't it?") or getting confirmation ("You're going to clean your room, aren't you?"), for the most part they indicate uncertainty. They are often used to leave oneself open to agree with others. Thus, a young girl may say, "That's a pretty good album, isn't it?" if she isn't sure how her listener will respond and wants to have a way of backing off from her statement.[11] The results of some of these styles of speech and the tendency of women to talk more softly and give more intonation have the result that women are often taken less seriously when they speak.

The sexes also differ in how they talk in mixed groups and in how much they talk. Contrary to the old stereotype of women chattering away while silent men try to squeeze a word in, men talk more in mixed groups. Indeed, in a mixed group where everyone is taking turns talking, men not only talk more but take their turns unfairly by interrupting women and answering questions not addressed to them. When there are overlaps—that is, when two people start a sentence at the same time—it is almost always the man who continues and the woman who drops out.[12] Lipman-Blumen argues that the belief that women talk too much is used to control women and to urge them to be silent and let men handle the conversation.[13]

Women tend to agree with statements during conversations and build on the statements of their conversational partners, while men tend to dispute a person's argument. Women also tend to do the listening and try to keep the

conversation going. They say more positive, reinforcing things such as "That's a good idea" and "Go on" to keep the speaker telling his or her tale. They laugh at the jokes men tell and nod in agreement even when they do not agree. In fact, women do much more of the conversational work, introducing subjects, keeping the conversation going, and reinforcing the speaker. In contrast, men may use techniques such as the delayed response to keep from actively encouraging women to speak. The woman says something like "You'll never guess what happened to me today." Only after a long pause does her male companion say, "Oh, what?" At other times the only response to the woman is silence. Thus, the woman is discouraged from talking further in spite of the fact that the man may have talked at length himself.[14]

If a woman keeps talking and insists on getting attention in a group, she may find herself simply not attended to. Indeed, she may hear an idea that she suggested and that was ignored taken up later by a man and suddenly found to be worthwhile. Specific studies show that women students are not listened to as much in the classroom either by their male peers or by their professors.[15] It is likely that the same pattern occurs in social relationships. If women persist in trying to talk, they may be seen as pushy or radical.

Although stereotypes of proper roles for men and women are probably more important, the words women use and their style of speech have much to do with their difficulty in commanding attention. We have noted that men use stronger statements than women do. In addition, women may use words that imply silliness or weakness or trivialize what they are trying to say.[16] Notice the difference in impact between "Oh, my, such a lovely idea!" and "Damn, yes, that's a tremendous idea!" It is not hard to guess the sex of the person saying each phrase. Research has shown that people who use the masculine style of communication are rated significantly higher in competence although lower in social warmth.[17] Women are often caught in a double bind: If they use weaker expletives or exclamations, they diminish the power of what they say; if they swear or speak assertively, they are condemned for doing so.[18]

Language thus is used to reinforce gender socialization. Men's speech reinforces the masculine gender role of being assertive and dominant, while women's speech reinforces the feminine stereotype of being polite, supportive, and reinforcing.

Nonverbal Communication

Women and men continue the pattern of different styles in their body language. Women use more facial expressions and show their emotions in gestures and movements. They smile more than men do and often smile not only with their mouths but with their eyes. Smiling is a submissive gesture that is often seen among apes and chimpanzees. "The smile is women's badge of appeasement," say Henley, Hamilton, and Thorne. Other submissive gestures are also found in the body language of women. When confronted with a stare, women avert their eyes and drop their eyelids. They also tilt their heads when talking, the beginning of a submissive gesture.[19]

In addition, women and men have different postures. A woman's space is more restricted than a man's. Women are supposed to be compact, not sprawled out. They sit with their legs crossed at the ankle or thigh; they may have their arms folded, and they keep their elbows at their sides. By contrast, a man usually sits with his legs crossed so that one ankle rests on the opposite knee or thigh, a much more open position. He may sprawl backward as he sits, with his arms along the back part of the couch. When he is standing, there is a similar pattern. Men stand with their legs apart, firmly planted. Women stand with their legs together, sometimes to the point of crossing one ankle over the other, so that the outside edges of their feet are together. (While the author did not believe that this was a posture women use often, she was surprised to find that while standing waiting for the elevator, she had assumed exactly that pose.)[20]

Part of the concept of body language is the element of space. There seems to be a direct association between the amount of space surrounding a person and that person's dominance.[21] An executive has the largest desk; the rich have large yards separating them from their neighbors. Women are usually accorded less body space than men are. Richardson reports a study by Willis in which 800 experiments showed that (1) women have more tolerance for invasion of their personal space than men have, (2) women stand closer to other women than men stand to other men, and when women get as close to men as they do to other women, the men retreat, (3) when men get as close to other men as they normally do to women, the male subjects "fight" (accuse the experimenter of being pushy or homosexual), and (4) both men and women stand closer to women than they do to men.[22]

Women are also more likely to move out of men's way if they approach men in a narrow passage. While chivalry would seem to dictate that a man step off a narrow walk into soggy ground and let a woman pass, the opposite actually happens.[23]

Just as higher-status people touch lower-status people significantly more often, women are more likely to be touched by others rather than initiate touching. Not only do men touch first, they are allowed to touch in an intimate way (an arm around the shoulders) without necessarily implying an actual sexual advance. Women cannot do the same thing. However, women use an affectionate touch more, especially with other women; men use more status touches, such as ritual handshakes.

In regard to the touch, certain things indicate the inferior position of women. One has only to think of a waitress to realize that women are subjected to many gestures usually used with children: cheek tweaking, hair mussing, pinching, or a spank on the bottom. Many hostile and painful touches are used on women in the guise of affection. Women are swung painfully at square dances and are chased by gangs of men and thrown in the water, spanked, or dunked at the beach. They are sometimes passed up the stands at football games. At the University of Michigan, the practice of "passing up" got out of hand when the games were boring; sometimes hundreds of women students were sent up hand over hand. Among the injuries were a dislocated shoulder, a broken arm, internal injuries, and severe bruises.

In a final perspective on body language, space, and active and passive roles, let us briefly consider the etiquette that prevails between men and women. While we often think of opening doors and other forms of chivalry and etiquette as trivial, they are important in reinforcing the passive and active nature of feminine and masculine roles. It is the man who is expected to do the active things: open the door, light the cigarette, hail the cab, and take the woman's arm to help her on a slippery sidewalk. The male is in control. In contrast, the female waits to have the door opened, have her cigarette lit, and be helped in dangerous territory.[24] The nonverbal communication indicates that she needs to be helped in everyday life. Thus the man practices his control and the woman her helplessness every time this type of etiquette ritual occurs. Usually the man and woman "feel" much more masculine or feminine because they have acted out their stereotyped roles.

Almost all body language suggests that women's role is that of a person of inferior status. One can see this more clearly by looking at general social status relationships. It is the boss who touches the employee first, and it is the lower-status employee who steps aside, nods in agreement when he or she does not agree, looks away, or is interrupted. Body language thus becomes a further extension of the gender-role stereotypes of dominance and submission in our culture.

Thus, whether communication is conveyed through words or body language or is learned by imitation or the rules of etiquette, communication sends different messages about the roles of females and males. Women learn that they are less important, linked to men, not taken seriously, and viewed sexually. These messages are important because language is always with us, although the messages may be subtle and not easily recognized. The different styles and vocabulary of each sex can be assimilated without question, yet vocabulary and language styles may influence a person's behavior and opportunities throughout life. Language is thus one of the most potent gender-role socializers, especially for young children.

TELEVISION

Television is an extremely important influence that molds children's views of how the sexes should behave. Between kindergarten and the sixth grade, children watch from ten to twenty-five hours of television a week. Preschoolers usually begin watching when they are about 3 years old, and a high level of watching continues until around age 12 years. During the teen years, television viewing declines, but it increases again in the young adult years after marriage. About 25 percent of all children watch as much as six hours a day. Television seems to drive out other leisure activities. Children spend more time watching television than they do reading books, listening to the radio, or going to the movies. They begin by watching children's shows such as *Sesame Street* and *Captain Kangaroo* and move on to detective shows, sitcoms, and movies. They see approximately 250 commercials in a week's television watching during which the set is on about six hours and eighteen minutes a day. The average child has spent 15,000 hours in front of a set by the time he or she is 16. That is 4,000 more hours than the child has spent in the classroom.[25] What does this "classroom of the air" teach children about their roles in the world?

Prime Time

In spite of some recent improvements, television overwhelmingly stereotypes masculine and feminine roles. A 1987 study reported that out of 7,000 characters in 620 prime time shows between 1955 and 1986, only one-fifth were female.[26] Women were disproportionately shown as young, unemployed, family-bound, and in comic roles. They were often sexual objects and the objects of violence. Only 2.9 percent of them were minority women, and only 20 percent were shown working. Even those shown in responsible roles were attempting desperately to get a man.

About 75 percent of the male roles in prime time represented tough, cool American men who were unmarried and without responsibility. These men engaged in violent, mobile occupations and had numerous female admirers.[27]

One of the disturbing trends on television is the overwhelming amount of violence shown. Between 1969 and 1983, 56 percent of all prime time characters and 80 percent of all weekend daytime characters (mostly on children's shows) were involved in violence. This portrayal of violence intersects with stereotyped gender roles in that women are almost three times more likely than men to be the victims. In particular, a disturbing number of older women are shown as the victims of crime.[28]

Soap Operas

At first glance it appears that soap operas give more equal time to women. There are usually equal numbers of women and men characters, but women workers are still shown as subservient to men. *The Doctors* shows surgery being performed by male physicians while female physicians fill out forms. Male lawyers try cases, and female lawyers research them. In the soaps, men even dominate in a female area by giving emotional advice to women.

Cantor points out that in soap operas, goals of love and romance predominate and both men and women are prisoners of their sexuality. These sexual images apparently influence viewers, especially the teenage girls who watch soap operas in the afternoon. A recent study which examined the sexual beliefs and values of teenage girls reported that those who were heavy watchers of soap operas were more likely to overestimate the number of people who engage in extramarital affairs and the number of times married people have sexual intercourse.[29]

Comedy Shows

In comedy shows males are portrayed as worldly, self-confident, and capable of leadership. Women seldom show these behaviors unless they take over in situation comedies, and then they are twice as likely as the men to demonstrate bungling behavior. Even in the "educational" shows, women are often shown in negative ways. The female puppets on *Sesame Street,* for example, are strident, loudmouthed types.[30] Children's cartoons include even fewer women or female characters than adult prime time shows do. The studies conclude that the message is that women don't matter much and are inferior to men in many ways.

Commercials

Television commercials portray even more stereotyped roles. Among 2,750 commercials looked at in one study, 94 percent used a male narrator, although over 50 percent of the products advertised were typically used by a woman. The man's voice would frequently be heard over the action telling the woman how to cook, clean, or wash with the particular product. Men told women what laundry soap or bleach to use, what cleaner to use on the floor, and how to wash windows. The implication is that even in domestic work, women are too dumb to know how to do things correctly.[31] Other research confirms that women continue to be shown in traditional occupations and roles.[32] A study in the late 1980s examined the occupations in which each sex is portrayed and identified which sex is shown in more professional roles. It found that conventional sex-role stereotypes persisted in television commercials in 1988.[33]

Minorities

How do black men and women fare on television? Among 2,226 characters surveyed in one research study, 75 percent were white, 19 percent were black, and 5 percent were nonblack minority members. Among all spot messages, only 40 percent had black characters and 10 percent had nonblack minority characters. Within each minority group, however, the representation of male and female characters was much more nearly equal than it was for whites. Of all the male characters, 22 percent were black and 6 percent were nonblack minority members; of all the female characters, 16 percent were black and 4 percent were nonblack minority members.[34]

Thus, the percentage of blacks and other minorities appearing on television is fairly close to those groups' percentages of the population. Indeed, the black female is portrayed more favorably in her roles than the white female is in hers. In all-white family interactions, men are more dominant than women; in all-black family interactions, women are more dominant.

While these data on the percentages of black men and women show that blacks are being represented approximately in proportion to their percentage of the population, we must not forget that whites fill 70 to 80 percent of the parts on the screen. They also predominate as newscasters' and in other important roles. Blacks, both male and female, are cast in the stereotyped roles we identified above.

Why This Portrayal?

Why does television show men and women in a way that obviously does not reflect reality? Gaye Tuchman hypothesizes that this portrayal may reflect a deeper issue: lack of power in society.[35] She calls it "symbolic annihilation" and points out that just as representation in the media signifies social existence, so lack of representation and trivialization signify annihilation. George Gerber believes that the similarity between yesterday and today's media is a matter of "cultural resistance." Much of the programming is aimed at the working class, among whom there is not much acceptance of women's changing roles. In addition, women's issues may be seen as unentertaining or too limited to interest the majority of viewers. There is also a desire to keep advertisers happy, and most advertisers appeal to traditional women who adorn themselves for men or keep house for men.[36]

How Much of an Effect Does Television Have on Children?

Gross and Jeffries-Fox point out that children are particularly susceptible to aspects of television that cultivate beliefs and knowledge. Most of what children see is not directly familiar to them; they have no "reality" with which to contrast it. Children also have a strong belief in the inherent reality of photographed and filmed images. Children who see slide shows often think they have seen something "real."[37] Other research shows that young children do not usually know the difference between a program and a commercial.[38] Children therefore take the images on television very much to heart.

Research also shows that what children watch *does* affect their view of the world. In one study, children who watched the most television had the most traditional gender-role development.[39] A study in 1988 reported that television viewing in the home can potentially affect infant behavior and development more than was previously believed.[40] Other studies indicate that television overwhelmingly reinforces children in adopting traditional gender roles.

In a 1970s report of sixty-three interviews with boys and girls between ages 3 and 6 some of the girls had abandoned their ambitions. When asked what they wanted to be, they replied that they would have liked to be a doctor or milkman but sighed and said they would never do it because they were not boys. In contrast, one boy said, "Oh, if I were a girl I'd have to grow up to be a nothing."[41]

There is some indication that the more recent portrayal of women in previously masculine occupations such as law has helped change these perceptions. Girls who watched shows that portrayed women in "nontraditional" occupations expressed a desire to enter those careers. However, girls who watched programs showing more traditional gender roles still expressed a preference for traditional feminine careers such as modeling.[42]

When children were shown a series of nontraditional commercials and tested for the effect of these presentations on sex-role stereotyping, the girls seeing nontraditional jobs portrayed were more likely to prefer those careers although the boys were not more likely to prefer traditionally female jobs.[43] In a subsequent study, over half the children who had seen a woman portrayed as a judge felt that it was appropriate for a woman to have that job; however, only 27 percent of the group who had not seen the commercial felt that it was appropriate for a woman to be a judge.[44] These studies show that commercials and traditional programming promote stereotyping in children and that less traditional portrayals of occupations lead children, at least female children, to see a wider range of choice.

Parental guidance and role models can outweigh the influence of television programs. O'Neil, Schoonover, and Adelstein tested children in a Montessori school and found that they were not affected by traditional television stereotypes. However, these children watched only half the average number of hours, their parents often chose programs for them, and the parents often had nontraditional roles.[45] More recent studies have shown that children seem to interact with television in terms of their existing gender schema, using their knowledge of traditional gender roles to process the activities they see on television.[46]

Women have come a long way on television from the time when they were shown only in the home. Series such as *Murphy Brown*, *L.A. Law*, and *Cagney and Lacey* have done much to improve the image of women on television, but a lot more needs to be done. As Sidney Sheldon, an author known for strong portrayals of women, stated, "What's needed is a series with a woman in control and who is good at what she does."[47]

For men, the violent, aggressive male is still the dominant figure on television. Although some shows portray men as wise, gentle fathers, the reality of men's lives is seldom depicted. In addition to a more positive portrayal for women, a more multifaceted role for men is needed on television.

GENDER ROLES IN ADVERTISING

Both children and adults look at advertisements in magazines and on billboards as well as on television. While the advertisements are aimed for the most part at adult men and women, children learn a great deal about adult gender roles from them. Some of the messages seem simple, but there is often more to them than meets the eye.

A great deal of advertising for women is aimed at getting them to buy products to make themselves more attractive. They are told they need to condition or color their hair to make it brighter, put on eye makeup to make their eyes look larger, and wear brassieres to lift and separate their breasts and girdles to slim their hips. The implicit message is that women who are natural are not good enough and can improve by using the product in question. There is also an emphasis on a woman staying young and staving off the signs of aging. The implication is that if she does age, it is her own fault for not trying hard enough to stop the clock; as an older woman, she will be unnoticed and unworthy.[48]

In many advertisements women are shown as childlike or cutesy. A recent Sears catalog shows three adult women in an ad for sportswear sucking on lollipops and kicking up their heels in an obviously childlike fashion. Sometimes women are shown as passive onlookers. An example is a Coca-Cola ad showing a couple with ski equipment and the caption "Melanie Loves to Watch Me Race." In other advertisements women are shown as dumb or at least uninformed. An ad which has a man giving a woman a diamond says, "A carat or more, because you were never good at fractions." Ads for cleaning products imply that women do not know enough to remove a ring of dirt from a collar. Interestingly, the ad for "ring around the collar" makes it sound like it is the woman's fault that her husband's collar got so dirty. Other ads for cleaning products show women in ridiculous positions crawling around the kitchen sniffing for odors or overjoyed about being able to see their faces in clean dishes. At worst, these ads convey the message that women are dumb and incompetent; at best, it is difficult to take women seriously in these childlike and trivializing portrayals.

Men are dominant in most ads that show both men and women. They are shown standing or as taller than women, while the women sprawl on the floor or on beds. Women cling to men and look adoringly at them, usually smiling, while men are in control of the action and look aloofly off into space or into the camera. Goffman points out that being higher in physical space is a sign of dominance, while smiling is a sign of submission. Women are often grabbed, tossed, or otherwise treated as childlike objects to be played with by a dominant "adult" male. Men also are likely to have women in a "shoulder hold," which shows the dominant person as being larger and as guiding and directing the person who is held.[49]

Particular attention should be paid to sexual appeals in advertising. In many advertisements targeted at men, partial or complete female nudity is used along with strong sexual innuendo. There is an implication that the woman shown is the man's reward for using the product. Women are also portrayed as sex objects in advertisements that have nothing to do with sex. One ad entitled "Sex and the Quality Instrument" shows a woman in her underwear with men on either side of her; the ad is for machine parts. Even in advertisements targeted at women, there are nude and sexually provocative women. Here the purpose seems to be one of identification: If the woman uses the product, she will appeal to men or give them pleasure. Another approach is to imply that a product increases female sexuality and that this is an essential part of a woman's personality. One recent example is the L'Eggs pantyhose ad declaring that "ladies with L'Eggs have choices" as the bottom half of a leggy lady stands between the bottom halves of two men. In a Calvin Klein advertisement for Obsession perfume, two nude men and a woman are tangled on a couch. In an advertisement for Hennessy cognac, a fully dressed young man is shown watching a football game on television. Behind him is a girl in a brief lacy black negligee, holding two snifters of cognac. The caption reads, "The civilized way to end the game."

Women against Pornography, a women's lobbying group, is concerned that such images of women incite sexual violence against them. One striking example is an ad that portrays a young blond woman, naked from the waist up and with her hands crossed over her chest, saying, "Don't do this to me." While it looks as though she were about to be raped, the text tells us that she doesn't want us to cancel our magazine subscriptions. A recent advertisement for Guess jeans adds an implication of force to the sexual suggestion. A casually dressed girl is slung over a man's shoulder and struggles as she is carried toward a garage. In the next scene her jeans are off, one breast is partially exposed, and she is tousled and dazed.[50]

Not only are women trivialized by this type of advertisement, the trend toward advertisements that show women in compromising positions that imply rape or assault is a dangerous and growing one. Some advertisements imply assault as women lie in vulnerable positions with their heads back and their throats exposed. Recent record covers show women bound and gagged. Still other ads show women with a fierce dog's teeth closed around their legs.[51]

A particular concern of women's groups is the use of young girls as symbols of sexuality. It is very common to see girls of 10 or 11 made up to look like sex objects, with hints of cleavage and other sexual teases. The author recently picked up a men's magazine which showed a naked girl of 6 or 7 in an ad for men's shirts. There was no connection between the print and the general image of the ad; the naked little girl was just in the background. Ironically, research shows that sexually explicit advertising does not increase brand attractiveness or recall. Attention tends to be focused on the model, to the detriment of the brand name.[52]

Over time, the advertising images of gender roles for men and women have changed. In the 1970s women were shown mainly in family roles. In the 1980s they were shown in more occupational roles and, when not working, as decorative objects. Men were portrayed mainly in work roles in the 1970s but were shown more in educational and recreational roles in the 1980s. However, men are still shown as cool, unemotional, and dominant, while women are still depicted as concerned with personal beauty and with household and family.[53]

BOOKS

Books are another influential element in the teaching of gender roles. Although children may not spend as much time reading as they do watching television, books are important because they may represent one of the first contacts an infant or very young child has with gender roles. From nursery rhymes onward, the stereotyped roles are clearly shown. Books are also important because the written work implies truth or authority which is accentuated when the book is selected or read by a parent. Finally, an older child may not have much choice about reading certain books. Children can escape a required schoolbook only by refusing to open it, leaving themselves open to punishment by the teacher.

Sex stereotyping starts in books for the very young. In books published in the 1970s, preschool and elementary school books overwhelmingly depicted men as providers and women as homemakers. In a study of preschool books, seventeen male characters were shown as providers but only one female (a schoolteacher) had an occupation. In contrast, eighteen female characters were shown doing domestic things and only three male characters were portrayed in the home.[54] More recent studies have shown that this depiction has changed a little, although not as much as one might hope. Girls are now depicted more often in picture books for children, but when adults or animals are shown, males are still predominate.[55]

The overwhelming emphasis on men as providers and women as homemakers was quite pronounced in earlier books. The limited range of career options shown for women is striking. In a large survey, men participated in 213 different occupations, and women in only 39 (one-fifth the number). Only seven of the female occupations were shown in more than one book, and the women most commonly shown were nurses, librarians, elementary school teachers, seamstresses, secretaries, mothers, and witches.[56] Frequently these women were not shown contributing to the income of the household, although 53 percent of married women now work.

A picture book entitled *I'm Glad I'm a Boy; I'm Glad I'm a Girl* makes one wonder if the girl really is glad. The book depicts appropriate occupations and roles for each sex. It says that "boys are doctors; girls are nurses," "boys are pilots; girls are stewardesses," "boys are football players; girls are cheerleaders," and "boys are presidents and girls are first ladies." Perhaps worst of all in terms of dealing with competence, it tells us that "boys fix things and girls need things fixed" and that "boys build houses and girls keep houses." How can a child not be affected by such a strong portrayal of stereotypes?[57] While the book was written in 1970, it is still on bookstore shelves.

Males not only are shown more, they also are shown in more positive roles. Again, while some things have changed, others have not. A 1972 study found that in many books, competence and activity seem to be reserved only for boys. In play activity, boys were overwhelmingly depicted as active and girls as passive (watching, sitting, and admiring). Boys were shown talking, and girls were shown listening. Boys were shown as logical and realistic; girls were shown as illogical and idealistic.[58] Even the animated characters in educational books such as the Dr. Seuss series reflect a difference in the presentation of males and females. For example, boys are always riding the bicycle, while girls are the passengers. In other stories, the inanimate objects that are personified as achievement-oriented (Toot the Tugboat) are male and male animals are portrayed as exciting tigers or horses while female animals are portrayed as sloths, geese, or squirrels.[59] Many of these books are classics which are still read by parents to their children.

The roles in which boys and girls or men and women are still shown also imply characteristics that go beyond simple occupational stereotyping. Girls not only are ignored but are depicted as passive, fearful, vain, and unable to make friends. They are told that they are not good at sports and are silly and boring. They usually watch the boys in action or are at home helping with household chores, caring for pets or other children, or doing things to improve their appearance. They are so clumsy that they drop dishes when they are drying them and fall down when they try to skate. They frequently must be rescued by boys, and they cry a lot.[60]

Boys, in contrast, do active and interesting things. They serve as school crossing guards, play sports, and help their fathers build things. They form friendships easily and have great camaraderie with each other. However, they are not allowed to express emotion. They are never shown crying and are seldom shown hugging animals or playing with younger children. There is an implied pressure to enjoy being active and to be good at the things they do. While boys are depicted indoors playing with chemistry sets and erector sets, they are still being active. There is no picture of a boy who would like to sit quietly and read or perhaps cook.

Girls also learn early that it is a boy's and/or man's world. One frequently quoted phrase from an elementary school reader advises girls to "accept the fact that this is a man's world and learn to play the game gracefully."[61] When the message isn't explicitly stated, it is often implied. In one story, Kristen, a newcomer who has been ostracized by a group of girls, bakes Danish cookies for the school fair and wins their approval. When complimented on her cooking, she says, "It's easy. Even I can do it and you know how dumb I am." The story seems to be a nice one but manages to convey that girls are mean and exclude newcomers, that the way to gain acceptance is to do something feminine such as cooking, and above all that girls must be modest and play dumb if they are to win friends.[62]

Mathematics books also promulgate this stereotyping. Girls are still shown as being not very good at math and confused by complicated problems. They are depicted using mathematics to do typically female tasks such as buying hair ribbons and grocery shopping. In some books, girls are shown earning lower salaries than those of boys even when doing the same work.[63]

In an update of the 1970 studies, Williams and his colleagues found that while more women were shown, males continued to be more visible. In this 1980–1985 sample, women accounted for 37 percent of the human illustrations and 29 percent of the nonhuman pictures; in 13 percent of the picture books there were *no* pictures of women. In the stories, about one-third of the central characters were female. Women were also portrayed outside the home, but not in occupations. They did not have career goals, and there were no adult female role models. Only one woman in the entire 1980s collection of books studied worked outside the home, and she worked as a waitress. Men were still shown as independent, persistent, and active, but women were portrayed as colorless. Only two males in the entire study showed tender emotions, and one of them was a mouse.[64]

Sometimes good-faith attempts are made to correct these depictions. Unfortunately, good intentions are not enough. One book that discusses "mommies at work" ends with "all mommies loving the best of all to be your very own mommy and coming home to you."[65] The depiction of working women is admirable, but the impression is that women are not serious workers and that motherhood is their primary job. In *The Snake in the Carpool*, a little girl finds a snake and fearlessly handles it. However, in the end the rightful owner of the snake is a boy who must show the girl how to feed it and build a house for it.[66] Again, the intention is good but the message clearly comes through that boys know more about these things.

There has been a recent trend among some publishers to go beyond sexism by showing the characters in their books as gender-neutral. However, researchers have found that parents who read these books to their children usually talk about the characters as "he" or "she." In 90 percent of the cases, the gender chosen is male.[67]

Few children's books depict the realities of family life. Not only do they ignore the 53 percent of married women who are in the labor force, few show single-parent families or locales outside white suburbia. This makes many students feel "different" and may contribute to lowered self-esteem. Nonwhite students in particular seldom get a chance to see the environment in which they live and the kind of family to which they belong depicted in schoolbooks. They also find no information about their cultural heritage.

Thus, one of the most authoritative sources of gender roles—books—reinforces traditional stereotypes. The limited range of occupations depicted for women depresses their aspirations, and the ones shown for men are often unrealistic although exciting. The implication that the sexes divide in other attributes is even more insidious. It is bad enough that girls are ignored and portrayed as passive and doing only household chores, but when they are shown as dumb, clumsy, vain, incompetent, and unfriendly, the chances of their having a poor self-image are greatly increased. The characteristics of boys which are depicted are more positive, but boys are denied quiet pastimes and expressions of emotion. Most children's books now available are hurting children by depicting gender-role behavior in this rigid manner.

Since the inequities in these books have been known for over twenty-five years, one wonders why publishers have not done more to correct them. One reason seems to be that girls will read stories about boys but boys are less willing to read stories about girls. Another reason is the expense involved in publishing new series of books: It is expensive for publishers and school systems alike to change books frequently. Things are changing slowly, but much more needs to be done if books are to stop reinforcing traditional roles for females and males.

The sexism and racism depicted in many of these books can be eliminated. Pressure can be brought on publishers, school boards, PTAs, and others who are instrumental in designing and adopting books for the schools. Parents need to be educated about these matters so that they can pick the right books for their children.

Sexism is not confined to children's books. Other printed media to which children are exposed also continue the stereotyping. In a study of newspapers, men were found to be shown far more often than women and the men were portrayed as professionals and sports figures while the women usually were portrayed as spouses.[68] News magazines such as *Newsweek, Time,* and *U.S. News and World Report* also have many fewer references to women and articles bylined by women. In the most equal of these magazines, *Newsweek,* only 17 percent of the references were to women; women accounted for only 33 percent of the photos and had only 32 percent of the bylines.[69]

SCHOOLS

Schools reinforce traditional gender roles in many ways. Differences between boys and girls and their behaviors are often stressed very early. In preschool, boys and girls usually line up separately, use different bathrooms, and may even have recess and physical education at different times. Sex may be used as a way to separate teams for spelling bees and other activities. Boys' groups are frequently chosen for physical activities such as carrying chairs and washing blackboards, and girls' groups may pass out cookies. This reinforces the idea that sex can be used as a way to divide people, and it isolates the sexes from each other. It also reinforces gender-role stereotypes.

The authority structure of elementary schools also serves as a model for children. While 85 percent of elementary school teachers are women, 79 percent of elementary school principals are men. The difference in status is quite clear to the pupils. As the grades get higher, the percentage of female teachers gets smaller, and men have correspondingly more influence.[70]

Female and male children are also affected by the expectations of teachers. At the nursery school level, teachers react differently to boys and girls. Both inside and outside school, girls are rewarded for neatness, docility, obedience, passivity, and amenability to following instructions. Boys are rewarded for obedience and docility as well, but teachers subtly encourage more aggressive behavior. There is a feeling that "boys will be boys." In one study, female teachers were explicitly shown to encourage independence and assertion in boys, although they rewarded dependence in both sexes. They would often give attention to nearby dependent girls, praising and assisting them and sometimes almost doing their work for them. They would praise nearby boys but then would send them off to work by themselves. There is some indication that teachers negatively evaluate the competence of less compliant girls.[71]

However, with the passive nature of much elementary education, boys get into trouble and become discipline problems more often than girls do. Therefore, boys get reproved by teachers more often. In one study, teachers responded to boys' class disruptions three times as often as they did to similar disruptions by girls. This disapproval was primarily for violation of the rules, however. When disapproval was for lack of attention, the sexes were treated approximately equally, and when disapproval was for lack of knowledge or skill, girls were criticized more than boys were.[72] When praise was given, girls were praised for the neatness of their work, and boys for the quality of theirs.[73]

In addition, although teachers disapproved of boys more, they also listened to them more, gave them more instruction, and approved of them more. In one nursery school, boys received more directions from the teacher and were twice as likely to get individual instruction on how to do things.[74] In an example quoted by Serbin and O'Leary, a teacher helped the children make Easter baskets. The pupils had progressed to the point where they were stapling the paper handles on the baskets they had made. The teacher approached each girl in turn, took her basket, and stapled the handle with the comment "Here, dear, let me do that for you." The teacher gave the boys the stapler and showed them how to staple the handles themselves. In another example, a girl and two boys were learning Piaget's concept of "conversion." To demonstrate this concept, water is poured from one container to another to show that different-shaped containers can hold the same amount of water. The teacher let one of the boys try to pour the water himself. When the girl asked to try, she was told to wait her turn. The teacher then let the other boy try, and the period ended. The materials were put away without the girl getting a chance to handle the containers and practice using the concept.[75]

Boys are also rewarded more than girls are. In the 1960s, Torrance asked teachers to describe situations in which they had rewarded creative behavior;

74 percent of the children rewarded were boys. This high percentage may have resulted from different perceptions of who is creative. When boys and girls played with science toys and suggested uses for them, the girls suggested many more interesting and creative uses. However, when the students were asked whether boys or girls had contributed the ideas, they all replied that the boys had done better.[76] More recent studies seem to show that teachers share this perceptive bias and see boys as more creative whether they are or not.[77]

As teachers expectations can become self-fulfilling prophecies, these data are important. While teachers are often not aware of what they are doing and may even be opposed to it in theory, they exercise a powerful influence on the gender-role behavior of their students.

Surprisingly, male and female teachers do not behave very differently. In one study, both male and female teachers approved of dependence for boys and girls. However, the male teachers approved of masculine behavior in boys more than the female teachers did. Therefore, while both boys and girls are getting a message to be passive and dependent in elementary school, boys are also being rewarded by their peers and by some teachers for operating in assertive, masculine ways.[78]

What are the results of this type of interaction with teachers during the early school years? One effect is that boys may get lower grades. Although boys seem to score as high as or higher than girls on standardized tests of achievement, their grades are significantly lower. The sex of the teacher does not seem to be as important as whether the child is a boy or a girl. Why the lower grades for boys? Perhaps teachers expect more of them or grade them more severely because they are not as neat or have disrupted the class more often.

Do boys suffer from the excessive amount of disapproval that they receive? Judith Bardwick speculates that boys learn that they can get attention through disruptive behavior; thus teacher criticism, although it may seem negative, may lead boys to greater independence and autonomy. Boys learn how to take criticism and assert themselves. They also seem to be more realistic about their achievements.[79] Educators speculate that boys are more likely to develop independent, autonomous behavior because they are disapproved of, praised, listened to, and taught more by the teacher. Many educators believe that adults respond as if they found boys more interesting and attention-provoking than girls. This message is not lost on either sex.

Bardwick speculates that because the criticism a girl gets is more general and personal, it may lead to oversensitivity to criticism and a tendency to do tasks only to get social approval rather than for the joy of achievement.[80] Some researchers speculate that girls may have lower ambition because they are ignored and are criticized for lack of skill. One study found that bright fifth- and sixth-grade girls are lower in self-concept and in their estimates of their mental abilities than are equally intelligent boys.[81] Even girls who do consistently well in subjects estimate that their future grades will be lower than those of boys who currently get similar grades. When girls do well, they attribute their success to luck, while boys attribute their success to their own skill and ability.[82] Girls seem to accept a negative stereotype of their abilities, often unnecessarily. Academic achievement increases the aspirations of boys and high-achieving girls as they progress through school, but the aspirations of average girls do not seem to be affected by solid evidence that they can achieve.[83] Although girls get better grades than boys do, they are less likely to believe that they can do college work or succeed in a career.[84]

This low sense of competency can apparently be changed by means of intervention. In an experiment in Colorado, a group of middle-class girls changed their feelings of internal control and perceived competence after exposure to a Life Choices program.[85] It is important that schools empower both boys and girls with feelings of competence and the ability to control their futures. Treating the sexes differently on the basis of outdated stereotypes of dependence or being a breadwinner shortchanges everyone.

Instead, children of both sexes need to learn to be independent as well as not disruptive in class. Teachers, especially elementary school teachers, are a very important link in the chain of gender-role socialization. Both sexes need equal amounts of time and attention and equal amounts of praise and disapproval. Feelings about self and patterns of action established in the early years are important indicators of adjustment and achievement in the future.

THE BLACK CHILD IN SCHOOL

The black child in the school setting faces some of the same gender-role stereotyped environments as the white child but often faces other problems aggravated by stereotyping. One problem is that the language used by the teacher and the other children may be slightly to considerably different from that of a black child. If the black child has been brought up using primarily street talk or black English and is now faced with the problem of talking, reading, and writing "standard" English, she or he is facing a language barrier as well as the other gender-related problems in school. For the male black child in particular, to revert to standard English may be to revert to what is considered feminine in his culture. His resistance to using standard English may thus hinder his learning.[86]

In a similar fashion, playing the role of the quiet, docile student may be particularly difficult for a male black child who bases his masculinity on being "bad" or "tough." While the same problem exists for the male white child, the black boy experiences even greater conflict between the definitions of masculinity and good student.[87]

The female black child, however, probably is free from some of the stereotype problems experienced by her white counterpart. Because female children in the black community are encouraged to be self-sufficient and are expected eventually to provide their own support, female black children are likely to be more assertive and independent in the school setting. Indeed, if they are in an all-black school or have a female black teacher, they, rather than the boys, may get the extra attention. If they are in integrated schools or have white teachers, the lack of attention may not hurt their self-image as much as it does that of their female white classmates.[88]

Some solutions recommended for these problems were suggested by Rodney J. Reed. They include implementing childhood education programs and recruiting competent caring teachers and administrators, with minority teachers visible as role models for minority students. These teachers should be aware of the importance of expectations for student achievement. Heterogeneous ability groups should be used to eliminate the stigma of "tracking" at low levels (Chapter 6) and to place emphasis on valuing school performance and parental involvement. While Reed suggested these changes for minority students, they would help all students regardless of race or gender.[89]

SUMMARY

We have seen that children receive gender-role socialization from the cradle onward. Some of this socialization is subtle and indirect, as in the role of language, but direct influences such as the messages sent by television, books, and schoolteachers about appropriate gender-role behavior reinforce more subtle pressures. Early pressure to conform to traditional roles limits the potential for both sexes, particularly in regard to emotional expression by men and achievement potential among women.

Psychologists are beginning to call attention to the great damage done to both men and women by our narrowly defined role models. A statement made by the Association of Women Psychologists in 1970 is still relevant today:

> Psychological oppression in the form of sex-role socialization clearly conveys to girls from the earliest ages that their nature is to be submissive, servile and repressed, . . . the psychological consequences of goal depression in young women—the negative self-image, emotional dependence, drugged or alcoholic escape—are all too common. In addition, both men and women have come to realize the effects on men of this type of sex-role stereotyping: the crippling pressure to compete, to achieve, to produce, to stifle emotion, sensitivity, and gentleness, all taking their toll in psychic and physical traumas.[90]

Many individuals would be happier and more creative if they could choose a wider range of behavior. If children are to see more kinds of behavior as sex-appropriate, socialization and the institutions that perpetuate sex-stereotyped norms—such as language, media, and the schools—will have to change.

ESSAY QUESTIONS

1. Give several examples of how the same kind of word may have different implications when applied to men or to women (for example, "master"

and "mistress"). Describe the different styles and vocabularies of men and women when they use language and when they respond to one another. How can this differentiation affect the way they are treated by others?

2. It is said that a smile is "women's badge of submission." Discuss other forms of body language that imply submissiveness on the part of women.
3. How are men and women portrayed in the three different areas of television: prime time viewing, commercials, and children's programming? Comment on occupational roles and behavioral characteristics as well as numbers. How are blacks shown?
4. Describe how men and women are portrayed differentially in advertisements and discuss the messages that are communicated.
5. Boys and girls are portrayed quite differently in children's books. Assess the relative numbers of boys and girls shown in these books. How are they portrayed in occupational or work roles? And (very important) what kind of characteristics are boys shown as having? What kind of characteristics are shown for girls?
6. How are adult men and women shown in children's books? Are women and men limited in their chosen occupations or in the behavior they are allowed to express? Give examples.
7. How can the different amounts and kinds of attention paid by teachers to boys and girls affect the kind of motivation to achieve they will have in the future?
8. List ten different ways in which a teacher can differentiate between boys and girls in an elementary school classroom (for example, different games at recess). How could these differences be eliminated?
9. Why does school seem particularly difficult for many black children?

EXERCISES

1. Develop a list of "parallel adjectives" that are used about men and women. If men are called "absentminded," then women are called . . . ("scatterbrained"), and so on. After you have done this, talk about your feelings.
2. In a newspaper, count the number of men and women both in news stories and in advertisements. Make a list of important and positive images versus unimportant or negative images. How do men and women stack up on these lists?
3. Watch several hours of television. Write down all the put-downs or insults to men or women ("Men can't cook; women can't drive"). Would any of them have been allowed if they were aimed at ethnic groups? *Hint:* It is interesting to watch children's cartoons.

4. Watch several hours of television again and develop nonsexist commercials to replace all the sexist ones you find. Is it possible to have nonsexist commercials for some of the products that are advertised?
5. Read three or four children's picture books. Compare the number of aprons your mother (or you) owns with the number shown in the books. What is the message?
6. Develop nonsexist materials that could be used with young children in elementary-school classrooms. For example:

   • Make a jigsaw puzzle in which the opposite of the usual sex is shown (for example, a girl in a job requiring physical strength, a father feeding a baby). After you have found the pictures, paste them on heavy cardboard and then cut the cardboard with a jigsaw. In putting the puzzle together, the idea that babies are associated with fathers will be reinforced.
   • Develop a lotto game in which boys and girls do the same activity (girls can run track, for example). The idea can be modified to fit any kind of game. Be sure that girls as well as boys get a chance to be doctors and that boys as well as girls get to do housework.

NOTES

1. Thomas Mann, *The Magic Mountain (Der Zauberberg),* translated from the German by H. T. Lowe-Porter (New York: Knopf, 1949).
2. Laurel Richardson (Walum), *Dynamics of Sex and Gender: A Sociological Perspective,* 3d ed. (New York: Harper & Row, 1988).
3. Michigan Women's Commission, "Sex Discrimination in an Elementary Reading Program," Lansing, Mich., 1974.
4. Wendy Martnya, "Beyond the `He/Man' Approach: The Case for Nonsexist Language," *Signs* 5, no. 3 (1980):482–493; Mykol C. Hamilton, "Using Masculine Generics: Does Generic `He' Increase Male Bias in the User's Imagery?" *Sex Roles* 19, no. 11/12 (1988):785–799; J. Briere and C. Lanktree, "Sex-Role Related Effects of Sex Bias in Language," *Sex Roles* 9 (1983):625–632.
5. Karen L. Adams and Norma C. Ware, "Sexism and the English Language: The Linguistic Implications of Being a Woman," in Jo Freeman, *Women: A Feminist Perspective,* 3d ed. (Palo Alto, Calif.: Mayfield, 1983), pp. 478–491; P. A. Smith and E. Midlarsky, "Empirically Derived Conceptions of Femaleness and Maleness: A Current View," *Sex Roles* 12 (1985):313–328.
6. Barrie Thorne, Cheris Kramarae, and Nancy Henley, eds., *Language, Gender and Society* (Rowley Mass.: Newbury House, 1983.)
7. Allen Nilsen, "Sexism in English: A Feminist View," *Female Studies VI* (Old Westbury, N.Y.: Feminist Press, 1972), quoted in Barbara Eakins and R. Gener Eakins, *Sex Differences in Human Communication* (Boston: Houghton, Mifflin, 1978), p. 123.
8. Adams and Ware, *op. cit.*
9. *Ibid.*

10. *Ibid.*
11. Thorne et al., *op. cit.*
12. Carol Edelsky, "Who's Got the Floor?" *Language in Society* 10 (1981):383–421.
13. Jean Lipman-Blumen, *Gender Roles and Power* (Englewood Cliffs, N.J.: Prentice-Hall, 1984).
14. Pamela Fishman, "Interaction: The Work Women Do," in Thorne et al., *op. cit.,* pp. 89–102.
15. R. Hall and B. Sandler, *The Classroom Climate: A Chilly One for Women* (Washington, D.C.: Project on the Status and Education of Women, Association of American Colleges, 1982).
16. Thorne et al., *op. cit.*
17. Kathryn Quina, Joseph A. Wingard, and Henry G. Bates, "Language Style and Gender Stereotypes in Person Perception," *Psychology of Women Quarterly* 11 (1987):111–122; A. Mulac, C. Incontro, and M. R. James, "A Comparison of the Gender-Linked Language Effect and Sex-Role Stereotypes," *Journal of Personality and Social Psychology* 49 (1985):1098–1109.
18. Eakins and Eakins, *op. cit.,* pp. 115–176.
19. Nancy Henley, Mykol Hamilton, and Barrie Thorne, "Womanspeak and Manspeak: Sex Differences in Communication, Verbal and Nonverbal," in Alice G. Sargent, ed., *Beyond Sex Roles,* 2d ed. (St. Paul, Minn.: West, 1985), pp. 168–185.
20. Eakins and Eakins *op. cit.,* pp. 115–176.
21. Henley et al., *op. cit.,* pp. 168–185.
22. Richardson (Walum) *op. cit.* p. 22.
23. Nancy Henley, *Body Politics: Power, Sex and Nonverbal Communication* (Englewood Cliffs, N.J.: Prentice-Hall, 1977); N. M. Henley, B. Gruber, and L. Lerner "Effects of Sex-Biased Language on Attitudes and Self-Esteem" (paper presented at a meeting of the Southern California Language and Gender Interest Group, Los Angeles, Calif., October 1984, cited in Hamilton, *op. cit.*).
24. Eakins and Eakins, *op. cit.,* p. 171.
25. Larry Gross and Suzanne Jeffries-Fox, "What Do You Want to Be When You Grow Up, Little Girl?" in Gaye Tuchman, Arlene Daniels, and Jane Benet, *Home and Hearth: Images of Women in the Mass Media* (New York: Oxford University Press, 1978), pp. 240–265; Gail Tuchman, "Women's Depiction by the Mass Media," *Signs* 4(1979)528–542.
26. Kevin Durkin, *Television, Sex Roles and Children: A Developmental Social Psychological Account* (Philadelphia: Taylor and Francis, 1985).
27. Nancy Signorielli, "Television and Conceptions about Sex Roles: Maintaining Conventionality and the Status Quo," *Sex Roles* 21, no. 5/6 (1989):341–352; George Gerber and Nancy Signorielli, "Women and Minorities in Television Drama, 1969–1979" (a research report in conjunction with the Screen Actor's Guild, Annenberg School of Communications, Philadelphia, 1979); Bradley S. Greenberg and Carrie Heeter, "Television and Social Stereotypes," *Prevention in Human Services: Rx Television* 2, no. 1/2 (1982):37–51.
28. Greenberg and Heeter, *op. cit.*
29. Muriel G. Cantor, "Popular Culture and the Portrayal of Women," in Beth Hess and Myra Marx Ferree, eds., *Analyzing Gender: A Handbook of Social Science Research* (New York: Sage, 1987), pp. 190–214.
30. Jane Bergman, "Are Little Girls Harmed by Sesame Street?" in Stacey et al., eds., *And Jill Came Tumbling After: Sexism in American Education* (New York: Dell, 1974), pp. 110–116.

31. G. Bretl and M. Cantor, "Portrayal of Men and Women in U. S. Television Advertisement: Recent Content Analysis and Fifteen-Year Trends," *Sex Roles* 18, no. 4/5 (1988):545–609.

32. F. L. Geis, Virginia Brown, Joyce Jennings (Walstedt), and Natalie Porter, "T.V. Commercials as Achievement Scripts for Women," *Sex Roles* 10, no. 7/8 (1984):513–525.

33. Lynn Lovdal, "Sex Role Messages in Television Commercials: An Update," *Sex Roles* 21, no. 11/12 (1989):715–727.

34. G. H. Hill and S. S. Hill, *Blacks on Television* (Metuchen, N.J.: Scarecrow, 1985).

35. Gaye Tuchman, "The Symbolic Annihilation of Women by the Mass Media," in Tuchman et al., eds., *op. cit.*

36. Gerber and Signorielli, *op. cit.*

37. Gross and Jeffries-Fox, *op. cit.*

38. Scott Ward, D. B. Wackman, and Ellen Wartella, *Consumer Socialization: An Information Processing Approach to Consumer Learning* (Beverly Hills, Calif.: Sage, 1978).

39. Michael Morgan, "Television, Sex-Role Attitudes and Sex-Role Behavior," *Journal of Early Adolescence* 7, no. 3 (1987):269–282.

40. Andrew Meltzoff, "Imitation of Televised Models by Infants," *Child Development* 59, no. 5 (1988):1221–1229.

41. Ann Beuf, "Doctor, Lawyer, Household Drudge," *Journal of Communication* 24, no. 2 (1974):142–145.

42. Charles K. Atkin, "Effects of Television Advertising on Children: Second Year Experimental Evidence," Report 2, (East Lansing, Mich.: Michigan State University, 1975).

43. Nora O'Neil, Sandra Schoonover, and Lisa Adelstein, "The Effect of TV Advertising on Children's Perceptions of Roles," summarized in T. W. Whipple, ed., *Children and Television: A Report to Montessori Parents*, mimeographed (Cleveland: Cleveland State University, 1980).

44. Roberta Wroblewski and Aletha Huston, "Televised Occupational Stereotypes and Their Effects on Early Adolescents: Are They Changing?" *Journal of Early Adolescence* 7, no. 3 (1987):283–297.

45. O'Neil, Schoonover, and Adelstein, *op. cit.*

46. Kevin Durkin, "Children's Accounts of Sex-Role Stereotypes in Television," *Communication Research* 11, no. 3 (1984):341–352; Faye Dambrot, Diana Reep, and Daniel Bell, "Television Sex Roles in the 1980s: Do Viewers' Sex and Sex Role Orientation Change the Picture?" *Sex Roles* 19, no. 5/6 (1988):387–394.

47. Jerry Burkick, "Women's Images on TV Still Need Fine Tuning," *Jackson Citizen Patriot* (Michigan) (February 13, 1983):C5.

48. Jean Kilbourne, *"Killing Us Softly: Advertising Images of Women.* Film available from Jean Kilbourne, P.O. Box 385, Cambridge, Mass.

49. Erving Goffman, *Gender Advertisements* (Cambridge, Mass.: Harvard University Press, 1979).

50. Jeffrey A. Tractenberg, "It's Become Part of Our Culture," *Forbes* (May 5, 1986):32 Judith Posner, "Sexual Sell: Or We Do It All For You," manuscript (Toronto: Atkinson College/York University, 1981), quoted in Courtney, *op. cit.*, p. 13.

51. Kilbourne, *op. cit.*

52. Alice Courtney and Thomas Whipple, *Sex Stereotyping in Advertising* (Toronto: Heath, 1983), pp. 3–30; Alice E. Courtney and Thomas W. Whipple, "Female Role Portrayals in Advertising and Communication Effectiveness: A Review," *Journal of Advertising* 14, no. 3 (1985):4–8, 17.

53. *Ibid.*
54. Janet Saltzman Chafetz, *Masculine, Feminine, or Human?* (Itasca, Ill.: Peacock, 1978).
55. Elizabeth Grauerholz and Bernice A. Pescosolido, "Gender Representation in Children's Literature: 1900–1981," *Gender and Society* 3, no. 1 (1989):113–125.
56. Lenore Weitzman and Dianne M. Rizzo, "Images of Males and Females in Elementary School Textbooks" (slide program produced by NOW Legal Defense and Education Fund, New York).
57. Whitney Darrow, Sr., *I'm Glad I'm a Boy; I'm Glad I'm a Girl* (New York: Simon & Schuster, 1970).
58. Women on Words and Images, *Dick and Jane as Victims: Sex Stereotyping in Children's Readers* (Princeton, N.J., 1972); Elizabeth Fisher, "Children's Books: The Second Sex, Junior Division," in Stacey et al., *op. cit.,* pp. 116–123.
59. *Ibid.*
60. Weitzman and Rizzo, *op. cit.*
61. Elizabeth Fisher, *op. cit.*
62. Weitzman and Rizzo, *op. cit.*
63. *Ibid.*
64. J. Allen Williams, Jr., et al., "Sex Role Socialization in Picture Books: An Update," *Social Science Quarterly* 68 (1987):148–156.
65. Eve Merriman, "Mommies at Work," quoted in Elizabeth Fisher, "Children's Books: The Second Sex Junior Division," in Stacey et al., *op. cit.*
66. Miriam Schlein, *The Snake in the Carpool* (London and New York: Abelard Schuman, 1983).
67. J. S. Deloache, D. J. Cassidy, and C. J. Carpenter, "The Three Bears are All Boys: Mothers' Gender Labeling of Neutral Picture Book Characters," *Sex Roles* 17 (1987):163–178.
68. Barbara F. Luebke, "Out of Focus: Images of Women and Men in Newspaper Photographs," *Sex Roles* 20, no. 3/4 (1989):121–129.
69. Linda Russman, "Survey of News Magazines Shows Little News Coverage of Women," *Media Report to Women* 17, no. 6 (1989):1.
70. L. V. Paradise and S. M. Wall, "Children's Perceptions of Male and Female Principals and Teachers," *Sex Roles* 14 (1986):1.
71. Delores Gold, Gail Crombie, and Sally Noble, "Relations between Teachers' Judgments of Girls' and Boys' Compliance and Intellectual Competence," *Sex Roles* 16, no. 7/8 (1987):351–362.
72. Shoshanna BenTsvi-Mayer, Rachel Hertz-Lazarowitz, and Marilyn P. Safir, "Teachers' Selections of Boys and Girls as Prominent Pupils," *Sex Roles* 21, no. 3/4 (1989):231–239.
73. C. S. Dweck, W. Davidson, S. Nelson, and B. Enna, "Sex Differences in Learned Helplessness," *Developmental Psychology* 14 (1978):268–276.
74. M. Sadker and D. Sadker, "Striving for Equity in Classroom Teaching" in A. G. Sargent, ed., *Beyond Sex Roles* (New York: West, 1985), pp. 442–455.
75. Lisa A. Serbin and K. Daniel O'Leary, "How Nursery Schools Teach Girls to Shut Up," *Psychology Today* (December 1975):57–58, 102–103.
76. E. P. Torrance, *Guiding Creative Talent* (Englewood Cliffs, N.J.: Prentice-Hall, 1962).
77. BenTsvi-Mayer et al., *op. cit.*
78. Dolores Gold and Myrna Reis, "Male Teacher Effects on Young Children: A Theoretical and Empirical Consideration," *Sex Roles* 8, no. 5 (1982):493–513.
79. Judith Bardwick, *Psychology of Women* (New York: Harper & Row, 1971), p. 113.
80. *Ibid.,* pp. 112, 158.

81. P. S. Sears and D. H. Feldman, "Teachers' Interactions with Boys & Girls," *National Elementary Principal* 46 (1966):30–35; Mzobanzi M. Mbova, "The Relative Importance of Global Self-Concept and Self-Concept of Academic Ability in Predicting Academic Achievement," *Adolescence* 24, no. 93 (1989):39–45.; C. M. Siddique and Carl D'Arcy, "Adolescence, Stress, and Psychological Well-Being," *Journal of Youth and Adolescence* 13, no. 6 (1984):459–473.

82. Nita Danziger, "Sex-Related Differences in the Aspirations of College Students," *Sex Roles* 9, no. 6 (1983):683–695.

83. Kip C. Alishio and Karen Schilling, "Sex Differences in Intellectual and Ego Development in Late Adolescence," *Journal of Youth and Adolescence* 13, no. 3 (1984):213–225.

84. Carolyn Simmons and Ruth Parsons, "Developing Internality and Perceived Competence: The Empowerment of Adolescent Girls," *Adolescence* 18, no. 72 (1983):917–922.

85. Rosalie Cohen, "The Language of the Hard Core Poor: Implications for Culture Conflict," *Sociology Quarterly* 10 (1968):19–28.

86. Claire Etaugh and Valerie Hughes, "Teacher's Evaluations of Black Students," in Janice E. Hale-Benson, *Black Children: Their Roots, Culture and Learning Styles* (Baltimore: Johns Hopkins University Press, 1987):47–69.

87. Rodney Reed, "Education and Achievement of Young Black Males," in Jewelle Taylor Gibbs, ed., *Young, Black and Male in America* (Dover, Mass.: Auburn, 1988), pp. 37–96.

88. John U. Ogbo, "Black Education: A Cultural-Ecological Perspective," in Hariette McAdoo, ed., *Black Families* (Beverly Hills, Calif.: Sage, 1982), pp. 146–149.

89. Reed, *op. cit.*

90. Association of Women Psychologists, "Statement Resolutions and Motions" (statement presented at the American Psychological Association Convention, September 1970), quoted in Women on Words and Images, *op. cit.*, p. 43.

Chapter 6

Socialization in the Teenage Years

An adolescent boy or girl must carve out an individual identity. The freedom of childhood and the comfort of being an unthinking part of a family are left behind. At this age, boys and girls are faced with new norms and values, new tasks, and a resultant concern about whether they are doing well in their new, freer environment. Changing bodies, combined with uncertainty about identity and behavior, often make adolescent boys and girls anxious. Prescriptions for certain kinds of gender-role behavior may be intensified; for example, boys may be pressured to control their emotions even more rigidly than they did before. In other instances, prescriptions for gender-role behavior are modified; for example, a girl who was a tomboy in elementary school may feel pressure to be more "feminine" and may sense an increased emphasis by her peers on being pretty and popular rather than being active.

Uncertainty about appropriate behavior may be increased because this society has few **rites of passage** to mark the transition from boy to man or from girl to woman. In many cultures, when girls can bear children and boys are large enough to hunt and provide for a family, they are considered adults. The adult roles and responsibilities they take on are well known, and their passage to adult status is usually marked with a ceremony. By contrast, the transition from childhood to adult status is not easily marked in this society. With our prolonged adolescence, marriage may be deferred until ten years or more after puberty. Because there is no strict definition of the transition from childhood to adulthood, the adolescent years may be marked by uncertainty and conflict as boys and girls try to separate from parental attachments.

The question of just when one becomes a man or a woman is always there. Does this occur when a person can bear or father children, when one has the first sexual experience, when one can earn a living, when one is old enough to vote or be drafted, or when one can drink legally or get a driver's license? There are no pat answers. While some norms exist, they vary by region, by the size of one's hometown, and by one's friends and family. Thus, individuals must develop their own answers to questions such as, When is one old enough to set one's own curfews and decide how one wants to spend one's time? and How much can one be seen with one's parents or do things with them and still have an identity of one's own?

Some people have characterized adolescence as a time of crisis and considerable emotional pain. The German expression *Sturm und Drang* ("storm and stress") has been used to characterize the psychology of adolescence. In a 1980s study, 27.5 percent of adolescents reported high levels of psychological distress, 39 percent reported mild distress, and 39 percent reported no symptoms of distress.[1] Many people believe that adolescent crisis is created by our culture.[2]

The most tumultuous period in adolescence seems to be early adolescence, or junior high school age. Children of this age appear to have a lower self-image, slightly lower self-esteem, and less favorable views of the opinions that others hold of them. Parents and adolescents both agree that the greatest turmoil in their lives occurred between the ages of 12 and 14.[3]

Many researchers have hypothesized that the gender-role attitudes of boys and girls during the teenage years are more conservative than they are in other parts of the life cycle. Uncertainty and the search for identity during this period make a ready-made set of prescriptions for behavior attractive. A study of children in the second, fourth, and sixth grades found that ideas of appropriate roles for men and women become more stereotyped as children grow older.[4] Other studies have found that students become more conservative with each older age and grade category.[5] In all these studies, boys were found to be more conservative than girls in their gender-role stereotypes. One study of high-school students found that boys saw males as having more advantages and fewer disadvantages than girls, while girls identified equal numbers of advantages and disadvantages for males.[6] Most studies have documented a consistency in conservative gender-role attitudes in adolescents in spite of the effect of more liberal attitudes in society at large.[7]

In all these studies there was a difference between the sex-role ideals of boys and those of girls.[8] One study differentiated the ideals of ninth-grade boys and those of girls. Girls saw the ideal man as "the chivalrous football player" (kind and honest, fun-loving, smiling, and bringing flowers); boys saw the ideal man as "the frowning football player" (fun-loving, frowning, and engaged in sports). Girls portrayed the ideal woman as "the smiling hard-worker" (kind and honest, smiling, intelligent, and having adult responsibilities); boys described the ideal woman as "the smiling sunbather" (good-looking, sexy, smiling, and engaged in leisure activities).[9] Boys pictured the ideal woman in traditional stereotyped activities (modeling and cooking); girls listed traditional activities and other roles as well. Girls were also more likely to picture a man engaging in nontraditional activities.

By the college years this trend toward conservatism seems to be moderated. A study of college students by Fabes and Laner in 1986[10] showed that although the men perceived females as having more disadvantages than advantages, they did not do so to as great an extent as the high school students had. Conversely, college females saw males as having significantly more advantages than high school females had. The older females may have had a more realistic perception of the greater social power and status of males. Advantages perceived for women included social expectations such as chivalry, courtesy, and not paying for dates; advantages perceived for men included greater social and occupational status. Women saw inexpressiveness as a distinct male disadvantage, but men saw women's necessity to be attractive, cope with the menstrual cycle and pregnancy, and be sexually abused and exploited as disadvantages. Both women and men perceived the *necessity* for men to take on the responsibilities and pressures of a breadwinner role as a disadvantage in spite of men's higher status in most occupational categories.[11]

Because these ideal perceptions become prescriptions for behavior, particularly for a young person who is searching for an identity, it is important to examine gender-role ideals. Because each sex views the ideal boy and girl somewhat differently, we will look at the ideal each sex depicts for itself and mention possible differences in how that ideal is viewed by the other sex.

THE MASCULINE WORLD IN HIGH SCHOOL

In many ways, values for adolescent boys are simply intensified versions of the values learned in early childhood. In particular, masculine, or "macho," themes intensify. A young boy was always expected to be tough and scrappy; now it is absolutely essential for him to hold his own in fights and to be physically tough enough to "take it" while participating in sports. A young boy ideally was expected never to cry or get upset in any but an angry fashion. He was always supposed to be good at sports and other activities; now that pressure is increased. In addition, there are new pressures to be good (but not too good) at activities that will lead to occupational success and to be good at sex and heterosexual relationships. These pressures are intense and are continuously present. The penalty for not living up to the norms of being tough, being "cool," and being good is severe: rejection or simply being ignored.[12] Let us look at each norm in turn to see how the pressures are applied. While there is individual variation in accordance with family, social class, and area, most of what we will describe, applies to all adolescents in American society.

Being Tough

Physical toughness is an important norm for males and can be expressed in a variety of ways. It can mean having a good body build and being in shape. A good body build is an obvious way for a boy to show he is tough and able to use force if necessary. For older middle-class men, the appearance of being tough is usually enough; it is not usually necessary to prove one's toughness by fighting or even engaging in contact sports.[13] This is not so true for blue-collar men, who may get into physical confrontations, or for adolescents. While some boys may get through high school without fights, most boys have some and some boys have many. Fights are a way to prove that one is tough, that one's ego cannot be stepped on, that one is "a man." Fights may be picked over inconsequential things for just that reason. In addition, any confrontation may end in a fight. My son has told me that junior high school is the worst time for confrontations and fights, and this is especially true for middle-class boys. Such children have big bodies but little social maturity to guide them in deciding when and how to use those bodies. One can also imagine the trauma of spindly seventh- and eighth-grade boys who have not yet undergone their growth spurt but must deal with adolescent norms of toughness. During this period many boys begin to lift weights or engage in body building. It is important to be tough enough to protect oneself and to look as though one can't be "messed with."

The pressure to be tough is greatly intensified for working-class and lower-class boys. Because these boys will probably not compete as much for academic and occupational success as middle-class boys do, toughness is the primary field of competition aside from the competition for women. Working-class and lower-class boys are likely to engage in many more fights than their middle-class peers do. Staples points out that fighting may be a means of gaining status among youths in the black community.[14] In the lower class, fights may become institutionalized with confrontations between gangs.

Body Build.   For boys as well as girls, satisfaction with one's body is related to self-esteem.[15] A good body build not only is a vehicle for proving toughness, it also enhances a boy's social prestige. For boys, popularity is associated with strength and athletic skills; thus, a strong, heavy, athletic body build is preferred. Physical attractiveness often determines interpersonal acceptance; studies show that people are less likely to make negative assumptions about attractive individuals. When subjects in one study were asked to identify a person with epilepsy from two different photos, 83 percent chose the less attractive person. In contrast, attractive people are described as having more desirable personalities and are seen as being likely to be successful both professionally and maritally.[16] The importance of physical attractiveness as a factor in determining social acceptance does not diminish even when a person has been known for a long time.[17]

The popularity enjoyed by attractive boys leads to greater self-esteem. Such boys are seen as having greater social power, and they perform more successfully within their groups. Successful group performance enhances self-esteem, which is also related to high masculine role identification. Therefore, we may agree at least partially with Gagnon's statement that "the primary power the young male has is his own body."[18] His attractiveness and body build seem to influence his popularity, social prestige, and ability to conform to prescriptions for the masculine role such as being tough and being good at sports, and these factors in turn affect his self-esteem.

Sports.   Participation in athletics goes hand in hand with a good body build in providing evidence of toughness. Coleman states that athletic ability in boys is directly associated with high status and membership in the adolescent elite and that an adolescent's position in relation to this elite has a direct bearing on his self-image, adjustment, and general development.[19] Athletic achievement is thus linked directly to prestige for males. It seems to be the most important factor determining a male adolescent's social standing in high school.[20]

Schools place an overwhelming emphasis on sports in terms of time and financial support. A great deal of the social life in school is organized around participating in or watching sports events. Boys are told that they should participate in sports and are encouraged or even pressured to do so. Offer describes a young man who was a very good athlete but was not particularly interested in sports; he liked music. The coach made fun of this student in front of the whole gym class, and some of the bigger boys pinned him against a wall and threatened to "cut your long hair and make you a real man if you don't join the group and fight for your high school."[21] Luckily, the student had a good deal of self-confidence, his own group of friends, and supportive parents, and so he was able to withstand this kind of pressure.

The pull to the sports world is reinforced by the fact that many teachers who are highly respected by faculty and students alike are also coaches.[22] Students often see these coaches as confidants and as being among the few teachers who treat them as individuals. The adolescent emphasis on athletics may be partially a reflection of the adult emphasis on sports. Boys frequently see adult males who are fanatic followers of all kinds of sports and teams, from the hometown league to professional franchises.

While there is some variation by social class, contact and team sports probably contribute the most to masculine prestige; general team sports (baseball) and general contact sports (wrestling) are next, and sports that are neither team nor contact (track) come last in the hierarchy. Snyder and Spreitzer suggest that in the lower rung of the hierarchy, track is more prestigious than gymnastics for men in most regions and social classes, because sports such as track involve endurance and the projection of the body through space with some force while sports such as gymnastics and tennis involve less force and more grace, although they require as much skill or more.[23]

Thus, the best way for a boy to gain prestige in the junior high or high school world of sports is to play football. The sacrifices boys make to play provide mute testimony to the need for this prestige. Smaller boys who get clobbered by their classmates on every play still go out for the team and take the punishment. Boys endure brutal training techniques and three or four hours of practice a day, giving up their weekends, giving up dating and drinking during the season, giving up summers for football camp or training—all to be a member of the team. In this way they show that they are tough enough and skilled enough to be accepted.

There are negative aspects to this overemphasis on toughness and work in sports. It has been documented that much of the spontaneous fun associated with childhood sports is eliminated in organized athletic leagues for children. Clearly, children become more negative about sports as the fun is gradually replaced by an emphasis on skill and success.[24] The high degree of organization and consequent lack of fun are certainly evident in sports in junior and senior high school. Sports are not fun, at least not very much fun; they are work. What they are all about is proving oneself.

Another negative aspect of the emphasis on sports and the greater pressure to win is the increasing use by athletes of steroids that build strength and muscle. Only about 2 percent of college athletes who responded to one questionnaire admitted steroid use, but other estimates put the percentage using performance-enhancing drugs much higher.[25]

The emphasis on group conformity, on being part of the team, may also be excessive. Although group identity provided by team membership may ease the transition to manhood and even be a rite of passage, belonging often has a price. Some teams have special "initiations" to show that a boy has arrived or has been accepted as a member. Needless to say, these rites emphasize that the boy must be a man among men, that he must be tougher than the tough. If he takes the initiation without complaining, he is a member of the team. Some teams do this informally by "making it tough" for the new guy, and others have mild initiations. One very difficult initiation was recently reported in the *Ann Arbor News.* Several members of the University of Michigan hockey team kidnapped a new team member from his dorm room, stripped him in twenty-degree weather, and shaved his body hair in front of the dorm. They then poured alcohol into the still-naked young man, stuffed him in the trunk of a car, and drove around for three or four hours in the freezing weather. When they finally dumped the initiate on his dorm steps, he could neither walk nor talk and had to be treated for exposure at the hospital. In spite of great pressure from administrative officials, he did not say who had initiated him.[26] Fraternity initiations in college have similar functions of strengthening ties to the in group, but the element of physical toughness is stressed especially in initiations for teams.

Violence.   Another element of being tough is the violence that is an illegal but common accompaniment of most sports. Hockey certainly has enough legitimate body contact, but many fans relish the extra checking against the boards, the fights, and the general violence that goes beyond the sport itself. One researcher reports that young hockey players perceive that their illegal behavior is supported by their coaches, parents, and nonplaying peers. In a court case involving hockey professionals, Boston's Dave Forbes claimed that another player had hit him first and he had to retaliate. He stated that if he hadn't fought back, he would have been an easy mark from then on. He pointed out that fighting back is an integral part of the game, taught to players as youngsters. "Before the trial (which ended with no verdicts), National Hockey League president Clarence Campbell defended fighting as a well-established safety valve for players, and even as an essential ingredient for the economic well-being of the game. . . . `Insofar as fighting is part of the show, certainly we sell it,' he said."[27]

Sports are not just an area in which an adolescent can prove his toughness; they are a reflection of the dominant values of society. The emphasis on being tough, working hard, winning at all costs, and working with the team continues into adult male life. While the majority of adult males may be watchers rather than participants in team sports, they still live by these values. Sports are therefore a way to socialize adolescents to learn the values of the adult male world. Betty Harragan has pointed out how the rules of the team player carry over into the corporate world. She notes that one learns to play by the rules, play one's own position, take criticism, and not talk back to the coach. The player learns that he can't win them all and sometimes the crowd will be against him, that he must play with those he doesn't like, and that he must cooperate and compete at the same time. These rules stand a boy in good stead in the business world.[28]

The slogans frequently used for athletics show how other adult male values of effort, coolness, not complaining, aggressiveness, and competition are socialized in sports:

It's easier to stay in shape than to get in shape.
It takes a cool head to win a hot game.
The guy who complains about the way the ball bounces usually dropped it.
The harder I work, the luckier I get.
No one ever drowned in sweat.
Anyone can be ordinary, but it takes guts to excel.
When the going gets tough, the tough get going.
Winning isn't everything; it's the only thing.
They ask not how you played the game but whether you won or lost.
If it doesn't matter whether you win or lose, why keep score?
There is no "I" in team.
Who passed the ball to you when you scored?
An ounce of loyalty is worth a pound of cleverness.[29]

The emphasis in sports is on achievement and success through competition, hard work, and discipline. Sports socialization also tells a young man that he must adopt certain behavior patterns to win: He must be cool and must keep trying.

For working-class or lower-class boys, success in sports becomes extremely important. Although only rarely, sports can be an occupation or a way out of the ghetto. It is also a way to gain acceptance by the larger society. Some black leaders have become worried about the overemphasis on sports for black children. Arthur Ashe points out in "An Open Letter to Black Parents: Send Your Children to the Library" that while black athletes constitute 60 percent of the players in the National Basketball Association, blacks account for less than 4 percent of the doctors and lawyers in the United States. Few can qualify at the top of the athletic heap, and the period of earning a high salary is a short one.[30] Nevertheless, sports are a route to achievement for some black youths.[31]

For all young males, sports represent a chance to prove themselves masculine and, if they are really good, to be sports heroes. There are few other paths to adulation for adolescent males. Success in sports implies approval of both peers and parents, social success, and even a future occupation.

The emphasis on toughness and athletic ability is especially difficult for a boy who does not have a spectacular body build or athletic skills. If what he can do physically determines to a great extent his social acceptance by others and his own self-esteem, a boy who is nonathletic may suffer. He is less likely to be a leader and is more likely to doubt his masculinity. For a boy who is large, strong, and talented, sports may provide an avenue toward a masculine identity. For a boy who is not athletically inclined, not playing sports deprives him of a culturally defined route to being masculine.

Being Cool

Not showing one's emotions—being cool—is an element of the ideal male role that carries over into many areas beyond the emotional realm. Part of the image of being tough is to be cool. A person who maintains a calm exterior during an exciting sports competition or in a physical encounter is also being tough. Lack of emotion is supposed to signal many things: that the person is not afraid of danger (as in skiing down a steep slope) or is keeping a cool and reasonable mind in the face of hot competition (as in a basketball game). Being cool is also interpreted as not expressing tender emotions, at least in public. This part of being cool may be a denial of the tender and gentle side of men, but it is also a denial of "feminine" characteristics.[32] Thus, a man who is cool has a perpetual poker face and keeps his feelings to himself.

Black teenage males in particular are pressured to be cool as well as tough. Hare points out that if black males do not do well in school, they increasingly seek recognition from their friends in nonacademic areas. He states that the black boy often develops a particular air of coolness and aloofness and a special style of walking and talking to prove his distinctiveness.[33]

It is often difficult for black boys (and girls) to do well in school because of the attitudes and expectations of high school teachers and officials. Black students are often perceived to be less capable and thus receive less attention in an integrated classroom.[34] They may also attend school in areas that have lower expenditures per pupil and where other factors make the learning environment a difficult one. These problems and the negative attitudes and low expectations held by school officials may get transmitted to the student and become self-fulfilling prophecies. While more black students are now graduating from high school, college enrollments for blacks as a percentage of high school graduates have actually declined since 1978.[35]

The Inexpressive Male.   The epitome of the "cool dude" may be Clint Eastwood, whose dialogue consists primarily of monosyllables. Actually, this type of inexpressive male is the "man's man," who is rugged, tough, and quiet. He enjoys men's activities and the outdoors and is a little uncomfortable around women. A more extreme example of the body-built, cool man would be Rambo, the movie figure played by Sylvester Stallone.

Women obviously have their place as mothers and housekeepers and should be respected, but they are not really a part of these men's intimate world. Male gangs of football players in high school may come the closest to fulfilling this image. While many of these high school boys date, they do not spend much time with girls and do not relate to them except in a sexual way. A quote from a high school boy shows this:

I don't allow myself to get involved with girls in any kind of meaningful relationship. I see girls as a softening agent to guys like me who can't afford to soften up in a love thing. The reason I can't afford to soften up is that I'm in sports and a degree of meanness and toughness is needed for me to excel.[36]

For this kind of male, the worlds of males and females are separate. We will see this style again in the blue-collar marriage.

Another type of inexpressive male is not so quiet, although he also rarely reveals his emotions. This type is epitomized by the James Bond character in films. Such a man relates to women and spends time with them. He is verbal and articulate, but he relates in an artificial way by using a "line." He does not really express his emotions or get involved in a relationship. He is not respectful of women but sees them as sex objects and is likely to use them.[37]

While most high school boys and adult men do not fall completely into either category of cool man, the models are there for them to copy. Because men must keep quiet if they are scared, are disappointed or hurt, or have tender feelings, not much is left for them to talk about that has deep, personal meaning. It is hard for them to become intimate with anyone in the sense of revealing themselves without breaking the code of being cool. Blier and Blier-Wilson report that significantly more boys than girls worry about controlling their emotions, especially the emotion of anger.[38] Perhaps because of messages they get about not showing emotion, men also perceive affiliative situations as being dangerous.[39] Men who disclose a great deal of personal information to another man are less well liked, and rejected male adolescents in one study were characterized by other men as pesky, noisy, conceited, silly, and effeminate.[40]

Researchers have different perspectives on the inexpressive male. Some have suggested that learned inexpressiveness is beneficial later in life. A man will modify his inexpressiveness somewhat with his wife, but it keeps him away from other women. Others have said that it is not a help in marriage and is often used as a weapon against women. In our discussion on language, we saw that men frequently do not answer women and cut off a woman's conversation. They also use silence to frustrate women and make them feel there is something wrong with them.[41]

Some studies show that men have increased their level of emotional expression in recent years.[42] However, the national Veroff study that measured changes between 1957 and 1980 showed that men had decreased their affiliative urges and increased their fear of losing power. Veroff suggests that these changes may reflect the changing role of women and the fact that men see this as threatening and therefore are not as willing to be open and expressive with women.[43]

Homophobia.   Another reason why it is difficult for men to get close to other men is the homosexual taboo. Too close a relationship with another man—perhaps one in which the other man cries or talks about fear and self-doubt—may make a friend fear that this man will abandon masculine role behavior. It is unnerving and frightening to many men when a man does reveal himself, and a frequent response is, "Get yourself together, man." If the man has cried on his friend's shoulder or has been given a hug at some point, the problem is compounded. Now there is a fear that latent homosexuality may come out. It has been proposed that this excessive fear of homosexuality may occur because of the excessively strong prohibition against boys doing feminine things such as hugging when they were small. As young boys must be weaned from identification with the mother and taught to identify with the male role, the prohibition against doing anything "feminine" is meant to ensure being "masculine." Any departure from aggressively heterosexual masculine role behavior is also seen as not being masculine, and feminine characteristics in a male are equated with being homosexual. Thus, a boy who looks effeminate in childhood may be called a "girl" or a "sissy," but he may also be called a "fag" or another derogatory homosexual term.[44]

The result of this homosexual taboo is that men often fear real closeness with one another. They fear homosexuality, and they fear losing status if they reveal themselves. The way to avoid getting close is to be cool. Men can have friends, but there is a limit to the emotions expressed and the topics discussed. There are also limits on when and where men can touch. Because one male touching another can imply homosexuality and is thus taboo, at least in this culture, touch between men seems to be governed by ritual. While men would never think of giving each other a pat on the fanny in any other situation, this certainly occurs when a football player makes a particularly good play or a hockey team skates onto the ice: As each successive player skates onto the ice, the player before gives him a pat on the rear with his stick. Athletic events represent the few situations in which men hold hands or hug each other in joy after a triumph. It is acceptable to do these things on the field; it would not be all right to do them in any other place. The hugs and even the hand holding are symbols of achievement in a competitive male domain; the athletic mystique and its connection to the masculine role protect men from charges of homosexuality. In a similar fashion, one of the few times tears are allowed for men occurs when their team has lost an important game. No one will fault a player or coach for a few quiet drops trickling down the cheeks or for burying his face in his hands, but the same tears would be unacceptable at a movie or even after the loss of a job.[45]

We will return later in this chapter to this idea of men experiencing discomfort in their friendships with other men. The prescription to be cool is one of the dominant rules of adolescence, and it means that adolescent boys keep a certain distance from their male friends as well as their female friends. Being cool is difficult in the context of the problems and stresses of this period, and in his struggle to be cool a boy may become oversocialized to be inexpressive.

When men do disclose themselves and talk about their troubles, they usually talk to a woman. Frequently they choose a woman who is a friend rather than a girlfriend. A woman is more likely to listen supportively and not "put them down" for showing emotions such as fear and self-doubt.[46] In contrast, it is very difficult for men to talk intimately with other men. They can be friendly, but it is hard for them to be friends. To admit to doubt, fear, or strong feelings may make them lose status with other men. Thus, many male conversations center on sports, business, war stories, or personal stories of achievement in the physical realm or with women.

Being Good at Something

After being tough and being cool, the next prescription for the adolescent boy is to be "good" at something. Preferably, the "something" will involve physical prowess in sports. It can also include being good at sex or, to some extent, being good in school. We have already looked at the need to achieve and to be good in sports, and we will look at sexual achievement later in this chapter.

Career Plans. When Douvan and Adelson asked boys what gave them high self-esteem, the boys talked about work and skill.[47] In particular, many mentioned contributing to a work group and achievement in school. Achievement and careers are still important to young men: A 1986 study found that school performance was still important for boys' self-esteem,[48] and the ideal male for most boys was achievement-oriented in both school and career.[49]

Boys are also consistently concerned about work roles and plan realistically for the work they will do, including choosing colleges and courses. Boys show particular interest in high-technology careers.[50]

However, there is a growing ambivalence in boys about academic success. Peers pull boys away from academic success to some extent, and adult cultural values do not always support academic achievement the way they are supposed to. One researcher believes that if adolescents and their parents were asked to choose between going to a football game and listening to a lecture by a famous scientist, the same percentage in both generations would choose each event.[51] While middle-class boys are expected to do well enough in school to get into college, they are not necessarily supposed to be "brains." It is shameful to flunk, but it is not appropriate to be a grind. Although it is acceptable to study for exams, turning down a chance to go out with the boys in order to study may be difficult. The prevailing tone in public high schools is somewhat anti-intellectual.[52] The praise goes to the athletes; those who are rewarded for academic achievement are not as popular.

More recently there has also been a recognition of the costs of success and fame, which often come only after one has spent many years in a professional school. As we will see, boys have increasingly shown a fear of success, citing stress, health problems, and lack of time for individual pursuits. Some researchers have suggested that while young people want to achieve, there is a certain unwillingness to work very hard which may reflect the values of the "me generation": It's time to have fun; life is too short to work so hard.[53]

Therefore, being good at something is a qualified ideal. In sports and in social and sexual interaction it is clear that an adolescent boy should do his absolute best. However, in academics the prescription is not so definite. The young man is supposed to prepare for a career, but there may be ambiguous messages in the high school years about what is really important.

Other Areas of Being Good at Something. For an adolescent male, being good extends into a variety of other areas. It may mean being a good driver, knowing about cars, and knowing about woodworking or cameras. It is very difficult for a boy of this age to admit to a lack of knowledge. It is part of being good and being cool to always be competent. Obviously, this is an impossible goal. However, the fact that the goal exists keeps up the pressure on a boy. He may feel the need to "act smart" even when he isn't. He may attempt to relieve the pressure by weeding out areas where competence is not considered absolutely necessary or may even be considered feminine, such as dancing. While some boys may gain prestige by being good dancers, many boys can keep from learning to dance without penalty.

Being good at something also means being good at sex. It is up to the boy to initiate social and sexual overtures and to be successful in interactions with women. This is one more pressure added to the many already mentioned. We will talk more about sexuality in Chapter 7.

By late adolescence, most boys are working at part-time jobs. They need to support cars and dates and perhaps to buy clothes or save for college. They may gain competence through these jobs and may gain social power by having money. Thus, work may be a way to gain skills. In this and other areas, the pressure to be good is very real, and the adolescent boy may figure out ways he can be good, tough, and cool in as many areas as possible.

THE FEMININE WORLD IN HIGH SCHOOL

Sources of Self-Esteem

There is some controversy among researchers about whether boys and girls have similar levels of self-esteem. Certainly the sources of their self-esteem differ. It seems more difficult for girls to gain self-esteem from concrete achievements that they can control. While more American girls are moving into sports and into jobs that were previously dominated by men, a primary source of self-esteem for girls seems to be popularity, relationships, and appearance.[54]

Being Pretty. Much like boys, girls gain a great deal of self-esteem from their physical appearance. Girls believe that physical appearance is crucial for popularity with boys, and to some extent they are probably correct. In a study done by Coombs and Kenkel in the 1960s, 500 men and women filled out a questionnaire about what they wanted in a date. Attractive physical appearance was a very important quality for the boys to find in their female companions.[55] Both women and men were happier with a "computer date" if that date was attractive.[56] We might think that personality becomes more important as we get to know someone better, but the influence of attractiveness on a person's desirability as a date does not diminish as that person becomes better known to us. More recent studies confirm that appearance is still the major factor in initial attraction, particularly for males.[57] Therefore, girls may perceive accurately that physical attractiveness is very important to popularity and dating success.

The original impulse behind this desire to be attractive was probably an attempt to attract a mate and thus to assure the perpetuation of the species. For women, perpetuation of the species was probably also a survival mechanism. As Nancy Baker points out in *The Beauty Trap*, women needed the protection of men to help them resist the elements and predators. As men have traditionally had control over economic resources, women also needed a mate to support them economically.[58] If women were not beautiful, they usually attempted to achieve physical beauty through physical artifice.

More recently, women have gained economic resources and can survive without male support and protection. However, the idea persists that beauty is the primary quality needed to attract a mate. Beauty also becomes a status symbol and even may be associated with being worthy.

Beauty has recently been linked with fitness and health. Nutrition, aerobic workouts, and general exercise have become important to a majority of the population, both men and women.[59] However, other developments show that slim is in and that being fit and healthy may not be the only reason for the exercise boom. Women are likely to take drastic measures to reduce their waists and thighs, such as using liposuction. They also still painfully remove body hair by waxing or by using a machine that pulls hair out by the roots. Women are more likely than ever before to color their hair and have permanents; there is also an unbelievable variety of makeup and beauty aids available. American women spend $2.5 billion on skin care products every year.[60]

Plastic surgery is also greatly on the increase in this society. Between 1970 and 1984, the number of cosmetic surgeries doubled, with a million an a half Americans, both men and women, trying to improve their looks. By 1984 this had become a $4 billion business.[61]

We seem to be getting increasingly preoccupied with our looks. Ninety-one percent of the college students in one survey were dissatisfied with their bodies.[62] The obsession with beauty or the lack of it becomes particularly acute for teenagers, who are already introspective and insecure about their changing bodies. Physical appearance is often the easiest place on which to pin these feelings of misery. "If only I had the right hair (or figure or clothes or face)," the teenager tells herself, "my life would be perfect." If she just *looked* perfect, she believes, she could *be* perfect.

There seems to be a link between race and gender-role orientation and concern about appearance. Black girls have been found to be more likely to be "satisfied with their looks" and to have higher self-esteem. One study found that while women in feminine and androgynous groups rate physical appearance as very important, feminine-typed women are more likely to feel bad about their bodies. Among all females, those with better self-esteem were found to have better body images.[63]

Anorexia and Bulemia.   There is a preoccupation with body weight and appearance among both men and women. As the saying goes, "One can never be too thin," and beauty is associated with being thin. The diet business takes in $14 million a year in this country.[64] Many teenagers go to great lengths to achieve a thin body that they think will make them more attractive. They starve themselves, or if they can't control their appetites, they binge and then vomit to get rid of the unwanted calories.

Anorexia nervosa is an eating disorder characterized by the loss of at least 25 percent of the original body weight, preoccupation with food, fear of fat, and hyperactivity; bulimia is characterized by binging on food and then vomiting or purging.[65] Both conditions can lead to severe nutritional deficiencies, abnormal thyroid functioning, kidney and blood dysfunctions, and even heart abnormalities. Over the long term, they can become life-threatening. In one study, a third of the patients remained chronically ill or died of anorexia.[66]

Recent studies have reported a dramatic increase in both anorexia and bulimia among high school and college students.[67] The American Psychiatric Association estimated in 1980 that approximately 1 in 250 females between the ages of 12 and 18 are anorexic and that between 1 and 3 percent are bulimic, indulging in at least weekly binging and purging.[68] One study found a threefold increase in bulimia from 1980 to 1983 in a college population in the Midwest.[69] These disorders are also beginning to occur in the lower social classes, in women over age 25, and among blacks, Hispanics, and East Indians.[70]

It is no accident that at least 90 percent of people who have eating disorders are women. One researcher stresses that this society values thinness in general and that thinness in women is associated with femininity.[71] Women who are in professions that require a certain body weight (models, dancers, actresses, and athletes) are also more likely to develop eating disorders.[72]

Good Looks as a Mixed Blessing.   Ironically, extreme measures to improve one's looks may constitute a mixed blessing. A beautiful woman may be a target of the jealousy of other women, and men may avoid her because they feel she couldn't possibly be interested in them. Because beautiful women have often wielded power, they may be the subject of antagonism from men and may even be victims of sexual assault.[73]

People may believe that a beautiful woman can't also be smart and may not take her seriously. A study that compared attractive and unattractive candidates for jobs found that good looks are an asset for male applicants but that good-looking women are less likely to be hired.[74] Other research shows that people will not support an attractive woman who has difficulties, believing that she already has more than her share of advantages.[75] Beautiful women may feel that they are not liked for themselves and can never trust the men with whom they have relationships.[76] These women may not develop their other talents, relying on their beauty, which of course will eventually fade.

However, most women do not have to worry about these problems; in fact, the majority of women may not feel a great deal of sympathy for the difficulties of their beautiful sisters. What about the woman who is not attractive? In a culture where beauty is highly valued, an unattractive woman may have very low self-esteem. Just as beauty sometimes is associated with being worthy, unattractiveness may become associated with being unworthy, with being "no good" as a person.

Worthiness.   Because being pretty and popular is so important to many female adolescents, good looks may become associated in a girl's mind with being worthy as a person. A girl who is not attractive or popular may develop low self-esteem.[77]

Ambiguous Definitions of Femininity. The definition of what is feminine has also become less clear, and this ambiguity can lead to stress. An adolescent girl's mother may be critical of her dress and of how she displays her body. At the same time, she sees Brooke Shields in a sexy jeans ad saying, "Nothing comes between me and my Calvin's." On a magazine cover she sees a pretty woman backpacking, but she hears her father say that he likes to see women in skirts and high heels. This lack of a specific definition of being feminine may lead to confusion and feelings of lack of control. A study that looked at the stress caused by the ambiguity in contemporary feminine sex-role norms reported that women who allow their identities to be defined or molded by their relationships with others are in a very vulnerable position that can affect their health and well-being.[78]

Being Popular and Being Nice

Girls base a great deal of their self-esteem on interpersonal relations rather than on achievement, work, or skill.[79] Girls consistently give high priority to being liked. They stress the value of interpersonal harmony and of desirable personality traits such as being likable, easy to get along with, friendly, sociable, pleasant, and popular.[80] A study of 24,000 students showed that females were more consistently cooperative in their attitudes during adolescence, while males were consistently competitive in theirs, with the greatest difference between the sexes occurring in grades 8 through 10. Females increase their orientation toward cooperation in grades 8, 9, and 10.[81] Girls and boys both agree that the most acceptable girls are good-looking, tidy, friendly, likable, enthusiastic, cheerful, quiet, and interested in dating.[82] For girls, being popular is inextricably linked with being nice. We will examine the idea of being nice in our discussion of the dating personality in Chapter 7.

Lack of Control over Outcomes

Girls may see being pretty and popular as the route to femininity. However, because they are operating in the realm of interpersonal relationships rather than concrete achievements, they have much less control over areas that are important to them. While beauty can be faked to some extent, it is difficult to change one's basic appearance. To be popular, a girl must have someone respond to her by calling her, talking to her, or asking her out. While a girl may do everything in her power to elicit the response she wants, she does not have the ultimate control over getting it.

Femininity and Future Roles

The goals girls hold for the future are more ambiguous and less consistent than those of boys. A study that explored how high school girls assess the advantages and disadvantages of employment and parenthood in the future found that they look at the drawbacks of certain roles rather than choosing a lifestyle because of all it has to offer. These girls consistently wanted children, and in thinking about the future they planned to combine work and parenting throughout their lives or to leave employment while the children were young. There was an element of feeling that they could do it all: have several children and pursue a demanding career.[83] In another study, 62 percent of the college-age women respondents expected to combine housework and work outside the home, 33 percent expected only to work outside the home, and 4 percent mentioned being solely homemakers. (Interestingly, both the male and female respondents in this study expected wives to do most of the household chores.)[84] In a third study, 86 percent of the girls and 80 percent of the boys expected to get married but only 74 percent of the girls and 54 percent of the boys mentioned having children. Sixty-two percent of the girls but only 19 percent of the boys mentioned combining household tasks with work outside the home.[85] Even college women who are pursuing nontraditional careers such as engineering and pharmacy still want "instrumental behaviors" in their mates and want to combine a career and marriage.[86] Black girls were more likely to plan to get a good education and to have high career ambitions.[87]

Although more college females have become interested in pursuing careers that are nontraditional for their sex, only a minority select jobs that are dominated by men.[88] They seem to be influenced by the potential negative costs of perceived sex discrimination.[89] In addition, women more than men value personal benefits (pride, self-fulfillment from the job they choose, and helping others), and this may explain the tendency for women to choose service occupations as careers. Time-scheduling factors are also more important to women than they are to men. Women are more interested in the availability of part-time work, the possibility of flexible schedules, and ease of reentry into a job. They believe more than men that job availability and job security are important. However, young college women also put a great deal of stress on financial reward,[90] and there was a steady increase between 1969 and 1984 in the number of college women seeking higher-paying male-dominated careers.[91] Studies differ as to whether women are as interested in occupational prestige as men are. Some have found that they are not as concerned with job prestige,[92] and others have found no difference.[93]

Thus, girls have become more career-oriented but have shown only a slight decrease in their desire to have a family. Many are still willing to modify career goals (take time out for parenting or consider part-time work), but many expect to have it all. It remains to be seen if they can.

FACTORS AFFECTING THE SELF-ESTEEM AND CAREER AMBITIONS OF WOMEN

During the high school years, several factors negatively influence the self-esteem and probably the career ambitions of women.

Negative Stereotypes

The stereotype of women includes unflattering ideas about their ability and competence. They are known as "terrible" drivers, are told that they are not logical, hear that they cannot balance a checkbook or do math, and are told that they swing (at baseballs) like "rusty gates." Most of these stereotyped ideas, of course, are untrue. For example, one only has to check with insurance companies about the rates for young male and female drivers to know which sex has the better driving record. These stereotypes, however, are very prevalent in our everyday culture: We hear them on television, read them in books, and see them in the movies. Women may come to believe that they are not good at many of these things.

Even when women do not actually believe they are unskilled, they may find themselves trying to fool the men in their lives about their abilities or holding back so that they will not seem unfeminine to the world in general. Playing this game means that they are not realizing their own potential, that their relationships may be dishonest, and that they are reinforcing the original notion that they cannot be admired for their concrete accomplishments, in other words, that they must be admired for what they *are*, not what they *do*.

Ironically, men *do* admire competent women, even women who are competent in masculine specialities. Some men admit to being threatened by intellectual women, but they usually find ways to compensate for the threat. They may pick an intellectual woman who is less attractive than the average women or has few social skills.[94] There is some evidence that men truly admire a woman who can stand on her own without leaning on them, balance a checkbook, or hold her own in a game of tennis. One study showed both men and women liking best a woman who was competent and had masculine interests. The one exception was very traditional men, who liked incompetent, feminine women the best.[95] Men seem to admire masculine skills in women, and women seem to admire feminine traits such as sensitivity and understanding in men.[96]

Girls may come to believe elements of the negative stereotype. Although girls get better grades than boys do until late high school, some research shows that girls' opinions of their own abilities grow worse with age and that their opinions of boys' abilities get better. Boys develop better opinions of themselves and worse opinions of girls' abilities.[97]

Girls also seem to be more sensitive to the values attached to achievement, and this may affect their motivation.[98] An early study done by Philip Goldberg and its replications indicate that women and men may not value the abilities of women as highly as they value those of men. Goldberg gave a college class of women a series of professional articles dealing with material in male- and female-dominated fields of study. Some of the articles listed the author as either John McKay or Joan McKay. Students were asked to rate the articles on value, writing style, and the like. The male authors came out ahead in every case, even in female-dominated fields such as dietetics. Replications of the study with classes of both men and women have had mixed results. Some of these studies have shown devaluation of women's work, and others have not.[99]

We should not be surprised at this devaluation of women's work. The fact that women have lower social status in our culture and are often devalued by themselves and others is not hard to document. Both sexes seem to value the characteristics, values, and activities of men more highly than those of women. They may also see success and achievement as male traits. Mental health professionals still characterize traits needed in the work environment as being similar to the characteristics that are associated with a "masculine" man. By contrast, "feminine" characteristics such as dependence and passivity are linked to adults who are associated with domestic and nurturing tasks.[100]

When girls do succeed, they attribute their success to luck or hard work rather than to innate ability. When they fail, however, they believe it is because of their innate characteristics. Thus, they seldom feel better when they do a good job but always blame themselves when they don't perform well.[101] Even when they succeed, they may feel that they are impostors and that their lack of ability will be discovered by others. The values attached to achievement and the motivation behind it seem particularly important for girls.

General Self-Esteem and Gender-Role Orientation

Many recent studies have found a relationship between masculine traits and higher self-esteem in both male and female adolescents. There is some question about an overlap between measures of masculinity and self-esteem, and measures of trait masculinity do not necessarily converge with masculine behavior.[102] Nevertheless, people who possess masculine traits, especially females, seem to feel both more socially competent and more physically competent than do people without such traits.[103]

School and Messages about Ability. Girls may get other messages suggesting that they are not competent. In a continuation of the pattern of the elementary school years, teachers pay more attention to boys. Many high school girls and college women claim that they are ignored or taken less seriously when they speak in class, particularly in male-dominated academic areas. Surveys show they are right: Teachers take them less seriously, and the girls get the message that they are not worth listening to.[104] By the end of the teen years, girls are more likely to be underachievers than boys are.[105] They are also less likely to see themselves as college material even when they get the same grades as boys.[106]

We saw in Chapter 5 that mathematics is an area in which girls are taken less seriously. High school girls may often feel incompetent in math compared with high school boys, and teachers think that girls lack mathematical aptitude. We have also seen that when girls are encouraged to take math courses and can work in a supportive climate, their mathematical skills are equal to those of boys. Yet in spite of equal skill, boys are much more likely to be advised to take advanced mathematics because they are expected to enter occupations such as engineering and physics.[107] Girls, in contrast, are seldom counseled to take math classes and are subjected to cultural stereotypes that tell them they cannot balance a checkbook much less do advanced mathematics. Girls do not have higher math anxiety than boys do and they see math as useful, but they are not as likely to select math-related fields as careers. They simply see math as a male domain. Even when they are good at it, they do not seem to relate their ability to a sense of self-competence in math-related fields, including the sciences.[108] Thus, even skilled girls take fewer advanced mathematics courses and are not prepared for careers in mathematics or the sciences.

This perception of a field as a male domain also holds true for computers. Both women and men view computers (and especially video games) as male activities. This view increases throughout the teen years. Even though college women were found to be more comfortable with computers than were high school girls, college men were even more at ease and felt they were more skilled in using computers.[109] Ironically, in the 1980s, 59 percent of computer operators, 31 percent of computer programmers, and 22 percent of systems analysts were women.[110]

Counseling and Tracking.   In all areas, most boys are counseled to take the proper sequence of courses "just in case." There is some evidence that counselors are gender-stereotyped and counsel girls to take a slower introductory algebra course that stretches over two years.[111] This may throw off the whole cycle of courses a girl has to take, so that she is not prepared for advanced work. Counseling women out of mathematics or preparation for engineering may not be a conscious decision, but it is an unconscious implementation of the stereotype that women do not need to be serious about or prepared for their careers. The stereotype persists even though over half of today's high school girls will work full-time for thirty years or more and 90 percent will work for other long periods of time.

Counseling in high school has been largely passive rather than active and has not reflected changing roles for women. Counselors often wait for girls to ask for help and do not understand the problems of poor self-concept and ambivalence about careers.[112] Yet counselors could publicize opportunities available for men and women in all fields. Encouraging a high school girl to go for an interview with a business or computer firm may be all that is needed to set her on the right career path.

The chilly classroom climate for women continues into college. Women get fewer fellowships and less financial aid than men do when applying for college, and very able female students are less likely to do college work than are similar male students. When they do go to college, women are more likely to be in sex-typed departments.[113] They continue to be ignored or belittled in the classroom.[114] The climate is particularly bad for black women, who may be seen as less competent both because they are female and because they are black.[115] After four years of college, women's ambitions have decreased, as they apparently internalize these expectations for their performance.[116]

On the college level, women have even fewer female role models. While men account for 57 percent of the teachers in high school, in college they constitute approximately 90 percent of the full professors, 80 percent of the associates, and 70 percent of the assistants.[117] This is true even though there is strong evidence that women teach as well and produce as much research.[118] This lack

of female instructors means that female students may not have role mo~~~
mentors to help them through the college years. The situation becomes ev~~
worse in graduate school.[119] In addition, 20 to 30 percent of female students
report being victims of sexual harassment in college.[120]

Fear of Success. The power motive seems to be the same in men and women
in terms of getting formal social power through office holding and careers.[121]
However, there has been a continuing debate about whether women's self-
devaluation and early socialization not to surpass men actually lead them to
fear success in masculine areas. This **fear of success** is *not* a fear of inability to
achieve in an area stereotyped as masculine but a fear of the negative consequences of success.

In 1965 Matina Horner had female students complete sentences about a
woman, Anne, who finds herself ranked at the top of her medical school
class and had male students complete stories about John, who is in a similar
situation. The content was coded to identify stories that anticipated positive
or negative results from the academic success Anne or John was having.
Horner found that women wrote many negative responses based on their perception of the feminine role in society and the negative consequences that
would ensue if Anne pursued her goal. A typical comment was that "Anne is
happy she is at the top of her class, but now she will have to make a decision
about whether or not she really wants to be a doctor or get married." One
revealing comment suggested that "Anne is not happy with her position at
the top of her class because she now fears she will be teased and excluded by
the other students." Approximately 65 percent of the women wrote sentences
that showed fear of success for Anne. In contrast, male students showed little
fear for John's success; only 10 percent expressed negative feelings about his
success.[122]

In this and similar studies that followed, the most sex-typed (feminine)
women showed the highest fear of success, particularly when competing with
males. Women with very high ability, who had a good chance of succeeding,
also showed a great fear of success. In some of the studies men also wrote stories portraying negative results for successful women, although neither men
nor women wrote stories that portrayed negative results for men. Thus, it was
not just women who saw women's success in negative terms.

Later studies that replicated Horner's research found a decrease in fear of
success among women but an increase in fear of success among men.
However, the men seemed to have a different content to their fears. They mentioned the health dangers and family problems that come with being successful. A typical quote said, "He graduates with honors and hates being a doctor.
He wonders what it was all for." In contrast, the women respected success but
saw continued problems for successful women.[123]

Fear of success does not seem to be as evident among black girls as it is
among white girls, although there are differences by social class and political
values. In several studies that combined lower- and middle-class black girls,
fear of success was very low, although it was present in black high school
boys. It has been suggested that fear of success is not prevalent among black

been socialized to think of themselves as being inde-
...g their own support. It has also been hypothesized that a
...nan creates a special situation: Such women are so few in
...y knows how to treat them, and they are not subjected to
...nation that a successful black man or white woman might

...n that black women have less fear of success because they are
mo.. ...at and independent and because they have had to succeed and
support ... ...nselves seems to vary with social class. Mednick and Weston
describe the black middle class as "out-middle-classing" the white middle
class in terms of values. They hypothesize that as middle-class life is usually
male-dominated and family life is more stable, black middle-class women may
be less aspiring and less dominant than black working-class women are.[125]
Although their study did not directly support this hypothesis, other studies of
upper-middle-class black women in sororities at the University of Michigan
did show fear of success. Perhaps fear of success affects black women when
they have less need to be successful.[126]

More recent studies that have duplicated Horner's research show much
less fear of success among all women but a continuing fear among men. The
fall in women's fear of success probably reflects changing cultural norms
about successful women. The degree of fear of success certainly varies with
the area of achievement, the geographic region, and the like. In addition, one
researcher hypothesizes that a factor that may make a difference in women's
fear of success is whether they accept achievement as being female-appropri-
ate. There is evidence that bright, academically oriented girls show achievement patterns and attitudes similar to those in males, while underachieving
girls or girls in mixed samples like Horner's do not.[127]

Women's career choices are also narrowed by their socialization. By high
school, women have learned a repertoire of behaviors and attitudes that make
it easier for them to function in some careers than in others. It is no accident
that women have traditionally gone into the nurturing fields: nursing, social
work, and teaching. Not only do they receive less flak if they choose appropriately feminine fields, they also have the behavioral characteristics that are necessary to do well in such areas. It is much more difficult for them to do well in
business or entrepreneurial jobs that require aggressive, competitive behavior.
Thus, the pressures of early socialization, discouragement by teachers and
counselors, ambivalence about their abilities, fear of success, and cultural values may discourage many women from choosing a nontraditional career or
preparing early for any career. While options are rapidly opening and these
generalizations do not apply to all women, they apply often enough that we
must be worried about some of the influences in high school.

Happily, studies show that the views of adolescents are significantly less
stereotyped today than they were in 1973. The beliefs of male adolescents
about which careers are sex-appropriate has been liberalized the most,
although this pattern is found mostly among middle-class and higher-income
students.[128] Women are also becoming more aware of the opportunities avail-

able in traditional male fields; the greater rewards of money and status are increasing their numbers in business and other occupations.

NEW DIRECTIONS

A New Emphasis on Sports for Women

Adolescents' perception of the role of women in sports is also changing. The advent of Title 1X and other legislation guaranteeing women equal opportunities in school has increased the funding, personnel, and equipment available for girls' sports, and girls have had unprecedented opportunities to participate and compete. However, a recent ruling held that schools that discriminate in one area can still get funds in other areas, and so many schools may see this as an opportunity to funnel money away from women's sports again.[129]

However, sports for girls have become more popular. Many girls who would not have participated and would have considered sports unfeminine are joining teams. Some women's sports have become extremely popular with spectators; women's basketball is well on its way to becoming a spectator draw to rival women's tennis. Women are beginning to have an opportunity to achieve recognition by participating in these physical, competitive activities. More important, they now have a chance to experience achievement personally as they learn physical skills and use their bodies.

How does participation in sports actually affect teenage females? Some stigmatizing of girls who participate in sports still occurs, although the stigma varies according to the sport. The most acceptable sports for women are aesthetically pleasing and do not involve direct body contact. Fifty-six percent of the women involved in basketball, 50 percent of those in track, 40 percent of those in swimming and diving, and 31 percent of those in gymnastics reported feeling stigmatized. Men who were questioned saw soccer, basketball, field hockey, fencing, track and field, and softball as the least desirable sports for women.[130]

Part of the stigma seems to come from a perception that women who engage in these sports are less "feminine" to begin with or become less feminine as a result of their participation. The research on whether this is true is contradictory. While the characteristics of the sports participants and their "femininity" are not necessarily important in and of themselves, it is important to know whether women who play sports suffer stigma and loss of self-esteem.

In one study, no differences in self-esteem were found between those who participated in what were considered acceptable sports for women and those who participated in unacceptable sports for women.[131] Indeed, the self-image and feelings of self-satisfaction of women athletes are exceptionally high. While stigma does exist, it does not seem to make participation in athletics psychologically stressful for women. Positive feedback and concrete achievements seem to outweigh negative sanctions.

Recent studies have shown that female athletes have a more masculine sex-role orientation.[132] Other studies have proposed a link between masculinity and measures of self-esteem. Part of the high self-esteem shown by female athletes may be an artifact of measurement. Nevertheless, measures of psychological well-being show that female athletes stack up very well against the population as a whole. Girls who participate in sports feel better about themselves and their bodies than do girls who do not participate. They report themselves as having more energy and better health and being in good spirits or satisfied with life considerably more of the time than nonathletes do. Female athletes in one study also seemed to be more independent, creative, and autonomous than nonathletes. In other studies they tended to have slightly higher grade averages and educational goals than did nonathletes. It has been hypothesized that their achievement may derive from the discipline and commitment learned in athletics.[133]

Therefore, participation in sports may be an important way for women to change their self-image, allowing them to get a sense of mastery by exerting control over their physical achievements. In addition, they learn the cooperation and competition that are so valuable later in life.

SUMMARY

We have seen that the teenage years are still a time of both pain and pleasure. An adolescent boy who must be tough, cool, and good at things is under constant pressure to prove himself. Being tough and cool also means repressing emotions, making it difficult to relate to other men or to women in an intimate and open way. Being good may entail a constant push to initiate social and sexual relations whether one wants such interactions or not. The equation of being tough, cool, and good with being masculine means that boys are pressured to succeed at being these things in spite of any adverse consequences, yet many boys cannot succeed in these ways and thus feel inferior.

While the feminine stereotype does not affect the experience of all girls in the same way or to the same degree, it can lead to anxiety for girls as they learn to value things, such as looks and popularity, over which they have little control. They may have to define their success as females by the extent of others' approval. Stereotypes of women as incompetent in many areas, less smart than men, poor at mathematics, unable to do well in male occupations, and uncoordinated in sports can be internalized by high school girls, who may limit their career and recreational choices. While girls seem be overcoming their fear of success and going into more occupations where men have predominated, the problems of early socialization and peer and teacher pressure may keep them from preparing early or seriously enough for a career. However, girls are participating more in sports, which seems to raise their self-esteem as they realize more concrete achievements. Black girls show higher self-esteem, more independence, and much less fear of success than do white girls.

High school is a time of testing oneself, trying new experiences, and developing socially. Unfortunately, the rigid sex stereotypes that are enforced by peer and cultural pressure limit the options of both boys and girls, so that they often become less than what they could be.

ESSAY QUESTIONS

1. Discuss the intensification of macho themes in the adolescent years. In what ways is a boy expected to act tough and cool?
2. Discuss the role of sports in high school as a way for a boy to show he is tough, cool, and good. What part do team initiations play in defining the male role in sports? What significance do gestures like tapping another player with a hockey stick as he skates onto the ice and holding hands in a football huddle have? How do sports help a boy play his role later in the corporate world?
3. Discuss the kinds of inexpressiveness a boy may be socialized to have. How is homophobia related to inexpressiveness?
4. What does Coleman mean when he says that high school boys are ambivalent about success in high school? How do adolescent peer pressures for being good conflict with adult expectations of being good?
5. Why does Gagnon say that "the primary power the young male has is his own body"? How does appearance fit in with other prescriptions for male behavior?
6. Discuss the relationship between appearance and self-esteem among girls in high school. Why may good looks be a mixed blessing?
7. Why is the need to be popular a problem in terms of a girl's sources of self-esteem?
8. What factors influence girls' feelings about academic success in high school? In particular, discuss stereotypes about ability, hidden messages, expectations for careers, and counseling and tracking practices.
9. What is fear of success, and how does it differ from fear of failure? Has the degree of fear of success changed in recent years among females? Among males? What groups show the greatest and the least fear of success, and why?
10. Discuss the relationship between participation in sports and self-esteem for high school girls.
11. Discuss the particular nature of black girls' feelings about prettiness, popularity, and career success and their relationship to self-esteem.

EXERCISES

1. Pretend that you are a 140-pound male who would like to try out for the football team in high school because girls look up to football players. Discuss your feelings about this choice.

2. In what way does a commitment to sports show in the physical atmosphere and social activities of schools? Do you believe that sports for males are treated differently from sports for females?

3. Suppose you want to be a biologist and have a big test in high school biology coming up. The guys have called and want you to go to a party when you need to study. How do you feel, and what decision will you make?

4. If you are a male, discuss your feelings about being a future breadwinner. Do you ever wish that you could work part-time, stay home and take care of children, or do other things that many women are able to do?

5. List five times when you or a male you were with chose to be inexpressive and hide personal feelings. How did you feel underneath? How do you think your friend felt?

6. List all the qualities you associate with your own sex. List the qualities you associate with the other sex. Put a plus before the qualities you think are positive and a minus before those you think are negative and discuss your choices. Are there some qualities of the other sex you would like to have? Are there some qualities of the other sex that you fear?

7. List five times when you (if you are a girl) or a girl you were with chose to hide anger and act "nice" in a group or dating situation. How did you feel underneath? How do you think your friend felt?

8. As a girl, discuss how you feel about your appearance. If you could be extremely pretty or extremely bright and successful, which would you choose?

9. As a girl, discuss how you feel about being "popular" or not being so. Would it bother you if you didn't have dates? Why?

10. As a girl, discuss your future career plans. What courses are you taking now, and what else are you doing to advance those plans? If you are not working toward your career plans or have not made such plans, do you expect to work? If so, full-time?

11. As a girl, discuss your feelings about succeeding in a field that is not a traditional one for women. Do you believe that fear of success affects you or your friends? If not, why not? If so, why?

12. For the boys and girls in the class to do separately: Discuss how you will (or how you do) combine career and marriage roles. After each sex has discussed this separately, compare the answers. Are males planning a different combination of these roles than females are? Discuss.

NOTES

1. C. M. Siddique and Carl D'Arcy, "Adolescence, Stress and Psychological Well-Being," *Journal of Youth and Adolescence* 13 (1984):459–473.
2. M. Rutter, *Changing Youth in a Changing Society* (Cambridge, Mass.: Harvard University Press, 1985); D. Mechanic, "Adolescent Health and Illness Behavior:

Review of the Literature and a New Hypothesis for the Study of Stress," *Journal of Human Stress* 9 (1983):4–13.

3. Janet Kay Bobo, Lewayne Gilchrist, John F. Elmer, William Snow, Steven Paul Schinke et al., "Hassles, Role Strain and Peer Relations in Young Adolescents," *Journal of Early Adolescence* 6 (1986):339–352.

4. J. P. Hill and M. E. Lynch, "The Intensification of Gender-Related Role Expectations during Early Adolescence," in J. Borrks-Gunn and A. C. Peterssen, eds., *Girls at Puberty: Biological, Psychological and Social Perspectives* (New York: Plenum, 1983), pp. 201–229.

5. J. Schnelmann, "The Ideal Man or Woman as Described by Young Adolescents in Iceland and the U.S.," *Sex Roles* 17 (1987):313–320.

6. R. A. Fabes, "Adolescents' Judgements of the Opposite Sex," *Adolescence* 18 (1983):535–540.

7. R. L. Helmreich, J. T. Spence, and R. H. Gibson, "Sex-Role Attitudes: 1972–1980," *Personality and Social Psychology Bulletin* 8 (1982):656–663; K. S. McPherson and S. K. Spetrino, "Androgyny and Sex-Typing: Differences in Beliefs Regarding Gender Polarity in Ratings of Ideal Men and Women," *Sex Roles* 9 (1983):441–451.

8. J. F. Curry and R. A. Hock, "Sex Differences in Sex Role Ideals in Early Adolescence," *Adolescence* 16 (1981):779–789.; K. Wells, "Gender Role Identity and Psychological Adjustment in Adolescents," *Journal of Youth and Adolescence* 9 (1980):59–73.

9. Deborah A. Stiles, Judith L. Gibbons, and Jo Schnellmann, "The Smiling Sunbather and the Chivalrous Football Player: Young Adolescent Images of the Ideal Woman and Man," *Journal of Early Adolescence* 7 (1987):411–427.

10. Richard A. Fabes and Mary R. Laner, "How the Sexes Perceive Each Other: Advantages and Disadvantages," *Sex Roles* 15 (1986):129–143.

11. McPherson and Spetrino, *op. cit.*

12. L. E. and V. L. Ryan, "A Reexamination of Masculine and Feminine Sex-Role Ideals and Conflicts among Ideals for Men, Women and Persons," *Sex Roles* 9 (1983):1223–1248.

13. Barry Glassner, "Men and Muscles" in Michael Kimmel and Michael Messner, *Men's Lives* (New York: Macmillan, 1989), pp. 310–320, reprinted from *Bodies: Why We Look the Way We Do and How We Feel about It* (New York: Putnam, 1988) pp. 310–320; Rupert Wilkinson, *American Tough: The Tough Guy Tradition and American Character* (New York: Harper & Row, 1986).

14. Robert Staples, "Masculinity and Race: The Dual Dilemma of Black Men," *Journal of Social Issues* 34 (1978):173.

15. Marcia McCaulay, Laurie Mintz, and Audrey Glenn, "Body Image, Self-Esteem and Depression-Proneness: Closing the Gender Gap," *Sex Roles* 18 (1988):381–392.

16. Susan Sprecher, "The Importance to Males and Females of Physical Attractiveness, Earning Potential, and Expressiveness in Initial Attraction," *Sex Roles* 21, no. 9/10 (1989):591–599.

17. N. Cavior and P. R. Dokecki, "Physical Attractiveness, Perceived Attitude, Similarity, and Academic Achievement as Contributors to Interpersonal Attraction among Adolescents," *Developmental Psychology* 9 (1973):44–54.

18. John Gagnon, "Physical Strength, Once of Significance," in Deborah S. David and Robert Brannon, eds., *The Forty-Nine Percent Majority: The Male Sex Role* (Reading, Mass.: Addison-Wesley, 1976), p. 173.

19. J. S. Coleman, *The Adolescent Society* (New York: Free Press, 1961).

20. Lloyd B. Lueptow, *Adolescent Sex Roles and Social Change* (New York: Columbia University Press, 1984), p. 254.

21. Daniel Offer, *The Psychological World of the Teenager* (New York: Basic Books, 1983).
22. *Ibid.*
23. Eldon Snyder and Elmer Spreitzer, *Social Aspects of Sport* (Englewood Cliffs, N.J.: Prentice-Hall, 1978), pp. 106–107.
24. A. Sluckin, *Growing Up in the Playground* (London: Routledge and Kegan Paul, 1981).
25. Harrison G. Pope, Jr., David Katz, and Richard Shampoo, "Anabolic-Androgenic Steroid Use among 1,010 College Men," *Physician and Sports Medicine* 16, no. 7 (1988):75, 80, 84; Marty Duda, "Female Athletes: Targets for Drug Abuse," *Physician and Sports Medicine* 14, no. 6 (1986):142–146.
26. *Ann Arbor News* (February 28, 1981):C-1.
27. Snyder and Spreitzer, *op. cit.;* Michael Smith, "Sport and Collective Violence," in D. Ballome and J. Loy, *Sport and the Social Order* (Reading, Mass: Addison-Wesley, 1975), p. 130.
28. Betty Harragan, *Games Mother Never Taught You* (New York: Warner Books, 1977).
29. Snyder and Spreitzer, *op. cit.,* p. 26.
30. *Ibid.,* quoting Arthur Ashe.
31. Rodney J. Reed, "Education and Achievement of Young Black Males," in Jewelle Taylor Gibbs, ed., *Young, Black and Male in America: An Endangered Species* (Dover, Md.: Auburn, 1988), pp. 37–96.
32. Michael J. Blier and Linda A. Blier-Wilson, "Gender Differences in Self-Rated Emotional Expressiveness," *Sex Roles* 21, no. 334 (1989):287–296.
33. Richard Majors, "Cool Pose: The Proud Signature of Black Survival," in Kimmel and Messner, *op. cit.,* pp. 83–87.
34. B. R. Hare, "Structural Inequality and the Endangered Status of Black Youth," *Journal of Negro Education* 56 (1988):100–110.
35. Reed, *op. cit.*
36. Majors, *op. cit.*
37. Jack W. Sattel, "The Inexpressive Male: Tragedy or Sexual Politics," in Kimmel and Messner, *op. cit.,* pp. 374–382.
38. Blier and Blier-Wilson, *op. cit.*
39. Joseph Veroff, Richard Kulka, and Elizabeth Douvan, "Comparison of American Motives: 1957 vs. 1976," *Journal of Personality and Social Psychology* 39 (1980):1249–1262.
40. Lawrence H. Ganong and Marilyn Coleman, "Sex, Sex Roles and Emotional Expressiveness," *Journal of Genetic Psychology* 146 no. 3 (1985):405–411.
41. Sattell, *op. cit.*
42. Blier and Blier-Wilson, *op. cit.*
43. Veroff et al., *op. cit.*
44. Gregory K. Lehne, "Homophobia among Men," in Kimmel and Messner, *op. cit.,* pp. 416–429.
45. Alan E. Gross, "The Male Role and Heterosexual Behavior," in Kimmel and Messner, *op. cit.,* pp. 452–460.
46. Blier and Blier-Wilson, *op. cit.*
47. Douvan and Adelson, quoted in Joseph Pleck and Jack Sawyer, eds., *Men and Masculinity* (Englewood Cliffs, N.J.: Prentice-Hall, 1974), pp. 169–170.
48. Lynn S. Walker and John W. Greene, "The Social Context of Adolescent Self-Esteem," *Journal of Youth and Adolescence* 15, no. 4 (1986):315–332.
49. Nira Danziger, "Sex-Related Differences in the Aspirations of High School Students," *Sex Roles* 9 (1983):683–695.

50. Thomas G. Erb, "Career Preferences of Early Adolescents: Age and Sex Differences," *Journal of Early Adolescence* (Winter 1983):349–359.
51. Offer, *op. cit.*
52. Robert A. Hock and John F. Curry, "Sex-Role Identification of Normal Adolescent Males and Females as Related to School Achievement," *Journal of Youth and Adolescence* 12, no. 6 (1983):461–470.
53. Kenneth Woodward, "Young Beyond Their Years," *Newsweek* (Winter/Spring 1990):54.
54. Hock and Curry, *op. cit.*; Elena M. Skaalvik, "Sex Differences in Global Self-Esteem: A Research Review," *Scandinavian Journal of Education Research* 30, no. 4 (1986):157–179.
55. R. H. Coombs and W. F. Kenkel, "Sex Differences in Dating Aspirations and Satisfaction with Computer-Selected Partners," *Journal of Marriage and the Family* 28 (1966):62–66.
56. Susan Sprecher, "The Importance to Males and Females of Physical Attractiveness, Earning Potential and Expressiveness in Initial Attraction," *Sex Roles* 31 (1989):591–603.
57. *Ibid.*
58. Nancy Baker, *The Beauty Trap* (New York: Franklin Watts, 1984), pp. 1–26.
59. Ann Jones, "Fit is Beautiful," *Ann Arbor News* (October 31, 1989).
60. Baker, *op. cit.*
61. *Ibid.* pp. 220–225.
62. Toby Mark Miller, Judith Gilbride Goffman, and Ruth A. Linke, "Survey on Body Image, Weight and Diet of College Students," *Journal of the American Dietetic Association* (November 1980), pp. 39–44.
63. L. A. Jackson, "Gender, Gender Role and Body Image," *Sex Roles* 19 (1988):605–618.
64. Marci McCaulap, "Body Image, Self-Esteem, and Depression Proneness: Closing the Gender Gap," *Sex Roles* 18, no. 7 (1988):381–391; Jill Rierdan, Elissa Koff, and Margaret L. Stubbs, "Depressive Symptomatology and Body Image in Adolescent Girls," *Journal of Early Adolescence* 7, no. 2 (1987):205–216.
65. Catherine M. Shisslak and Marjorie Crago, "Primary Prevention of Eating Disorders," *Journal of Consulting and Clinical Psychology* 5, no. 5 (1987):660–667.
66. E. L. Bliss and C. H. Branch, *Anorexia Nervosa: Its History, Psychology and Biology* (New York: Paul B. Hoeber, 1960).
67. D. M. Kagan and R. L. Squires, "Eating Disorders among Adolescents: Patterns and Prevalence," *Adolescence* 19 (1984):15–19.
68. M. D. VanThorre and F. X. Vogel, "The Presence of Bulimia in High School Females," *Adolescence* 20 (1985):45–51.
69. R. L. Pyle, J. E. Mitchell, E. D. Eckert, P. A. Halvorson, P. A. Neuman, and G. M. Goff, "The Incidence of Bulimia in Freshman College Students," *International Journal of Eating Disorders* 2 (1983):75–85.
70. P. E. Garfinkel and D. M. Garner, *Anorexia Nervosa: A Multidimensional Perspective* (New York: Brunner/Mazel, 1982); T. J. Silber, "Anorexia Nervosa in Blacks and Hispanics." *International Journal of Eating Disorders* 5 (1986):121–126.
71. R. H. Striegel-Moore, L. R. Silberstein, and J. Rodin, "Toward an Understanding of Risk Factors for Bulimia," *American Psychologist* 41 (1986):246–263.
72. D. M. Garner and P. E. Garfinkel, "Socio-Cultural Factors in the Development of Anorexia Nervosa," *Psychological Medicine* 10 (1980):647–656; L. H. Hamilton, J. Brooks-Gunn, and M. P. Warren, "Sociocultural Influences on Eating Disorders in

Professional Female Ballet Dancers," *International Journal of Eating Disorders* 4 (1985):465–477.

73. Baker, *op. cit.*, pp. 39–62.
74. Madeline E. Heilman and Lois R. Saruwatari, "When Beauty Is Beastly: The Effects of Appearance and Sex on Evaluations of Job Applicants for Managerial and Nonmanagerial Jobs," *Organizational Behavior and Human Performance*, quoted in Baker, *op. cit.*, p. 50.
75. Adele Schele, quoted in Baker, *op. cit.*, p. 53.
76. Baker, *op. cit.*, p. 105.
77. Walker and Greene, *op. cit.*; Jill Rierdan, Elissa Koff, and Margaret L. Stubbs, "Depressive Symptomatology and Body Image in Adolescent Girls," *Journal of Early Adolescence* 7, no. 2 (1987):205–216; McCaulay, Mintz, and Glenn, *op. cit.*
78. Diana M. Zuckerman, "Stress, Self-Esteem and Mental Health: How Does Gender Make a Difference?" *Sex Roles* 20, no. 7 (1989):429–443.
79. Walker and Greene, *op. cit.*
80. Stephanie A. Tesch, "Sex-Role Orientation and Intimacy Status in Men and Women," *Sex Roles* 11, no. 5/6 (1984):451–465.
81. Andrew Ahlgren and David Johnson, "Sex Differences in Cooperative and Competitive Attitudes from Second through Twelfth Grade," *Developmental Psychology* 15 (1979):45–49; David G. Winter, "The Power Motive in Women and Men" *Journal of Personality and Social Psychology* 54, no. 3 (1988):510–519.
82. Sprecher, *op. cit.*
83. Leigh A. Leslie, "The Impact of Adolescent Females' Assessments of Parenthood and Employment on Plans for the Future," *Journal of Youth and Adolescence* 15, no. 1 (1986):29–49; Gisela Konopka, "Young Girls: A Portrait of Adolescence: I. Life Goals," *Child and Youth Services* 6 no. 3/4 (1983):14–29.
84. Carolyn Stout Morgan, Maggie P. Hayes, and Marilyn Affleck, "Differences in Life Expectations of College Students" (paper presented at the meetings of the North Central Sociological Association, Pittsburgh, 1988); A. Machung, "Talking Career, Thinking Job: Gender Differences in Career and Family Expectations of Berkeley Seniors" (Berkeley Center for the Study, Education and Advancement of Women, 1986).
85. Cherlyn Granrose, "Plans for Work Careers among College Women Who Expect to Have Families," *Vocational Guidance Quarterly* 33, no. 4 (1985):284–295.
86. C. Aneshensel and B. Rosen, "Domestic Roles and Sex Differences in Occupational Expectations," *Journal of Marriage and the Family* 42 (1980):121–132; Lenahan O'Connell, Michael Betz, and Suzanne Kurth, "Plans for Balancing Work and Family Life: Do Women Pursuing Nontraditional and Traditional Occupations Differ?" *Sex Roles* 20, no. 1/2 (1989):35–45; Linda L. Lindsey, "Career Paths in Pharmacy: An Exploration of Male and Female Differences" (paper presented at the Midwest Sociological Society Meetings, Chicago, 1985).
87. John U. Ogbo, "Black Education: A Cultural-Ecological Perspective," in Harriette McAdoo, ed., *Black Families* (Beverly Hills, Calif.: Sage, 1982), pp. 146–149.
88. R. Fiorentine, "Increasing Similarity in the Values and Life Plans of Male and Female College Students? Evidence and Implications," *Sex Roles* 18 (1988): 143–158: Norma Ware, Nicole Steckler, and Jane Leserman, "Undergraduate Women: Who Chooses a Science Major," *Journal of Higher Education* 56, no. 1 (1985): 73–84.
89. J. S. Bridges and M. S. Bower, "The Effects of Perceived Job Availability for

Women on College Women's Attitudes toward Prestigious Male-Dominated Occupations," *Psychology of Women Quarterly* 9 (1985):265–277.

90. Judith S. Bridges, "Sex Differences in Occupational Values," *Sex Roles* 20, no. 3/4 (1989):205–211.

91. Fiorentine, *op. cit.*; T. A. Lyson, "Sex Differences in the Choice of a Male or Female Career Line," *Work and Occupations* 11 (1984):101–116; N. E. Betz and L. F. Fitzgerald, *The Career Psychology of Women* (Orlando: Academic Press, 1987).

92. J. Block, E. R. Denker, and C. K. Tittle, "Perceived Influences on Career Choices of Eleventh Graders: Sex, SES and Ethnic Group Comparisons," *Sex Roles* 7 (1981):895–904; Machung, *op. cit.*

93. Bridges, *op. cit.*

94. Mirra Komarovsky, "Cultural Contradictions and Sex Roles," in Arlene S. Skolnick and Jerome H. Skolnick, *Family in Transition*, 4th ed. (Boston: Little, Brown, 1983), pp. 190–200.

95. Sprecher, *op. cit.*

96. Thomas A. Widiger and Shirley A. Settle, "Broverman et. al., Revisited: An Artifactual Sex Bias," *Journal of Personality and Social Psychology* 53, no. 3 (1987):463–469; Debra A. Poole and Anne E. Tapley, "Sex Roles, Social Roles and Clinical Judgements of Mental Health," *Sex Roles* 19 (1988):265–272.

97. E. Crandall, "Sex Differences in Expectancy of Intellectual and Academic Performance," in C. P. Smith, ed., *Achievement-Related Motives in Children* (New York: Russell Sage, 1969).

98. Donna Martin, "Relationship of Motivational Differences of Male and Female Community College Students to Academic Achievements" (Masters Thesis, University of Missouri, Kansas City, 1985).

99. P. Goldberg, "Are Women Prejudiced against Women?" in J. Stacey et al., *And Jill Came Tumbling After* (New York: Dell, 1974).

100. Widiger and Settle, *op. cit.*

101. Crandall, *op. cit.*

102. Bernard E. Whitley, Jr., "Masculinity, Femininity, and Self-Esteem: A Multitrait, Multimethod Analysis," *Sex Roles* 8 (1988):419–431.

103. Rodney Cate and Alan Sugawara, "Sex-Role Orientation and Dimensions of Self-Esteem among Middle Adolescents," *Sex Roles* 15 (1986):145–158.

104. Roberta M. Hall and Bernice R. Sandler, "A Chilly Climate in the Classroom," Project on the Status and Education of Women, 1982.

105. S. Greenberg, "Educational Equity in Early Educational Environments," in Susan Klein, ed., *Handbook for Achieving Sex Equity through Education* (Baltimore: Johns Hopkins University Press, 1985), pp. 457–469; L. Sundal-Hansen, "New Age Roles: Are We Preparing Girls and Boys for Personal and Social Change?" *International Journal for the Advancement of Counseling* 8, no. 1 (1985):5–15.

106. C. Cordos, "Tent Tilt: Boys Outscore Girls on Both Parts of the SAT," *American Psychological Association Monitor* (June 1986):30–31; R. Ekstrom, "Girls Are Usually Higher Achievers than Boys. . . ." (Paper presented at the annual Research on Women in Education Conference, Boston, 1985).

107. Kathryn R. Wentzel, "Gender Differences in Math and English Achievement: A Longitudinal Study," *Sex Roles* 18, no. 11/12 (1988):691–698; Elizabeth Fennema, "Girls, Women and Mathematics: An Overview" (Project on the Status and Education of Women Association of American Colleges, Washington, D.C.); Center for Early Adolescence, "Girls, Math and Science: Research & Resources" (paper pre-

sented at the University of North Carolina at Chapel Hill, 1984; Darrell Sabers, Katherine Cushing, and Donna Sabers, "Sex Differences in Reading and Mathematics Achievement for Middle School Students," *Journal of Early Adolescence* 7, no. 1 (1987):117–128.

108. Joan M. Singer and Jayne E. Stake, "Mathematics and Self-Esteem: Implications for Women's Career Choices," *Psychology of Women Quarterly* 10 (1986):369–402.

109. Gita Wilder, Diane Mackie, and Joel Cooper, "Gender and Computers: Two Surveys of Computer-Related Attitudes," *Sex Roles* 13 (1985):215–230; Irene T. Miura, "Gender and Socioeconomic Status Differences in Middle-School Computer Interest and Use," *Journal of Early Adolescence* 7, no. 2 (1987):241–254; Elizabeth C. Arch and David E. Cummins, "Structured and Unstructured Exposure to Computers: Sex Differences in Attitude and Use among College Students," *Sex Roles* 20, no. 5/6 (1989):245–252.

110. Marlaine F. Lockhead, "Women, Girls and Computers: A First Look at the Evidence," *Sex Roles* 20, no. 5/6 (1989):112–115.

111. M. M. Marini and M. Brinton, "Sex Typing in Occupational Socialization," in B. F. Reskin, ed., *Sex Segregation in the Workplace: Trends, Explanations, and Remedies* (Washington, D.C.: National Academic Press, 1984), pp. 192–232.

112. Iris M. Tiedt, "Realistic Counseling for High School Girls." in Stacey et al., *op. cit.*, p. 236.

113. Joni Seager and Ann Olson, *Women in the World Atlas* (New York: Simon & Schuster, 1986).

114. Hall and Sandler, *op. cit.*

115. Nijole V. Benokritis and Joe R. Feagin, *Modern Sexism: Blatant, Subtle and Covert Discrimination* (Englewood Cliffs, N.J.: Prentice-Hall, 1986).

116. D. M. Bush, "The Impact of Family and School on Adolescent Girls' Aspirations and Expectations: The Public-Private Split and the Reproduction of Gender Inequality" (paper presented at the annual meeting of the American Sociological Society, Chicago, 1987); F. Vollmer, "Why Do Men Have Higher Expectancy than Women?" *Sex Roles* 14 (1986):351–362.

117. Myra Sadker and David Sadker, "Striving for Equity in Classroom Teaching," in Alice Sargent, ed., *Beyond Sex Roles,* (2d ed. (New York: West, 1984), pp. 442–455.

118. Laurel Richardson, Judith A. Cook, and Anne Statham, "Down the Up Staircase: Male and Female University Professors, Classroom Management Strategies," in Laurel Richardson and Verta Taylor, eds., *Feminist Frontiers: Rethinking Sex, Gender and Society*, 1st ed. (Reading, Mass.: Addison-Wesley, 1983), pp. 280–286.

119. Sadker and Sadker, *op. cit.*

120. B. W. Dzeich and L. Weiner, *The Lecherous Professor: Sexual Harassment on Campus* (Boston: Beacon, 1984).

121. David G. Winter, "The Power Motive in Women and Men," *Journal of Personality and Social Psychology* 54, no. 3 (1988):510–519.

122. Matina S. Horner, "Sex Differences in Achievement Motivation and Performance in Competitive and Noncompetitive Situations" (Ph.D. dissertation, University of Michigan, 1968), p. 58.

123. Lois Hoffman, "Fear of Success in Males and Females: 1965 and 1972," *Journal of Consulting and Clinical Psychology* 42 (1974):353–358.

124. P. Weston and M. T. Mednick, "Race, Social Class, and the Motive to Avoid Success in Women," *Journal of Cross-Cultural Psychology* 1 (1973):284–291.

125. *Ibid.*

126. M. Mednick, P. Carr, and V. Thomas, "Evaluations of Sex-Typed Tasks by Black

Men and Women: A Second Look" (paper presented at the meeting of the Eastern Psychological Association, Philadelphia, 1983).

127. Marini and Brinton, *op. cit.*
128. *Ibid.*
129. Roger LeFievre, "Judge Deals Blow to Women's Sports," *Ann Arbor News* (February 25, 1981):1.
130. Snyder and Spreitzer, *op. cit.*, p. 108.
131. Gloria Desertrain and Maureen Weiss, "Being Female and Athletic: A Cause for Conflict?" *Sex Roles* 18(1988):567–582.
132. Janice Butcher, "Adolescent Girls' Sex-Role Development: Relationship with Sports, Self-Esteem and Age at Menarche," *Sex Roles* 20 (1989):575–593.
133. E. Snyder and Elmer Spreitzer, "Correlates of Sports Participation among Adolescent Girls," *Research Quarterly* 47(1978):804–808.

Spencer Grant/Stock, Boston

Chapter 7

The Teenage Years: Friendship, Dating, and Sexuality

Much of the interaction between boys and girls before and during the early teen years is platonic. They engage in activities together and see each other as friends rather than persons of the other sex. At some point, however, there is a recognition that there is indeed another sex, which cannot be easily included in plans. Dear Abby once ran a letter from a concerned father whose sixth-grade son was having a birthday party and had invited the members of his baseball team to spend the night. One of the team members was a girl. Although the boy wished to invite her, the father was dubious about having her spend the night with the boys. Dear Abby agreed that it would not be appropriate for the girl to be invited. One can imagine the feelings of the girl who was left out, but the boys, too, were made aware that a difference existed and that their former pal could not always be included.[1]

A story in a popular magazine told of a girl who had routinely played baseball with a group of neighborhood boys. Every Saturday morning some of the "gang" would come by her house and whistle to get her up, after which they would all head for the nearby sandlot field. She awakened one Saturday when the sun was high and realized that it must be midmorning. She wondered why no one had come by, figured that there had been a mistake, threw on her clothes, and ran down to the field. The game was in progress, and another boy was playing her position. When she asked them what was going on, her former pals responded that they didn't want any girls on their team because "girls swing like rusty gates." Until that morning she had been considered one of their most valuable players.

In the preteens and early teenage years girls are often excluded from previously coed activities, which are no longer considered suitable for females. Boys also face stricter prohibitions about not doing anything "sissy," that is, feminine. Thus, the members of the two sexes give up their few shared activities and move further apart into same-sexed groups.

However, absence may spark interest. With the beginning of puberty comes a stirring and awakening of interest in members of the other sex just because they *are* the other sex, not because they are Mary or John or a former pal. Sixth-grade or junior high school girls will gather on a corner, giggling and talking about boys as they pass by. The boys, who are often considerably shorter and smaller at this age, strut by self-consciously, ignoring "those silly girls," poking one another, and trying to be cool. Some of the boys may still be unconscious of the girls' attention and uninterested in them. I remember my sixth-grade daughter coming home from school and announcing that a certain boy was her boyfriend. Thinking it would be nice to meet her first boyfriend, I suggested that she bring him by some day after school. Her reply was, "Oh, Mom, *he* doesn't know he's my boyfriend!"

The first tentative steps made in interacting with the other sex can be anxious ones. In the stylized heterosexual interaction of early puberty, boys and girls test themselves and their social skills and seek confirmation of whether they are being appropriately masculine or feminine. The reactions an individual gets from the other sex may have a great effect on that individual's ego and self-image. One colleague tells of a sixth-grade daughter who was upset when he picked her up from an after-school mixer. When he asked her if she had danced, she burst into tears. The boys she had asked to dance had refused her but had danced with other girls.

These early interactions are wrapped up with feelings about the adolescent's changing body, budding sexual desire, and cultural norms for appropriate appearance and behavior. It is not surprising that in the years from 11 to 13 or so both boys and girls prefer coed groups where they can get reinforcement from their same-sexed peers while taking tentative steps toward the other sex. Interaction between the sexes varies by individual, social class, ethnic background, and even geographic area, but research shows that some commonalities occur in the experiences of all adolescents.

FRIENDSHIP

Boys' Friendships

Friendship patterns are somewhat different for each sex. Boys in early adolescence are less sophisticated about friendship and less eager for intimacy than are girls of the same age. The gang is more important to the boy than is close friendship. Boys state that they want a friend who controls his impulses, makes few demands for closeness, and has special traits such as athletic ability or good looks. In contrast to girls, boys at this age do not seek loyalty and empathy in their friends and are not threatened by the loss of a friend. A friend is seen primarily as a person to do things with, and the friend must "go along with the crowd."[2]

For both boys and girls, friendships progress in terms of stability between the ages of 5 and 18. Boys, however, show less conflict in their friendship relations at every age but 15.[3] The ages of 14 and 15 seem to be critical for friendship for both boys and girls, probably because they spend so much time with their friends.

As age goes up, conformity to the peer group seems to go down and the relationship with friends changes as well. In the early ages of adolescence, friends are mostly same-sex people to do things with. By middle adolescence, same-sex groups are common but more interaction occurs with the other sex. By late adolescence, a boy is doing more with girlfriends than he is with same-sex friends.[4]

Girls' Friendships

In early adolescence, girls seem to choose friends for companionship, seeking people to do something with. The focus is more on the activity than on the friend. Girls mention that they want a friend who is amiable, easy to get along with, cooperative, and fair. Leisure time is spent more often with the family than with friends, and boys do not have much importance.[5]

When girls are 14 through 16 their friendships are different in content, researchers report. Girls spend more time with friends at this point, and they want friends in whom they can confide and who will offer emotional support. They particularly want friends who will be loyal and trustworthy, who will not abandon them in a crisis or gossip about them behind their backs.[6] Girls at this age want a friend who will be like them in terms of trials and tribulations suffered and with whom they can identify. A girl looks for responses from friends to help her form her own identity and self-evaluation. Loyalty is important because this is a time when a girl reveals her fears and doubts, particularly in the area of sexuality. A friend must be someone she can trust not to use information against her or abandon her in favor of boys.[7]

The later adolescent girl of 17 and 18 seems to establish calmer friendships. She is more secure about herself and less insistent that the loyalty of a friend be a prime consideration. Girls of this age are also more secure with boys and can turn to them as intimates and friends. In all their friendships, girls seem to have more intimacy than boys do.[8] However, they also have more conflict, possibly because of dating and jealousy. They show about the same degree of conformity to the peer group that boys do, with the greatest degree of conformity occurring at ages 11 to 13 for both sexes. Increasing autonomy and ability to withdraw from the group occur at later ages.[9]

DATING

Marita McCabe has shown that dating has a number of functions. It is fun and provides companionship, it is a way of determining status, it is a means of socialization leading to personal growth, and it can be used as a means of sexual experimentation and a way to achieve intimacy. Finally, it is a way of mate sorting, whether or not this is a conscious motive. Current styles of dating have changed and include more group activities in the early stages of a relationship. Also, girls and boys approach dating from somewhat different perspectives. According to McCabe, boys approach dating with a sexual and affectional orientation but desire a lower level of affection than that desired by girls. Girls approach dating from a stronger affectional perspective but adopt a strong sexual orientation as the relationship deepens.[10] Because of these different orientations and the different gender roles implied in dating, we will look separately at dating for males and females.

Dating from a Boy's Perspective

Boys start dating later than girls do. A typical attitude toward girls was expressed by one of Offer's subjects, who was on the football team and who by the end of his sophomore year had never dated. He stated that he did not feel that anything was wrong and that he would have a lot of time for "that sort of thing" in college. Yet when the interviewers pointed out to him that his level of anxiety went up even while he was expressing indifference, he admitted that he simply did not understand girls and wanted to be left alone by them.[11] In contrast, by the end of the senior year 95 percent of the boys in Offer's research project were dating, and they liked their dates and enjoyed their relationships with girls. Those who were not dating stated that they wanted to do so but lacked the courage to try.[12]

Therefore, for the first two years of high school dating was not a major issue for boys in this research group. Later it became more important. If a boy was not dating, he could not exchange experiences; he was not part of the social group. Asking a girl out was very painful for these boys.[13] Indeed, dating emphasizes the active, "need to perform" role of boys. First of all, a boy had to perform by making the social overture of asking for a date. While girls would call the boys and ask for rides to parties, it was almost always the boys who did the asking on actual dates. They were anxious about what to say, wondered if the girl would say yes only out of politeness or would reject them, and wondered what the girl would say to others about them. (Given the difficulty of this role, it is little wonder that many boys develop bravado and thick skins about rejection.) However, the boys' curiosity about girls and desire to be part of a social group enabled them to overcome their fear of girls. They reported great satisfaction from their dates and enjoyed the social sharing of experiences with their peers afterward.

Offer believes that the "minute dissection" that goes on among boys telling each other what they did right or wrong is extremely helpful and suggestive. They try to do better the next time not only because they enjoy kissing or petting but also so they can tell their male friends about it. As their anxiety diminishes in relationships with girls, they begin to enjoy the encounters more and eventually can look forward to a date simply because they like the girl and want to share their experiences with her and her alone.[14]

Boys also have to take an active role in the sense of providing transportation and planning entertainment. It is usually considered preferable to have one's own car, and this has far-reaching consequences. It means that by the time a boy is dating on a regular basis, he may have to work long hours to support a car. At the very least, he must pay for gas, and if it is his own car, he may have to make car payments and pay for repairs and insurance. As the boy is also usually expected to pay for many of the expenses of a date, dating can become a heavy financial burden. While the situation often varies by locality and social class, middle-class boys may even attempt to outdo each other in entertaining their dates. At a tenth-grade dance, the boys not only got corsages for their dates but took them to dinner at a nice restaurant and out for pizza later. As some of the boys could not drive, they also rented a limousine. The senior prom at the same school involved the necessity of a rented tuxedo and more elaborate after-dance entertainment and was estimated by the boys to cost at least $150 a couple. Many boys opted to stay home rather than spend that kind of money.

A boy has the power to decide what to do and to set certain standards of behavior on a date, but with this power comes responsibility.[15] He may make the decision about where to go on a date, but he must live with the results of that decision. If he has displeased his date, he may feel like a fool. He may also have to perform by protecting his date in certain circumstances. If they go to a rowdy rock concert or if someone makes remarks to her on the street, it is up to him to defend her and possibly fight on her behalf. He is also expected to be in charge and know what to do. If the car breaks down, he is expected to know what is wrong. There is a subtle expectation that he can "tell her" about things. This, of course, makes bright girls threatening. It is not surprising that boys often date girls who are a year or two younger; the traditional roles are more easy to establish with that age difference.

Therefore, especially for boys, a great deal of anxiety may come with the early stages of dating.[16] Yet most boys persist because of all the positive factors drawing them into the dating scene. In time, they may develop special relationships or steady dates. Some research shows that steady dating adds to a boy's self-esteem and esteem with peers even more than it adds to a girl's esteem.[17]

Dating from a Girl's Perspective

The active role for the boy in dating is paralleled by a passive role for the girl. While she may make herself available and give every indication that she would like to be asked out, she usually has to wait for the boy to ask for a formal date. She can, however, arrange to "accidentally" be at a place where the boy will be, and in some circumstances she can even ask him to do things. Yet she cannot be too aggressive. Women who initiate dates are still seen less positively.[18]

American girls start dating sooner than boys do, at about 14 for most girls and a year or so later for boys, although there are ethnic and class variations. (Young people in Europe and other areas begin dating much later.) As a young girl is likely to be ahead of boys her age in social maturity and secondary sexual characteristics, she is likely to date boys a few years older. In the early years of dating there is a preference for coed activities in groups.

During this period real friends continue to be same-sex friends. However, by age 17 or 18 most girls are dating regularly.[19]

As popularity with boys is part of general popularity and builds esteem with peers, the girl is eager to be asked out again. To this end she may develop a "dating personality." Both sexes believe that the other sex wants them to live up to gender-role stereotypes whether or not this is true.[20] According to these stereotypes, the female good date is amiable and verbal; she should be gay and bright but not too serious and intellectual. She is the boy's audience for his offerings of entertainment; she must be polite and, if possible, enthusiastic about his plans.[21]

In intensive interviews with girls of 15 and 16, Dorothy Pearce describes the dating personality further. Girls make themselves available and look interested in the hope that a boy will ask them out. They try to respond to his moods. "If he is quiet, they attempt to remain low key and ladylike; if he is interested in sports, the girls quickly develop an interest in sports.[22] In certain situations they adjust their behavior to that of their date. For example, if a girl is unsure that a boy is going to open the car door for her, she uses a ploy. As one girl says, "You just sort of walk along and if he walks the other way, you know you are going to open it yourself." These girls learn to manage unwanted attentions and turn down dates gracefully. They try not to embarrass the boy unless he is too persistent. They agree, however, that if he is persistent, it is all right to be rude. They also try to encourage shy boys by moving closer or saying something like, "Gee, don't I get a good night kiss?" They agree that the right words and the right behavior come with experience. One says, "I change my behavior and manners according to the date I am with and the kind of date I am on. There are times you can do things and times you can't."[23] While this information comes from a 1975 study, the college freshmen in my classes in 1990 agreed that the same kinds of things are still done.

Elizabeth Graverholz points out that to some degree these ideas about the dating personality are based not only on gender-role stereotypes but also on exchange theory. *Exchange theory* says that people will dominate in a relationship if they have more resources such as attractiveness and money than the partner has. Boys have often had a lot of resources, including the fact that gender-role stereotypes indicate that they *should* be dominant in a relationship. However, Grauerholz points out that stereotypes and exchange theory do not usually function in the same manner in longer-term relationships. As the couple get to know one another well, things such as trust and commitment become more important than superficial standards in determining behavior.[24]

The basis of power in dating relationships seems to be different for males and females. If men perceive themselves as having access to alternatives to the present relationship, they perceive themselves as being more powerful. Women feel more power when they seem to be in control of the reciprocation of love but do not necessarily get power from contributing affection and companionship.[25]

The 14- and 15-year-old girls in Pearce's study saw the qualities of preferred male dates as, in descending order, physical attractiveness, a good personality, a good physique, and sincere and considerate behavior.[26] There is no longitudinal study to determine whether these desired qualities change as girls get older. However, girls do tend to spend more time with their dates than with their girlfriends. Girls are not as likely to retain a number of "girls-only" activities as boys are to retain "boys-only" activities.[27] While it is acceptable for a boy to enjoy the company of other boys, a girl who goes out with other girls is often seen as one to be pitied: She doesn't have a date tonight; she has to go out with "the girls." We see the reflection of a cultural standard suggesting that men are more important than women and that men's company is more valued.

Thus, the dating scene reflects the other pressures of adolescence in pushing girls into feminine stereotyped behaviors. If one wants male companionship and such behavior is what boys expect, there is great pressure to conform. The pressure may be accentuated because the average age of boys dated is a few years older than that of girls. An older boy may intimidate a girl and make it hard for her to move beyond a dating personality. The whole dating situation, and to some extent general heterosexual interaction, reflects the pressure to be feminine by being pretty, popular, nice, and unassertive. There are negative sanctions for those who don't conform: They can't go to the prom without a date; if all their girlfriends are dating, they may sit home without anyone to do something with; and they may be excluded from parties and other social events.

Some progress has been made in equalizing dating and social relationships. For one thing, the casual dating that goes on today is not done just in couples. Sometimes it is a form of group dating that seems to be an extension of early adolescent coed activities. As Reiss describes it, "a group of several males and females will be at a party, a dance, or a bowling alley together, but not as couples. As the evening wears on, some of the males and females may pair off."[28] When couples start going out with each other steadily or exclusively, however, more formal dating still takes place. Even in this formal dating, however, girls have a few more social options. They can telephone boys without stigma today, and they are more likely to pay for some of the expenses; this gives them some leverage as to what they do on a date.

However, a great deal has not changed. Boys still do most of the asking, decide where to go, and initiate sexual activities. The boy is still to a great extent the guardian of the girl's social life and reputation. Many girls still try to be nice and develop a dating personality so that they will be popular. A letter to Joyce Brothers shows the continuing lack of control of the social situation experienced by many girls. The writer, a teenage girl, described herself as "not a raving beauty" but said, "My friends tell me that I'm pretty," and went on to say that she almost never had a date. She stated that she was particularly perplexed about her unpopularity because she "tried hard to always be sweet and nice."[29]

SEXUALITY

Changing Bodies

The concern about physical appearance shared by many girls and boys during adolescence is accentuated by norms about what is an appropriately "feminine and beautiful" or "masculine and tough" body. Unfortunately, the ideal male and female physiques seem to have been generated by the Action Jackson and Barbie dolls of childhood. While they may try their best to live up to the ideal of rippling biceps or big breasts and slim legs, it is difficult for most teenagers to come close to this ideal. As we have seen, girls are particularly discontented with their appearance.

The beginning of puberty also involves the acquisition of secondary sex characteristics. The bodily changes that occur at this time can be socially painful and anxiety-producing for many adolescents. Life is particularly difficult for an adolescent who does not reach puberty at the same time as his or her friends. A girl who starts developing her figure early may be unmercifully teased or even accused of being overly interested in sex. One teacher was overheard to remark about a young girl who had developed early, "With that figure, she'll be the first one in seventh grade to get pregnant." A girl who develops late may be teased about her flat chest. She may feel unattractive and different and wonder whether she is really feminine. The passage through early puberty seems to be easier for some than for others, but in all cases it is marked with some degree of uncertainty and anxiety about the changes that are taking place.

Menstruation. During early adolescence, a young woman also begins to menstruate and may feel some ambivalence about her role as a female. Many reach **menarche** (the first menstruation) without knowing anything about it. Some studies show that up to 17 percent of girls from upper socioeconomic brackets may experience menarche without having been told about it.[30] Many more learn only minimal facts from parents, friends, or "the movie" shown in sixth grade. Even then, the information communicated is seldom accurate.

However, adolescent girls do learn attitudes about their bodies and about menstruation. These attitudes are seldom positive and bear all the negative weight of cultural tradition that was described in Chapter 1. They hear the menstrual period called "the curse" and are told to hide their tampons or napkins. They may hear negative references to raging hormones or unstable premenstrual moods or overhear a boy saying with disgust that a girl "has her period." At the very least it is a messy business, and they may have cramps and some discomfort. Menstruation may carry with it a feeling of uncleanliness and unattractiveness.

However, there is an element of delight and of having achieved an aspect of adulthood when a girl has her first period, particularly if she is one of the last in her group to do so. In any case, the ambivalence about this new biological part of her life may fit in with her general ambivalence about being female.

Changes in Boys.   Boys are as much concerned with the changes in their bodies during this time as girls are. There are outward, visible signs of the many inward changes taking place. Facial and pubic hair begins to grow, the voice changes and becomes unreliable, and acne often appears on the face. Sexual arousal may mean unwelcome erections during classes and at other inappropriate times. (Boys are usually very much concerned with their ability to have erections and to ejaculate. They may compare notes and even have contests to determine who can ejaculate the first or the farthest.) Boys are frequently concerned with penis size, and a large penis is equated with virility and masculinity. This concern with size seems to be only a male preoccupation. Linda Lovelace and *Deep Throat* to the contrary, females are very little concerned about the size of male genitals.[31] The following quotes are typical of male feelings at this time:

> About seventh grade these impromptu erections became more frequent, though, and I would always dread having to get out of my seat in class when I had one. It usually happened when the class was boring, and would sometimes last the whole hour. I was afraid that everyone would notice. Luckily nobody did. . . .
>
> Junior high was a rather god awful time in the life of most guys I know, myself readily included. What a drag puberty was. . . . I had greater questions. . . . When am I going to get pubic hair on my genitalia? Junior high locker rooms were particularly grotesque, especially when some of the more physically mature dudes, who were not always the most intelligent, made fun of the younger, less physically mature guys.
>
> When I was thirteen I had my first ejaculation which was kind of a shock since at this time I still didn't know anything about sex.[32]

When Sexuality Means Sex

For teenage girls, sexuality is as tied up with cultural taboos and stereotypes about the nature of males and females as it is with their own bodies and desires. The cultural good girl and bad girl images can be clearly seen at this time. Throughout the 1950s and into the early 1960s good girls were not supposed to have sexual intercourse until they got married. Actually, many girls during this period did have intercourse in late high school or college. However, they didn't tell people, even their best friends. As contraceptives could not be openly bought and used, they frequently got pregnant. When they did, they had a quiet wedding, had the baby in a home for unwed mothers, or had an illegal abortion. Legal abortion was not an option, and many women died from having an illegal abortion or trying to abort themselves. One remained a good girl as long as one did not get a bad reputation (that is, one's boyfriend did not talk) or as long as one did not get pregnant and stay unmarried.

Stereotypes about female sexuality went hand in hand with the good girl image. A nice girl wasn't that interested in sex and tried to fend off boys' advances. She was not supposed to respond strongly even when aroused, and no one worried about her having an orgasm. While stereotypes of female sexuality had changed by the 1990s, there is still a different standard for boys and girls. In spite of acceptance of sex within a committed relationship, girls are still looked down on for having too much casual sex.

Unfortunately, the stereotype of masculinity still demands that boys be "on the make." Boys who try to live up to the stereotype or to fulfill their own desires attempt to have dating include as much sexual activity as possible, starting with kissing and petting and ending with intercourse. Pressure is put on the girl to allow sexual liberties. A female adolescent is thus put in a very delicate position. Dating and male companionship are rewarding to her, and she wants to gain the approval of her date and keep him around. In addition, she may be sexually aroused and want to have sexual activity with her partner. However, if she is "easy," she will get a bad reputation; she will be increasingly pressured for sex and treated with little respect by the boys she dates. She may also be shunned by many girls and by the "nice crowd." Sadly, many girls get bad reputations without deserving them when boys lie to their friends about how they "scored."

Boys and girls seem to enter relationships for different reasons. In the Simon, Berger, and Gagnon study of 1972, 46 percent of the young men were not emotionally involved with their initial sexual partners; only 31 percent said that they were in love with the girl or planned to marry their first coital partner.[33] Subsequent research by Gagnon and Simon also showed that females are more likely to grant sexual access to serious suitors in order to secure a commitment to marriage.[34]

Whether she does or does not allow sexual liberties, a girl may be faulted. If she protects her reputation and is totally cool to sex, she may be labeled as frigid. If she gives in (or even if she doesn't), she may get a bad reputation. The path between these two extremes is very narrow. A girl can neck or pet with casual dates, but if she wants to have intercourse, she had better wait for a very special boyfriend who is not as likely to talk about her. For boys indeed do talk. In the Simon, Berger, and Gagnon study, 60 percent of the males but only 40 percent of the females had shared information about their sexual experiences with someone else within a month after the experiences took place. Apparently, a double standard existed. Eighty-six percent of the boys, compared to 67 percent of the girls, had an approving audience.[35]

One study shows the ambivalence that women may feel about sexual touching. Forty male and female undergraduates were questioned to see how they felt about touch on different body areas. For females, "the more a touch was associated with sexual desire, the less it was considered to imply friendliness, warmth, friendship, and pleasantness." Thus, while touching should be pleasurable, sexual touching may raise warning flags because of the need to exercise control. In contrast, men saw a sexual touch by a woman as being loving, warm, and pleasant.[36] Women must worry not only about their reputations but about pregnancy or even the use of physical force by the male. To add to the ambivalence, it is unlikely, in the early years of adolescence at least, that a girl will be able to get total physical satisfaction from sexual intercourse. It is usually several years after menarche before girls are likely to achieve orgasm.[37] By contrast, a girl may enjoy the love, warmth, and intimacy associated with sex and may want to please her partner. Her own ambivalence, combined with pressures both to have and to refrain from having sexual intercourse, makes the whole area of sexual experience an emotional and anxiety-producing situation for many girls.

A boy is pressured to perform. It is up to him to initiate sexual action. It is also up to him to be competent and cool and to appear to know what he is doing. To ensure his masculine image, he must press for sexual liberties. Whether he talks about them afterward depends on the closeness of the relationship.

A boy may not know much more about sex than his date does, but he has to be the one to tentatively reach his hand over her shoulder and let it drop casually on her breast. He has to risk rejection at every stage. He also has to be sure that he doesn't fumble or seem unsure of himself. He is put into the role of the leader and teacher. (The author heard about a boy who practiced unhooking bras on his mother's dressmaker dummy. He practiced until he could separate the hooks casually with one hand. Unfortunately, front-hooking bras made their appearance at just about the time he started dating.)

Whether or not sexual intercourse occurs between a dating couple, there is a great temptation for the boy to lie about his exploits to prove himself with the other guys. While all the participants recognize that locker room talk is not necessarily accurate, they listen and participate. The great danger is that feminine reputations may be slurred, often without reason (girls still get reputations even in this supposedly liberated age). Another problem is faced by the younger male who listens and believes without question that this is the way "men" behave and then wonders about himself.

Date Rape

There is a temptation for a boy to use force to satisfy his desires. The line between persuasion and force is a fine one. In a study of 400 unmarried male college students, 23 percent had attempted to have intercourse on a date by using physical force. A majority of 261 female college students said they had encountered some sort of physical sexual aggression of this kind. In most cases, they felt terror, fright, disgust, and anxiety.[38]

The high incidence of date rape or acquaintance rape is frightening. In a study at Kent State University in Ohio, one in eight women students had been raped and another one in four had been victims of attempted rape. Only 4 percent reported the rapes. At Auburn University in Alabama, the University of South Dakota, and St. Cloud State University in Minnesota, independent studies found that one in five female students were raped by men they knew. One in twelve of the men surveyed admitted to using force to obtain sex, but virtually none of these men felt they were rapists. One stated, "I didn't rape the chick, she was enjoying it and responding," and later said, "I feel that sex is a very pleasant way to relieve stress. Especially when there are no strings attached."[39]

Many men deny that rape has occurred by referring to such myths as "women like rape (so there's no such thing as rape)," "women provoke it (and men can't help themselves)," "yes, it happened, but no harm was done (she wasn't a virgin)," and "women deserve it anyway."[40]

In the Koss survey, which included 7,000 students at thirty-five schools, preliminary results show that 52 percent of all the women surveyed had experienced some form of sexual victimization. Forty-seven percent of the rapes were committed by first or casual dates. Three-quarters of the women raped were between the ages of 15 and 21, with the average age being 18. More than 80 percent of the rapes occurred off campus, with more than 50 percent happening on the man's turf: home, car, and the like. More than a third of the women did not discuss this experience with anyone; 90 percent did not tell the police. Denial was almost as typical for the women as it was for the men, although the women suffered guilt and anxiety.[41]

Beliefs about the right of men to use force to obtain sex seem to be widespread in all age groups. Fifty-one percent of the men and 42 percent of the women in the college study believed that it is all right for a man to force sex on a woman if "she gets him excited."[42] In a different survey grade schoolers answered questions about whether it was all right for a man to force a woman to kiss him if he had spent a "lot of money" on her. Fifty-one percent of the boys and 41 percent of the girls said it was acceptable. In a junior high survey, 65 percent of the boys and 47 percent of the girls said it was acceptable for a man to force sex on a woman if he had been dating her for more than six months. Eighty-seven percent of the boys and 79 percent of the girls said rape was permissible among married couples.[43]

These studies show the accuracy of Susan Griffiths in calling rape "the all-American crime." Beliefs about rape reflect power relationships between men and women that are also reflected in traditional sex roles.[44] When we look at rape, we see stereotypes about male and female gender roles as well as ideas about the nature of privilege and consent.

Rape

Rape is a violent rather than just a sexual act. Rape and the fear of rape are power mechanisms by which men seek to control women or humiliate other men. Rape has always been considered a crime more against the man to whom the woman "belongs" as daughter or wife than against the woman herself. Fear of rape has compelled women to seek the protection of men and to be good girls in the hope that they will be protected from rape or at least not accused of inciting it.

Many myths surrounding the act of rape relate to this idea of the good girl and the bad girl. Many people believe that only bad girls get raped and that any woman who has been raped was probably asking for it. The truth of the matter is, of course, that women of all ages, from 3-month-old babies to 90-year-old grandmothers, get raped and that few of them did anything to provoke the crime.[45] Yet victims who are even moderately attractive continue to be treated as though they provoked their own assault. They are often not believed when they report a rape, or they are harassed or intensively questioned by police officers who want to hear the lurid details of the attack. Griffiths goes so far as to propose that many police officers, lawyers, and judges identify with the rapists and, while they would not personally commit rape, enjoy hearing about the reaffirmation of male potency.[46]

The corollary of the "only bad girls get raped" myth is the belief that "all men are potentially rapists and will rape if too greatly sexually aroused." This belief is used to ensure that women remain demure, modest, and under the protection of "their" men. It is also used to excuse men who just "couldn't help themselves" and thus raped because they were sexually excited. Indeed, most rapes are planned: Fifty-eight percent of rapes by one man, 83 percent of rapes by pairs of men, and 90 percent of gang rapes were found to have been planned ahead of time in an extensive study of rapists.[47] Thus men do not assault their victims in the heat of desire but coolly and premeditatedly plan their attacks.

Most of the men who rape are not convicted and punished. The rape victim is put in the position of having to prove that a crime was even committed and having to show that she resisted the rape. Again, the assumption is that unless she has suffered great physical abuse other than rape, she probably cooperated in the rape attempt or did not resist enough, even if she was threatened with a knife or gun. One judge remarked that "you can't thread a moving needle" as he dismissed the case against an accused rapist. It is also assumed that if the rape did not occur during prime daytime hours at a PTA meeting, the woman asked for it by being in the wrong place at the wrong time or by being the wrong kind of woman. A judge in Oregon dismissed a case in which a woman jogger had been raped while being threatened with a broken bottle. The judge held that the woman should not have been out in the early morning jogging and that by so doing she had incited the rapist. A lawyer defending the rapist of a cocktail waitress said the victim was "familiar with alcohol" and implied that she was an unfit mother.[48]

Thus, rape can be used as a method to keep women indoors at night or in the early morning, keep them out of certain occupations, make them dress in demure and inconspicuous ways, make them act like a good girl, and make them seek the protection of a man. It is an effective way for men to exercise power and show their hostility against women or their antipathy toward the other men to whom the women "belong."

People are becoming more aware of the myths surrounding rape, and in many areas the treatment of rape victims is changing. Many localities have established rape crisis centers and hot lines where victims can seek immediate help. Police officers have been sensitized to the problems of a rape victim and are trained to take a more gentle approach while questioning her. Frequently female officers are assigned to help a victim. In many courts the victim's past sexual history can no longer be used as evidence that "she was a bad girl and deserved what she got." Women are also taking self-defense courses and becoming aware of the need to defend themselves and not just seek the protection of a man. All these things help, but the primary fact of rape remains: It is a power move used by men in an attempt to control and subdue women. Our cultural beliefs about rape help perpetuate the blaming of the victim and the excusing of the rapist and reinforce the power differential between the sexes.

Teenage Sexuality

Thus, we see that adult norms regarding power and sex influence the sexual misunderstandings that occur between teenage boys and girls. Times have changed, however, and sexual activity for girls is not as stigmatizing as before. While the possibility of a bad reputation can still be used as a social control, the limits by which one can get a bad reputation are different today.

Has there really been a sexual revolution? The answer depends on whom one asks and whether one is talking about attitudes or behavior. Some general patterns seem to have emerged since the mid-1960s, however, and have continued into the early 1990s. Teenagers are having the first sexual experience at slightly younger ages and are having it with more casual partners. While the norm, at least for girls, is only for permissiveness with affection, one no longer has to be engaged or going steady to validate sexual relations. Also, the rates of premarital sexual experience are tending to converge between men and women.[49]

A national random survey done by Robert Coles in the early 1980s yielded some specific information about current teenage sexual behavior. One has to allow for some overreporting on the part of boys and underreporting on the part of girls as well as a possible skewing of the results resulting from who was willing to respond to the questionnaire. According to Coles's survey, 50 percent of the boys had had intercourse by age 13, and by age 17, 98 percent were sexually experienced. Only 18 percent of the girls had had intercourse by age 13, but by age 17, 100 percent of these respondents had experienced sex. A public television special on teenage sex reported almost the exact same statistics for 1989.[50] Genital petting and oral sex frequently came before intercourse. Those who were very religious or who didn't drink were more likely to delay sex. Most of the respondents said that the first sexual intercourse was a positive experience for them, although girls were more ambivalent than boys. After the first time, most of the respondents stayed active sexually.[51] Forty-one percent believed that being in love makes it all right to have sex (at 13, 53 percent said they had been in love; at 18, 85 percent said so). Eighty-five percent reported that they had had a boyfriend or girlfriend, and 45 percent had one currently.[52]

The respondents reported that sex is more acceptable as a relationship gets more serious. While only 3 percent said that intercourse with strangers is all right, over 60 percent reported that intercourse between two people planning marriage is acceptable. Boys are accorded a little more freedom to have casual sex, but other than that, there is little difference between the sexes in terms of what is considered acceptable. It is particularly interesting that only 60 percent thought that intercourse before marriage is all right for either boys or girls but that far more than that were active sexually. They also believed that their parents had much stricter views about sexual freedom.[53] One can only wonder about the guilt and anxiety among the 40 percent who did not approve of what they themselves were doing.

Contraceptives

We can see the result of this ambivalence when we look at contraceptive use today. Among the respondents to the survey, only 45 percent used birth control during the first sexual experience and only 55 percent used it regularly thereafter. About a fifth of the 55 percent who reported using birth control were using rhythm or withdrawal; most were using a condom or the pill. When asked why they didn't use contraceptives regularly, the most frequent responses were that (1) they didn't have intercourse that often, (2) contraceptives were embarrassing to get, (3) contraceptives interfered with sex, (4) they didn't believe it was right to plan for sex, and (5) their parents would find out and (for the girls) they were afraid of the side effects.[54]

In the belief that it is not right to plan ahead for sex, we see the continuation of the good girl–bad girl dichotomy. In the views of some of these teenagers, only a bad girl plans ahead for sex; a good girl just gets swept off her feet by the passion of the moment. A girl who uses contraceptives on a regular basis is thus risking feeling like a bad girl. If she comes prepared for sexual intercourse, her date may wonder what she has done before. A girl who does not use contraceptives does not have this problem, but if she depends on the sporadic use of condoms by her boyfriend, on rhythm, on cola douches, or on any of the other very uncertain ways of preventing conception, she is likely to get pregnant. The usual solution for this dilemma in high school is to rely on the boyfriend to use condoms. Unfortunately, condoms used without foam have a high failure rate.

By the college years, norms and behavior regarding sexual activity have become similar between men and women. Women are still not supposed to be as aggressive sexually as men and the label of promiscuity is still more likely to be applied to women than to men, but women are relatively free to engage in sexual activity without being labeled. Living-together arrangements and to some extent coed dorms constitute an acknowledgment of what often went on covertly in the past.

There is not much evidence that the use of contraceptives has increased greatly in spite of liberalized values. Part of the problem is the attitude of parents, educators, and legislators. Until recently many schools that had sex education classes could not teach about contraceptives or preventing pregnancy. There was a feeling that it was all right to tell young people about the basic facts of life but that to talk about sexual intercourse and its results would encourage experimentation with sex. Many states have even attempted to remove sex education from the schools. It is common in Southern states to see billboards saying, "Remove sex education from the schools, elect ——— in November." Other attempts to limit sexual information and access to contraception have increased as well. National and state legislatures have tried to pass legislation requiring parenthood clinics to notify a parent within ten days if they give a minor contraceptives. The effect of the so-called squeal rule will be to prevent many young people who do not wish their parents to know about their sexual activity from getting contraceptives.[55] Right-to-life forces have introduced legislation that will allow states individually to ban abortion, which has been legal since a Supreme Court decision of 1973. In twelve states, teenagers must now get parental consent or court permission to have an abortion. Conservatives believed that these measures would help immature teenagers get official guidance before abortion and probably hoped that it would encourage sexual discretion. However, after the 1981 passage of a Minnesota law requiring parental notification, the birthrate for 15- to 17-year-olds went up 38.4 percent. Opponents are fighting many of these laws in court.[56]

Unfortunately, parents do not do a much better job with sex education than the schools and probably teach considerably less than the schools might, especially about contraceptive use. Nancy Friday in *My Mother, Myself* describes the different perceptions held by mothers and their daughters about what the girls were told about sex. The mothers all felt they had fulfilled their parental duty by telling their daughters important information; the daughters did not feel they had been told anything at all.[57] Quotes from Morrison support the belief that parents tell their children very little:

Female: When I was in the sixth grade, a film about sex education was shown at my elementary school, but I never saw it. For some reason unknown to me, my mother felt I should not see it.

Female: When I asked a group of grown-ups what Midol was, I guess my mother decided it was time for me to be lectured on where babies come from; she provided me with "What Every Teenager Must Know" and a question-and-answer period.

Female: My mother had a pretty hard time talking about the little she did talk about. The only reason she did it at all was because my Girl Scout troop was showing a movie talking about menstruation. . . .

Male: Because sex was taboo at our house, you couldn't say that "dirty" three-letter word without somebody blushing, trying to hush it up, or giggling. . . .

Male: I thought it was tough in childhood to get information about my own sex, but there was none to be found concerning the female! A sense of guilt accompanied acquisition of information about the sexuality of women which I today attempt to deal with.[58]

Although parents may offend their children by offering information before the children are ready, greater efforts need to be made by parents and children to talk about their bodies, sex, and contraceptive use.[59] In particular, there is a need to talk about the emotional aspects of sex and what can be expected. The lack of information about sex and the easy availability of contraception has led to an increased rate of teen pregnancy and illegitimate births. It is estimated that almost 50 percent of teenage girls will be pregnant before they are 18, and the present illegitimacy rate among teens is 33 percent. The United States has the highest rate of teen pregnancies among the developed, industrialized nations.[60]

AIDS

The spread of acquired immune deficiency syndrome (AIDS) has raised other important questions in regard to teenage sexuality. Recent reports show that the AIDS virus is slowly working its way into the age group from 15 to 24, yet teenagers know little about the virus and are taking few precautions to prevent getting it. A 1986 survey of over 800 Massachusetts teenagers 16 to 19 years old found that 29 percent of the respondents did not know that the virus can be passed from females to males. Seventy percent of this group said they were sexually active, but only 15 percent had made any changes in their sexual behavior because of concern about AIDS. Among those who had done so, only one in five had changed in ways that could be considered effective. As one 17-year-old boy explained, "From what I can see, all this fuss about AIDS is pretty much exaggerated. I've only slept with three girls this year, and I knew them all pretty well."[61]

Homosexuality and Homophobia

Sexuality may sometimes mean homosexuality for an adolescent. Sexuality seems to lie on a continuum, with homosexuality at one end and heterosexuality at the other. Most people are not totally at either end but somewhere in between. Adolescence is a time for the awakening of sexual urges and the exploration of feelings, including one's feelings toward the same sex. We will see examples of feelings of attraction to or arousal by the same sex: One girl writes of being "turned on" by the nude bodies of other females, and a boy writes about a dream in which a friend sucks his fingers. Almost all young people go through a stage in which they explore their own bodies, often in the company or with the aid of friends of the same sex. Girls may play doctor, and boys may masturbate together. In a large percentage of adolescents this type of interaction has occurred earlier, and by the adolescent years they are primarily attracted to the opposite sex. However, for others the attraction to the same sex persists. It may be a mild and fleeting thing, as described in the following quotes, or it may be the person's primary sexual orientation.

> *Male:* Lately I have become more scared of my (latent, thank God) homosexual tendencies. The main thing that made me worry about myself was a dream I had in which a (male) friend of mine was sucking my fingers, and giving me pleasure (pretty obvious symbolism). Intellectually, I realize that this is OK, but it still frightens me a little. Emotionally, I still feel that homosexuality is perverse.

Female: Many other feelings I had I really felt were abnormal, especially for a woman. I used to see pictures of nude women or would see them in movies and get sexually excited. . . . It is good now to find out that other women also have similar feelings, and that it is OK and I am not necessarily perverted or a homosexual.[62]

We do not know what causes homosexuality or heterosexuality, but doctors and scientists have come to accept the fact that homosexuality is a normal expression of sexuality for many people. It has recently been discovered that a great deal more of the population is homosexual or "gay" than we ever thought before. If those who are bisexual are included, estimates range from 10 to 20 percent.[63] Our concern with homosexuality in this book is limited to its relationship to **gender roles**. As gender-role norms have strong things to say about sexual behavior, identifying oneself as a homosexual may make it difficult to act in ways that society defines as masculine or feminine. According to these norms, girls are to gain approval by seeking popularity with *boys* in order to be defined as feminine and boys are to seek sexual prowess with *girls* in order to be defined as masculine. A person who defines himself or herself as homosexual or even worries about having homosexual interests or desires may be partially rejecting what the culture defines as masculine or feminine. The fear of many people about not being masculine or feminine enough leads to strong fears about homosexuality in our culture. This is particularly true for boys since being masculine has been depicted as *not* being feminine, and this lesson has been carefully taught from birth onward. At the same time, stereotypic masculinity is conceived of in terms of being heterosexual. Thus, if one departs from the norm of masculinity, one may be depicted as feminine, homosexual, or even both. The popular conception of a male homosexual is that of an effeminate person. Thus, the boy learns by implication that to be masculine is not to be feminine *or* homosexual.

Society's norms and popular conceptions do not represent reality in most cases. Very few gay men are effeminate in looks or behavior, and most cannot be distinguished from straight males. Similarly, most lesbians are not "butch" in style and usually cannot be distinguished from straight females. In addition, "butch-fem," or male-female, roles are seldom played in homosexual relationships. Many homosexuals are quite comfortable with their sexual preference and feel perfectly masculine or feminine in spite of what society says.[64] The real problem for most gay people is the oppression that comes from a heterosexual norm for behavior. This norm means that many gays have to keep their sexual preference secret or face stigma and even job or housing discrimination.

The fear of not living up to the heterosexual norms of gender-role stereotypes affects many straight people and leads to a related fear of homosexuality, or **homophobia**. The fear of being called homosexual and thus stigmatized as not masculine or feminine enough is so strong that people can play upon it and use it as a social-control mechanism. For example, a woman who is successful in sports or a career may be called a lesbian by those who are angry at her for not playing the female role. However, the threat or implication of homosexuality is not as likely to be used against women. This probably occurs because our culture does not put a great deal of emphasis on the sexual nature of women and because there is an assumption that all women would really prefer a man if they could have one. This assumption is not valid, but it eases society's fear of female homosexuality, and lesbianism has been more easily accepted in this culture than has male homosexuality. This does not make it easier for a lesbian woman to resolve the questions she may have about herself and her femininity, but she is not as frequently the target of open hostility as is the male homosexual. Women are also able to touch, hug, and be intimate without being accused of homosexuality.

It is the male who suffers most from intimations of homosexuality, as such hints are a threat to his masculinity. Gregory Lehne states that in his childhood, leaps from trees and rocks at the swimming area were tests of masculinity. Boys who hesitated were encouraged with a taunt such as "I done it three times. Come on fellas. What are you, a fag? Jump!"[65] A man who fears the label must attack first by proving he is straight and strong, possibly by teasing others or by denouncing gays.[66] Men are often so afraid of the parts of themselves that are attracted to other men and so afraid of having their masculinity demeaned that they constantly deny their homosexuality by saying how much they hate "fags" or even by looking for fights with them. When they do this, they deny an important part of their emotional structure and cannot become close to other men. They may pass these feelings on directly and indirectly to their male children, usually by ceasing to hug or even touch them once they reach 10 or 11. Psychologists have demonstrated that people need a certain amount of touching and stroking,[67] and the lack of physical closeness between boy and father hurts both of them.

Many men are willing to go to almost any lengths to avoid threats to their masculinity. Therefore, many repress affectionate or kind feelings toward other men. They make sure they don't touch other men or express any tender feelings toward them. As we saw in Chapter 6, this repression of emotions carries over into the repression of emotions in general and fits in with the cultural prescription to be cool. It keeps men from getting close to other men and expressing their real feelings to another male. Aside from the fear of homosexuality, such an expression of emotion may be considered sissy or effeminate, and so there is a double reason for many men to be inexpressive. Thus, men have kept a certain distance from one another, although this distance is papered over with ritual work and sports talk.

Men are thus denied an important part of their psychological well-being when they cannot touch and cannot express their tender feelings for other men. Needless to say, gay men are damaged by the negative implications of homophobia. They hear their sexual preference jeered at and derided, and they may be physically attacked.[68] Adolescence is the time when young men are most strongly affected by homophobic fears, as this is when they are trying to establish a sexual and gender-role identity. It is also the time when peer group pressure is strongest and a young man may suffer the most by deviating from society's norms. A modification of gender-role stereotypes that would allow a greater range of behavior for both men and women would enable many more people to enjoy their real potential without penalty. Interestingly, it is the rigidly "masculine" or "feminine" person who is likely to be the most homophobic. Those who are less stereotyped in their gender roles are able to accept a greater range of behavior in others as well.[69]

SUMMARY

It is difficult for both boys and girls to establish an identity in adolescence. The adolescent girl is socialized to need love and approval. She forms much of her identity from a reflection of the opinions of others, and this makes her uncertain about her body, her popularity, and her abilities. She may be afraid to succeed academically, in a career, or in sports because she wants to remain feminine. Yet without these concrete achievements, she may not find a foundation on which to base her self-esteem. She must also negotiate the new and precarious world of dating and sex with the handicap of needing approval from others. While women are now achieving more in sports and careers, it remains difficult for an adolescent girl, who is still establishing her identity, to become clear about the choices that are open to her. The messages about femininity are ambiguous. What the teenage girl hears is a little like the old dictum that "any man can become President," even though a presidential campaign requires millions of dollars and high-placed contacts. In a similar way, the adolescent girl is told that she can do what she wants, that this is the "era for women." The message is not totally dishonest, but it ignores many realities. It ignores the socialization that makes it difficult for her to fit into masculine roles and jobs, the socialized need to be loved and approved of and the fact that she may feel isolated if she does not do feminine things; and the real prejudice against women that is still in effect in schools and in the business world. Seward points out these problems:

> American core culture overtly offers its girls the same social role choices in the competitive status hierarchy as its boys, while covertly expecting them to decline the more challenging instrumental roles in favor of low-status domestic roles for which they are paradoxically both overqualified and untrained. Here is a case of cultural discontinuity, where preparation for adult participation in society is followed by regression to dependency upon husband and children. Her situation constitutes a double bind in which either alternative leads to frustration: if she accepts at face value the invitation to share all areas of responsibility with men, she does so at the cost of denying herself as a woman. If on the other hand, she responds to the hidden message, leaving the broader social field for the protection of the home, it is too frequently at the cost of denying herself as a person.[70]

There is evidence that many girls are now fighting the odds and valuing their concrete achievements. This may mean that they will have less desire for approval from others and will develop higher self-esteem. It is hoped that changes along these lines will continue.

Adolescence continues to be a difficult time for boys as well as girls. For the boy, the greatest change has been an increasing ambivalence about the demands of achievement, although the norms for success may be reinstated in more difficult economic times. However, most prescriptions for the male role still remain: be tough, be cool, be good. In this period of conformity to peer pressure, an adolescent boy learns to repress his feelings and build his body. He seeks esteem through achievements in sports, school activities, and sex. As the norms push him to seek sexual activity, his interaction with girls on dates may provoke anxiety and produce conflict. Also, his fear of homosexuality makes it unlikely that he will get close to other men.

The changing roles for girls that ease the good girl constraints and allow for more concrete achievements may ease the difficulty of female adolescence. In a similar way, the ambivalence about career success *may* take some pressure off the male and allow him to consider other options. On the whole, however, adolescence is still a mixture of pleasure and tension. It is made more difficult by pressures to conform to nonfunctional gender-role stereotypes.

ESSAY QUESTIONS

1. Discuss the different approaches to friendship taken by teenage boys and girls. Why do girls put so high a premium on loyalty? What do boys want in their friends? Do the approaches to friendship change as a teenager gets older?
2. Discuss the relationship of boys and girls to dating, in particular the active role taken by boys and the passive role taken by girls. How is the dating personality an example of this passive role?
3. Compare how adolescent boys and girls feel about their bodies. What things do they like and dislike and how satisfied are they with them?
4. Drawing on the material in Chapter 1, how do cultural ideas about menstruation affect a young girl's view of herself and her developing body?
5. What general trends can you cite in sexual behavior among teenagers (for example, first intercourse at a younger age)? Why are girls' rates of nonvirginity beginning to converge with boys' rates in the later teen years?
6. What different attitudes do boys and girls have toward the first sexual partner? How are these attitudes carried over in the sexual part of the dating relationship?
7. Are teenagers using contraceptives more as they become more sexually active? If not, why aren't they? What recent trends do you see that may affect contraceptive use?
8. Why does Susan Griffiths call rape the all-American crime? How do adult attitudes about rape show up in the teenage dating culture?
9. How common is homosexuality among adolescents, and how does it relate to the gender-role stereotypes of masculinity and femininity?

10. How is homophobia a social-control mechanism? What does this mean for men's relationships with one another?

EXERCISES

1. Discuss the rituals of dating. Do you believe that dating is still "active" for the boy and "passive" for the girl? Do you believe that the dating personality still exists? Do you think that as teenagers do more in groups, there is an effect on their relationships in dates?
2. Discuss your feelings about your body and the things you might like to change. In your experience, are girls more dissatisfied with their bodies than boys are?
3. *For females:* Plan to ask someone out on a date and make plans to use your $25 weekly money to provide transportation, pay for what you will do, and so on. (Draw up exact plans.) Think of approaching your date at first and be aware of having to ask if you are going to go out again. Also be aware of having to initiate any sexual overtures. During all of this, you do not know for certain whether the date likes you. (*Note:* This exercise can apply to an older person reentering the dating world as well as to young adults.)
4. *For males:* Try to show that you want to be asked out on a date without saying anything about it directly. Then assume you are out on the date and, without saying anything, communicate your desire to be a nice, pleasant good girl. What do you do if your date gets mad at you? (*Note:* This exercise is also effective for older males.)
5. To get a stronger feeling about gender-role stereotypes, complete the following exercise (for males and females):
   I feel attractive when _____.
   I feel angry when _____.
   I feel feminine when _____.
   Being feminine is irrelevant to me when _____.
   I feel masculine when _____.
   I feel afraid when _____.
   I feel alone when _____.
   I feel competent when _____.
   I feel I have little or no control over my life when _____.
6. Discuss why teenagers use contraception so infrequently. Do you see any connection between this low rate of use and the active and passive roles of boys and girls in dating?
7. Discuss your feelings about homosexuality and homosexuals. If you are afraid of homosexuals, dislike them, or feel anything else that is negative, explore why you feel that way. Is this feeling realistic in terms of what you know about homosexuals? Discuss your feelings about changing heterosexual norms for many kinds of behavior in this society that

will make homosexuals more comfortable in enjoying their sexual preference.

8. Complete the sentence. If I could change one thing about how I relate to the other sex, it would be _____.

Discuss what you have written. Now do the same sentence completion, but substitute "same sex" for "other sex." Compare your answers and discuss why they are different.

NOTES

1. Abagail Van Buren, "Dear Abby," *Detroit Free Press* (January 23, 1982):A–3.
2. H. T. Reis, M. Senchak, and B. Solomon, "Sex Differences in the Intimacy of Social Interaction: Further Examination of Potential Explanations," *Journal of Personality and Social Psychology* 48 (1985):1204–1217; D. Williams, "Gender, Masculinity-Femininity and Emotional Intimacy in Same-Sex Friendship," *Sex Roles* 12 (1985): 587–600.
3. J. M. O'Neil, B. J. Helms, R. Gable, R. Stillson, L. David, and L. S. Wrightsman, "Data on College Men's Gender Role Conflict and Strain" (paper presented at the meeting of the American Psychological Association, Toronto, Canada, 1984).
4. E. J. Aries and F. L. Johnson, "Close Friendship in Adulthood: Conversational Content between Same-Sex Friends," *Sex Roles* 9 (1983):1183–1196; R. R. Bell, "Friendships of Women and of Men," *Psychology of Women Quarterly* 5 (1981): 402–417; L. R. Davidson and L. Duberman, "Friendships: Communication and Interactional Patterns in Same-Sex Dyads," *Sex Roles* 8 (1982):809–822.
5. K. E. Davis, "Near and Dear: Friendship and Love Compared," *Psychology Today* (February 1985):22, 24–28, 30; F. W. Schneider and L. M. Coutts, "Person Orientation of Male and Female High School Students: To the Educational Disadvantage of Males?" *Sex Roles* 13 (1985):47–63.
6. Aries and Johnson, *op. cit.*
7. *Ibid.*
8. S. G. Candy, L. E. Troll, and S. G. Levy, "A Developmental Exploration of Friendship Functions in Women," *Psychology of Women Quarterly* 5 (1981):456–472.
9. Reis et al., *op. cit.*
10. Marita McCabe, "Toward a Theory of Adolescent Dating," *Adolescence* 19 (1984): 160–170.
11. Daniel Offer, E. Ostrov, and K. Howard, *The Adolescent* (New York: Basic Books, 1981).
12. *Ibid.,* p. 80.
13. *Ibid.,* p. 81.
14. *Ibid.,* p. 82.
15. *Ibid.*
16. Marshall Prisbell, "Factors Affecting College Students' Perceptions of Satisfaction in and Frequency of Dating," *Psychological Reports* 60 (1987):659–664.
17. Naomi Samet and Eugene W. Kelly, Jr., "The Relationship of Steady Dating to Self-Esteem and Sex Role Identity among Adolescents," *Adolescence* 20 (1987): 231–246.

18. S. K. Green and P. Sandos, "Perceptions of Male and Female Initiators of Relationships," *Sex Roles* 9 (1983):849–852.
19. R. Braito, D. Dean, E. Powers, and B. Bruton, "The Inferiority Games: Perceptions and Behavior," *Sex Roles* 7 (1981):65–72; L. R. Davidson, "Pressure and Pretense: Living with Gender Stereotypes," *Sex Roles* 7 (1981):331–347; D. Scher, "Sex-Role Contradictions: Self-Perceptions and Ideal Perceptions," *Sex Roles* 10 (1984): 651–656.
20. B. L. Alperson and W. J. Friedman, "Some Aspects of the Interpersonal Phenomenology of Heterosexual Dyads with Respect to Sex-Role Stereotypes," *Sex Roles* 9 (1983):453–474.
21. L. O. Lavine and J. P. Lombardo, "Self-Disclosure: Intimate and Nonintimate Disclosures to Parents and Best Friends as a Function of Bem Sex Role Category," *Sex Roles* 11 (1984):734–744.
22. Dorothy Pearce, "The Dating Experiences for Adolescent Girls," *Adolescence* 10 (1975):157–174.
23. *Ibid.*
24. E. Graverholz and R. T. Serpe, "Initiation and Response: The Dynamics of Sexual Interaction," *Sex Roles* 12 (1985):1041–1059.
25. Letitia Anne Peplau, "Power in Dating Relationships," in Jo Freeman, *Women: A Feminist Perspective* (Palo Alto, Calif.: Mayfield, 1984), pp. 100–112.
26. Pearce, *op. cit.*
27. McCabe, *op. cit.*
28. Ira Reiss, *Family Systems in America*, 3d ed. (New York: Holt, Rinehart & Winston, 1980), p. 102.
29. Joyce Brothers, "Sound Off," *Detroit Free Press* (February 19, 1982):A–7.
30. E. B. Grief and K. Ulman, "The Psychological Impact of Menarche on Early Adolescent Females," *Child Development* 53 (1982):1413–1420.
31. Eleanor Morrison, Kay Starks, Cynda Hyndman, and Nina Ronzio, *Growing Up Sexual* (New York: Van Nostrand, 1980.)
32. S. F. Newcomer, J. R. Udry, and F. Cameron, "Adolescent Sexual Behavior and Popularity," *Adolescence* 18 (1983):515–522.
33. W. Simon, A. S. Berger, and J. S. Gagnon, "Beyond Anxiety and Fantasy: The Experiences of College Youth," *Journal of Youth and Adolescence* 1 (1972):203–222.
34. J. H. Gagnon and W. Simon, *Sexual Conduct* (Chicago: Aldine, 1973): R. A. Lewis and W. R. Burr, "Premarital Coitus and Commitment among College Students," *Archives of Sexual Behavior* 4 (1975):73–79.
35. Simon, Berger, and Gagnon, *op. cit.*
36. T. Nguyen, R. Jeslin, and N. L. Nguyen, "The Meanings of Touch," *Journal of Communication* 25 (1975):92–103.
37. Morrison et al., *op. cit.*
38. Ellen Sweet, "Date Rape: The Story of an Epidemic and Those who Deny It," *Ms.* (October 1985):56–59, 84–85.
39. *Ibid.*
40. *Ibid.*
41. Women's History Research Center, "Information on Date Rape," Women's History Research Center, Inc., 2325 Oak Street, Berkley, CA.
42. Sweet, *op. cit.*
43. Claude Lewis, "Date Rape is O.K., Grade Schoolers Say," *Philadelphia Inquirer* (May 3, 1988):A–3.
44. Susan Griffiths, "Rape, the All-American Crime," *Ramparts* 10 (1971):353–381.

45. Diane Hermann, "The Rape Culture," in Freeman, *op. cit.,* pp. 20–44.
46. Griffiths, *op. cit.*
47. Amir Menachem, *Patterns in Forcible Rape* (Chicago: University of Chicago Press, 1971).
48. Hermann, *op. cit.*
49. Robert Coles and Geoffrey Stokes, *Sex and the American Teenager* (New York: Harper & Row, 1985), pp. 72–80.
50. *Ibid.,* pp. 56–64.
51. *Ibid.,* pp. 44–49.
52. *Ibid.,* pp. 121–144.
53. *Ibid.*
54. "Teenagers and Birth Control," *Newsweek* (April 5, 1982):33; Judith Burns Jones and Susan Philliber, "Sexually Active but Not Pregnant: A Comparison of Teens Who Risk and Teens Who Plan," *Journal of Youth and Adolescence* 12 (1983):235–242; P. J. Milan and P. R. Kilmann, "Interpersonal Factors in Premarital Contraception," *Journal of Sex Research* 23 (1987):289–301.
55. Barbara Kantrowitz, Ann McDaniel, and Rick Kushman, "Teenagers and Abortion," *Newsweek* (October 12, 1987):81.
56. *Ibid.*
57. Nancy Friday, *My Mother, Myself* (New York: Dell, 1977).
58. Morrison et al., *op. cit.,* pp. 51–53.
59. Elizabeth Stark, "Young, Innocent and Pregnant," in *Readings in Social Problems, 1988/1989* (Guilford, Conn.: Dushkin Press, 1988), pp. 15–18.
60. *Ibid.*
61. "The AIDS Threat: Who's at Risk," *Newsweek* (March 14, 1988):42–52, excerpted from W. H. Masters, Virginia Johnson, and Robert Kilodny, *Crisis: Heterosexual Behavior in the Age of Aids* (New York: Grove Press, 1988): L. Carroll, "Concern with AIDS and the Sexual Behavior of College Students," *Journal of Marriage and the Family* (1988) 50:405–411; R. W. Winslow, "Student Knowledge of AIDS Transmission," *Sociology and Social Research* 72 (1988):110–113.
62. Morrison et al., *op. cit.,* pp. 159–160.
63. Craig Christensen, "Discrimination and Sexual Preference," in Jerome H. Skolnick and Elliott Currie, *Crisis in American Institutions,* 7th ed. (Boston: Scott, Foresman/Little, Brown, 1988), pp. 218–231.
64. Bernard E. Whitley, Jr., "The Relationship of Sex-Role Orientation to Heterosexuals' Attitudes toward Homosexuals," *Sex Roles* 17 (1987):103–113.
65. Gregory K. Lehne, "Homophobia among Men," in Deborah S. David and Robert Brannon, eds., *The Forty-Nine Percent Majority: The Male Sex Role* (Reading, Mass.: Addison-Wesley, 1976), p. 66.
66. *Ibid.* pp. 66–86.
67. Marshall, Forstein, "Homophobia: An Overview," *Psychiatric Annals* 18 (1988):33–36.
68. John C. Gonsiorek, "Mental Health Issues of Gay and Lesbian Adolescents," *Journal of Adolescent Health Care* 9 (1988):114–122.
69. Whitley, *op. cit.*
70. Georgene H. Seward, "Sex, Identity and the Social Order," in J. Bardwick, ed., *The Psychology of Women* (New York: Harper & Row, 1971), p. 153.

Part III

SOCIETAL INSTITUTIONS, NORMS, AND CONTROL

Owen Franken/Stock, Boston

Chapter 8

The Family Over the Life Cycle

Changes have been taking place in the American family that have profound consequences for gender roles. Consider the following statistics:

- Only 13 percent of all American families consist of a married couple in a first marriage and their own children in which the husband is the provider and the wife is a homemaker.
- In the majority of married couples (62 percent), both spouses are in the work force (52 percent of the mothers of preschool children work).
- More people are staying single longer, and more will stay single permanently.
- In 1984, there were nearly 2 million cohabiting households, more than three times the number that existed in 1970. By 1991, one-third of all women had cohabited at some time.
- There is roughly a 50 percent chance that people marrying today will divorce. However, the divorce rate has been declining slowly since 1980.
- About 75 percent of those divorcing will eventually remarry.
- In 1984, about 20 percent of white families and 59 percent of black families were headed by a single parent.
- Among children born in 1986, 23.4 percent were born to unmarried mothers.
- Among those who marry, many are remaining childless, having only one child, or delaying childbearing.
- About 60 percent of today's children will spend some time in a stepfamily, and in 1990, 15 percent of all families were stepfamilies.
- By the year 2030, almost one-fifth of the population will be over age 65, and this figure will include many older families.

One can see that the American family has changed dramatically from the "traditional" family consisting of two adults in a first marriage who have several children, with a working father and a homemaker mother. These changes are likely to continue and to accelerate in the future.

It is ironic that Americans have never quite accepted the changing family and tend to think of any variation of the traditional family as deficient or even deviant. In actuality, the traditional family of the American dream has often been just that: a dream or a myth. The cozy, large family of the past is usually a figment of our imagination. In reality, colonial families were often broken by death if not divorce, and remarriages were a necessity if people were to survive. While women had many children, those children often died soon after birth, and children 12 years old were usually sent out of the household to learn a trade. Violence in the family was not unusual, and in many ways family lives were much harder than they are today. Marriages tended to be for economic necessity, and love grew after marriage, if at all.

Yet the belief in the traditional family persists, and we keep trying to get back to the "good old days." The media push its desirability, and people who do not have such a family may believe that they have somehow failed.

As society has changed so dramatically in the last fifty years or so, it is inevitable that the family has changed as well. Yet in many ways the institution of marriage is one of the places where stereotyped masculine and feminine roles have changed the least.

In this chapter we shall look at how stereotyped masculine and feminine roles are intertwined with and emphasized by the institution of marriage. We will first look at how changing patterns of marriage influence gender roles and how these changing gender roles in turn influence the pattern of interaction within a marriage. We will examine how the institution of marriage influences the behavior of men and women and how the addition of children, the occupational roles of husband and wife, and other elements of reward and tension in a marriage influence gender roles.

STAYING SINGLE

As we examine male and female roles in the twenties age group, we are struck by the increase in the number of people in this group who are staying single. In 1970, 54.7 percent of the men and 35.8 percent of the women who were 20 to 24 were single; by 1986, 75.5 percent of these men and 57.9 percent of these women had not married. In the age group from 25 to 29 the trend is even more marked. In 1970, 19.1 percent of these men and 10.5 percent of these women remained single. By 1986, 41.4 percent of men age 25 to 29 and 28.1 percent of women in that age group had not married.[1]

However, the increase in people who have never married seems to represent a postponement of marriage rather than a denial of the institution. Among those who are 30 to 34, 9.4 percent of the men were single in 1970 and 22.2 percent were single in 1986. Among the women in that age group, 6.2 percent were single in 1970 and 14.2 percent had not married by 1986. For both men and women, the numbers remaining single until they were over 34 years of age had doubled. Among 35- to 39-year-olds, the increase in the number remaining single is much lower.[2] First marriage in this country now occurs about three years later than it did a generation ago. Men are traditionally a little older than women when they get married. For men the median age of marriage in 1988 was 25.9, and for women it was 23.6. We must remember, though, that the trend toward later marriage is not unusual. Later marriage is typical of what occurred in this country in its formative years and is typical of developed countries in general.

Will there be an increase in the number who stay single as well? Paul Glick says that projections of current population trends show an increase in those remaining single. Of those who were in the "marriage years" (20 to 29 years old) in 1950, only 3 to 4 percent have remained single. Predictions for those who were in that age group in 1980 show 10 percent of the men and 12 percent of the women remaining single. The possible tripling of people who remain single means that this country will be "changing from one of the developed countries with the smallest proportions never marrying to a country with one of the largest proportions never marrying."[3] It is likely that some increase in those remaining permanently single will occur. The longer young adults postpone marriage, the more likely they are to remain single.

Why are more young adults postponing marriage or staying single today? Ambivalence about marriage and fear of the destructiveness of divorce have pushed both men and women toward staying single. Sex is more easily, or at least openly, available to the single person today than it was to his or her parents. Birth control methods are now more available and more acceptable, so that fewer "shotgun" marriages occur. Instead of taking the leap into marriage, it is easier to postpone commitment by just living together; one can have an intimate relationship without the ties that bind. As couples also want fewer or no children, it is not as important to get officially married.

Women have been influenced to stay single by other developments as well. Because women now have more of an opportunity to engage in fulfilling careers, they have remained in school longer and subsequently have been more committed to their jobs and less willing to make concessions to get married. Better-educated men have always married a little later; now better-educated women are also postponing tying the knot. Women, at least those who were born during the baby boom years (1950 to 1965 or so), have also been victims of what is known as the **marriage squeeze**, which occurs because women traditionally marry men a few years older than themselves. As the numerous women of the baby boom generation seek mates, they are looking among a smaller group of slightly older men who were born before the baby boom. However, for women who are in their twenties now, this factor is not as important.

Increasing inflation has also made it difficult to settle down in a marriage. Houses are priced out of the range of many young couples, two incomes are often needed for necessities, and children become a postponed luxury.

However, there is more to this change than demographics. Jessie Bernard in "The Rise and Fall of the Good Provider Role"[4] and Barbara Ehrenreich in *The Hearts of Men*[5] attempt to explain the change in commitment that has taken place. Bernard points out that settling down and providing for a family were a sign of maturity for men before the 1960s and that being a breadwinner for a family was intimately associated with masculinity. Ehrenreich suggests that the hippies of the 1960s that questioned the establishment and traditional lifestyles changed this. People began to talk in terms of "inner selves" and "true meanings" rather than "duty." This sense of wanting to find an inner satisfaction beyond obligations pushed men away from the duties of the breadwinning role. The new literature on the type A personality and the health hazards confronting men in the workplace increased men's disillusionment with family breadwinning. Ehrenreich postulates that the media, especially magazines such as *Playboy*, stepped in to provide a different definition of masculinity: being hedonistic and sexual. She also points out that this change in male values—"the male revolt"—scared traditional women and resulted in an antifeminist backlash. Traditional women wanted to keep their men in breadwinner roles, but instead of attacking the men, they cast working women and feminists in the role of scapegoats.

Ann Swidler states that there is a fear of adulthood as well as commitment. To today's young person, commitment means shutting off the process of liberating personal growth. There is a fear of limiting oneself by merging with another person. She comments about this phenomenon:

> If the self can no longer find definition in a single set of adult commitments, a set of roles which consolidate identity, what can the self be? . . . [W]e have an ideal of the self cut off from meaningful connections to others. This is a model of human relationships in which people are not willing to take the risks of disappointment and defeat that inevitably accompany meaningful love or work.[6]

We can see that American young people are staying single longer or permanently for a number of reasons. Personal fears about commitment and the work of adulthood are aided and abetted by demographic changes, particularly women entering the work force, and keep both sexes away from the altar.

Influences of Longer Singlehood on Gender-Role Behavior

As women stay single longer, get more education, and work in varied and demanding careers, it is likely they will become more independent and assertive. Certainly they will not have to depend on others to support them and will not feel that fulfillment comes only from marriage. They are likely to be willing to sacrifice a career for marriage only if they can get a truly equal marriage.

Men who have lived alone have had more time to practice domestic chores. Perhaps they have had time to develop friendships with other men and women in a way they would not have done if married. However, there is little indication that most of these men are ready to enter an equal marriage arrangement.[7]

Ehrenreich's analysis is particularly pessimistic. She sees men abandoning emotional responsibility toward women at the same time that they have abandoned the idea of financially supporting women. However, there is still an expectation of female nurturance and submissive service, and women do not earn wages that enable them to support families on their own.[8]

LIVING TOGETHER

As greater social approval makes **cohabitation** easier, many men and women are opting for living together before or instead of marriage. The number of living-together couples has risen from 523,000 in 1970 to 2,590,000 in 1988, increasing about 15 percent a year.[9]

Even if that growth rate slows, it is likely that the number of cohabiting couples will continue to increase during the 1990s. Some researchers have suggested that cohabitation is now institutionalized and is an intermediate step between dating and marriage. This step is available for people considering remarriage as well as those considering a first marriage.[10] The kind of living-together relationship varies, however, with the age of those involved. Sixty-three percent of those who live in a romantic relationship with someone of the other sex are under 35, and 18 percent are under 25.[11] Among college students, approximately 25 percent of the undergraduate population have cohabited and 50 percent more say they would do so if they found an appropriate relationship. For younger college students, cohabitation does not necessarily mean a commitment to marry, although it does imply a strong, affectionate, usually monogamous relationship. It is usually drifted into, not planned. College students see this kind of relationship as a way to develop real intimacy with another person and to grow and test themselves. While the average length of such relationships is only four and a half months, students usually feel they have benefited from the relationship. Many of the younger group who cohabit, however, are not college students; data show that 43 percent are working-class. For this group, economic necessity, along with the desire to test an intimate relationship, may pull couples into cohabitation.

For the age group in the middle and late twenties, cohabitation seems to have a slightly different meaning. For some, it is a way to test a relationship and see if they want to get married; for others, it is a more or less permanent alternative to marriage. In this age group, the hopes of men and women may diverge. Men may prefer to continue the relationship without stronger ties; women may hope that it will be a step toward a traditional marriage with children.

Among those in all age groups who cohabit, 53 percent have never been married, 35 percent are divorced, 4 percent are widowed, and the rest are separated. In one study, three of ten cohabiting couples had children in the household.[12]

Cohabitation is also common among the elderly. Because of economic necessity, it is often an alternative to marriage. A widow who remarries will lose her previous husband's Social Security allowance, and the new couple may not be able to live without it.

How does cohabitation affect gender-role attitudes? It seems to be those who are more liberal in their social attitudes and values who cohabit. Contrary to what might be expected, however, these individuals are not more androgynous in their sex-role orientations or more equalitarian in the sharing of labor than married couples are.[13]

People who have cohabited and then married also seem to have problems similar to those of people who have not lived together before marriage. The same degree of satisfaction, conflict, egalitarianism, and emotional closeness has been noted in most studies. Only in one study were differences found between couples who had cohabited before marriage and those who had not. The differences were interesting in terms of gender roles as they included more willingness to disagree about things such as finances and housework and the fact that the spouses were not as dependent on each other. In this study, those who had cohabited did not depend on marriage to be such a large part of their lives—they had other interests and friends.[14]

At least two studies indicate that cohabitation is not a guarantee of marital bliss. One of the studies, which included older students as well as college students, showed that the marital adjustment scores of couples who had cohabited before marriage were slightly lower than those of couples who had not lived together.[15] Another study has shown that those who cohabited with a marriage partner before marriage are more likely to divorce than are those who did not. Eleanor Macklin points out that this finding probably derives from the nature of persons who are willing to cohabit in the first place (less traditional, not willing to make an immediate strong commitment) rather than from any finding that cohabitation predisposes to divorce.[16]

LOVE AND MARRIAGE

Many people do not realize that most marriages throughout history, including our own historical past, were not based on love. Marriages were arranged for economic necessity or to cement relationships between various groups. In spite of the romantic ideal in our culture, many marriages continue to emphasize security and/or companionship rather than love. In Cuber and Harroff's description of five kinds of marriage, 80 percent were "utilitarian" in nature.[17] In particular, many couples had a "passive-congenial" type of marriage in which they did not marry for love or expect much love in the marriage. Others had a "devitalized" marriage which once had an intimate emotional relationship but lost it to the rigors of married life and the passage of time. Still others were "conflict-habituated," or centered on fighting. Only in "vital" and "total" marriages did the couples have a real emotional bond. However, only 20 percent of the marriages were found to be vital—to contain an ongoing, real emotional commitment—or total, with the couple totally absorbed in each other.

AMERICAN MARRIAGES: A MYTH OF EQUALITY

Some people believe that **norms** about equality of persons in the United States extend into the institution of marriage and mean that husband and wife are more nearly equal in this country than they are in many others. We will not attempt a cross-cultural comparison, but we should determine whether the supposed equality of American marriages does in fact exist. What *is* equality? One way to think of equality in marriage is in terms of the division of work and the ability to make decisions.

Differences in Power

Equality, Power, and Resources. Several well-known sociologists have proposed that equality of roles depends on equality of *power,* or the ability to achieve one's desires in the face of opposition from others. They also believe that such power, or the ability to tell who what to do in what circumstances, is one of the main issues in marital satisfaction.[18] Blood and Wolfe believe that power in turn is based on resources. They define **resources** as anything brought to the marriage that enables one and one's family to satisfy needs. Thus, resources can consist of money, education, attractiveness, social status, or even the ability to be a good hostess.[19]

The concept of power based on resources requires some qualifications. First, how do we measure power? In the 1960s Blood and Wolfe measured power by determining who makes the decisions in such areas as what job the husband should take, what car to get, where to go on vacation, whether the wife should work, what doctor to call when someone is sick, and what to fix for dinner. However, there are difficulties with this type of measurement. For one thing, these decisions are not all equal in importance. A decision about a husband's job is much more important than one about where to go on vacation. Some decisions are made frequently, while others are made only once in a while. In addition, there are different levels of decision making. For example, who makes the decision about whether to go on a vacation at all so that someone else can make the decision about where to go?[20] There are also different kinds of power to be measured, such as coercive power, expert power, and reward power.

A more recent study confirmed that economic power is the key variable in the power balance within a marital relationship but also looked at "discount factors," which essentially boil down to (1) the structural variables or institutional values that may repress women and keep them from equaling the economic contributions of their spouses, (2) the sex-role ideology of a couple and its particular reference groups (younger couples have reference groups that support a more equalitarian ideology), (3) the attractiveness of the partner, (4) how interested each person is in maintaining the marriage (those who are less interested have more power), and (5) the husband's perception of the need for the wife's income. Blumberg and Coleman also suggest that whether a couple is in a state of stability or change influences power. For example, a husband may feel threatened and reassert power if the wife's income suddenly rises to equal or surpass his own.[21]

In addition to power, there are other important aspects of decision making. Scanzoni and colleagues[22] looked at the decision-making process and the kind of control[23] each spouse has (possibly reflecting verbal abilities or implied use of physical force). In addition, there is the question of how important each particular issue is to a spouse.[24] Finally, there are intangible variables such as self-esteem and self-confidence, respect from others, and self-assertiveness. Blumberg and Coleman propose that the working wife not only brings in economic resources but also gains in intangible esteem variables that enable her to assert her will.[25]

Women's traditional resources have been physical attractiveness, home-making and mothering skills, and sometimes the social status they bring to a marriage. Men still value attractiveness in women and consider it important to have an attractive wife who will aid them in their career climb. A 1987 study showed that wives' physical attractiveness was a strong determinant of husbands' sexual interest and even faithfulness, while the husbands' physical attractiveness did not affect the wives in the same way.[26]

Wives have a difficult time equaling the resources of their husbands in other ways. Traditionally, men have always had an edge in possessing the most usable resources. They are older than their wives, are physically stronger and can threaten to use force, usually have greater income (only 11 percent of working wives make more than their husbands),[27] and usually have more education. They also have the advantages of social status outside the home, social contacts and interaction at work, and the ability to find an attractive alternative to marriage more easily than their wives can. In addition, men's dominance is guaranteed by the legal system as well as by cultural norms about men "wearing the pants" in the family.

While wives may wield informal, manipulative power, they may not be willing to use this power if it threatens the marriage.[28] Even children are not a resource for the wife. On the contrary, they detract from her power and make her more dependent on her husband.

However, wives today are likely to have more resources than they did in the past. They are likely to be closer in age to their husbands, to have an equal education, and to have greater incomes than they had in the past. Roughly 60 percent of all wives now work outside the home, and they usually gain some power from contributing to family resources, especially when their income is needed. Their work outside the home may also increase their status, their social skills, and even their attractiveness when they "dress for the office." Their self-confidence is likely to increase, and their need for approval and attention is likely to decrease. They are more likely to have an attractive alternative to marriage in a career, with the possibility of supporting themselves in a single life or cohabitation. In addition, modern gender-role ideology may support a wife's having a greater share in decision-making power.

The alternative of working and supporting herself is a particularly important resource for a woman. It gives her options she could not consider if she were dependent on the support of her husband. It is important to recognize, however, that the position of a single woman may still be difficult in our culture and that a career may not be a sufficiently attractive alternative to marriage for many women. If women are married and employed, they seldom earn as much as their husbands. If they divorce, their standard of living is likely to decrease considerably.[29]

Kranichfeld has criticized the resource model of marital power. She believes that women actually have more power within the family in terms of influencing children and keeping kin ties together and that power would be better defined as the capacity to influence others.[30]

Kranichfeld's point about the skewed emphasis on male power resources that come from outside the family is well taken, and a woman's power base within the family may be very important in terms of influencing other human lives and keeping close ties with children as the parents age. Acock and Bengtson found, for example, that mothers rather than fathers consistently influence their children's ideologies and behaviors.[31] However, in the short run women are probably disadvantaged in terms of marital power and may have to struggle to have their voices heard, to get leisure time, and in the case of marital breakup, to support themselves.

Why Discuss Power? The discussion of power makes it sound as though all marriages were battles, with people fighting for every scrap of authority. Of course this is not true. Considerations of power may be outweighed by respect, concern for the needs of others, and love and loyalty. However, power is always an underlying factor in a marriage. Its influence may surface only in times of conflict, but both partners are aware of their underlying power positions. These positions strongly influence gender roles.

Decision Making and Division of Labor

Usually decision-making power in a family changes toward the equalitarian model before the division of labor does. There seem to be many reasons for this. To paraphrase the argument of Scanzoni and Fox in their review of sex-role literature in the 1970s, **preference and process** are interwoven in such a way that some behaviors change more rapidly than others do. They believe that a questioning of traditional gender-role arrangements and preferences is taking place. This questioning causes potential conflict because some arrangements can no longer be taken for granted, but behavior is not changing as rapidly as preferences are because many people—especially women—do not wish to engage in conflict to change behavior. Nevertheless, some behavioral change is taking place because norms are changing. Thus, if men believe that they should listen to their wives and give them a voice in decision making and the wives believe that they should have such a voice, the decision-making process may change even though the wife's power has not really changed.[32] However, while women increasingly prefer to work outside the home, neither men nor women have significantly changed their preference for doing household work. Thus, the division of household tasks remains more traditional than does the power to make decisions.

Approximately 80 percent of husbands and wives believe that child care should be shared equally, and 50 percent believe that housework should be split as well.[33] In actuality, women do two to three times as much as men, usually about 70 percent of the work. They also take almost full responsibility for deciding what needs to be done and dividing up the work.[34] Almost every source agrees that wives typically do much more than husbands.[35] Berk found that only men whose wives were employed full-time and whose families included many small children did equal family work (about 10 percent of all husbands).[36] In general, men do so little in the way of housework that Miller and Garrison have called studies measuring such work "much ado about nothing."[37] Some research claims that men are doing more, and other studies say that husbands' contributions have not changed. Pleck believes that husbands have increased their share of family work from about 20 percent to 30 percent.[38] A 1986 study reports, however, that husbands' time in child care and housework did not change between 1965 and 1975 even though husbands worked fewer hours in the paid labor force.[39] A 1987 study concluded that husbands do about as much now as they did in the last century.[40]

Men are more likely to do nonroutine household work such as household repairs and outside chores, and women are more likely to do the daily repetitive tasks.[41] When they help with domestic chores, men are most willing to share cooking and child care, which happen to be the activities that women most enjoy.[42] They are more likely to play with children, while mothers are more likely to handle the practical activities of feeding and dressing.

Women and men also experience household work differently. Women are more likely to see family work as a test of their worth[43] and to be anxious about it. However, they also see it as mixed with love and as a part of the family ties.[44] They may not mind taking care of family members even though they do not like the actual activities. Women are also more likely to do family work alone and to find it isolating.[45]

Whether a wife works outside the home does not seem to have a great effect on the family work a husband does. Husbands with employed wives spend the same amount of time in housework as husbands whose wives are full-time homemakers.[46] However, as employed wives do less than full-time homemakers do, the percentage of family work that husbands do in two-worker families actually increases. When they do help, husbands with working wives are more likely to help with child care.[47]

The number of hours worked by each of the spouses does not seem to affect the division of labor, nor does the money earned by a working wife.[48] Even when wives earn more than their husbands, the division of labor does

Reprinted with special permission of King Features Syndicate, Inc.

not change.[49] In fact, wives are likely to step back and not use the power they have gained. The one variable that seems to influence whether husbands of employed wives participate more in family work is whether the wives' income is seen as necessary. Husbands who feel their wives' income is necessary even if they are ambivalent about her working and husbands who see their wives as coproviders do more family work.[50]

There are some differences in husbands' helping behavior by class and by race. Middle-class husbands believe that the wife is working for her own fulfillment and think of themselves as unselfish for supporting her.[51] They are thus reluctant to help much around the house, although many couples in this group can afford to hire help. Working-class wives may get less help than others do. Blue-collar men who earn higher incomes are less accepting of their wives working outside the home. Those whose wives are employed may resist doing housework because they feel that their identity as a provider is already threatened by their wives' work. These women may accept traditional roles, and they know that they must stay married as their income would not support a family.[52] Many black men see the earnings of their wives as essential[53] and are thus more willing to help with family work, especially child care.

Expectations are important predictors of which roles will be performed. In particular, husbands' expectations of how work should be divided are powerful predictors of what would be done. One study showed that perceptions of a partner's expectations significantly influence a spouse's role performance and that the husband's expectations in particular are powerful predictors of how housework is divided.[54] Men were more satisfied with their marriages and less critical of their wives when the wives did more than their "fair share" around the house.[55] However, wives whose husbands did their fair share were happier.[56] In fact, employment brings more well-being for wives only when their husbands pitch in.[57]

In general, one-fourth to one-third of wives feel that the division of labor is unfair.[58] Why don't more wives complain? Their expectations seem to be so low that they are satisfied with even minimal help; women also may be ambivalent about pushing for help if it leads to family conflict, and wives may be unhappy about giving up power in the one area of their lives where they have control.[59] A 1986 study shows that marriage partners often do not want to give up their traditional gender roles even though they may be willing to participate in the work of the other sex. Husbands may be reluctant to help if they are criticized for doing it poorly.[60]

Thus, many factors influence the division of labor in the home, including perceived traditional or more modern roles for men and women that vary by age, class, and race; the need for the wife's earnings; and the need for the husband's help. It is clear that many husbands are still unhappy about their wives working outside the home and are not eager to share labor inside the home whether or not their wives are employed. Wives still do 70 percent of the household work and take 90 percent of the responsibility for seeing that it is done.

Why the Difference between Decision Making and Division of Labor?

Why are men more willing to grant decision-making power to women than to help around the house? Why are women willing to engage in conflict about decisions rather than conflict about household chores? It seems that the answers are rooted in the American historical past. There is a tradition in this country that all *men* are created equal. This is interpreted to mean all "persons," and while it is seldom lived up to in practice, the concept of men and women as equals in making decisions is still operative in our democratic political tradition. However, no tradition holds that men and women should do equal work, and certainly none states that they should do the same work. In our historical past, women and men have done different and unequal work.

Determining what is men's work and what is women's work is also tied directly to gender roles. As we have seen, people are defined as masculine or feminine in accordance with the tasks they perform. Many women have learned that it is feminine to do child-care tasks, cook, sew, and even do housework. They may feel their femininity is reaffirmed when they bake bread or make dresses for their daughters. They also may have learned that women who do not do these things or who ask men to do them may be thought of as not quite feminine. Judith Laws has described the mystique of the housewife role. It becomes an extension of love, and therefore it is not permissible to analyze it as an exchange of labor. If a woman does not do these tasks for her husband and children, it may be assumed that she does not love them.[61]

In contrast, most men have been socialized to believe that it is not masculine to do things women do. *They* are not masculine if they do them! The mythology says it is all right for a man to help out with the dishes or baby-sit, but if he is directly responsible for any household work or child care, his self-definition of being masculine may be threatened. It is no accident that men choose cooking or grocery shopping as the household chore they are most willing to perform. Great male chefs have an esteemed profession, but great housecleaners do not. (Needless to say, housecleaning is also less desirable work.) The norms are enforced by peer group pressure. Even men with good intentions can be teased out of those intentions by their friends. Researchers have shown that lack of social support is an important factor in preventing men with equalitarian attitudes from changing their behavior in regard to helping in the house.[62]

Several other considerations also enter the picture. Men may have a vested interest in continuing women's personalized services at home so that the men can be free to pursue their careers. Also, housework is not valued labor, and no one wants to do work that is not valued. General housework is seldom exciting, fulfilling, or creative, and so there is not a natural incentive to do it. In addition, each sex has had more practice at doing certain tasks and may feel more comfortable doing them. Even with good intentions, both sexes have blind spots when it comes to the traditional areas of the work of the other gender. A man may not notice the dust in the living room, and a woman may not notice that the lawn needs to be fertilized. Ultimately, each knows that society will blame the traditional sex if that chore goes undone. People are not likely to enter a home and think that John sure is a lousy housekeeper no matter how the chores are actually divided.

The division of labor has changed little in most families. Feelings about doing gender-appropriate work, comfort with familiar roles, and societal pressure keep labor in traditional molds. In reviewing the literature, Scanzoni and Fox say that the following conclusions emerge from research on this question: (1) Wives continue to have prime responsibility for the organization and functioning of the family, (2) the employment status of wives only minimally affects husbands' participation in domestic tasks, (3) the length of a woman's day increases at the expense of her leisure and sleep time, (4) the aggregate amount of family time spent in housework decreases when the wife works (it is unclear whether this is because of an increase in efficiency, a decrease in standards, or both), and (5) to some extent the participation of older children in domestic tasks increases when the wife works.[63]

Decision making and the division of labor are not the only areas where traditional gender roles may strain a marriage. Jessie Bernard shows how some of the different perceptions that cause difficulties relate to gender roles. In *The Future of Marriage*, she shows that men and women perceive marriage differently. When a couple are asked questions about marital problems or decisions or even about specific mathematical counts of how much sexual activity they have had in the last month, the man and the woman answer so differently that Bernard has termed their marriage the "his" marriage and the "her" marriage. In general, the differences show that men seem to be happier in marriage than women and that marriage is actually better for them.[64]

The "His" Marriage

You may be surprised by that last sentence. This culture has generally believed that a woman is "better dead than unwed" and that she therefore chases a man until she catches him. Conversely, we believe that bachelors are lucky, happy men who avoid marriage at all costs until they are trapped into it. Contrary to these societal beliefs, however, it is the man who seems to be the happiest in marriage and to benefit the most from it. Insurance companies have known for years that married men are better risks than single men: They live longer, are healthier, have fewer accidents, are much less likely to commit suicide, have better mental health, are less likely to commit crimes, make higher incomes, and report themselves as being happier than any other group. They are twice as likely as their wives to say they would marry the same person again, and when widowed or divorced, they remarry quickly.[65]

In contrast, the lively, happy bachelor has a terrible record: "In general the 3,320,000 male single workers hardly earned enough to feed themselves and buy *Playboy*, let alone follow its philosophy."[66] They have poorer physical and mental health than married men do, are more likely to be in mental or penal institutions, and are much more likely to commit suicide. They seem to have a difficult time building and keeping friendship networks, at least in comparison to single women.[67] By comparison, the married man is in much better shape and seems to prefer to be married.[68] While health and accident statistics are still unfavorable for single men, a 1988 study shows that they report increased happiness from the past.[69] The authors suggest that changes such as increases in premarital sex and nonmarital cohabitation have weakened the benefits of being married. Greater social acceptance of single adults may also be a factor in the increased happiness of the nonmarried.

The "Her" Marriage

What about the married woman? Bernard says that she starts out with some advantages that marriage reverses. Women, both single and married, have much better physical health than men and live longer. However, in comparison to their single sisters, married women have poor mental health. Married women report much higher rates of anxiety, phobia, and depression than any other group except single men. Marriage does not protect them as much from suicide as it does their husbands. They do not make incomes that are as good as those of their single counterparts, have fewer friends, and report themselves as being much less happy. When a husband and wife are interviewed about their marriage, the wife is likely to say that the problems in it are more numerous, started sooner, and are more severe. Wives are also only half as likely as husbands to say that they would marry the same person again. Indeed, only half of married women say they would marry the same person again. Ironically, many of the same wives report their marriages as happy.[70] However, between 1972 and 1986, there was a significant decline in the reported happiness of married women.[71] Perhaps these women realized the problems they were facing and were more likely to admit their discontent about the structure of the married role

Why are married women so much less happy than their husbands and their single sisters? If it were a matter of gender alone, we would certainly expect single women, who are not only female but stigmatized as being unwanted and unchosen, to be less happy, yet single women seem to cope better than married women. Conversely, married women seem to fare more poorly in marriage than their husbands do. What kinds of constraints does the institution of marriage impose that change the happiness of women but not that of men?

We have seen that employed wives may carry an unfair burden of household work. Jessie Bernard also points out that women who become wives in this culture frequently lose legal and personal identities and, if not employed, become dependent. This dependence may lead to depression. In fact, Bernard asserts that housewives are among the most depressed group in the country. As we have noted, they exhibit much higher rates of dysfunctional mental symptoms such as anxiety, paranoia, and phobias than do either men or single women.[72] In a national study of mental health, Walter Gove corroborates

Bernard's findings and hypothesizes that the structure of the marital role leads to women's depression. In particular, he mentions that the expectations for women's roles are unclear and that this ambiguity creates anxiety for many women. If women are housewives, they may find themselves in a low-status job without structure and dependent on their husbands, and even when married women work, they may not have the status and salary of their husbands.[73] Other, more recent studies have confirmed these ideas.[74]

The Shock Theory of Marriage

Bernard takes Gove's hypothesis and elaborates it in what she calls the "shock theory" of marriage. She describes some of the legal, social, and personal changes that occur in women's lives when they become wives. In most instances the changes can be divided into three main categories of problems: (1) changes that create dependence in women, (2) changes that affect women's success or self-esteem, and (3) the nature of the housewife role. We see in these problems an elaboration of Nielsen's thesis (Chapter 1) that the structure of society's institutions creates gender-role behaviors.

Changes That Create Dependence: Becoming a Legal Nonentity. Many of the changes that create dependence in women are legal in nature. When a woman marries, she gives up a good portion of her legal identity as an individual. As one lawyer put it, "The wife and husband are assumed to be one and that one is the husband." A more elaborate version of that notion states:

> Whatever may be the reason of the law, the rule is maintained, that the legal existence of the wife is merged in that of the husband, so that, in law, the husband and wife are one person.
>
> The husband's dominion over the person and property of the wife is fully recognized. She is utterly incompetent to contract in her own name. He is entitled to her society and her service; to her obedience and her property. . . .
>
> In consideration of his marital rights the husband is bound to furnish the wife a home and suitable support.[75]

Specifically, what does this mean? First, it means that traditionally the husband has been the legal head of the family in most states. He has had the legal authority to determine the family's standard of living, including the allowance for the wife and the kind of house that is lived in; the child-rearing method; and household management. He must support his wife, but it is he who decides what the level of support should be. The courts have refused to intervene even when husbands with plentiful resources have let their wives be undernourished and underclothed. Second, in the past a wife was supposed to provide services as a companion and housekeeper without compensation. In return, she was *not entitled* to a share of the family assets, including the property, or even an allowance. The courts presumed that all household goods were the husband's even if the wife had, through her service, enabled him to buy them. Until the late 1800s wives could not sue in court, enter into contracts, or own or control their own property. Some states still limit women's rights in this regard, although the Married Women's Property Act in the late 1800s gave women the right to own and control their own property, including their earnings from outside employment.[76] A woman can do little to change this situation. Even marital contracts entered into by a married couple have not been enforced by the courts. A wife has few ways of enforcing the provision that her husband support her, since it is he, as head of the household, who determines the level of support. As the Citizen's Advisory Council on the Status of Women summed up the case, "a married woman living with her husband can, in practice, get only what he chooses to give her."[77] Even community property laws do not help because the husband has control of the use and disposal of the community property funds.[78] The homemaker's dependence is further increased by other legal considerations that make women dependent on their husbands' health insurance, pension funds, and Social Security.[79]

While the U.S. Bureau of the Census now lets either spouse be declared the head of the household and legal decisions have improved women's legal status vis-à-vis property and contracts, tradition still persists. As we will see, it influences current court decisions, including those involving divorce.

Dependence has insidious effects. A person who is dependent on another person for "daily handouts" or decisions about general welfare loses a sense of control over her life and experiences anxiety, depression, frustration, and stress. Even when a devoted husband gives a wife everything she wants, she is still taking handouts and has no assurance that they will continue and no sense of management of her own life. She is even more helpless because getting out of the marriage may reduce her income as well as her social status.

Even for a woman who has her own source of external support, as many women now do, there are still legal traps. For example, wives who have their own income may have their credit reported separately, but many do not know this and end up without a credit rating if they divorce.[80]

Changes That Affect Self-Esteem.   A married woman may find that her status has changed in terms of social interaction. Vendors of appliances, cars, and sporting goods who previously paid attention to her may defer to her husband as though she did not exist. At social events, her husband's opinion may be solicited about politics or economics. Although she may have been a bright political science major, she is asked, "What does John think about the election?" If she is not working outside the home, she may find no social confirmation of her skills and intelligence.

A wife may also find that her husband is one who determines the interests and friends of the family. He may keep playing baseball and bowling, but she is likely to give up her skiing if he doesn't ski. Studies show that wives adjust their patterns of behavior to those of their husbands. In a similar fashion, she may see her friends for lunch, but it his friends they entertain for dinner. Married women consistently report fewer friends than do their single counterparts.[81] If the couple moves frequently, her only friends may be the wives of her husband's office colleagues, and she will lose these friends if she loses her husband.

Finally, another factor enters into the picture: that of the *sources* of self-esteem for women. Bernard suggests that most young women are used to receiving a good proportion of their self-esteem from the admiration and approval of others, particularly men. When they marry, they are not likely to send out "available" kinds of vibrations. They may also mute their sexuality and wear their necklines higher and their skirts longer as society and their husbands believe befits a wife and mother. As this happens, the attention they get from other men is likely to diminish. Married women often do not realize why this has happened and feel they are getting fat or need new clothes. As women are trained to find their self-esteem in the approval of others, lack of approval may be a substantial element in a new wife's discomfort, although she may not be aware of its source.[82]

The Nature of the Housewife Role.   Thus far we have looked at legal changes in the status of women and changes in the sources of their self-esteem. Married women who do not work may also be unhappy and frustrated because of the nature of the housewife role. Compared to most housewives, married women who work outside the home report themselves as being more satisfied and happier.

While women who work outside the home gain resources and power, the trade-offs in tension and stress seem to cancel out at least some of these benefits. Thus, something about the nature of the housewife's role may make women unhappy. If we look at the role, we can certainly see elements that cause distress. A young woman with small children may be isolated in her home. She may not have a car at her disposal, may not have funds to pay a baby-sitter, and may have little chance to get out, be with adults, and do things. Solitary confinement is considered a punishment in prison, and confinement with small children may be punitive as well. Her isolation may also lead her to depend excessively on her husband for companionship and emotional support. His approval and his interaction with her may be tremendously important to her, and she may become depressed if they are not forthcoming.

As we saw above, the housewife's *work* is also a source of distress: It has low status, it is not paid, and it is never really done but just done enough to be done over. It has also been pointed out that the housewife's work is interrupted by the demands of her schedule so that she often has to go from activity to activity without finishing any of them. People who are unable to finish activities are left without a sense of completion or fulfillment.[83] Labor-saving devices have not decreased the number of hours spent on housework. The housewife is also more likely to spend time chauffeuring the children and participating in community affairs.[84]

The phrase "just a housewife" may also describe a married woman's feelings about what she does. Her work is noticed only if it is not done, and it is seldom valued when it is done. She must go way beyond the boundaries of the ordinary to achieve recognition as a "gourmet cook," "marvelous seamstress," or "wonderful hostess." Even here, there is little possibility for growth or advancement. It is certainly true that society gives housework little status. In Great Britain, for example, housework is legally *not* defined as work because no wages or salary are received for it.[85] Oakley points out that housework is the most disliked aspect of the housewife role. In her study, women reported the job as monotonous, fragmented, and isolating, although they appreciated the ability to regulate their own time. Women who had the financial resources to counteract the boredom and loneliness of the housewife role did not report the same discontent, however.[86]

We have painted the bleakest possible picture. Not all young housewives live far from others and suffer from lack of companionship. Many enjoy at least some of the tasks associated with the housewife role and the control it gives them over their time. Others escape housework by hiring outside help. If these women do not work outside the home, however, they still suffer the personal and legal consequences of being dependent.

As we have shown, their sisters who combine outside jobs and housework may escape much of the dependence, but they usually end up doing the better part of two full-time jobs. Wives who were employed full-time were reported to spend approximately sixty to seventy hours a week in work inside and outside the home.[87] Many report no leisure time at all. This dual burden reduces their ability to compete in the work world. (We will look at some of the consequences of this dual burden in Chapter 10.) For now, suffice it to say that for women who cannot afford to hire household help and who must do almost all of the housework and child care on top of another job, this dual burden is a crippling one.

Are Wives Employed Outside the Home Happier?   With this dual burden, how do working wives fare in terms of satisfaction? Most studies say that a woman who does what she wants to do in terms of working outside the home is the happiest. Yet most wives who work outside the home report themselves as being happier than housewives, even though the demands on them are greater. The main reasons for this seem to be the enhanced self-esteem of working wives and their greater ability to have social contact with others. They are also doing work that is valued; no matter what kind of work it is, it is paid, whereas housework is not. They have control over resources of their own; they are not dependent. Wives who work outside the home also get more decision-making power, specifically the ability to make large, far-reaching decisions.[88] Working wives seem to gain power relative to their husbands. They are more satisfied with their marriages and get along better with their spouses,[89] and they report better mental and physical health than housewives do.[90]

We must be careful to distinguish between women who "just have a job" and women who have a satisfying career. For many women in difficult, dead-end, low-paying jobs, the idea of staying home may be very attractive.

What Is the Solution to Problems in the "Her" Marriage?

What is the significance of all this? Is the structure of marriage so bad for women that they should avoid it? Obviously, this is not a feasible solution.

While the trend seems to be that women are staying single longer and while more women are staying single permanently, most still want to get married. They still want to have legitimate children, and they want the level of intimate emotional involvement symbolized by marriage. They also want companionship and more control over social interaction in this "couples society" than they can get as single women.

Is the solution that every woman should work outside the home and have her own funds so that she will not be dependent? This may be a solution for many women, but it is unrealistic for others. Some women like housework and the associated tasks of the housewife's role, and others want to stay home with their children, especially when the children are young.

In addition, it may be difficult for women in traditional marriages to work outside the home. As the provider role is an extension of "masculinity," many men express discomfort when that role is threatened. Few men are delighted at the prospect of sharing household duties with a working wife. Some husbands of wives who work outside the home express dissatisfaction with their marriages, their health, and even their jobs. Even though they communicate more with their wives and are in general agreement with them, they do not perceive themselves to be as happy as are the husbands of women who stay home.[91] However, more recent studies show that the benefits accruing to couples in which the wife is in the labor force outweigh the disadvantages. Men report a feeling of relief that they are not solely responsible for the support of the family. They also report that their working wives are more interesting people and more fun to be with[92] and that the family has greater resources and flexibility.

The message in regard to gender roles is clear. People who participate in work that is valued and fulfilling are happier, particularly if they have a support system to do other things for them. Those who are forced into dependent positions and made to live vicariously through the accomplishments of others have little self-esteem and are likely to be unhappy. This lack of happiness is not a matter of gender. When roles are reversed and men do the jobs that many housewives do, they too are unhappy.[93]

Thus, the solution does not lie in reversing roles. Nor can the problem of overly demanding or frustrating marriage roles be solved simply by sharing traditional kinds of labor between both sexes. It sounds ideal to have both sexes share the burden of providing and the frustration of housework, but it may be unrealistic for some couples given the way the economic world is structured. Later on we will see how dual-career couples manage.

This solution is probably the one most likely to be tried in the near future, as it is the one over which individual couples have the most control. Many women may insist on shared work before they will even consider marriage. As their monetary contribution to the household is more and more needed, they will have the power to enforce change in the direction they wish. Men may also be more willing to share the housework when they find themselves relieved of some of the stresses and strains of producing enough income to support a family.

Changing the Values Implied in Different Kinds of Work

Perhaps the best way to encourage change in the definitions of masculine work and feminine work and to encourage both sexes to enjoy all kinds of endeavors is to change the value placed upon work and the opportunities to do it. As "masculine-style" participation in the labor force is already valued, it seems that the way to achieve a more equitable valuation is to increase the value placed upon housework. The Swedes have partially solved the dilemma by recognizing that housework makes a valuable contribution to the economy. Sweden pays housewives and househusbands and gives them two weeks' paid vacation a year. The government also arranges for couples to have rotating work shifts so that husbands can share household and child-care duties. Either partner can take maternity or paternity leave or take time off from work for sick children. While any change that challenges general cultural norms is difficult to implement and the Swedes do not claim to have all the answers, their approach seems to be a logical solution to changing values regarding housework.[94]

Oakley points out the potential for similar change in this country. Housewives as a group are dissatisfied with their tasks and working conditions. There even seems to be some degree of class consciousness, such as that manifested by the current International Wages for Housework Movement (IWHM). People in this movement demand that the government pay housewives for their work and award them back pay for years of past labor. Adherents of IWHM argue that housework is really an aggregation of services, such as cooking, waitressing, chauffeuring, and janitorial work, that are paid when done outside the marriage tie, and they reject the idea that housework should be an unpaid service or an extension of the love of a woman for her family.[95] The Displaced Homemaker Movement demands support for divorced women who have devoted unpaid labor to their families for years and are left after divorce without a source of self-support. Alice Cook has proposed legislation that would compensate women for the advantages given up during their child-raising years.[96] There is also a trend in court cases now to recognize the contributions of housewives to their husbands' success and to award them portions of the husbands' future earnings if they divorce.

There is much to be said for paying for housework. It would not only reduce the dependence of the "housespouse" on the provider but also raise the status and self-esteem of those engaged in this work. It is likely that the work could then be shared more equally between the genders. Housewives would not necessarily be isolated in an all-female world. A spin-off from the entry of more men into housework is that its esteem would probably be increased. Studies show that college students downgrade the esteem of an occupation when the proportion of women in it increases, and it is likely that the prestige of an occupation will increase as men participate more fully. Of course, there are the difficult questions of how housework should be valued (by the job? by hours of labor? at what rate?) and who should pay the housewife (her husband? the government?).

There has been a proliferation of companies that do housework for pay. One of them, Molly Maid, is among the fastest-growing and most profitable service-oriented corporations in the United States. The commercialization of housework may mean that it will get some status at last. Another interesting part of this trend is that many young men work as housecleaners in these companies.

This trend and others may modify ideas about what kinds of work are masculine. Another possibility is that as the breadwinner role declines, masculinity may not be linked as forcibly to economic achievement. The ethic of hard work seems to have been modified. People are enjoying leisure now and not feeling guilty about it; they are not willing to work and slave for an undefined future. This is not true of the majority of young men, and the work ethic may return with hard economic times, but some modification of the desire to work hard and achieve seems to have occurred. In addition, as more women enter occupations, paid work may not be defined as masculine. Work may come to be seen as something that all adults do to support themselves and find fulfillment. If success and achievement can be both masculine and feminine, then perhaps care of a house and children can be both feminine and masculine too. We will see that many men are entering more actively into a fathering role or even taking complete care of a family as custodial fathers in single-parent homes.

Thus, changing the definitions of masculine work and feminine work and changing the values placed on that work by pay or other means may be our best ways to modify traditional family roles. These roles are being modified by the economic situation and by women's increasing awareness of their opportunities. They are also being modified by men's awareness of the physical and emotional burdens they have carried.

GENDER ROLES AND MARITAL SATISFACTION

As one might suspect from the above analysis, changing gender roles are related to marital happiness. We have seen that fewer married women reported themselves to be happy in 1986 than did so in 1972.[97] There is also evidence that women who have a more modern gender-role ideology are less likely to be happy in marriage.[98] This lesser happiness of married women with nontraditional gender roles seems to hold in spite of age, education, and work status. We should not be surprised by the fact that women who hold strong beliefs about equality are particularly upset by the inequities in marriage; interestingly, men with a modern gender-role ideology are no less happy than are their more traditional peers.

Other research confirms that men are more likely to believe in innate traditional gender roles which justify their advantaged position. Yet when couples disagree, there is still an opportunity for one to influence the other. The mutual influence of husbands' and wives' beliefs reduced their disagreement on gender roles by about 30 percent in one study.[99] Yet it is particularly important that husbands and wives hold congruent gender roles if they are to be happy in marriage. The marriages that have been found to have the lowest rating of marital quality are those with a traditional husband and a modern wife.[100] The highest levels of adjustment and satisfaction in married couples are reported by those who consider their marriages equitable.[101]

Another element of gender roles that is related to marital satisfaction is marital self-disclosure leading to intimacy. We have talked at length about men being socialized to be inexpressive and keep their feelings inside. By contrast, women are socialized to prefer intimate, self-disclosing relationships. The nature and difference in the communication between spouses is very important in marital happiness. Happily married couples spend more time interacting with each other and have more companionship;[102] they are also likely to say that the amount of disclosure by themselves and their spouses is high.[103] Not surprisingly, wives are more likely than husbands to want more expressiveness and communication in a marriage.[104]

THE TRANSITION TO PARENTHOOD

Opting Not to Have Children

Parenthood is not always the option chosen by young couples today. More couples are opting for childlessness, and many more are delaying the time when they have the first child or are having fewer children.

While it cannot be known how many couples will stay childless, we do know that fewer couples want or expect to have children. According to one study, about 10 percent of couples in their early twenties do not expect to have children.[105] Add to this the one of every six couples in the United States who are child-free because of infertility. Statistics show that about 13 percent of women in their middle forties in 1986 will end their childbearing years without having had children; in 1960, that figure was 11 percent. The Census Bureau's fertility expert, Martin O'Connell, is quoted as expecting 20 to 25 percent of the women born in the 1950s and 1960s to remain childless.[106] Neal and associates determined in a 1989 study that there is an increasing ambivalence toward having and rearing children and that hostile and negative images of children exist among many young adults. In their study, the potential reward value of having children had only a slight edge over alternative values such as having extra money to invest and spend and having a neat household.[107] Thus, we might expect that a trend toward more people remaining childless will continue. Childless marriages have special implications for gender roles because of the possible interaction of childlessness with a wife's career plans and the possible greater equality of gender roles between spouses.

Most studies of couples who are considering or have opted for childlessness have included relatively small samples and are dated. Nevertheless, the results of these studies are very similar. Frequently the wives are the ones who make the decision not to have children and are firm in sticking to it. In one study, approximately one-third of the wives had reached the decision to remain childless and had chosen partners with that decision in mind. The other two-thirds had reached the decision to remain childless with their husbands after a series of postponements of parenthood.[108] Such wives are quite strong in their opinions that the costs of a child are high and the satisfactions low.[109]

DINKS (double income, no kids) is an acronym that has been coined to describe a new brand of voluntarily childless couples. These couples often have high incomes and demanding careers, and most of them stress the importance of marital interaction and the opportunity to work, travel, and enjoy leisure as their primary reasons for not wanting children.[110] There is a tendency for higher-income men and women to marry each other, resulting in an extremely high joint income and dedication to their careers.[111] Highly educated women are more likely to remain childless than are women with less education. Between 7.3 and 14.3 percent of college-educated women in one study expected no children, while 4.9 percent of high-school-educated women expected none. This relationship held up at all age levels, so it did not just represent a postponement of having children. The highly educated wives tended to be more successful at their jobs than most wives in the paid labor force, and they also had higher-status, better-paying occupations.[112] We might infer that women who are highly educated and have careers are less likely to want children because of the perceived conflict with their work roles.

Some studies show that those who do not intend to have children are equalitarian in their gender-role attitudes,[113] although to get any real measure one would have to compare their attitudes with those of couples who have had children. Most of the studies that have compared childless marriages and marriages of the same duration with children have found that childless marriages are happier in all stages of the life cycle.[114] Their greater happiness is largely due to the companionship and marital interaction they are able to maintain.[115]

Even though the percentage of families without children is growing, it is predicted to remain under 10 percent of all marriages through the mid-1990s.[116] It is not clear whether this low birthrate simply represents a delay in having the first child as couples marry later and establish their careers or a firm decision to remain childless.

Having Fewer Children

The birthrate in the United States has declined steadily since 1800. It hit a low during the 1970s and has since climbed a little. Table 1 describes the trend.

There are many reasons for the smaller families of today. Marriage occurs at a later age, and this means fewer childbearing years. The high divorce rate also reduces the number of childbearing years for many women. With women working outside the home, many couples choose to limit the number of their

Table 1   Declining Birth Rates in the United States: 1900–1985

Year	Births per 1,000 Population	Average Number of Births per Adult Woman
1800	58.0	7.0
1850	48.0	5.4
1900	32.0	3.5
1925	25.1	3.0
1936	18.4	2.1
1950	24.1	3.2
1957	25.0	3.6
1970	18.4	2.4
1975	14.8	1.7
1980	15.8	1.0
1985	15.7	1.9

SOURCE: U.S. Bureau of the Census: *Statistical Abstract of the United States: 1986* (Washington, D.C.: U.S. Government Printing Office, 1986).

children so that the wife will have more time to devote to her career. Another possible factor is the desire of many young couples to use their resources for their own satisfaction rather than to raise a family.[117] More certain methods of birth control have meant that parenthood can be postponed or avoided. In a national fertility study done in 1975, at any one time about 80 percent of all married couples stated that they used contraception. Among couples married five to nine years, only 2.1 percent had not used contraception at some time.[118] The January 1973 Supreme Court ruling that the decision about abortion should be left to a woman and her physician has made it easier for women to use this method as a backup when contraception fails, although pending state laws may change this in some areas.[119]

In addition, there is a trend toward delaying having the first child. In 1970 women under age 25 accounted for 81.2 percent of first births; by 1980 the proportion was 68.4 percent. About one-third of first births are now to women of 25 years of age or older.[120] Some couples who delay childbearing are unwilling or unable later to have children, and so the delaying trend increases the number of childless couples.

This trend has significant interactions with gender roles. On the one hand, it may be partially a result of changing work roles for women as well as changing expectations about individual fulfillment. On the other hand, the trend may itself affect gender roles in the family. A couple who remain childless or even delay childbearing are likely to be more equalitarian. A wife who is not burdened with child-care responsibilities is more likely to have a better income and higher occupational status and thus has more power in the family. A young couple who depend on each other for companionship are also less likely to develop stratified roles. The longer the period of equality, the less likely it is that the couple will revert to traditional roles even when they have children.

Parenthood and Crisis

However, for many couples the transition to parenthood is likely to mean a move toward more traditional gender roles in the family. Even for couples with equalitarian values, there is likely to be a realignment of gender roles after the first child is born.[121] Alice Rossi has discussed the process and difficulties of this transition.

Rossi points out that one of the things that make the transition to parenthood so difficult is its abrupt nature: One day a person is childless, and the next day that person is a parent.[122] Even the long months of pregnancy and preparing a nursery cannot prepare a couple for the responsibility and time and energy demands that will suddenly be thrust upon them. The demands are made more difficult by the fact that there is little preparation for parenthood in our culture. We live in small, nuclear families in which we may never take care of little babies.[123]

Parenthood, and particularly motherhood, is also romanticized in this culture. Motherhood is seen as completing a woman's identity, and all women are supposed to want to be mothers and know instinctively what to do with a small infant. The practicalities and difficulties of caring for a new infant are seldom discussed. Many couples with new babies often imagine themselves as perfect parents and try to achieve this image,[124] yet most young couples report some disruption of marital roles and some feeling of crisis when the first baby arrives. In several studies, over 80 percent of the respondents have reported at least a slight crisis.[125]

The parenthood crisis includes disrupted marital roles and communication as well as the physical demands made upon the parents.[126] Many researchers report that the presence of children in the home has a negative impact on the parents' well-being and on marital satisfaction in particular. The addition of the first child especially disrupts intimacy and marital communication.[127] Some researchers say that decreasing marital satisfaction is just part of a general decline in love, marital satisfaction, and the frequency of husband-wife activities over the life of the marriage,[128] but others find that parents experience more of a decline in marital satisfaction than do nonparents.[129] When a decline in marital satisfaction is found, it is more pronounced for wives,[130] although couples followed different patterns according to their individual characteristics.[131] One study reported high well-being a month after the birth but a significant decline six months afterward.[132] In at least one study, all the husbands and wives experienced declines in their feelings of love, marital satisfaction, and the frequency of couple activities. Their activities became more instrumental and child-oriented, and the division of tasks became more traditional.[133] While all couples seem to experience some decline, the degree of decline in satisfaction depends largely on factors such as prebaby marital adjustment, adequacy of finances, and planning and preparation for the baby.

This drop in marital satisfaction can be traced to several important causes. In all cases, the amount of household work rose and the mother did more.[134]

Mothers expected shared child care but often didn't get it. Indeed, the father often worked longer hours outside the home than before,[135] and the mother saw this as his defaulting on promises of equality. Nontraditional wives[136] and men who were traditional but had to help with child care were the least happy.

Another reported cause of decline in marital satisfaction was the gender specialization that occurred after the birth. Women whose husbands earned sufficient incomes and women who lacked job opportunities were more likely to quit work, but many women cut back on their hours.[137] Middle-class women in particular felt the loss of status, opportunity, and freedom. While they felt good if their husbands appreciated their mothering,[138] they often had to depend on their husbands' help and believed that they had to be more deferential to get it. One study found that women with children were more likely to give in during disagreements.[139]

Parenthood makes it difficult to maintain the equality that was established when the couple were both working and contributing resources to the family. Even if a woman plans to return to work quickly, it is more feasible for her to stay home with a newborn infant than it is for the father to do so. Most businesses give maternity leave but not paternity leave, and men are not as likely to take such a leave even when it is offered. Once she is at home without income or social status, a woman's power drops drastically. Because she is at home and the father is working, it is also "logical" that she do the housework and get up with the children at night. It is difficult for the couple to do things together, and so they may separate their chores and recreation. He baby-sits while she "goes out with the girls," for example. A young wife who is isolated with a baby may be without funds for sitters or without a car. Her friends may be working or far away. She must regulate her schedule according to the needs of the baby, and she is left with the housework. She is also left with no income and status of her own.[140]

Spouses were also found to be likely to focus more on instrumental tasks and less on emotional maintenance.[141] They were more likely to report increased conflict and less likely to see each other as lovers.[142] Fathers were often worried about being replaced in the wives' affections and resented the fact that the wives were not more available to them.[143] Mothers often resented their changed roles. Time together, intimacy, and communication dramatically decreased.

There is also evidence that while men are participating more with their children, women are still doing the bulk of child-care work. Even highly involved fathers characterize 50 percent of the time they spend with children as play and 50 percent as work. By contrast, mothers say they spend 10 percent of their time with children playing and 90 percent working.[144] Fathers see child care as the mother's primary responsibility and view their role as "helping out"[145] and being the primary provider. They often use gender-specific excuses for being with children less than mothers are, such as the fact that work keeps them away or that they are impatient with young children.[146] Interestingly, women often collaborate with men in maintaining the belief in large-scale father involvement with children in spite of evidence to the contrary.[147]

Thus, parenthood has a tendency to initiate or perpetuate traditional gender roles. Even when the wife returns to work, she is usually held responsible for the greatest part of child care and housework. The couple's beliefs about the importance of being home with small children and cultural expectations perpetuate this system.[148] Even young women with very high career aspirations say that they want to take at least some time off with their children and that they expect their husbands' careers will come before their own. While they expect to share the housework and child care equally, young men of their age are convinced that their wives will be the ones to take time out for children and do the primary caregiving.[149] Businesses also expect a mother to take time off but look askance at a man who does so.

THE MIDDLE-AGED FAMILY

A Changing Orientation to Masculine and Feminine Behavior

Gender roles undergo a different kind of a change in middle-aged families. Middle age appears to be a time of taking stock of one's life. Men are at a crucial point in their careers and are actively moving up the job ladder or are aware that they are unlikely to ever have the occupational success they have dreamed about. Women who are mothers recognize that their role will be different as the children leave home. For women who have been primarily mothers and homemakers, the loss of the mothering role may represent a significant change. For women who are employed outside the home, there may be an increasing emphasis on careers and a pulling away from family responsibilities.

Men in the Middle Years

Neugarten points out that middle age is not so much a specific time of life as a perception of age. Men may become aware of their advancing years when they see colleagues twenty years younger moving up the career ladder. They may come to a recognition of their age the first time a son beats them at tennis or a friend has a heart attack. While the time of the perception of middle age varies, it comes in the late thirties and the first few years of the forties for most men.[150]

While some researchers disagree,[151] Levinson and other researchers believe that the awareness of middle age and the evaluation of personal goals and of one's total life that takes place at this time represent a midlife crisis. As the masculine striving for career success may be stymied by outside forces, the pause in a man's move up the career ladder may give him time to think about other things he is missing.

Levinson describes four concerns of men going through this evaluation.[152] While he does not deal with women in his study, other studies have shown

For Better or For Worse®   by Lynn Johnston

that women have many of the same anxieties. The first concern is with mortality. Men (and women) feel the vulnerability of their aging bodies and have a much stronger sense that time is passing and that they will die. Neugarten talks about the change in measuring time as "time left to live" rather than "time from birth." A person is concerned that he or she must do things now because there is so little time left in the future. This feeling is based somewhat on the belief that sudden death may occur but more on a sense that the vigor of youth may not hold out long enough for a person to accomplish things.

The second concern of this period is trying to make an appropriate transition from being young to becoming older. For some people this transition is not easy and is marked by a desperate attempt to stay young. Men may work frantically at being physically fit, try younger styles of dress, take up dangerous sports, or look for young sexual partners.

The third and fourth concerns relate more directly to sex roles. There is an attempt, particularly by men, to deal with real feelings and relationships with others, something young men may have done only at a superficial level. In one sense, this represents an attempt to get in touch with the more feminine parts of the self, with the emotions and tender feelings that may have been repressed. The fourth concern may involve "feelings" but consists primarily of an emphasis on doing the things one did not do in the past, possibly because they were "feminine" or because of lack of time. This may entail more involvement with one's family, more of a desire to try artistic and cultural things, and less of an emphasis on achievement and ambition. The physical, competitive world cannot usually be dealt with at the same pace, and the integration of the masculine and feminine parts of his nature (Levinson's terms) may give a man more depth and satisfaction.[153]

For a man who is able to achieve integration, work may take on new meaning. He may mentor or help protégés and perhaps become more satisfied with his present job situation rather than continually strive to get ahead. For some men, it is a period of rethinking and restarting rather than integration. Old job choices and old marriages may give way under the stress of the period, and new ways of working and living may be found.[154]

Women in the Middle Years

Women may experience many of the same concerns, particularly the vulnerability of the body and the sense of passing time. Faced with the realization that their mothering roles are not as important as before, women may begin assessing what they want to do with the rest of their lives.[155] Some women who formed their identity and sense of self entirely around the finding of a suitable mate and around motherhood may find themselves "bankrupt" at this time whether they have married or not. If they feel less needed by husbands whose interests are taken up with careers and by children who are grown, they may suffer an identity crisis and even depression and may need to reevaluate their lives.[156] At least one researcher believes that the wife probably has more problems adjusting during the postparental years than does the husband, who may be occupied with his career while he takes stock of his life.[157] Some researchers hypothesize that the husband's power will rise during this period and that the wife will depend more for emotional exchange on her husband, who does not have the same needs. At the same time, health concerns surface, and the wife may be aware of the possibility of losing her husband and of what that loss will mean to her.[158] As the health of middle-aged women is better than that of men, the man does not have similar concerns about his wife. There is considerable evidence that stereotyped housework roles do not change in middle age,[159] although personality traits seem to move in a less stereotyped direction.

However, Neugarten reports that the most common feeling of women from age thirty through the fifty is one of freedom. They have time and energy for themselves, and they feel a satisfying change in self-concept.[160] This improvement in self-concept comes in spite of factors that seem to work against it. Bell describes the "double standard of aging," in which men are described as getting "character lines" and distinguished gray hair while women are seen as becoming old and wrinkled.[161] However, women do not seem to suffer from poor body image. Many report that menopause, which may start during these years, does not affect them adversely. While some have physical discomfort, most see it as a period to be gotten through and as a relatively unimportant factor in their lives.[162] As one woman put it, "If it's not the pause that refreshes, it at least is not the pause that depresses."[163] Many women raised in the days before "sure" contraception actually find that after menopause they have a renewed enjoyment of sex without fear of pregnancy. Parenthetically, the sexual enjoyment of middle-aged and older couples who have always enjoyed their sex life does not seem to decrease.[164]

The degree of difficulty that women seem to have in getting through the midlife crisis and assuming new identities may actually be based more on exterior than on interior causes. There is still discrimination against older women in the labor force, and it may be difficult for a woman who has never worked or a woman with rusty skills to find a job. Family reactions to a woman's decreased availability to her husband and children may be relatively hostile. As men may also be going through midlife changes, some instability in the family may occur as a result of envy or dissonance in roles. One professor expressed his feelings this way:

> I'm afraid I'm a bit envious of my wife. She went to work a few years ago when our children no longer needed her attention, and a whole new world has opened to her. But myself? I just look forward to writing another volume, and then another volume. . . .[165]

Even for a woman who has always combined a work identity with her home roles, the midlife transition may not be easy. While work can have an important integrative function when women are losing a motherhood role, women have the same concerns about their careers that men do.[166]

Perhaps as a result of these life assessments, the personalities of men and women change during these years. The changes seem to be the reverse of the traditional stereotyped personality traits for each sex. "Men seem to become more receptive to affiliative and nurturant promptings" and cope with the environment in more contemplative and abstract ways. Women, in contrast, seem to become more aggressive and self-assured. They are less guilty about egocentric impulses,[167] although they continue to cope in their accustomed affective and expressive manner. Many researchers believe that personality and behavioral differences between the sexes tend to moderate as people age.[168]

What is the effect of reassessment and gender-role changes on the marital satisfaction of middle-aged couples? When we look at marital satisfaction, we must remember that families that have survived to the empty-nest stage may be happier to start with. A great deal of happiness in the postparental stage may depend on the type of relationship the couple has maintained. For couples who have had traditional marriages, the postparental stage may mean that marriage becomes something of an empty shell.[169] For couples who have shared activities and communication all along, the postparental years may become more meaningful.

Most studies of the postparental years show an increase in marital satisfaction as the children leave home.[170] In spite of the problems of midlife transition and the difficulty in finding new directions, family tension decreases and companionship increases during this period. While the increase in companionship is small (some researchers have noted that it is lower during this period than it is during the first fifteen years of marriage and probably does not increase significantly until after the retirement of the husband), it seems enough to offset the negative aspects of this period. Data from six national surveys show that women in particular are happier in the postparental period and get more enjoyment out of life than do women of similar ages who still have a child at home.[171] More recent studies show even greater satisfaction, probably because of the changing role of women. More middle-aged women are reentering the labor force, and they see freedom from child care as an opportunity to pursue their neglected interests.

OLDER MEN AND WOMEN

The Stigma of the Elderly and Gender Roles

Both elderly men and women lose the status of being young as they age. Preoccupation with and glorification of youth is apparent in this culture. One study found that 57 percent of monitored television ads promised "youth, youthful appearance or the energy to act youthful."[172] By contrast, seniors in the same ads were shown dealing with backaches, loose dentures, and constipation.

Women suffer more from losing the beauty that is associated with youth. As women "are associated with the girlish qualities of young, firm bodies, the wrinkles and flab of the older years is seen as particularly revolting on the female body. In men, those wrinkles are often called 'character lines' and the flab gets such euphemisms as 'the beer belly.'"[173] Ironically, women are told to get rid of telltale age spots and stop wrinkles, but they are also ridiculed if they attempt to look young by wearing too much makeup or dying their hair.

Both sexes suffer from a loss of financial resources in the later years, but women are likely to suffer more than men. Men are more likely to have substantial retirement benefits, and while married women may share a husband's pension, widowed, single, and divorced women may have very low incomes. Because women live longer, they are also likely to lose marital status and the companionship of a spouse.

Studies done in the 1950s and 1960s showed that women in the middle and later years are very unhappy. In a 1958 study that asked, "What are things you do that make you feel useful or important?" a substantial group of respondents answered, "Nothing."[174] Another study of four age groups of men and women pointed out that empty-nest women are strikingly low in well-being.[175] Happily, this low self-esteem was not found in the studies done in the 1980s. In a replication of the study by Gurin and associates of 1960, Veroff and associates found that the decline in women's self-esteem with age was no longer evident.[176] The change may be due to the fact that older people now have more resources, that the marital status is not as important, and that women who have been working may have sources of self-esteem other than traditional roles.

The effect of retirement on morale may differ for men and women. Some studies have shown that retirement from one's career does not hold the significance for women that it does for men,[177] but this is no longer true.[178] Women who had made social and economic plans for retirement seem to suffer the least; of course, the same is true for men. Couples who have experienced leisure-time activities together are the most satisfied.[179]

One study showed that there were variations according to age among people who had been married many years. Positive interaction was highest and negative sentiment lowest among those aged 63 to 69. The researcher speculated that retirement may occur in the mid-sixties and couples may enjoy the "honeymoon stage" of retirement with the release from the pressures and constraints of occupational pursuits. Later, health and income may decline and affect marital satisfaction.[180]

Androgyny and the Elderly

Changes in the personality traits and interests of men and women are accelerated in the postretirement years. With a larger percentage of the population living past age 65, studies have focused on mature role development and increasing evidence that older adults are more androgynous in personality traits. Sinnott believes that elderly people who experience this variation in sex roles show a general flexibility which is associated with more successful aging.[181]

Cause and effect are not clear in this integration of roles among the elderly. Perhaps those who survive were always androgynous in their sex roles; to put it another way, perhaps the sex-role flexible person is the one who survives. Another possibility is that this integration of sex roles in older people is an adaptation to functional needs in the older years or at least an adaptation to having less of a need for differentiated roles. The old man does not need to be aggressive and competitive in the same way; the older woman may need to move beyond nurturant activities and cope with society in an instrumental way.

Studies show that older persons see themselves as changing their personality traits,[182] and many researchers agree that this change is taking place.[183] The change seems to lie not in the direction of losing original, more traditional gender-role orientation but in adding characteristics of the other gender role.[184] Men seem to add the feminine social skills that enable them to develop a support system, and women seem to add the instrumental traits and assertiveness that help them cope with everyday problems.

Both younger and older persons agree that there is a difference in the gender-role characteristics perceived as ideal for older men and women.[185] The change in the ideal toward more neutral, androgynous characteristics may hasten any gender-role change that is occurring or may simply make its expression more acceptable, thus affecting life satisfaction that is dependent on "fitting in."[186]

Other studies show that there may be class differences in the possible changes toward increased androgyny.[187] Apparently, special life circumstances such as divorce or the loss of a spouse can hasten such change.[188]

Sometimes a pattern of contradictions occurs so that it is not unusual for an older person to proclaim stereotyped roles but act in a more androgynous way. An older person may counsel a young man to be competitive and a young woman to be domestic because she still sees these as ideal roles. At the same time, she may be doing different things because these roles are no longer functional for her.[189]

Studies show that greater androgyny leads to greater life satisfaction. Those with the best adjustment were found to have both active and passive traits, with neither group of traits dominating. They were active, independent, and competitive but also nurturant and aware of feelings.[190] Other research reported that androgynous older individuals were more stable and less neurotic and that masculine and androgynous subjects had higher self-esteem.[191] Different studies reported that traditional sex roles were associated with the symptoms of poor mental health.[192]

The Older Family

Gender roles continue to change in the older family. The change involves a reorientation of personality rather than a changing orientation toward tasks. While older women become more assertive and older men become more passive, they are unlikely to greatly modify their provider and housekeeper roles. The gender-role orientation that is changed is manifested across all activities rather than in particular sex-stereotyped activities. Retired men increase their involvement in male tasks such as taking care of the car and yard but do little more around the house.[193] Wives who are or have been employed often expect a more equal division of labor after retirement but do not get it.[194] As one might expect, men generally see their marriages more positively than do women, although the marital satisfaction scores for both are relatively high for this age.[195]

The reasons for the change in personality traits in the older years have not been fully explored. It is generally assumed that this change in traits is associated with the freeing of women from their motherhood responsibilities and the contemplation induced in men by midlife stocktaking of their career achievements. Why changes in gender-role orientation take the direction they do is not completely clear. Why have men become aware of the emotional relationships they have missed and not taken the path of denying those emotional needs even more firmly so that they can concentrate on the career success that has eluded them? Why do women not seek further expressive and affiliative bonds but instead become more assertive? What is the relationship of these changes to physical strength and to cultural norms regarding age and status? It may be that the older family holds clues to many questions about gender-role norms and behavior in our society.

Some researchers have looked beyond the immediate questions of family roles and the possible benefits of androgyny in the older years and have developed theories about androgyny as part of a pattern of role development over the life span. According to them, the early part of life is a period of undifferentiated gender roles which are functional for early socialization, the middle part of life is a period of very polarized gender roles which are more functional for the breadwinning-parenting division of labor at least in traditional two-parent families, and the older years are a period of undifferentiation again as polarized roles are no longer needed and integrated roles may be more functional.[196]

SUMMARY

When we look at the American family today, we see that many changes are affecting gender roles. Men and women are more likely to stay single or at least to postpone marriage, and this is likely to mean more independence for women and a trend toward more equalitarian marriages. With greater education and more time on their own before marriage, women are more likely to have started careers and to have learned the kind of assertiveness that makes it difficult to revert to dependent relationships. Men may learn to take care of domestic chores themselves and later, with pressure, may be more willing to have equalitarian marriages. With more contraception available and fewer social taboos against cohabitation, marriage has become more a symbol of commitment than a necessity. Marriages based on this kind of emotional commitment tend to be more equalitarian.

As we have seen, couples who do not have children or postpone childbearing are likely to have equalitarian marriages. Women are not as likely to have the career interruptions they had because of their children and are more likely to maintain their resources. Established patterns of shared decision making and division of labor are not as likely to be changed by the addition of children.

It is also likely that all married couples will be pushed more toward equalitarian modes of interaction. Women are marrying men closer to their own age and are getting educations, incomes, and occupational statuses that are closer to those of their spouses. They will have more resources that will give them power in a marriage. Norms are also changing, at least in the middle class. There is some indication that men are more interested in fathering, and there is more pressure on them to share child-care and household responsibilities. Although this period of changing gender roles may create ambiguous expectations and conflict between spouses, these changes may actually increase marital satisfaction in the long run. However, there is a long way to go. Men and women of all ages still have different expectations about who will do what tasks in a marriage, and women are suffering from the dual burden of employment outside the home and family responsibilities.

We have seen that there has been a move toward androgyny in older families in regard to the personalities of the spouses, if not in the sharing of tasks. The wide variety of family forms found today also has an interactive influence on gender roles. We will look at some of these family forms in Chapter 9.

ESSAY QUESTIONS

1. Why are men and women staying single longer? Discuss the effect this has on sex roles.
2. Why has the traditional family of the American dream been a myth rather than a reality in our culture?

3. According to Blood and Wolfe, power in marriage is determined by the resources one brings to a marriage. What resources do they cite for the husband and for the wife? How is their resource theory modified by the beliefs of a couple and the cultural norms of the society in which they live?

4. Contrast the experiences of married men and single men. How is marriage good for men? Why do myths exist about how bad marriage is for men?

5. Discuss the reasons why a woman may be shocked when she enters marriage. Be sure to include legal, social, and personal reasons for her shock and possible loss of self-esteem. Are men shocked too?

6. Discuss the "her" marriage as described by Jessie Bernard. Why does she say about housewives that "if their symptoms belonged to any other group in American society, their condition would be considered a social disaster of the worst magnitude"?

7. Why are married women who work outside the home apparently happier than housewives even though they may have longer hours and more work to do? What aspects of housework contribute to the unhappiness of a woman who stays at home? Be very specific and quote studies where possible. What suggestions do you have for changing this situation?

8. When wives work outside the home, there is usually a realignment of power because the wife is contributing resources. Why does decision-making power change faster than the division of labor? How much help can a working wife usually expect with household chores?

9. When couples become parents, there is often a reversion to traditional gender roles. Why does this happen, and what could be done to prevent it?

10. How have changes in the number of persons opting to remain childless affected gender roles?

11. Discuss the changing orientation toward gender roles in the middle-aged family. Would you expect this change to affect power and marital satisfaction?

12. Discuss why you think changes in sex-role orientation in the older family take the direction they do. Why don't the spouses cling to their traditional roles in a time of change?

EXERCISES

1. To understand how you learned assumptions about marriage roles, list below how you saw the interaction in your family.
   My mother typically made decisions about _____.
   My father typically made decisions about _____.
   They both made decisions about _____.

My mother typically did the following kinds of household or outside-the-house work (yard work and the like): _____ .
My father typically did the following kinds of household or outside-the-house work: _____ .
Both typically did the following kinds of work: _____ .

2. Have both the men and the women in the class answer the following questions and compare their answers: Did your mother work outside the home when you were a child? How did you feel about this? How did your father feel about it?

3. What are your feelings about the following words?

   Housewives   Single parents
   Women managers   Househusbands
   Working mothers   Men managers
   Divorced women   Unemployed men

4. According to what you learned in childhood, what do responsible men do? What do responsible women do? Do you believe the same things now? If not, why not?

5. Have the men and women in the class answer the following questions and compare their answers.

   a. In my marriage, I have to _____ .
                    I need to _____ .
                    I want to _____ .
   b. I may not want to get married because _____ .

6. You are a husband in a white middle-class family in which the last child has just graduated from college. Your wife, who has never worked, is talking about finishing her college education and getting a job. You have just been passed over for a promotion at work and pulled a muscle in your leg while playing tennis last weekend. How do you feel about your age, your life, and your marital relationship?

NOTES

1. U.S. Bureau of the Census, "Current Population Reports: Population Profile of the United States, 1987," Special Studies, Series P-23 no.150 (Washington, D.C.: U.S. Government Printing Office, 1988).

2. *Ibid.*; Paul C. Glick, "The Family Life Cycle and Social Change," *Family Relations* 38 (1989):123–129.

3. Paul C. Glick, "Marriage, Divorce and Living Arrangements: Prospective Changes," in Arlene Skolnick and Jerome Skolnick, eds., *Family in Transition* 5th ed. (Boston: Little, Brown, 1986), pp. 89–103; Arthur J. Norton and Jeanne E. Moorman, "Current Trends in Marriage and Divorce among American Women," *Journal of Marriage and the Family* 49, no. 1 (1987):3–14.

4. Jessie Bernard, "The Good-Provider Role: Its Rise and Fall," *American Psychologist* 36, no. 1 (1981):1–12.

5. Barbara Ehrenreich, *The Hearts of Men: American Dreams and the Flight from Commitment* (Garden City, N.Y.: Anchor/Doubleday, 1983).

6. Ann Swidler, "Love and Adulthood in American Culture," in Skolnick and Skolnick, *op. cit.*, pp. 286–305.

7. Peter Stein, "The Never Marrieds," in Peter Stein, ed., *Unmarried Adults in Social Context* (New York: St. Martin's, 1981).

8. Ehrenreich, *op. cit.*

9. U.S. Bureau of the Census, *Statistical Abstract of the United States: 1987* (Washington, D.C.: U.S. Government Printing Office, 1988).

10. Patricia Gwartney-Gibbs, "The Institutionalization of Premarital Cohabitation: Estimates from Marriage License Applications, 1970 and 1980," *Journal of Marriage and the Family* 48 (1986):423–434; Graham Spanier, "Married and Unmarried Cohabitation in the United States," *Journal of Marriage and the Family* 45 (1980):277–288.

11. U.S. Bureau of the Census, *op. cit.*, Table J, p. 12; "Adults in Unmarried Couple Households by Age and Marital Status," *Population Profile of the United States*, Washington, D.C.: U.S. Government Printing Office, 1987.

12. *Ibid.*; Spanier, *op. cit.*

13. Roy E. L. Watson, "Premarital Cohabitation vs. Traditional Courtship: Their Effects on Subsequent Marital Adjustment," *Family Relations* 32 (January 1983): 139–147.

14. *Ibid.*

15. Alfred DeMaris and Gerald R. Leslie, "Cohabitation with Future Spouse: Its Influence upon Marital Satisfaction and Communication," *Journal of Marriage and the Family* 46 (1984):77–94.

16. Eleanor Macklin, "Nontraditional Family Forms: A Decade of Research," *Journal of Marriage and the Family* 12 (1980):905–922.

17. John Cuber and Peggy Harroff, *The Significant Americans* (New York: Penguin, 1965).

18. David Heer, "The Measurement and Bases of Family Power: An Overview," *Journal of Marriage and the Family* 25 (1963):134; Robert Blood and Donald M. Wolfe, *Husbands & Wives: The Dynamics of Married Living* (New York: Macmillan, 1960).

19. Blood and Wolfe, *op. cit.*

20. *Ibid.*

21. Rae Lesser Blumberg and Marion Tolbert Coleman, "A Theoretical Look at the Gender Balance of Power in the American Couple," *Journal of Family Issues* 10, no. 2 (1989):225–250.

22. Wayne Hill and John Scanzoni, "An Approach for Assessing Marital Decision-Making Processes," *Journal of Marriage and the Family* 44 (1982):927–941; Cynthia Arnett and John Scanzoni, "Enlarging the Understanding of Marital Commitment via Religious Devoutness: Gender Role Preferences and Locus of Marital Control," *Journal of Family Issues* (1987):136–156; John Scanzoni and Karen Polonko, "A Conceptual Approach to Explicit Marital Negotiation," *Journal of Marriage and the Family* 42 (1980):31–44.

23. John Scanzoni and Maximiliane Szinovacz, *Family Decision-Making: A Developmental Sex Role Model* (Beverly Hills, Calif.: Sage, 1980); Maximiliane E. Szinovacz, "Power" in Marvin B. Sussman and Suzanne K. Steinmetz, *Handbook of Marriage and the Family* (New York: Plenum, 1987), pp. 651–694.

24. Deborah D. Godwin and John Scanzoni, "Couple Decision-Making: Commonalities and Differences across Issues and Spouses," *Journal of Family Issues* 10, no. 3 (1989):291–310.
25. Blumberg and Coleman, *op. cit.*, p. 239.
26. Leslie Margolin and Lynn White, "The Continuing Role of Physical Attractiveness in Marriage," *Journal of Marriage and the Family* 49, no. 1 (1987):21–27.
27. Rosanna Hertz, *More Equal Than Others: Women and Men in Dual-Career Marriages* (Berkeley: University of California Press, 1986).
28. Blumberg and Coleman, *op. cit.*
29. Lenore Weitzman, *The Divorce Revolution* (New York: The Free Press, 1985).
30. Marion L. Kranichfeld, "Rethinking Family Power," *Journal of Family Issues* 8, no. 1 (1987):42–56.
31. Alan C. Acock and Vern I. Bengston, "On the Relative Influence of Mothers and Fathers: A Covariance Analysis of Political and Religious Socialization," *Journal of Marriage and the Family* 40 (1978):519–530.
32. John Scanzoni and Greer Litton Fox, "Sex Roles, Family, and Society: The Seventies and Beyond," *Journal of Marriage and the Family* 42 (1980):743–758.
33. Dana Hiller and William Philliber, "The Division of Labor in Contemporary Marriage: Expectations, Perceptions and Performance," *Social Problems* 33 (1986):191–201.
34. Grace Baruch and Rosalind Barnett, "Consequences of Fathers' Participation in Family Work: Parents' Role Strain and Well-Being," *Journal of Personality and Social Psychology* 51 (1986):578–585.
35. Sarah F. Berk, *The Gender Factory: The Apportionment of Work in American Households* (New York: Plenum, 1985); Yoshinori Kamo, "Determinants of the Household Division of Labor: Resources, Power and Ideology," *Journal of Family Issues* 9 (1988):177–200; Rebecca Warner, "Alternative Strategies for Measuring Household Division of Labor: A Comparison," *Journal of Family Issues* 7 (1986):179–195.
36. Berk, *op. cit.*
37. Joanne Miller and Howard H. Garrison, "Sex Roles: The Division of Labor at Home and in the Workplace," in David Olson and Brent Miller, eds., *Family Studies Yearbook,* vol. 2 (Beverly Hills, Calif.: Sage, 1984), pp. 323–348.
38. Joseph Pleck, *Working Wives/Working Husbands* (Beverly Hills, Calif.: Sage, 1985).
39. Shelley Coverman and Joseph Sheley, "Change in Men's Housework and Child-Care Time, 1965–1975," *Journal of Marriage and the Family* 48 (1986):413–422.
40. Ruth Schwartz Cowan, "Women's Work, Housework and History: The Historical Roots of Inequality in Work-Force Participation," in Naomi Gerstel and Harriet Gross, eds., *Families and Work* (Philadelphia: Temple University Press, 1987), pp. 164–177.
41. Berk, *op. cit.*; Pleck, *op. cit.*
42. Catherine Berheide, "Women's Work in the Home: Seems Like Old Times," in Beth Hess and Marvin Sussman, eds., *Women and the Family: Two Decades of Change* (New York: Hayworth Press, 1984), pp. 37–55; Laura Lein, *Families without Villains: American Families in an Era of Change* (Lexington, Mass.: Lexington Books, 1984).
43. Robert S. Weiss, "Men and the Family," *Family Process* 24 (1985):49–58.
44. Berheide, *op. cit.*; Myra M. Ferree, "Family and Job for Working-Class Women: Gender and Class Systems Seen from Below," in Naomi Gerstel and Harriet Gross, eds., *Families and Work* (Philadelphia: Temple University Press, 1987), pp. 289–301.

45. Berheide, *op. cit.;* Susan M. Shaw, "Gender Differences in the Definition and Perception of Household Labor," *Family Relations* 37 (1988):333–337.
46. Berk, *op. cit.;* Miller and Garrison, *op. cit.;* Pleck, *op. cit.*
47. Baruch and Barnett, *op. cit.;* Ann C. Crouter, Maureen Perry-Jenkins, Susan McHale, "Processes Underlying Father Involvement in Dual-Earner and Single-Earner Families," *Developmental Psychology* 23 (1987):431–440.
48. Joan Huber and Glenna Spitze, *Sex Stratification: Children Housework and Jobs* (New York: Academic Press, 1983); Kamo, *op. cit.*
49. Maxine Atkinson and Jacqueline Boles, "WASP (Wives as Senior Partners)," *Journal of Marriage and the Family* 46 (1984):861–870.
50. Myra M. Ferree, "The View from Below: Women's Employment and Gender Equality in Working-Class Families," in Hess and Sussman, *op. cit.,* pp. 57–75; Maureen Perry-Jenkins and Ann Crouter, "Husbands' and Wives' Concepts of the 'Provider Role': Implications for Men's Involvement in Family Work" (paper presented at the annual meeting of the National Council on Family Relations, Atlanta, 1987).
51. Weiss, *op. cit.;* Michael Fendrich, "Wives' Employment and Husbands' Distress: A Meta-Analysis and a Replication," *Journal of Marriage and the Family* 46 (1984):871–879.
52. Ellen Rosen, *Bitter Choices: Blue-Collar Women in and out of Work* (Chicago: University of Chicago Press, 1987); Patricia Zavella, *Women's Work and Chicano Families* (New York: Cornell University Press, 1987).
53. Charles V. Willie, *A New Look at Black Families,* 3d ed., (Dix Hills, N.Y.: General Hal, 1988); Noel Cazenave, "Black Male–Black Female Relationships: The Perceptions of 155 Middle-Class Black Men," *Family Relations* 32 (1983):341–350.
54. Hiller and Philliber, *op. cit.*
55. Baruch and Barnett, *op. cit.*
56. Graham Staines and Pam Libby, "Men and Women in Role Relationships," in Richard Ashmore and Frances DelBoca, eds., *The Social Psychology of Female-Male Relations: A Critical Analysis of Central Concepts* (New York: Academic Press, 1986), pp. 211–258.
57. Neal Kraus and Kyria Markides, "Employment and Psychological Well-Being in Mexican-American Women," *Journal of Health and Social Behavior* 26 (1985):15–26.
58. Baruch and Barnett, *op. cit.;* Rosen, *op. cit.;* Sara Yogev and Jeanne Brett, "Perceptions of the Division of Housework and Childcare and Marital Satisfaction," *Journal of Marriage and the Family* 47 (1985):609–618.
59. Mary G. Boulton, *On Being a Mother: A Study of Women with Pre-School Children* (London: Tavistock, 1983); Janice Saltzman Chafetz, "The Gender Division of Labor and the Reproduction of Female Disadvantage: Toward an Integrated Theory," *Journal of Family Issues* 9 (1988):108–131; Michael Geerkin and Walter Gove, *At Home and at Work: The Family's Allocation of Labor* (Beverly Hills, Calif.: Sage, 1983); Elizabeth Maret and Barbara Finlay, "The Distribution of Household Labor among Women in Dual-Earner Families," *Journal of Marriage and the Family* 46 (1984):357.
60. Ferree, *op. cit.;* Mary Benin and Joan Agostinelli, "Husbands' and Wives' Satisfaction with the Division of Labor," *Journal of Marriage and the Family* 50 (1988):349–361.
61. Judith Laws, *The Second 'X': Sex Role and Social Role* (New York: Elsevier, 1979).
62. Anne Johnson, "Men and Housework: Do They or Don't They?" *New York Times* (November 1, 1980):20Y.

63. Scanzoni and Fox, *op. cit.*

64. Jessie Bernard, *The Future of Marriage* (New York: Bantam, 1973).

65. Bernard, *op. cit.*

66. George Guder, "The Single Man: He's in Bigger Trouble Than You'd Ever Guess," *Detroit Free Press* (November 10, 1974): 1D.

67. Peter Stein, *Single Life: Unmarried Adults in Social Context* (New York: St. Martin's, 1981).

68. George Gallup, "Most Women Want Marriage and Babies," *St. Louis Post-Dispatch* (June 15, 1980):3F.

69. Norval D. Glenn and Charles N. Weaver, "The Changing Relationship of Marital Status to Reported Happiness," *Journal of Marriage and the Family* 50 (1988): 317–324.

70. Bernard, *op. cit.*

71. Glenn and Weaver, *op. cit.*

72. Bernard, *op. cit.*

73. Walter Gove, "The Relationship between Sex Roles, Marital Status, and Mental Illness," *Social Forces* 51 (1972):34–44; W. R. Gove and J. Tudor, "Adult Sex Roles and Mental Illness," *American Journal of Sociology* 78 (1973):812–835.

74. Janice M. Steel, "Marital Relationships and Mental Health: The Psychic Costs of Inequality," in Jo Freeman, ed., *Women: A Feminist Perspective* (Palo Alto, Calif.: Mayfield, 1984), pp. 113–123.

75. Joan M. Krauskoph, "Partnership Marriage: Legal Reforms Needed," in Jake Chapman and Margaret Gates, eds., *Women into Wives: The Legal and Economic Impact of Marriage* (Beverly Hills, Calif.: Sage, 1977), p. 94.

76. Jo Freeman, "Women, Law and Public Policy," in Freeman, *op. cit.*, pp. 381–401.

77. Chapman and Gates, *op. cit.*

78. *Ibid.*, pp. 98–99.

79. *Ibid.*, p. 101.

80. Margaret Gates, "Homemakers into Widows and Divorcees: Can the Law Provide Economic Protection?" in Chapman and Gates, *op. cit.*, p. 226, quoting the 1975 International Women's Year Commission Poll; Krauskoph, *op. cit.*, p. 99.

81. Bernard, *op. cit.*, p. 43.

82. *Ibid.*

83. Ruth Swartz Cowen, *More Work for Mother; The Ironies of Household Technology* (New York: Basic Books, 1983).

84. Joann Vanek, "Keeping Busy: Time Spent in Housework, U.S. 1920–1970" (Ph.D. dissertation, University of Michigan, 1973).

85. Anne Oakley, *The Sociology of Housework* (New York, Pantheon, 1974).

86. Vanek, *op. cit.*; Patricia Freudiger, "Life Satisfaction among Three Categories of Married Women," *Journal of Marriage and the Family* 45 (1983):213–219; Carin Rubenstein and P. Shaver, *In Search of Intimacy* (New York: Delacorte 1982).

87. Sharon K. Houseknecht and A. S. Macke, "Combining Marriage and Career: The Marital Adjustment of Professional Women" *Journal of Marriage and the Family* 43 (1981):651–661.

88. R. Kessler and J. McRae, Jr., "The Effects of Wives' Employment on Men and Women," *American Sociological Review* 47 (1982):216–226.

89. Zick Rubin, "Are Working Wives Hazardous to Their Husbands' Mental Health?" *Psychology Today* 17 (1983):70–72.

90. Freudiger, *op. cit.*

91. Alan Booth, "Wife's Employment and Husband Stress: A Predication and a Refutation," *Journal of Marriage and the Family* 39 (1977):645–650.
92. Carol C. Nadelson and Theodore Nadelson, "Dual-Career Marriages: Benefits and Costs," in Fran Pepitone-Rockwell, ed., *Dual Career Couples* (Beverly Hills, Calif.: Sage, 1980), pp. 91–110.
93. William Goode, "Why Men Resist," in Barrie Thorne and Marilyn Yalom, eds., *Rethinking the Family: Some Feminist Questions* (New York: Longman, 1982).
94. "Sweden: The Western Model," in Ira Reiss, *Family Systems in America*, 3d ed. (New York: Holt, Rinehart & Winston, 1980), pp. 435–452; Ira L. Reiss, "Sexual Customs and Gender Roles in Sweden and America: An Analysis and Interpretation," in H. Lopata, ed., *Research on the Interweave of Social Roles: Women and Men* (Greenwich, Conn.: JAI Press, 1980), pp. 343–357.
95. S. S. Simister, "Out of One Kitchen into Another," in *Wages for Housework* (Toronto: Amazon Press, 1975), quoted in Laws, *op. cit.*, p. 158; Oakley, *op. cit.*
96. Judith Laws, *Wages for Housework* (Toronto: Amazon Press, 1975); Alice Cook, "Working Mothers: Problems and Programs" (unpublished, School of Industrial Relations, Cornell University), quoted in Laws, *op. cit.*, p. 159.
97. Glenn and Weaver, *op. cit.*
98. Lloyd B. Lupetow, Margaret B. Guss, and Colleen Hyden, "Sex Role Ideology, Marital Status and Happiness," *Journal of Family Issues* 10 (1989):383–400; Mark Whisman and Neil Jacobson, "Depression, Marital Satisfaction and Marital and Personality Measures of Sex Roles," *Journal of Marital and Family Therapy* 15 (1989):177–186.
99. John Mirowsky and Catherine E. Ross, "Belief in Innate Sex Roles: Sex Stratification versus Interpersonal Influence in Marriage," *Journal of Marriage and the Family* 52 (1987):527–540.
100. Gary Lee Bowen and Dennis K. Orthner, "Sex Role Congruency and Marital Quality," *Journal of Marriage and the Family* 46 (1983):223–230.
101. Bernard Davidson, "A Test of Equity Theory for Marital Adjustment," *Social Psychology Quarterly* 47 (1984):36–42.
102. Lynn K. White, "Determinants of Spousal Interaction: Marital Structure or Marital Happiness," *Journal of Marriage and the Family* 45 (1983):511–519.
103. James M. Honeycutt, Charmain Wilson, and Christine Parker, "Effects of Sex and Degree of Happiness on Perceived Styles of Communicating in and out of the Marital Relationship," *Journal of Marriage and the Family* 44 (1983):395–406.
104. Joe F. Pitman, Jr., Sharon Price, and Patrick C. McKenry, "Marital Cohesion: A Path Model," *Journal of Marriage and the Family* 45 (1983):521–531.
105. J. Blake, "Demographic Revolution and Family Evolution: Some Implications for American Women," in P. W. Berman and E. R. Rainey, eds., *Women: A Developmental Perspective* (Washington D.C.: NIH Publication No. 82-2298, 1982).
106. L. P. Salazar, *Infertility: How Couples Can Cope* (Boston: Resolve, 1986).
107. Arthur G. Neal, H. Theodore Groat, and Harry W. Wicks, "Attitudes about Having Children: A Study of 600 Couples in the Early Years of Marriage," *Journal of Marriage and the Family* 51 (1989):313–328.
108. Jean Veevers, "Voluntary Childless Wives: An Exploratory Study," *Sociology and Social Research* 57 (1973):356–366.
109. Veevers, *op. cit.*; Ellen M. Nason and Margaret M. Paloma, *Voluntary Childless Couples: The Emergence of a Variant Lifestyle* (Beverly Hills, Calif.: Sage, 1976).
110. S. Koep, G. Bolte, and J. D. Hull. "Is the Middle-Class Shrinking? *Time* (November 3, 1986):54–56.

111. N. Callan, "The Impact of the First Birth: Married and Single Women Preferring Childlessness, One Child or Two Children," *Journal of Marriage and the Family* 48 (1986):261–269.

112. Reiss, *Family Systems in America, op. cit.,* p. 358.

113. Population Reference Bureau, "U.S. Population: Where We Are: Where We Are Going," *Population Bulletin* 37, no. 2 (1982): 3–51; L. C. Harriman "Marital Adjustment as Related to Personal and Marital Changes Accompanying Parenthood," *Family Relations* 34 (1986):233–239; Jay Belsky, Mary Lang, and Michael Rouine, "Stability and Change in Marriage across the Transition to Parenthood: A Second Study," *Journal of Marriage and the Family* 47 (1985):855–865; E. L. Worthington, Jr., and B. G. Buston, "The Marriage Relationship during the Transition to Parenthood," *Journal of Family Issues* 7 (1986):443–473.

114. U.S. Bureau of the Census, *Statistical Abstract of the United States: 1986* (Washington, D.C.: U.S. Government Printing Office, 1987).

115. *Ibid.*

116. *Ibid.*

117. Ann Swidler, "Love and Adulthood in American Culture," in A. Skolmad and J. Skolnick, eds., *Family in Transition,* 4th ed. (New York: Little, Brown, 1983), pp. 223–228.

118. Lawrence L. Santi, "Change in the Structure and Size of American Households: 1970–1985," *Journal of Marriage and the Family* 49 (1987):833–837.

119. Reiss, *op. cit.,* p. 362.

120. Andres Hacker, ed., *U/S: A Statistical Portrait of the American People* (New York: Viking, 1983); Jane Riblett Wilkie, "The Trend toward Delayed Parenthood," *Journal of Marriage and the Family* 43 (1981):583–591.

121. Alice Rossi, "Transition to Parenthood," in Peter Rose, ed., *Socialization and the Life Cycle* (New York: St. Martin's, 1979), pp. 132–145.

122. *Ibid.*

123. *Ibid.*

124. Ellen Galinsky, *Between Generations: The Six Stages of Parenthood* (New York: Times Books, 1980).

125. Robin Palkovitz and M. Sussman, eds., "Transitions to Parenthood," *Marriage and Family Review* 12 (1988); Martha Cox, ed., "Progress and Continued Challenges in Understanding the Transition to Parenthood," *Journal of Family Issues* 6 (1985):395–408; Carolyn Cowan, P. Cowan, G. Heming, E. Garrett, W. Coysh, H. Curtis-Boles, and A. Boles, "Transition to Parenthood: His, Hers and Theirs," *Journal of Family Issues* 6 (1985):461–481.

126. Worthington and Buston, *op. cit.*

127. Cowan et al., *op. cit.;* Graham L. Staines and Pam L. Libby, "Men and Women in Role Relationships," in Richard D. Ashmore and Frances K. DelBoca, eds., *The Social Psychology of Female-Male Relations* (New York: Academic Press, 1986), 211–258; Jay Belky, Mary Land, and Ted L. Huston, "Sex Typing and Division of Labor as Determinants of Marital Change across the Transition to Parenthood," *Journal of Personality and Social Psychology* 50 (1986):517–522; Jay Belsky, Graham Spanier, and Michael Rovine, "Stability and Change in Marriage across the Transition to Parenthood," *Journal of Marriage and the Family* 45 (1983):567–577; Diane N. Ruble, Alison S. Fleming, Lisa S. Hackel, and Charles Stangor, "Changes in Marital Relationship during the Transition to First Time Motherhood: Effects of Violated Expectations Concerning Division of Household Labor," *Journal of Personality and Social Psychology* 55 (1988):78–87.

128. Lynn K. White and Alan Booth, "The Transition to Parenthood and Marital Quality," *Journal of Family Issues* 6 (1985):435–449; Susan M. McHale and Ted L. Huston, "A Longitudinal Study of the Transition to Parenthood and Its Effects on the Marriage Relationship," *Journal of Family Issues* 6 (1985):409–433.
129. Cowan, et al., *op. cit.;* Shelly M. MacDermid, Ted L. Huston, and Susan M. McHale, "Changes in Marriage Associated with the Transition to Parenthood: Individual Differences as a Function of Sex-Role Attitudes and Changes in the Division of Household Labor," *Journal of Marriage and the Family* 52 (1990): 475–486.
130. Holly Waldron and Donald K. Routh, "The Effect of the First Child on the Marital Relationship," *Journal of Marriage and the Family* 43 (1981):785–788; Belsky et al., *op. cit.*
131. Jeffrey P. Wright, S. W. Henggeler, and I. Craig, "Problems in Paradise? A Longitudinal Examination of the Transition to Parenthood," *Journal of Applied Developmental Psychology* 7 (1986):277–291; Sylvia W. Sirigano and M. S. Lachmen, "Personality Change during the Transition to Parenthood: The Role of Perceived Infant Temperament," *Developmental Psychology* 21 (1985):558–567.
132. Pamela M. Wallace and Ian H. Gotlib, "Marital Adjustment during the Transition to Parenthood: Stability and Predictors of Change," *Journal of Marriage and the Family* 52 (1990):21–29; MacDermid et al., *op. cit.*
133. Cowan et al., *op. cit.;* Staines and Libby, *op. cit.;* Ruble et al., *op. cit.*
134. Cowan et al., *op. cit.;* McHale and Huston, *op. cit.;* Ralph LaRossa and Maureen Mulligan LaRossa, *Transition to Parenthood: How Infants Change Families* (Beverly Hills, Calif.: Sage, 1981); Ruble et al. *op. cit.*
135. Judith M. Gerson and Kathy Peiss, "Boundaries, Negotiation, Consciousness: Reconceptualizaing Gender Relations," *Social Problems* 32 (1985):317–331; Cowan et al., *op. cit.*
136. Belsky, et al., *op. cit.;* MacDermid et al., *op. cit.*
137. Gerson and Peiss, *op. cit.*
138. Kathryn Backett, "The Negotiation of Fatherhood," in Charlie Lewis and Margaret O'Brien, eds., *Reassessing Fatherhood: New Observations of Fathers and the Modern Family* (London: Sage, 1987), pp. 74–90; Mary G. Boulton, *On Being a Mother: A Study of Women with Preschool Children* (London: Tavistock, 1983).
139. Waldron and Routh, *op. cit.*
140. Worthington and Buston, *op. cit.*
141. Belsky, *op. cit.*, 1985.
142. Cowan et al., *op. cit.*
143. Cowan, et al., *op. cit.;* MacDermid, et al., *op. cit.*
144. Staines and Libby, *op. cit.;* Ruble et al., *op. cit.*
145. McHale and Huston, *op. cit.;* LaRossa and LaRossa, *op. cit.*
146. LaRossa and LaRossa, *op. cit.;* Lorna McKee, "Fathers' Participation in Infant Care, A Critique," in Lorna McKee and Margaret O'Brien, eds., *The Father Figure* (London: Tavistock, 1982), pp. 120–138.
147. LaRossa and LaRossa, *op. cit.*
148. Shirley Hanson and Frederick Bozett, "Fatherhood: A Review and Resources," *Family Relations* 36 (1987):333–340.
149. A. Machung, "Talking Career, Thinking Job: Gender Differences in Career and Family Expectations of Berkely Seniors," *Feminist Studies* 15 (1989):35–58.
150. Bernice L. Neugarten, "Adult Personality: Toward a Psychology of the Life Cycle," in Bernice Neugarten, ed., *Middle Age and Aging* (Chicago: University of

Chicago Press, 1968), p. 144; B. Neugarten and D. A. Neugarten, "The Changing Meanings of Age," *Psychology Today* 21, no.5 (1987):29–33.

151. Nancy C. Schlossberg, "Taking the Mystery out of Change," *Psychology Today* 21, no. 5 (1987):74–75.

152. Daniel Levinson with Charlotte Darrow, Marie Levinson, Edward Klein, and Braxton McKee, *The Seasons of a Man's Life* (New York: Ballentine, 1978).

153. *Ibid.*

154. *Ibid.*

155. Ellen Goodman, *Turning Points* (New York: Fawcett-Columbine, 1979).

156. Kathleen M. Mogul, "Women in Midlife: Decisions, Rewards, and Conflicts Related to Work and Careers," *American Journal of Psychiatry* 136 (1979):1139–1143.

157. Rueben Hill, *Family Development in Three Generations* (Cambridge, Mass.: Schenkman, 1970), p. 48.

158. Anne Foner, *Aging and Old Age: New Perspectives* (Englewood Cliffs, N.J.: Prentice-Hall, 1986).

159. *Ibid.*

160. Neugarten and Neugarten, *op. cit.*

161. Inge Powell Bell, "The Double Standard of Age" in Freeman, *op. cit.*, pp. 256–263.

162. Jean Silligmann, Deborah Witherspoon, Nadine Joseph, and Lauren Picker, "Not Past Their Prime," *Newsweek* (August 6, 1990):86–88; Carol Tavris, "Old Age Is Not What It Used to Be," *New York Times Magazine* (September 27, 1987), pp. 5–6.

163. Bernice Neugarten, Vivian Wood, Ruth Kraines, and Barbara Loomis, "Women's Attitude toward the Menopause," in Neugarten, *op. cit.*, pp. 195–201.

164. Edward M. Brecher, *Love, Sex and Aging* (Boston: Little, Brown, 1984).

165. B. Neugarten, "The Awareness of Middle Age," in Neugarten, *op. cit.*, p. 97.

166. Maxine Szinovacz, *Women's Retirement: Policy Implications of Recent Research* (Beverly Hills, Calif.: Sage, 1982).

167. Neugarten, *op. cit.*, p. 96.

168. Jan D. Sinnott, *Sex Roles and Aging: Theory and Research from a Systems Perspective* (New York: Kaerger, 1986); Cynthia Dobson, "Sex-Role and Marital-Role Expectations," in Timothy H. Brubaker, ed., *Family Relationships* in *Later Life* (Beverly Hills, Calif.: Sage, 1983), pp. 109–126.

169. Rosalie Guilford, "Contrasts in Marital Satisfaction throughout Old Age: An Exchange Theory Analysis," *Journal of Gerontology* 39 (1984):325–333.

170. *Ibid.*

171. *Ibid.*

172. J. S. Francher, "It's the Pepsi Generation: Accelerated Aging and the Television Commercial," *International Journal of Aging and Human Development* 4 (1983): 245–255.

173. N. Cobb, "What's Ahead after the Twenties: Not-so-Sweet 16," *Boston Globe* (January 24, 1982); Bell, *op. cit.*

174 Linda George, *Role Transitions in Later Life* (Monterey, Calif.: Brooks/Cole, 1984), p. 130.

175. Pauline Bart, "Depression in Middle-Aged Women," in Vivian Gornick and B. K. Moran, eds., *Women in Sexist Society* (New York: Basic Books, 1972), pp. 162–186.

176. J. Veroff, R. Kulka, and E. Douvan, *Mental Health in America: Patterns of Help-Seeking from 1957–1976* (New York: Basic Books, 1981).

177. M. F. Lowenthal, C. Thurnher, and D. Chiriboga, *"Four States of Life: A Comparative Study of Women and Men Facing Transitions* (San Francisco: Jossey-Bass, 1975).

178. Timothy H. Brubaker and Charles B. Hennon, "Responsibility for Household Tasks: Comparing Dual-Earner and Dual-Retired Marriages," in Szinovacz, *op. cit.*, pp. 205–219.

179. Linda K. George, Gerda G. Fillenbaum, and Erdman Palmore, "Sex Differences in the Antecedents and Consequences of Retirement," *Journal of Gerontology* 39 (1984):364–371.

180. Guilford, *op. cit.*

181. Sinnott, *op. cit.*

182. R. W. Hubbard, J. F. Sanos, and B. J. Farrow. "Age Differences in Sex-Role Diffusion: A Study of Middle-Aged and Older Adult Married Couples" (paper presented at a meeting of the Gerontological Society, Washington, D.C., 1979).

183. K. Douglas and D. Arenberg, "Age Changes, Cohort Differences and Cultural Change on the Guilford-Zimmerman Temperament Survey," *Journal of Gerontology* 33 (1978):737–747.

184. L. M. Breytspraak, *The Development of Self in Later Life* (Boston: Little, Brown, 1984).

185. Sinnott, *op. cit.*

186. *Ibid.*

187. Marie Richmond-Abbott, "The Interaction of Gender-Role Convergence in Seniors with Coping Skills and Life Satisfaction" (paper presented at the National Council on Family Relations, Atlanta, 1987).

188. Marie Richmond-Abbott, "Sex-Roles of Mothers and Children in Divorced, Single-Parent Families," *Journal of Divorce* 8, no. 1 (1984):23–34.

189. Sinnott, *op. cit.*

190. J. M. Patterson and J. J. McCubben, "Gender Roles and Coping," *Journal of Marriage and the Family* 46 (1984):95–104.

191. J. K. Antill and J. D. Cunningham, "Self-Esteem as a Function of Masculinity in Both Sexes," *Journal of Consulting and Clinical Psychology* 47 (1979):393–400.

192. M. Windle, "Sex-Role Orientation, Cognitive Flexibility and Life Satisfaction among Older Adults," *Psychology of Women Quarterly* 10 (1981):263–273.

193. Norah C. Keating and Pricilla Cole, "What Do I Do with Him 24 Hours a Day?: Changes in the Housewife Role after Retirement," *The Gerontologist* 20 (1980): 84–89.

194. Brubaker and Hennon, *op. cit.*

195. Guilford, *op. cit.*

196. R. Hefner, M. Rebecca, and B. Oleshansky, "Development of Sex-Role Transcendence," in Alexander Kaplan and Joan Beam, eds., *Beyond Sex-Role Stereotypes: Readings toward a Psychology of Androgyny* (Boston: Little, Brown, 1976), pp. 89–97.

Chapter 9

Diversity in American Families

The family as we know it is not a "natural" group created by the claims of "blood" but a sphere of human relationships shaped by a state that recognized families as units that hold property, provide care and welfare and attend particularly to the young—a sphere conceptualized as a realm of love and intimacy. . . .[1]

This quote captures the essence of the contemporary American family. Both the structural form of the family and the gender roles within it have changed dramatically in the past twenty years. This chapter describes some of these changing family forms. It focuses primarily on certain variations in which gender roles and family structure have intersected to produce change or, occasionally, to sustain the traditional roles.

DUAL-CAREER FAMILIES

In Chapter 8 we looked at changing power relations and the division of labor in families. We saw that one of the most important factors that has caused change in these areas is the employment of women outside the home. However, for the majority of women with part-time or full-time jobs, equality has been elusive. Let us now look at a group of people who, in the words of Rosanna Hertz, are "more equal than others." Dual-career couples are distinguished from the majority of two-earner couples by a number of factors: Both partners are committed to long-term professional careers, their joint income is well above the average, and they make family adjustments so that they can sustain both careers.

In these marriages, both spouses are committed to demanding and time-consuming work. It is instructive to see how these couples deal with gender roles and conflicts between work and family.

Many women in dual-career families are highly educated, but they did not go directly from college or graduate school into their jobs. Rather, they entered their careers by a meandering path, often starting at lower-level jobs and part-time work and later adding education that led to increased responsibility. By contrast, the men in these families usually moved directly into their careers.

Researchers agree that a woman's career line is different from a man's in most cases.[2] Paloma and associates distinguish various types of careers. The *regular career* is one in which a person pursues professional training just after graduating from college and, after completing that training, begins work and continues it full-time without long interruptions. An *interrupted career* begins as a regular career but is interrupted, usually for child rearing. *Second careers* begin after a divorce or after the children are grown, and a *modified second career* is one in which professional training and a career come after the last child is old enough not to need full-time mothering, usually at the beginning of school or nursery school.[3] Obviously, women are more likely to have one of the last three career lines. Paloma and associates found that only 38 percent of the professional women in their sample had regular careers. These women had had to make extensive compromises, although they were able to maintain a full-time uninterrupted work schedule. Usually the compromises included eliminating the "extras" of evening work, travel, and annual meetings. Sometimes the compromise was on the family side: having no or few children and spending minimal time with them. Thirty-six percent of the sample had interrupted career lines, having substituted part-time work for full-time involvement while the children were young; 27 percent had second careers or modified second careers.[4]

Most men in dual-career families are supportive and proud of their wives' careers, although some admitted that they would feel reservations if their wives earned more than they did.[5] Many of these families gradually made the transition from traditional roles to a more equitable system as the demands of the wife's career became greater. In *More Equal Than Others*, Rosanna Hertz explains that it is

> not feminist ideology that leads these couples to construct new marriages or new approaches to family roles; instead, their employers' demands and their own desires for individual and combined career success lead them toward these changes. The ideology of equality, particularly in marital roles, emerges out of common opportunities and constraints. . . .[6]

Hertz points out that one can see the persistence of traditional roles in her Chicago sample of dual-career couples, in which the husband handles the family finances and the wife is responsible for establishing the child-care arrangements.[7]

Almost every researcher who has examined the dual-career family has pointed out that women and men do not handle the conflict between work and family demands in the same way. Being married and having a family is much more likely to affect a woman's career than a man's. Most women in dual-career families were not willing to give up having children altogether. They compromised by limiting the number of children and frequently by postponing having children for a long time. They also compromised in other ways. One woman typified these compromises when she said, "I turned down a chance for an administrative, eleven-month, time-consuming job to keep the flexibility of a normal academic year for my spouse and children."[8] Although this respondent regretted her decision, most of the women interviewed accepted compromise as a necessary part of combining career and marriage. They did state, however, that they envied their husbands, who did not have to make similar compromises. In addition, almost all the professional women with children reduced their professional involvement during the child-rearing years. Some cut their workload back to part-time work; almost all cut out extras such as professionally related travel, speaking engagements, and research and publication.

For women, the conflict between work and family is particularly disturbing because work demands usually give way to those of the family. Joseph Pleck points out that

> for women, the demands of the family role are permitted to intrude into the work role. . . . For husbands, the work-family boundary is likewise asymmetrically permeable, but in other directions. Many husbands literally "take work home."[9]

Thus, many women find that their lives are subject to the overlapping demands of home and work. These career women say it is necessary for them to be very well organized and have a great deal of physical vitality. They often mention feeling physically fatigued, however, and say they have to give up leisure and even seeing their friends to pursue their careers.[10] Many dual-career wives feel that their careers have suffered because of family demands. If they spend fewer hours in the office or take time off from their careers, they feel isolated, especially from access to new ideas and social support from a professional group.[11]

A particularly difficult problem for all dual-career couples is finding quality child care.[12] Most of the women in Hertz's sample hired a one-on-one child-care worker to come into the home. (Ironically, to pursue their careers, these dual-career mothers often used the labor of other, more unfortunate women. Most of the day care workers were recent immigrants or very young or elderly women.) Most dual-career wives were worried about the day care that was available,[13] although most research shows that the children of employed mothers generally do not suffer.[14]

Being in a dual-career family affects the attitudes of family members.[15] Both sons and daughters of employed mothers hold more equalitarian gender-role attitudes;[16] and view women as more competent,[17] and the daughters are likely to be independent[18] and to plan to work outside the home themselves.[19] Incidentally, there has been no consistent finding that the children of employed mothers feel deprived.[20] While these women spend less time with their children, the gap is smallest among the most educated, who spend time with their children even at the expense of sleep and leisure time.[21]

A second major problem for dual-career couples is how to allocate time. Most studies find no difference in division of labor between dual-career couples and dual-earner couples, in which the wife earns significantly less than the husband does. In either case, the husbands of employed women spend little or no more time in housework than do the husbands of nonemployed women.[22] Pleck cites data showing that husbands of employed wives spend 1.8 more hours per week in housework and 2.7 more hours in child care but admits that this probably occurs because employed women cut corners and do less so that the husband's relative contribution seems to increase.[23] Another study reports that men spend very little time with their children, approximately 25 minutes a day.[24] Apparently, any difference in hours spent on housework and child care is linked to the hours the wife has available. Husbands fill in if they absolutely have to because the wife is unavailable, but they do not take on significantly more housework when they themselves have more time.[25]

Most dual-career couples solve the problem of housework by hiring outside help. To find time to spend with the children at home, many wives adjust their schedules to the family's needs. They spend the evening hours with their children but then get up earlier than the rest of the household in order to get work done. They also try to work when the children are napping.[26] Unfortunately, while most of the literature shows that dual-career wives are physically and emotionally healthy and have high self esteem,[27] the dangers of physical and emotional exhaustion are evident.[28]

Patterns of Accommodation

Some couples cope by lowering their aspirations and stepping off the fast career track, thus reducing the career role;[29] or they may have no children or only one child, thus reducing the domestic role.[30] Another possibility is "recycling" either a career or peak family commitments. Usually the most demanding years of family and career coincide, but couples can decide to have children later or to have careers that peak later so that these peak demands do not occur at the same time.[31] Finally, one pattern of **accommodation** that fits into many dual-career couples' lives is "segmentation," or compartmentalizing each area so that the couple is not dealing with family and work demands during the same hours or days. Segmentation may mean that a certain time at home is allocated for the family and nothing else is allowed to interfere.[32] These are all "ideal" types, and many couples combine styles.

If both spouses want total career commitment, it is probably essential that one or both careers be very flexible, with flexible hours or work that can be done at home. It may also be easier if the spouses are at different phases in their careers. If one is settled and secure, that person can take over more of

ARLO AND JANIS ® by Jimmy Johnson

Reprinted with permission of NEA, Inc.

the home role while the other person is moving up.[33] In the later years, couples may be happier because of the reduced demands of family, work, or both.[34]

Commuter Marriages

Sometimes segmentation may require geographic separation or commuting, where the couple work in separate locations during the week and get together on weekends. In spite of the seriousness of the problem of deciding where to work, one study found that only half the career wives had discussed the issue of geographic location with their prospective husbands before marriage.[35] When the decision was made after marriage, it was primarily influenced by where the husband could best work. The husband took account of the wife's interests, but usually in a secondary way. For example, he would take a position in a large metropolitan area because his wife would be more likely to find work there; however, she was the one who had to look for another job.[36] At the same time, the husband's employment was more contingent upon his wife's career than many couples realized. The career interests of the wife might threaten the husband's employment in cases where the employer was afraid the husband would move if his wife could not find work. Particularly when the wife was in a high-status occupation, her career interests restricted the husband's geographic mobility.[37] If the dual-career couple opted to remain where they were for family reasons, both spouses might share the professional costs of limited geographic mobility.[38]

A person who moves or stays because of a spouse's opportunities contrary to his or her own best choices is called "tied." At the present time, a tied mover is most likely to be a wife and a tied stayer a husband. Researchers speculate that as men and women's market positions approach equality, family migration in dual-career couples may decrease.[39]

Benefits and Burdens

We have detailed the burdens of the dual-career family, particularly the dual-career wife, yet recent literature shows little reduction of marital satisfaction in such families.[40] While some researchers have emphasized the stress placed upon the dual-career family during the peak years of child rearing, findings from a national sample show that the extra income from the working wife is particularly beneficial during the parental stage of the family.[41] This study also points out that the extrafamily work role seems to keep wives from concentrating exclusively on their children. Simpson and England have introduced the theory of **role homophily**, in which very similar marital roles (both spouses combining work and family commitments) build marital solidarity. They have tested their theory on traditional families, in which the greatest marital satisfaction occurs before childbearing and after the children have been launched and thus the greatest satisfaction coincides with the period of

ARLO & JANIS® by Jimmy Johnson

Reprinted by permission of NEA, Inc.

least gender-role differentiation. They believe that the small gender-role differentiation in dual-career marriages is similarly likely to promote marital solidarity.[42]

Other variables that affect the marital satisfaction of dual-career couples include the attitudes of the spouses toward each other's work. The wives emphasized that the husband's supportive attitude was extremely important in allowing them to advance their careers.[43] Most dual-career couples said that they did not feel directly competitive in their work because they were in different fields or because they made it a point to cooperate. Those who did feel competitive were competitive in many areas, such as general status and hours worked, as well as in professional accomplishments.

There was no real equality of the sexes in terms of role sharing when one compared the obligations of the women in dual-career couples with those of the men. The men had much more freedom and opportunity to pursue their careers than the women did. Some researchers suggest that the future holds the promise of greater development of equality in dual-career marriages.[44] Young people are starting married life more committed to an equal relationship, the concern about occupational equality for women is pushing many employers to adopt policies that more readily accommodate family roles, and men seem to have lessened their work involvement as the health hazards of excessive involvement have been documented and thus have more time for family roles. The woman may also gain equality because she has more leverage and is appreciated and needed. In addition, a married wage earner does not have to live with the fear that she will not survive without the marriage; she has an attractive alternative.

SINGLE-PARENT FAMILIES

One structural variation in the family that seems to affect gender roles is the single-parent family. Whether the single-parent family originated as such or became a single-parent family after divorce or the death of one of the spouses, gender roles in this type of family are necessarily different from those in two-parent families. Obviously, one parent must do the traditional tasks usually performed by both sexes. We will look at how these single-parent families vary in accordance with their reasons for coming into being. While the number of unwed, single-parent mothers has increased tremendously in the last decade, most single-parent families in this country originate after a divorce.

Divorce

The low point in the divorce rate in the United States in this century was reached during 1933, at the height of the depression, when people could not afford to get divorced. The rate gradually rose again and hit a peak at the end of World War II. It increased gradually until 1965 but more than doubled in the next fourteen years to reach a record level in 1979. (In 1973, the number of marriages ending in divorce surpassed those ending in death for the first time.) Since 1981 the divorce rate has stabilized and even declined a little bit.[45] It was down 3 percent in 1982 and another 4 percent in 1983.[46] How can we explain the decline? One possibility is that the bulk of the baby boom generation is past the late twenties, the most likely divorce years. The lower divorce rate may also reflect the drop in marriages during the mid-1970s.

In spite of this stabilization, approximately half (49 percent) of all marriages end in divorce. For those with a college degree, the proportion is closer to 40 percent; for those without a degree, the proportion is closer to 60 percent. Most demographers predict little dramatic movement upward or downward in the divorce rate in the next ten years.[47] The later age at marriage (possibly making young adults more mature), the increasing education of those who marry, a growing fear of the consequences of divorce, and the trend toward a lower remarriage rate (reducing the pool of those eligible to divorce) may all lead to a lower divorce rate. Counterbalancing factors that may lead to a higher divorce rate include the continuing high level of employment of women (who are able to support themselves if divorced), the continued high level of cohabitation outside marriage, the continuing low birthrate (people do not hesitate to divorce because they have children), and the growing cultural acceptance of divorce. These various factors seem to balance out and lead to the stabilization that has been predicted.[48]

Single Parenthood

The single-parent family is the fastest growing family form in the United States. Since 1960 the proportion of single-parent families has doubled, and it is currently growing at two and one-half times the rate of growth of husband-wife families.[49] About 60 percent of all divorces now involve children. In fact, 40 percent of the children growing up in the 1980s had divorced parents (one of every three white children and two of every three black children). An additional 5 percent will be affected by a long-term separation, and about 2 percent will lose a parent by death.[50] Twelve percent will have a mother who has never married. In 1984, 23 percent of children under age 18 were living with only one parent. Projections show that nearly 60 percent of the children born this year can be expected to spend a year or more in a one-parent family before reaching 18 years of age.[51] Fathers who have custody of their children have become more common as well. Single-parent families headed by fathers now constitute about 12 percent of all single-parent families. Let us look at the changes that come about when a two-parent family becomes a single-parent family.

Special Problems

Poverty.   Single-parent males with custody seldom suffer a debilitating loss of income, but for single custodial mothers, the biggest family burden is usually an economic one. Many single-parent mothers have never worked, have outdated skills, or are now working at jobs that have relatively low average pay. They are subject to the problems of low income, few fringe benefits, occupational segregation, and discrimination that face all working women. In 1987, the mean family income of two-parent families was $34,700 while that of female-headed families was $14,620.[52] After divorce, the income of the custodial single-parent mother falls an average of 73 percent and that of the noncustodial father rises 41 percent.[53] Fifty-one and a half percent of children under 18 years of age in female-headed families fall below the poverty level. These statistics result from the prevalence of divorce and death among poor families, low and irregular levels of alimony and child support, a lack of public assistance, and fewer opportunities for female heads of families to work. If these women are not able to have their children cared for by family members or friends, they must often pay exorbitant rates for day care.

Role Overload.   A study by Mavis Hetherington and colleagues found that another major problem for single-parent mothers and fathers is role overload. This is a problem particularly for the single-parent mother, as she is often unable to buy replacement services such as housecleaning help as most single fathers are able to do. Custodial mothers have to deal with the tasks normally performed by two parents: earning an income, taking care of a house, having time for children, and doing all the errands and maintenance chores that are needed. They are concerned about areas that may be new to them, such as insurance, mortgages, taxes, wills, and judging the appropriateness of charges by service people.[54]

In contrast, single-parent fathers with custody found that their major problem was adjusting to household routines and combining the demands of home and work roles. However, most of these fathers had mastered this combination by a year or so after the divorce and felt comfortable in their new roles. They were also more likely than mothers to get household and child-care help from paid employees or female relatives and friends.[55] A continuing issue for many custodial fathers is the problems and needs of adolescent daughters, particularly in the realm of sex education and sexuality.[56] In general, girls in father-custodial families tended to be less well adjusted than were those in mother-custodial families; boys tend to be less well adjusted in mother-custodial families.[57]

Stigma and Loneliness.   A single-parent mother also has to deal with stigma and loneliness. Many of these women found that while their married friends were supportive for a while, they excluded these women from couples' gatherings. At times these mothers were even viewed with suspicion and fear as a threat to existing marriages. The single-parent mother usually found that she made new friends among other single and divorced people who acted as a support system. In most cases, it was difficult for her to get into social situations where she could meet men without intimating that she was encouraging sexual advances; it was often difficult for her to get and pay baby-sitters so that she could leave for entertainment. Many of these women also felt the loss of identity connected with the ex-husband's status and their status as a wife. Many felt unattractive and rejected.[58]

Fathers without custody reported that they felt lost and isolated after divorce; they especially felt the loss of their children. In the first year after divorce many suffered from self-doubt and depression and tried to overcome these problems with frantic dating and social activities. Many tried various forms of self-improvement, such as going on diets and taking courses. Single-parent custodial fathers, though, suffered less from isolation. A single man with custody is viewed with approval by the community and also has more of a chance to lead an active social life.

Hetherington describes single-parent fathers as having gone through a "hip, hirsute, and Honda" syndrome in which they put great emphasis on clothes, often grew beards or long hair, and bought motorcycles and sports cars. These fathers were more likely to keep a support system of married friends because they wanted to have companions to do things with when the children visited. Even fathers without custody saw their children more than they did before the divorce and reported that their relationship with their children had improved.[59] However, poor parenting practices included extreme indulgence with an "every day is Christmas" approach to the children. Contact with the children gradually became less frequent among most fathers, although they continued to see their sons more than their daughters.[60] These fathers also seemed less concerned about their adolescent children than about their preadolescents.[61]

In spite of the problems, most single parents seemed to feel that they were coping well. In one study, mothers reported that they derived "considerable satisfaction from their successful negotiation of the progression of problems that confronted them as they went about the business of earning a living, caring for their children, and attempting to meet their needs for intimacy and adult interaction." Many mentioned increased autonomy and independence. There was also a feeling of individual achievement and self-fulfillment on the part of many divorced women.[62]

While some wished to remarry to regularize their positions, others deemphasized remarriage in their newfound independence.[63] This willingness to stay single was reinforced by bonds with other single parents. The leveling off of the remarriage rate, especially for women in higher economic, occupational, and social strata, reflects this newfound autonomy.[64]

Similarly, in many studies single-parent fathers with custody reported relative confidence and satisfaction. However, Keshet found that men who took care of their children often made this a major focus in reorganizing their lives.[65] In general, studies report that single parents are forced into less stereotyped behavior. Many of the mothers were forced to assume certain parts of a male parent's role: They had to work at paid employment, be authority figures to their children, and cope with bills, insurance, and household repairs. In a similar way, fathers did nurturing, maternal tasks, and household chores.

Gender-Role Attitudes

How does being forced into less stereotyped behavior affect the gender-role attitudes of single parents and their children? We have more information about families headed by women than we do about those headed by men. Brown and colleagues report that women who have less traditional gender-role attitudes adjust more easily to divorce and the housework role and are more likely to take a job to support themselves and their children.[66]

The psychological theory of *cognitive consistency* states that people come to hold values that support the behavior that they have to perform. If this theory is applied to single parents who are doing both masculine- and feminine-stereotyped tasks, it seems likely that the parents would modify traditional sex roles in a more liberal direction. Children might also modify their attitudes and behavior as they modeled themselves after their parents.

A study which tested whether the gender-role attitudes of single parents go along with the more androgynous behavior they are forced to adopt found that both male and female single parents were more liberal in their attitudes than would be expected in the population as a whole. However, the custodial fathers were generally more conservative than were the mothers, and girls of single-parent fathers were considerably more conservative in their attitudes than were girls of single-parent mothers. Boys' scores did not differ markedly no matter who the custodial parent was, but boys were more conservative than girls. The correlations between the adults' and children's scores showed that children have attitudes similar to those of the custodial parent and that this similarity increases greatly when the child and parent are the same sex.[67]

In this same study, neither fathers nor mothers were good at translating their attitudes into behavior with their children. Mothers declared that they wanted to see nonstereotyped characteristics in their children. They hoped that their boys would be thoughtful and their girls would be independent. Fathers desired cross-sex traits in their daughters but seldom asked for them in their sons. However, both mothers and fathers gave their children neutral or traditional toys most (90 percent) of the time. While girls got sports equipment such as ice skates and skis, they did not get footballs, baseball bats, and basketballs. There was only one instance of a boy getting a doll, although some younger boys got stuffed animals. Similarly, parents often gave their children chores that were stereotyped by sex: Boys were more likely to carry out the garbage, while girls vacuumed. Although chores tended to be switched around when more than one child was present, older girls did more housework than older boys did.[68]

The single parents in this sample were unaware that they were not living up to their own nonstereotypic values when they assigned chores and gave gifts. The fact that this kind of behavior occurs among very liberal parents gives some indication of how traditional the gender-role socialization of most children is.

Effect on Children

The effect of single-parent families has been extensively studied with respect to gender-role preferences and sex-typed behavior among children. Many of these studies emphasize the importance of the father in developing certain sex-typed behaviors in both boys and girls. Some studies have found that boys reared by warm, dominant, masculine fathers in nuclear families are more masculine than other boys are.[69] Other studies report that girls who receive warmth and high evaluation of their feminine behaviors from their fathers are more feminine.[70] However, adolescent boys from single-parent homes show no differences in sex-typed behavior or gender-role preferences in most studies.[71] They may show a "compensatory masculinity" in which they manifest excessively masculine, assertive forms of behavior at some times and show feminine behaviors such as dependence at others.[72] Hetherington argued that such compensatory masculinity "is a result of the father-absent boy's attempts to maintain a masculine identification when no masculine role model is present,"[73] but others have claimed that this is an erroneous assumption because fatherless boys are not as lacking in role models as is commonly assumed.[74] Adolescent girls from fatherless homes may show some discomfort and either aggression or shyness in their sexual interaction with men in later years.[75]

Thus, the studies indicate that early absence of a father may affect the behavior of young boys and later that of adolescent girls. However, some of the behavioral differences seem to be due as much to the custodial mother's attitudes and the behavior occasioned by divorce as to absence of the father. Children may get less help with schoolwork or monitoring of social activities, although there is some evidence that single-parent mothers are restrictive and overprotective.[76] However, in a longitudinal study, Hetherington found that mothers who encouraged independent, mature behaviors and who were warm and nurturing had children who were highly androgynous.[77] Thus, most of the studies show little or no difference between children from single-parent families and those from two-parent families. The differences that do occur seem to be due as much to the attitude of the parent as to the structure of the home.

In conclusion, children do not seem to suffer in single-parent homes, and most single parents cope relatively well with their situation. Indeed, they may develop some of the assets of the androgynous person, such as confidence and a more flexible repertoire of behaviors with which to face the world. Judging from the Michigan study, some single-parent families hold more liberal gender-role attitudes than the population as a whole and model a greater variety of behaviors to their children, although they do not seem to consciously train the children to be more androgynous.[78] Even with all their problems and difficulties, single-parent families may end up being in the vanguard in adopting more liberal gender-role attitudes and more liberal behavior.

REMARRIAGE

Most of those who divorce in the United States eventually remarry (Table 1). Forty percent of all new marriages are remarriages,[79] and more than 20 percent of households that contain a married couple are remarried-couple households.[80] In 1987 there were 5.24 million remarried households in the United States. Eighty-four percent of divorced men and 77 percent of divorced women remarry, most within five years. The remarriage rate is highest for those in the youngest age brackets and tends to decline sharply at older ages. It declines the longer a person remains divorced. Young women with less education hasten to remarry and consistently represent the highest proportion of

Table 1   Remarried Families and Stepfamilies in the United States: 1987–1980

Type of Family	Percent	Millions
All families	100	64.49
Married-couple families with children under 18	79.9	51.54
	38.2	24.65
Remarried families:	17.1	11.00
with children under 18	8.1	5.24
Stepfamilies*	6.7	4.30
Not stepfamilies	1.4	.94
First-married families with children under 18	62.8	40.54
	30.1	19.41
One-parent families	11.3	7.25
Other families†	8.8	5.70

*An estimated 18 percent of remarried parents had all their young children after remarriage.
†Families of unmarried adults with no children under 18 in the household but with young adult children or other relatives sharing living arrangements.

SOURCE: U.S. Bureau of the Census, "Living Arrangements of Adults and Young Children," PC 80-2-4B (Washington, D.C.: U.S. Government Printing Office, 1985); U.S. Bureau of the Census, "Households, Families, Marital Status, and Living Arrangements: March 1987," Advance Report, Current Population Reports, Series P-20, no. 423 (Washington, D.C.: U.S. Government Printing Office, 1988).

those remarrying. Glick suggests that this may occur because they cannot support themselves. Women who have a college degree and who are childless are the least likely to remarry. Even among this group, however, more than 60 percent remarry.[81]

Goode states that the divorced status in this society is not a "regularized one; there are no specific rules and customs relating to divorced persons. They are set aside from the great majority of married couples and their role is not clearly defined."[82] Coping without a partner may be difficult for the single-parent mother in particular. Thus, there is a push to remarriage: Not only does the divorced person find a companion with whom to share work and pleasure, he or she becomes a member of the couples world again and has a "regularized" position. Therefore, the proportion of marriages that are remarriages has climbed steadily. In 1985, in 45 percent of marriages, the bride and groom were remarrying; in 6 percent, the bride and groom were marrying for the third time (up from 3 percent in 1970).[83] The time between divorce and remarriage is on the average three years.

We will concentrate on divorced people who remarry and on the changes in their lives that affect gender-role behavior. Serious adjustments often have to be made when a person remarries. Sixty percent of all remarriages fail, and the average length of these unions is only five years; when children are involved, 75 percent fail.[84] A reconstituted family has many problems. Finances are often a problem, with a remarried husband making child support payments to his former family and having less left for the new family. A former husband may stop sending child support payments when the wife remarries, and the new family may suffer a lower standard of living. Other problems are also evident. Each spouse comes to the marriage with patterns of behavior that were established in the first marriage. If the remarriage includes children, the partners are faced with the adjustments of dealing with each other's children and frequently with ex-spouses as well. While the children are usually those of the custodial mother, many fathers also have their children present at least some of the time. More than half the fathers in one study had children from a former marriage living with them.[85]

A recent analysis looked at some of the factors related to marital satisfaction in remarriages and concluded that people in remarriages are slightly less likely to report marital satisfaction and that married women in both first marriages and remarriages are more likely to be dissatisfied than are men. Remarried families in which only one parent is a stepparent are likely to report slightly greater satisfaction than are those in which there are two stepparents and two sets of children. However, there did not appear to be any difference in marital satisfaction between remarried couples who had children living with them and those who did not and between stepmothers and stepfathers.[86]

What are the implications of remarriage for gender roles? Because of the financial situation of most remarried couples, it is likely that the wife will continue working. It is also likely that she worked and supported her single-parent family before the remarriage, although this is not always the case. Her participation in the labor force is thus well established, and it is unlikely that she will be relegated to a domestic role. Her financial contribution means that she is more likely to gain power as the remarried pair make decisions.

Routines facilitating her employment have also been established; she is likely to have had some help with housework from children or paid employees and to expect to share the burdens of her domestic role. A study by Weingarten found that remarried men do more household chores than do men in first marriages.[87] In this study, it was found remarried spouses of ten years or less who have primary responsibility for housework are twice as likely as first-marrieds to report that their spouses often help with the housework. The study suggests that the remarried are more likely than the first-married to feel that the work they do in and around the house contributes a great deal to their "most important values"; at the same time, men may be less involved with parenting, at least parenting someone else's children. Weingarten reports that remarried men are less likely to report satisfaction with the parenting role.

Children in remarriages have a tremendous effect on the interaction between the spouses, and this may also affect gender roles. Eighty-eight percent of remarried families with children are raising some combination of natural children and stepchildren.[88] In the majority of remarried households where the children are those of the mother (90 percent), the mother probably has greater power. Her routines have been established, and she has the immediate support of her relatives.

However, other factors may erode her bases of power. She may be extremely dependent on the financial contribution of her husband or on the help with her children. She may be placed in the role of stepmother, which is conceded to be more difficult than that of stepfather, and she may be an outsider to the unit of her husband and his children.

There has recently been a small decline in the remarriage rate; this is attributed by some researchers to the greater likelihood that divorced people will cohabit and not remarry. Glick predicts, however, that this decline will only reduce the proportion of people who remarry after divorce from 80 percent to perhaps 75 percent.[89] Remarriage, with its attendant opportunities and problems, will thus remain an important part of the family system.

GAY RELATIONSHIPS AND FAMILIES

There is a new awareness that a family does not mean just a heterosexual couple. For years homosexual couples have considered themselves married, and many are now forming families. These families include adopted children, children from previous heterosexual marriages, and, for lesbians, children conceived deliberately by means of artificial insemination.

Although many gay couples frequented the bars and were more likely to have short-term relationships in the 1960s and 1970s,[90] recently gay male couples have joined lesbian couples in forming long-term, committed relationships. These couples think of themselves as a family, and their network of similar friends often constitutes an extended family.[91]

Accurate knowledge about such relationships is still hard to achieve, but recent research, especially a major study by Blumstein and Schwartz which compared lesbian couples, gay male couples, cohabiting heterosexual partners, and married couples, has provided a great deal of information.[92] Because their relationships are not based on traditional societal sexual scripts, homosexual couples are more free to establish new ways of doing things. They are likely to have more equal relationships and do less role-playing than heterosexual couples. They often divide chores on the basis of who has the most time or on the individual's inclination for doing a certain task. Lesbian couples in particular are concerned about maintaining an equitable division of labor, and in lesbian couples there is more concern with having power shared equally even when one partner is not contributing as much financially.[93] Blumstein and Schwartz point out that it is harder for gay men to become interdependent and give up things such as dominance and submission and competition because they have been socialized to have male cultural values.[94]

About one-third of lesbians and one-fifth of gay males have been heterosexually married, and many have children from these marriages.[95] While it is difficult for lesbian parents and especially for gay men) to gain custody of their children, some have done so. Others have adopted, and some lesbians have had children by means of artificial insemination. More children are thus growing up today in households where both parents are of the same sex. The research on such families shows that children who are loved and valued grow up normally and happily with homosexual parents.[96] In particular, there is no evidence that gay parents raise children with conflicts involving gender identity.[97] There are obvious problems of societal stigma in rearing children in a gay family, but on the whole such families seem to be succeeding very well.[98]

In addition to the gay male and lesbian couples described above, one study details another kind of couple in which a gay man is married or committed to a heterosexual woman. She knows about his homosexuality but understands it, and they share companionship and intimacy.[99]

Homosexual couples, of course, face many problems that heterosexual couples do not. Societal stigma and homophobia may be internalized by parents who are gay. Curran and Renzetti point out that such self-hatred may cause self-destructive behavior such as substance abuse[100] and may even be at the root of hostility toward partners and cause violence in the relationship.[101]

The AIDS epidemic has also been a major problem for the homosexual community. While it primarily affects gay men, homosexuals of both sexes have suffered from the resulting resurgence of homophobia. Gay bashing has been on the increase, with 15 to 20 percent of gay men reporting being attacked. This and other forms of hostility have resulted in a retrenchment in the gay community, with even more solidarity and an emphasis on monogamous relationships.[102]

There has always been institutional discrimination against gays.[103] They have been denied their right to parent, there has been a refusal to extend Fourteenth Amendment protection to homosexuals,[104] and twenty-three states and the District of Columbia still have laws against homosexual acts.[105] However, homosexual couples have recently been winning more legal rights.

In 1988, Madison, Wisconsin, approved sick leave and bereavement leave for domestic partners of city employees. In 1989, San Francisco passed legislation recognizing homosexual and unmarried heterosexual couples as families, and New York State decided that a long-term, live-in gay couple would be considered a family under the state rent control ordinance.[106]

In spite of the AIDS scare and renewed hostility toward the gay community, there seems to be a growing acceptance of gay rights and lesbian and gay families.[107] One specific sign of this was an extensive article on gay and lesbian couples and families in a special edition of *Newsweek* that dealt with the family.[108] As this alternative family form becomes more visible, we may learn more about the nature of gender roles.

BLUE-COLLAR FAMILIES

The working class, which constitutes at least two-fifths of American workers, has a lifestyle and gender-role interactions that differ in many ways from those of the middle class. Who are these working-class families? Eshleman describes them by saying that the men in these families not only have manual skills but earn wages by the hour and are dependent on swings of the business cycle for employment. Most have little formal education beyond high school, and many of their wives work.[109] The working class is distinguished from the lower class by steadiness of employment and relatively stable family lives; it is distinguished from the lower middle class by the fact that the working class is largely made up of skilled and semiskilled manual workers, while the lower middle class includes lower white-collar workers such as clerical and sales workers. However, there is some overlap between these two groups, as working-class wives may work in clerical or sales jobs and some working-class people move up into the lower middle class.

Some of these families have good incomes that they spend on consumer goods such as campers and boats. However, many others barely scrape by. The working-class level of life includes an element of economic insecurity that is seldom found in higher-income groups. The central goal of life for people in this class is to create a secure place for self and family; ill health and unemployment frighten them, as they have little chance to move to other jobs. The insecurity leads to an emphasis on traditional values that extends through the political scene into gender roles in the home.

Let us look at the life cycle of these blue-collar men and women and see how their gender roles differ from those of the middle class. Several excellent books have described the blue-collar way of life, including Rainwater, Coleman, and Handel's *Workingman's Wife*, Komarovsky's *Blue-Collar Marriage*, Rubin's *Worlds of Pain*, Luxton's *More Than a Labour of Love*, Rosen's *Bitter Choices*, and Zavella's *Woman's Work and Chicago Families*.[110] Although many of these books were written fifteen to twenty years ago, most of the basic features of working-class life they describe continue to exist today. The title of Rubin's book describes accurately the life of these working-class couples. Most marry young. Life in the parental home is hard, with poverty and sometimes drunkenness and violence. Forty percent of those interviewed in Rubin's survey had at least one alcoholic parent.[111] Parents try to maintain control by restricting the behavior of their growing daughters, and the daughters try to escape from that control. Marriage is seen as liberation,[112] as a way of getting out of the family home and having one's own home and family. For the male, it is seen as a confirmation of adult status.[113]

Most couples marry sooner than they expect, usually because the girl is pregnant; in 44 percent of the couples studied by Rubin, the girl was pregnant before marriage. Ninety-two percent of the men and 65 percent of the women had had premarital sex, and few had regularly used contraceptives; thus, the pregnancy rate is not surprising. In this group there is a definite split in views of the sexual nature of good girls and bad girls. Working-class people believe that only so-called bad girls plan to have a sex life and use contraceptives; thus, many girls get pregnant. The prevailing norm for the men is that if one gets a girl pregnant, one must marry her. Few consider abortion.[114] They are not stopped by religious scruples but simply say that it is "not a choice" or that "it never occurred to me." Luxton reports the same kind of thing in her sample of Canadian steelworkers and their wives:

> I never thought it would happen to me. I didn't want kids then. But when I realized I was that way [pregnant] then I was trapped.

> I wouldn't have married Mike if we hadn't got caught. He was fun to date for awhile, but not to marry. But we got stuck and here we are.[115]

Luxton's sample included women from three generations. Many in each generation, including those who were born in the 1960s, reported that unplanned pregnancies led to unexpected or early marriage.

Special Problems

The early years of marriage are particularly difficult for these young couples. The men, who are just out of high school or may not have finished it, have insecure jobs and little money.[116] They often move from job to job in the early years, trying to find work with meaning and dignity as well as good wages.[117] Many hold eight or ten jobs in six years. The women, who are still in their teens, frequently have several children in quick succession. Both feel the duty and responsibility of providing for a family. Although they wanted to get married, they feel tied down and regret having lost the fun of the premarriage years. They are also faced with the problem of making very little income go a long way; a couple frequently have to live with in-laws because they cannot afford a place of their own.[118]

The problems they face are exaggerated by several factors. Both spouses are very close to their mothers and spend a great deal of time phoning and visiting them. The ties of the husbands to their mothers frequently hurt the marital relationship.[119] One wife tells of a stormy first year of marriage. No sooner did they marry, she says, than "he started going out with his four buddies every night, just as if he was still single. Sometimes if he drank too much he would go to his mother's house to sleep and not come home at all."[120]

The women are frustrated and angry that the men leave them alone to cope with the house and children while they are out having fun with their friends. The men, who feel tied down, maintain their male status by going out with the boys and not being henpecked. Thus, each spouse maintains close ties to his or her family of origin and to a same-sex friendship group. The woman has little freedom to do things with her girlfriends, but she often visits with them at length by phone and in person. While Komarovsky says that the clique of friends is a group in which the spouses can complain and thus drain off resentments about their mates, the clique also serves to draw the couple apart.[121] However, recent studies have found that women have been tolerating fewer absences by their husbands.[122]

Friendship

The couple expect separateness to some extent; they do not believe that marriage is for friendship. The couple's families push them into conforming to traditional segregated roles.[123] They counsel the wife to have patience, insisting that the husband will settle down; they counsel the husband to take more interest in his wife and children. In the meantime, the spouses do little together. Leisure hours are usually spent watching television, or the husband may be busy on do-it-yourself projects around the house or cooperate with his friends in fixing a car. Weekends are frequently spent visiting with one or the other's family, where the men will watch a ball game and the women will talk.[124]

The following excerpts from Rubin's *Worlds of Pain* give an insight into the interaction between husband and wife.

> Frank comes home from work; now it's about five, because he's been working overtime every night. We eat right away, right after he comes home. Then, I don't know. The kids play a while before bed, watch TV, you know, stuff like that. Then, I don't know . . . maybe watch more TV or something like that. I don't know what else—nothing, I guess. We just sit, that's all.

> The husband: I come home at five and we eat supper right away. Then, I sit down with coffee and a beer and watch TV. After that, if I'm working on a project I do that for a little while. If not, I just watch TV.[125]

Rubin found that by the middle years, the couples compromise more and show greater acceptance of their roles. The men settle down and like marriage[126] and do not go out with their male buddies as often. The wives often accept their lot with more or less resignation. They rationalize that they could have it worse and say about their husbands, "I guess I shouldn't complain; he's a steady worker, he doesn't drink, and he doesn't hit me."[127] However, these wives feel discontented with the emotional aspects of marriage. They want more communication from their husbands, but there is little about which these couples can communicate. Rubin says, "Despite the yearning for more, relations between husband and wife are benumbed, filled with silence; life seems empty and meaningless; laughter, humor, fun is not a part of the daily ration." She quotes a couple married seven years. The wife says:

> There is plenty of time [to talk], we just don't do it. He doesn't ever think there's anything to talk about. I'm the one who has to nag him to talk and then I get disgusted.

The husband says:

> I'm pretty tight-lipped about most things most of the time. . . . Sometimes I'm not even sure what she wants me to be telling her. And when she gets all upset and emotional, I don't know what to say or what to do.[128]

In Luxton's sample there is some difference between the older generation and the expectations of the younger generation in regard to togetherness. One young woman says of her parents,

> They didn't seem to expect much of each other. They lived together and I know they cared, but they each went their own ways. I don't think that's right. I want to have more closeness with my husband. I think husbands and wives should be best friends.[129]

Yet, another 1980s study reaffirms that most of these women do not think of their husbands as friends. One young woman says,

> Sometimes I think of Richard as not only being my husband, [but] as being a helper and a friend, someone to talk to, where a lot of my friends don't feel that way about their husbands. That's just their husband. . . .[130]

Sex

Sexual communication in blue-collar families is usually minimal. Traditional inhibitions have limited their sexual interests and repertoire until recently. The spouses in a traditional blue-collar marriage have seldom discussed their feelings or desires:

> One wife says, "Experimental? Oh, he's much more experimental than I am. Once in a while I'll say, 'Okay, you get a treat; we'll do it with the lights on.' And I put the pillow over my head."[131]

An interesting aspect of this quote is that it suggests the degree to which sexuality can be used as a vehicle for power negotiations. Women who are not in the paid work force are often left with no other base of power. This kind of sexual negotiation can have long-term negative effects on marital communication and satisfaction.

A common theme in the comments in Rubin's American sample and Luxton's Canadian sample is women who are tired and distracted by the house and children and want less sex than the man does. They are seldom satisfied afterward but feel that they must please their husbands out of duty or to keep them from straying. These wives typically make comments like the following:

> Then he wants to make out, but I just can't. . . . I'm tired and just want to collapse asleep. And part of me is always listening for the baby.[132]

> Sometimes I get real excited and I really want it, but what we do doesn't really do it to me so then I feel frustrated and irritable.[133]

> I try to act real interested and sexy just as he's leaving for work so he'll be interested and come straight home after work.[134]

With the recent emphasis on sex in the media and the proliferation of sex manuals, there has been pressure on the blue-collar couple to change its ways. The men are interested in more variety in their sex lives and press their wives to try new kinds of sexual behavior.[135] Yet the hangover from the good girl–bad girl stereotype inhibits many wives from enjoying the new sexuality. Many wives particularly resist oral sex and are worried that their husbands will think they are cheap if they engage in such activities. One wife says:

> Sometimes I enjoy it, I guess. But most of the time I'm worried thinking about whether I ought to be doing it and worrying what he's really thinking to get much pleasure.[136]

Some husbands reassure them, but others show their own ambivalence about the new sexual standards. One husband commented as follows when asked whether he and his wife practice oral sex:

> No, Alice isn't that kind of girl. . . . She wasn't brought up to go for all that fancy stuff. . . . There's plenty of women out there to do that kind of stuff with. You can meet them in any bar any time you want to. You don't have to marry that kind.[137]

In spite of this attitude, there has been a change, and greater mutuality in sex appears to occur between more modern blue-collar spouses who are isolated from the traditional pressures of relatives.[138]

Women's Work and Men's Work

There is little disagreement in the blue-collar family about what is men's work and what is women's work. Women expect men to provide a decent living for their families, and if the men are underemployed or unemployed, the women show their resentment.[138] Both men and women agree that a man's life is easier than a woman's, especially when the woman works. It is the "woman's job" to do everything in the house: cleaning, cooking, child care, and even bill paying. She is likely to do a large portion of the yard work as well. The husband seldom gives regular assistance, although he will help out if asked by the wife. Men with high school educations or better are more likely to help with shopping and infant care. For the most part, however, the home is considered the woman's job by both sexes. When one woman was asked if she would change places with her husband, she replied:

> I guess I wouldn't like to change places with him because I couldn't support the family like he does. . . . On the other hand, that's all men have to do. I don't mean it's easy, but it's all they do. We—women, I mean—have a lot more to do and worry about all the time. I guess what it boils down to is that the man does the harder physical work, but the woman does the harder emotional work.[139]

Another woman, a mother of three who had been married seven years, said:

> The man's life is a lot easier; there's no doubt about it. He gets up in the morning; he gets dressed; he goes to work; he comes home in the evening; and he does what he wants after that.
>   As for me, I get up in the morning; I get dressed; I fix everybody's breakfast; I clean up the kitchen; I get the children ready for school and the baby ready to go to his babysitter; I take him to the babysitter. Then I go to work. I work all day; I pick up the baby; I fix dinner; I do the dishes; I clean up; I get the kids ready for bed. After the kids are finally asleep, I get to worry about the money because I pay all the bills. . . .[140]

A miner who worked for a Canadian steel company for forty-one years expressed his feelings about not doing work at home:

> I work hard, see. And its not great work. And when I gets home I'm tired and fed up and I want to just rest until I feel better. . . . I want to do what I want for a change.[141]

More recent studies show that wives have to work to keep their families afloat in difficult economic times and that their contributions frequently are appreciated and lead to reciprocal help from the man of the house.

In Rosen's sample of unionized factory workers in New England, the women earned good money and frequently made the difference between living on the edge of poverty and having the extras to have a comfortable life. In Rubin's 1970s study, the women earned about 25 percent of the family income but their contribution made little difference in the work they did around the home. In Rosen's 1980s sample, the women earned almost half (45 percent) of the family income. They worked all year, were committed to their work, and saw it as a way of ensuring that their families got ahead. Frequently their work enabled the family to put a down payment on a house or send the children to school. They had definite authority in deciding how money was spent.[142]

However, even in this sample, one-third of the husbands would have preferred that their wives didn't work and another one-third were ambivalent about it. Men who made good money were particularly likely to say they disliked having their wives work; men whose wives made good money also felt threatened and preferred that their wives not work.[143]

Both Rosen and Hood found that families often handled this ambivalence about the wife's work by defining the husband as the major provider and saying that the wife worked for extras, to help out. This definition allowed the women to keep working yet avoid tension at home. Rosen suggests that the idea of separate spheres of work also reinforces a husband's obligation to continue to support the family. She says that these wives are very conscious of the plight of the divorced woman.

Therefore, working-class women are not necessarily committed to an equal sharing of housework even if they work outside the home. However, they believe that if they "help" their husbands, the men in all fairness must help them. When negotiating that help, they appeal to a sense of fairness and reciprocity. One wife in Rosen's sample says,

> My husband helps me a lot too. That's the thing I told him. If you want me to help you out, then you'll have to help me. That way we can help each other. So far its been working pretty good.[144]

In practice, the women still do the majority of the housework, but the men participate in child care, shopping, and housework such as vacuuming. Wives who work get more help than do wives who are unemployed, but the level of earnings that a working wife brings in does not seem to influence the amount of help she gets.[145]

In many cases, the way in which the wife and husband define their obligations influences their attitude about what each should do. Rosen points out that among the Portuguese families in her sample, the women were seen as having an *obligation* to work outside to support the family and that this work did not entitle them to any more help with housework.[146] In Hood's sample, couples variously defined the wife as a secondary provider or a coprovider. Wives who were secondary providers (earning 30 percent or less of the income and being seen as providing temporarily and possibly quitting in the near future) got less help. Those who were seen as coproviders often got more help, but having the husband depend on the wife's income did not always lead to more sharing of housework. Increased income resulted in more help from husbands only when wives wanted it and asked for it. Some wives were afraid to provoke confrontation; wives who felt better about themselves when working bargained for more help.[147] Husbands were also more likely to help when the family was one in which the couple shared leisure activities rather than going their separate ways.

Violence in the Family

Although the problem isn't confined to these working-class couples, petty tyranny and even violence are built into some of these marriages. The men feel powerless at work and want to control their households. They insist that their wives be home when they return from work and that the children be quiet or playful according to the men's needs. Occasionally, they take out their work frustrations in violence. One wife said, "My husband beats me, usually on pay day. He gets real mad and hates me."[148]

These wives feel that it is important to manage the tensions in the household and keep things running smoothly. To some extent they understand the tension their husbands are expressing. A wife who was beaten so severely that her husband broke her arm reported,

> He hates his job. He's got all that mad locked up inside with nowhere for it to go. So sometimes he takes it out on me and the kids. Well I sort of don't blame him, I guess.[149]

Working wives in all studies were likely to be happier in spite of the dual burden of job and housework. They enjoyed the sociability at work, the sense of competence that working gave them, and the fact that they were contributing to the family's welfare. Myra Feree's study of 135 working-class wives whose last children were in school and who thus were free to work also showed that wives in the paid labor force were happier. Almost twice as many housewives as employed wives said they were dissatisfied with their lives. Feree points out that satisfaction with the housewife role in particular may have deteriorated as more and more working-class families have moved away from relatives and the women have become isolated in the home. Housewives who had social support groups and felt appreciated for their contributions (25 percent of the total) enjoyed their role.[150]

Changes in Blue-Collar Families

Some blue-collar families seem to be shifting away from highly segregated conjugal relations. About one-third of the families surveyed in the Rainwater, Coleman, and Handel study said that the husband participated more in the family, particularly in terms of involvement with the children.[151] These couples have often moved away from relatives and rely on each other for social resources. Hood found that couples typically had an interaction style: husband-centered, child-centered, or couple-centered. In the first two styles, communication centered on the children. In the couple-centered marriage, both husband and wife were active parents but had shared leisure activities.[152]

There seems to be a new attitude toward children in working-class families. The parents want to spend more time with their children and give them the good things that they themselves never had. Rainwater points out, however, that the parents are not really socializing their children to grow up differently; they are still stressing conformity to external standards, orderliness, neatness, and obedience instead of the more white-collar emphasis on individuality, initiative, and creativity.[153]

Blue-Collar Women and the Women's Movement

There is little support for the women's movement among working-class women. They believe in equal pay but do not believe that a woman should get a job if a man needs it. They see the movement as "putting down" housewives and feel alienated from most of its goals. While they would like to talk to other women about their discontentment with their lives and marriages, they are afraid to do so for fear they would be considered "women's libbers."[154] They know they are unhappy with their lives, but they do not see the women's movement as articulating their discontentment.

Thus, in the working class the division between the sexes is rigidly defined, whether as parents, workers, or lovers. The roles are more rigid than is usually the case in the middle class. However, there is pressure for change toward more liberal gender-role behavior in the blue-collar family as families move away from relatives and the media teach them to expect more companionship, affection, and sex. Any real modification of gender-role behavior, however, will probably depend on an extended period of prosperity and security for the working class.

BLACK FAMILIES

Writing about the black family is difficult because there is not one black family any more than there is one white family. The literature reflects this confusion. Some studies deal with the black middle class,[155] and others deal with ghetto socialization.[156] Between these two extremes, however, there is a black working-class family that can be described and compared with the white working-class family.

Demographic Approaches

With these perspectives in mind, let us look at recent information about certain characteristics of the black family. Staples has pointed out that gender roles in the black family are constrained by **demographic** characteristics. One of these characteristics is an imbalanced sex ratio among blacks. For every 100 young eligible women in the marriagable age group, there are considerably fewer than 100 young men. This imbalance has been brought about partly by the higher mortality rates among young black males and is accentuated by the number of black men who are in prisons or mental hospitals or who have married outside their race. Staples also points out that black men may be in a different class from single black women. Ironically, many black men do not have an opportunity to marry because of low income.[157] In 1987, black family income was only 56 percent of white family income (an $18,100 median for black families compared with $32,270 for white families). It has been reported that 33.1 percent of black families but only 10.5 percent of white families were living below the poverty line of $11,611 for a family of four. Forty-three percent were headed by female householders. The poverty rate for black families maintained by a woman with no spouse present was about 51 percent, compared with 27 percent for white female householders.[158]

This sex-ratio imbalance and the economic constraints of poverty have led to higher rates of singlehood for blacks as well as a later age of marriage and increased rates of separation and divorce. There has been a sharp drop in husband-wife families among blacks from 74 percent in 1960 to 51 percent in 1987.[159] Estimates of the overall proportion of women who will marry range as low as 70 to 80 percent.[160]

Marriage is approached with ambivalence by many young blacks. Staples and others point out that for a woman in a black working-class family, marriage may mean giving up a familiar and comfortable home that places few restrictions on her behavior (in contrast to a white working-class home) to marry a man who will not be a good provider. The woman may be reluctant to be tied down by a man she feels is not worth the restrictions. He may be reluctant to take on the role of provider, particularly if he feels that he will not be able to fulfill it well.[161]

Staples points out, however, that willingness to marry rises with a young black man's ability to fulfill his breadwinning role.[162] The provider role is extremely important for black husbands in both the middle class and the working class.[163] A 1989 study reports that the decline in marriage among blacks is not due to a lack of desire for romantic involvement and a stable relationship, but can be traced to structural problems.[164]

All this has implications for gender roles. Cazenave points out that young men who cannot achieve success in the breadwinner role may demonstrate their masculinity on the street or in sexual conquests.[165] Young women are raised to believe that they will have to provide for themselves and perhaps raise children on their own. Partially as a result of ambivalence about marriage, illegitimacy rates have risen; in 1987, 55 percent of all black births occurred out of wedlock. Half of all black families with children live in female-headed households.[166] The reaction to a premarital pregnancy is seldom a resort to abortion or marriage. It is expensive to have an abortion, and federal funding is no longer available in most areas; as pointed out above, a black woman may also see little sense in marrying a young black man who has no job and little ability to support a family. Children are seen as a positive good, and having a child is a mark of adult female status. Little stigma is connected with illegitimacy, and the pregnant girl's mother and extended family system often help her care for a child.

The Situation of Black Men

As we have seen, economic opportunity is a vital factor for black men if they are to fulfill husband and father roles. Staples has pointed out the irony of a culture that values high masculine achievement orientation and job success and an economic situation that allows black men very little chance of success. It is difficult for black men to fulfill the provider role when they are subject to periodic unemployment and earn low wages even when they do have jobs. He explains that some of these men deal with the dilemma by abdicating the role and leaving home. Both Staples and Cazenave assert that black fathers who are not beset by economic difficulties play viable, important roles in their families. According to Staples, "the black father is not simply a shadowy figure who provides . . . [children] with money or metes out punishment. He is a frame of reference, the person in general most respected and admired, and the most likely to be emulated by the children."[167]

Cazenave also emphasizes that while employment may be a problem for many working-class black men, the provider role is still very important in their lives and their concept of masculinity. He examined middle-income letter carriers in New Orleans and discovered that these men see the provider role as their most important one (47 percent), with husband next (28 percent), and father after that (22 percent). They also felt that the most important part of the father role is being an economic provider. Cazenave believes that for these men, the provider role was not emphasized in and of itself, as in the case of cultural norms for masculine job success. Rather, the role was emphasized as a means to an end, a way to carry out father and husband roles. He confirmed these findings in a sample of black men in professional, white-collar jobs. Husband was chosen as the most important role by the married men in this sample (34.5 percent), the provider role was second (31 percent), and the father role was last (19 percent).[168]

He points out, however, that black men in all social classes have certain traits in common that do not fit neatly into the cultural stereotype of masculinity. Black men put an emphasis on success and achievement, but they also are high in expressive dimensions such as being warm and being gentle. In addition, they are likely to emphasize the value of other characteristics that are related to their reactions against racial discrimination and prejudice, characteristics such as "stands up for beliefs" and "fights to protect family."[169]

The Situation of Black Women

Another characteristic of the black family that affects gender roles is the fact that the wife is more likely to be employed. In 1987, 74 percent of black wives were employed and were likely to work even when the husband's income was good. Black middle-class wives are more likely to work than are white middle-class wives, and some researchers have suggested that their income is needed to keep a black family in the middle class.[170] Both black wives and black husbands assume that the wife will work. Black men seem to have a less stereotyped view of the female sex role than white men do; they believe their wives have the knowledge and competence to hold a job. Being a good provider is seen as an essential part of the mother role as well as the father role, and black women believe that they can combine employment and good relations with their children. Black women also believe that their men want them to work.[171]

This high degree of maternal employment has many implications for black families and gender roles. Black children report that they see both parents as fulfilling instrumental (provider) and expressive functions. Similarly, McAdoo reports shared child rearing and decision making by black husbands and wives when the wives work.[172] Others, however, have declared that the employment of black women has led to the establishment of a **matriarchy.**

The Black Matriarchy: Myth or Reality?

Some people believe not only that black families are more equal but that black women dominate their households and their men. Black women who have struggled to support their families have been accused of emasculating the "real" breadwinner, the male. Staples decries the myth of the matriarchy and says that

> black men do have an egalitarian attitude toward that institution [marriage]. As early as adolescence, they expect egalitarian marriage roles concerning authority, housekeeping, and care of children. In comparison to white males, black husbands are more accepting of a wife's employment outside the home. . . . [In studies where] differences were found, they were related more to class than race. In general, blue-collar husbands of both races exercised more power in decisions in such areas as recreation, joint purchases and household tasks than their white collar counterparts.[173]

Most researchers agree that employment among black women has led to greater equalitarianism in black marriages. As black women can work where black men often cannot, there has been an alteration of the traditional division of labor over the decades: Employment behavior in wives has become more institutionalized in black society. In a Midwestern sample that included 25 percent blacks, black women saw themselves as more capable than white women saw themselves and black men and women both saw themselves as more nurturant *and* more instrumental than white men and women saw themselves.[174]

However, in spite of generally equalitarian husband-wife relationships, maternal control over most family matters is probably greater in all socioeconomic black groups than in similar white groups. Heiss did a study that assessed who had control in the family by asking questions such as, "When you did something wrong, who punished you?" "Who kept track of family money?" "Thinking back now, who do you think made the important decisions in the family when you were a child?" He found maternal dominance in all these areas in all black families.[175] However, Heiss and others emphasize that this situation does not seem to have the detrimental effect on black males that some people have assumed. Both families with maternal control and those with parental control produced males who achieved the same grades and had the same number of years of schooling.[176]

Division of Labor

Most studies find that, in a parallel to white families, division of labor in the black family is not as equalitarian as decision making is. A 1988 study found that black women do most of the cooking, cleaning, and laundry and that many feel overworked.[177] Findings differ on whether black husbands do more or less household work than white men. Older studies found that black men do approximately the same amount of housework as white men; however, most studies show them doing slightly more child care.[178]

Another comparison of black and white families found very little difference in the interaction of black and white fathers with their children and in the goals they held for the children. White fathers emphasized the importance of helping with homework; black fathers tended to emphasize the importance of giving their children money and training them athletically. However, black fathers seemed to be more expressive in interacting with their children and to enjoy them more.[179] As Cazenave points out, this expressiveness increases as men have better incomes, can concentrate less on the provider role, and have more time for expressive parental activities. Even the low-income respondents, however, spent more time with their children and thought of themselves as being closer to their families than their fathers had been. They reported that they played more with babies, were more involved in child-care activities such as baby-sitting, and helped more with homework than their fathers had been.[180]

Companionship and the Black Marriage

The black family parallels the white working-class family in the degree of conjugal role segregation. In the working class, the husband and wife tend to think of themselves as having very separate kinds of functioning in the family organization. As long as the husband fulfills his provider role, he does not expect to do much around the house; conversely, if he is unemployed, his wife may not do much for him. The separate incomes earned by wife and husband are treated as separate money, and both sexes seem to have an equal but separate right to peer group activity outside the home and are likely to engage in separate activities. Heiss states, "It appears that the norm of togetherness is not universally accepted in the black community and its absence does not cause much in the way of dissatisfaction."[181] Komarovsky similarly reports a dearth of joint activities inside or outside the family and suggests that it is not just a lack of enabling income that keeps these activities from taking place but a real difference in values.[182]

Marital Satisfaction

Given these facts, we might ask what is the nature of marital satisfaction in the black family. Most of the research confirms that black women who are married, widowed, or divorced are somewhat more satisfied than are those who are separated or single,[183] although one study found that when age, health, social participation, and education were not considered, there was no relationship between marital status and life satisfaction among black women.[184] In one study, black females were found to be three times as likely as black males to report that their marriages were not happy,[185] although several studies have reported that black men who are married are the least satisfied of all groups with their lives in general. While one study of newlyweds attributed such findings to the early stage of marriage[186] and to men feeling "trapped," the same result is found in a sample of black couples who had been married various lengths of time.[187] Black husbands who had greater education and income were more likely to be satisfied, however.[188] Several studies reported that children are not a factor in family life satisfaction for either sex.[189]

Satisfaction varies by sex and social class. Women and high-status men give more value to shared activities in their concept of a good marriage.[190] A 1989 study that compared black and white newlyweds found that higher education and income were positively correlated with marital happiness for blacks and whites.[191] However, Scanzoni found that lower-status black men seem quite content with a system of very separate marital roles.[192] Other literature traces marital satisfaction to economic variables and finds marital tensions among lower-class husbands and wives as a result of economic strain.[193]

The Extended Family: Support System or Deterrent to Upward Mobility?

A unique part of the black family which affects gender roles as well as many other facets of family life is the prevalence of the *extended family*. Although approximately 75 percent of black families are nuclear (including a single parent with children), approximately 25 percent can be classified as extended, or including relatives other than just husband, wife, and children living with the family.[194] The term "extended family" is used rather loosely by some researchers; many seem to define an extended family as a kinship network whether or not the members of this network all live in the same household. Eugene Litwak coined the term "modified extended family" to represent patterns of networks that develop among related nuclear families.[194] If we use this latter definition, many extended families can be found in higher socioeconomic groups as well as in the lower classes.

Researchers suggest that many people in the black community could not survive without such helpful ties. Martin says:

> The economic interdependency of family members is a main element of the extended family structure. Many have no choice but to depend on relatives for economic assistance. Others maintain a stance of economic dependency out of habit or to ensure that aid will be available if they need it. The built-in mutual aid system in black extended families . . . is a major survival component. Without this mechanism, the extended family structure would be jeopardized.[195]

There is no doubt about the prevalence of these extended-help networks in the black community. Scanzoni's 1971 study showed that although a large majority of working-class respondents had been raised in a nuclear family, one-third had received task-oriented help and two-thirds had received expressive help from other relatives.[196] Staples states that 48 percent of elderly black women have related children living with them. Stack found that such an extended kin network often operates through a core of women and offsets economic strains.[197] Several researchers have documented the existence of such cultural systems of help even in families whose finances are more secure. The degree of mutual aid depends on the degree of kin relationship and the distance between members, but reciprocal obligations are always implied.[198]

While researchers agree that the extended family is a survival mechanism for poor blacks, they are divided on whether such ties hamper upward mobility.[199] McQueen and Stack think that an extended kin network places such a drain on the resources of the upwardly mobile that they have to cut themselves off from it to move upward. Such isolation does not necessarily exclude causal visiting or shared holiday celebrations, support of aged parents, or occasional help, but it does mean separation from meeting the everyday needs of many relatives.[200] Hill, however, believes that upwardly mobile families keep their kin ties even after gaining more secure status.[201] McAdoo says that the "extended family pattern is not just a structural coping tactic, but has evolved into a strong and valuable cultural pattern,"[202] although others point out that middle-class families who are not close to their kin do not seem to suffer for it.[203]

We need to stress again the great class variation among black families. In most black families, however, although women contribute more income to the family and power is somewhat more equally shared between husband and wife than is the case in white families, a traditional division of labor is still evident. Women do almost all the housework and the great bulk of the child care. Men may be more expressive toward their children, but this does not seem to carry over into expressiveness with their wives. While a matriarchy is not evident, the black woman has achieved a degree of equality by taking care of herself and claiming her social and sexual rights.

THE VIOLENT FAMILY

The Epitome of Male Dominance: Wife Abuse

> The first time Frank hit me, I was three months pregnant . . . that was the first indication of his tremendous jealousy. There were times when I didn't dare go shopping for groceries; *I felt like a prisoner in my own home.* I was afraid of his accusations and abuse when I got back.
>
> (These words were spoken by an abused wife, Martha, as she recalled the shoving, punching, kicking, and choking she had received from her husband.)[204]

Something that is never mentioned when talking about the ideal family of the American dream is violence in the family, yet the statistics on interspousal violence indicate that the problem has reached epidemic proportions. According to a 1980s study, over 2 million women are abused every year. Many estimates indicate that the number is twice that, and other estimates say that at least one-third of all women will be battered at some time.[205] The statistics on husbands abused by their wives are more difficult to ascertain. Gelles reports that men are more likely to admit abuse than are women, but others say that husbands are less likely to report abuse.[206] All sources agree, however, that husbands are much less likely to be hurt by abuse.[207] However, husbands may be murdered by wives who are defending themselves. In 1984, nearly half of all intrafamilial homicides (one-eighth of all homicides) involved husbands and wives. Two-thirds of these homicides involved wives killed by husbands, and one-third involved husbands killed by wives.[208] While husband abuse may occur more than is realized, we will confine ourselves to talking about wife abuse because of its implications for gender roles.

Wife abuse is the epitome of male power and female submissiveness. Because of a long cultural history of women being considered men's property and men having power over them, many men feel they have the right to abuse their wives and many women are socialized to submit to such abuse. Laws and the economic situation perpetuate the dominance of men and make it difficult for women to escape an abusive situation. Married women may have few economic resources and may be totally dependent on their husbands for support. Other researchers contend that being married makes women feel powerless; many women are taught that their effectiveness and creativity don't count and that only their beauty and ability are worthwhile. Such women may develop "learned helplessness" as a result of their general dependence and low self-esteem.[209] This helplessness is intensified by the verbal and physical abuse of the battering situation. Let us look at some of the myths about wife abuse.

Contrary to popular belief, few people who use violence in the family can be considered mentally ill.[210] Family violence also occurs in all social classes, although it is probably more prevalent in the working class. In a study of applicants for divorce, 23 percent of middle-class couples and 40 percent of working-class couples listed physical abuse as a major complaint.[211] Violence is not usually provoked by a major trauma; in a family with a cycle of violence, any minor incident can provoke it.[212] However, certain variables are connected with the use of violence. One in four women are hit when pregnant[213] (some recent studies show an incidence of one in three hit while pregnant), alcohol is connected with 50 percent of batterings,[214] and it is likely that hard economic times and high unemployment provoke the use of violence.[215]

Abusers are often persons who were abused themselves as children and who use violence in other parts of their lives.[216] Many authorities have suggested that when wives are abused, the husbands are sadistic and the women are masochistic—that is, they like being beaten—but this is not borne out by the facts. Other myths that protect the wife abuser are that the wife must have done something to deserve the violence and that arguments between husband and wife are a family matter that should not be interfered with by friends, neighbors, or the legal system. The fact that many women do not report abuse or leave home after they are beaten makes many of these myths seem legitimate.

Legal, Economic, and Social Systems Encouraging Abuse

Many times women do not report abuse or do not escape from it because the legal, social, and economic systems fail to support them when they do report it. Police hate to respond to domestic disturbance calls. Almost 20 percent of police fatalities occur in these situations, sometimes when a wife who is afraid of her husband's anger turns on the police officer.[217] However, a study in Kansas City shows how necessary a police response is. Forty percent of that city's homicides were found to be cases of spouse killing spouse. In more than 85 percent of these homicides the police had been summoned once before the murder, and in 50 percent the police had been called to quell disturbances five or more times within the two-year period before the homicide.[218]

In past years officers were usually directed by their superiors to avoid making arrests in domestic disputes except when a person was severely injured. In many cases they could not make an arrest unless there was a witness or the injuries were extremely obvious. Even then, only one in about a hundred cases finally went to court, and women were often threatened by their husbands with injury or death if they prosecuted. By the time a case did get to court, the wife's injuries had usually healed, there was no witness, and beliefs about family arguments being private matters prevailed. If the wife had the knowledge and money to get a restraining order (they often cost $75 and are issued during office hours, not when the wife may need it), she was still not protected. If the husband violated the order and beat his estranged wife, he was usually only cited for contempt of court. To get the order, the wife usually had to show that she had initiated divorce proceedings.[219]

The legal system has improved in most states, but the social and economic systems are still failing women so that they cannot leave abusing husbands. They may have no job or economic resources of their own and no safe shelter where they can go. They are often threatened with injury or death if they leave. The self-esteem of many of these women has eroded, and they have developed a sense of helplessness in coping with the outside world. Frequently, marriage counselors or others tell them that they should stay with their husbands and try to work things out. They are also ashamed of their situation and withdraw after abuse rather than seeking help. They often do not see the alternatives available to them. These women may suffer from depression and anxiety and engage in substance abuse.[220] Those who do leave are more likely to be employed, to have not had models of violence in their childhood homes, to have been in the relationship a shorter time, and to have suffered more severe violence in the relationship.[221]

Lenore Walker describes the cycle of family violence that makes it difficult for a wife to leave home. There is usually a three-stage cycle of violence, she says. It starts with a tension-building stage in which the wife accepts the husband's criticisms (she *did* burn dinner) and unconsciously reinforces his aggressions. He fears his behavior will make her leave, so he becomes oppressive and jealous. It is usual to have verbal harangues and psychological humiliation during this phase. The second, or "explosion," phase follows, in which the man batters his wife when he loses control. He wants to "teach his wife a lesson" and often does not realize the harm he has done. If the wife resists, she is often hurt more; arms raised in defense get broken. The third phase is calm and loving: The batterer tries to make up with his wife and may apologize profusely. He is afraid she will leave him and pleads that he needs her and promises to reform. Such behavior makes it very difficult for the wife to leave, especially when she is ambivalent about such a departure anyway.[222] Women who do leave may find themselves drawn back to their husbands because they can't cope on their own.[223] If they stay or return, they reinforce the husband's behavior so that is likely to occur again and to escalate. If she stays, the wife may eventually be killed or may kill her oppressor.[224]

Characteristics of Abusers

Who are these men who abuse their wives and sometimes their children? Shupe and colleagues point out that the common characteristic shared by them is a dependence on women that they are reluctant to admit. They believe they can keep their wives by controlling them.[225] They may also have seen a model of violence in their parental families.[226] They usually lack communication skills and impulse control, and some may suffer from unemployment or stress at work.[227] Some have alcohol problems as well, although this is not the primary reason for abuse.[228] Frequently these men are insecure and have traditional gender-role attitudes. Abusive situations are particularly likely to occur if these traditional men have nontraditional wives.[229]

One link between wife abuse and gender roles is an obvious one: Men demonstrate their physical power over women. There are also links with the credo that men be independent and self-sufficient emotionally and that they be breadwinners. A man who believes in this version of masculinity yet finds himself emotionally dependent on a woman may become angry. A man who is unable to succeed at the breadwinning role may also develop anger that is taken out on those in his life who cannot defend themselves. Stereotypes for women—that they are responsible for maintaining relationships in the face of adversity, that they are subservient in the home, and that they are passive and masochistic—also perpetuate abuse. As gender roles are changing, these underpinnings of wife abuse may change as well. However, the ambivalence—or even resentment—about changing roles on the part of men and women may engender more abuse, at least temporarily.

Yet there are hopeful changes. A late 1980s study compared national samples from 1975 and 1985 and found that rates of abuse declined by about 27 percent in that period. The authors are hesitant to specify the reasons for the possible decline, which may have resulted from a methodological problem in the comparison. However, they suggest that there may have been a better economic climate and more equalitarian marriages in 1985. They also admit that with the new stigma attached to wife abuse, people may simply be more reluctant to report it.[230]

New laws have been enacted on both the federal and state levels that punish abusers but also provide funds for treating them and assistance for the victims.[231] In 1985, Congress passed the Family Violence Prevention and Services Amendment, which allocated $65 million over a three-year period to assist states in preventing violence and providing services to victims. Unfortunately, some of this money has since been cut. Laws in forty-three states enable battered women to obtain civil protection without initiating divorce, as was previously required.[232]

In July 1986 the U.S. Department of Justice called on police departments nationwide to treat spouse-beating cases as violent crimes and to set up specific programs to deal with them.[233] Officers are required to arrest suspected offenders, who are then kept in jail or removed from their homes until their victims can be protected. For these angry men, a brush with the law may have a sobering effect. Advocacy follow-up visits to the victim also help women find the resources to get out of abusive situations.[234] A study of such programs in southern California found that arresting the batterers dramatically reduced the likelihood that they would commit abuse again.[235]

There have also been important changes in the alternatives available to women trying to get out of an abusive situation. Over a decade ago, when Erin Pizzey wrote *Scream Quietly or the Neighbors Will Hear*,[236] little attention was paid to the problem of wife beating and there were few places a wife could go in an emergency. The number of shelters has since grown from 2 in 1974 to 780 in 1985, and there are even more crisis hot lines.[237] The need for shelters is demonstrated by the fact that each shelter was filled almost as soon as it was opened and hot lines were overloaded. For example, Fort Worth, Texas, had to install a social worker to handle the wife-beating calls, which were coming in at a rate of over 400 a month.

Most shelters attempt to make their women clients self-sufficient with job training and arrangements for alternative living arrangements. One measure of the effectiveness of shelters has been the fact that 45 to 50 percent of the women using them do not return to their abusers. Some researchers have even estimated that those not returning constitute two-thirds to four-fifths of the victims. Even those who return may have gained skills which will enable them to get out of the abusive situation.[238]

Intervention for abusers has developed more slowly; there were approximately 150 programs in 1982.[239] Some programs emphasize consciousness raising, and others work on restructuring behavior. Many report lack of motivation and commitment by the men. Many of these men do not recognize battering as a problem until their women have left them; if the partner returns, the motivation for treatment is often ended.[240] There are also programs for couples that emphasize family systems and treat the whole family. While all these programs can be helpful in many cases, there has been little evaluation of their overall effectiveness.[241]

Certainly public awareness has been heightened and attempts are being made to reduce spouse abuse, yet recent cutbacks on funds for social services have forced many shelters to reduce their services or close. Seventy-six percent of domestic violence programs have reduced their services, and 79 percent are not able to meet the needs of battered women in their communities.[242] If women cannot stop abuse or escape from it, they risk severe injury and even death as the violence escalates. It is also likely that their children will be abused and will grow up to become wife and child abusers. Those who deal with wife abuse say it is imperative that there be immediate public and private funding to provide shelters and job retraining and that there should be a wide range of intervention programs.

SUMMARY

We have seen that the variety of family forms and behavior is far greater than the homogeneity implied in most discussions of the American family. This variety is likely to increase as fertility continues to decline, women enter the work force in greater numbers, and the percentage of those divorcing and remarrying continues to be high. There are important implications for gender-role behavior in this variation. The general trend seems to be toward more equalitarian relationships, dual-career families, and remarriages. Single-parent families provide an important training ground for female independence and male appreciation of what it takes to run a household. While gender roles in the black family have always been more equalitarian, blue-collar family interaction is also becoming somewhat more equal. Many of the demographic trends noted in Chapter 8 will aid this trend toward more equalitarian roles in the family. While progress probably will be slow, in the future family power differences between men and women may be less noticeable.

ESSAY QUESTIONS

1. How do you think power relationships in dual-career families differ from those in families in which the wife is a homemaker or works at a part-time job to which she is not committed? How do the various styles of interaction between spouses (accommodation, equal sharing, and the like) relate to power in the family?
2. How do sex-role attitudes in single-parent families differ from those in two-parent families? Is the behavior of a single parent usually consistent with his or her attitude?
3. How do the attitudes and behavior of girls and boys of custodial single-parent fathers and mothers vary?
4. How does remarriage affect the sex-role attitudes of the single parent? How do you think power relationships would develop in a family where

the mother was a single parent for six years, has teen-aged children, and has just remarried a man of moderate income who has no children of his own?

5. Why don't abused wives leave their husbands? (You should deal with both cultural beliefs and economic realities in your answer.) What happens when they stay with their husbands? What do you think is the most urgent need in changing the cycle of violence?

6. Describe the interaction between couples in a blue-collar marriage. Why is it said that the working-class marriage is characterized by separateness of roles and lack of communication? What role do the families of the spouses play in sustaining their children's marriage?

7. Is the black extended family a deterrent to upward mobility for its members? What evidence can you give to support your answer?

8. Is the black matriarchy a myth or a reality? Discuss the variation in power relationships in black families as they vary by social class. Does the division of labor in the black family reflect the existence of a matriarchy?

9. Compare the role of women in white working-class and black working-class families. How are their attitudes similar or how do they differ toward marriage, sex, work, interaction with parents, and child rearing?

EXERCISES

1. Do you want to have children when you marry? If you are a woman, do you think that having children would affect your career success or your relationship with your husband? If you are a man, discuss the same issues. Compare the answers of men and women in the class and comment on any differences.

2. In a dual-career marriage, the wife has an offer to move to a new job in another city a thousand miles away. The move will mean doubling her salary and a chance at increased upward mobility; she may never again get such an opportunity. If the husband moves with her, he will have to give up his job as a university professor and try to find another one in a new city. (There are several universities there, but the job market for professors is very tight.) Do you think the couple should make the move? Should she move without him? How would you resolve the issue?

3. Assume you are a single parent who believes in more liberal gender roles. How would you organize your household and your behavior toward your children so that you would be teaching them liberal gender-role attitudes and letting them practice nontraditional gender-role behavior? What would you do if the children wanted to do traditional things or if their friends laughed at them for nontraditional behavior and told them they were "odd"?

4. Assume you are a single mother who is remarrying a man with a 13-year-old daughter and an 11-year-old son. His children live with his ex-wife, but your children, two girls who are 10 and 12, live with you. What problems do you foresee in the remarriage? In what ways might your gender-role attitudes and behavior change, and how might you transmit them to your children? (*Hint:* Little behaviors like letting the man drive the car when you are going out may show the children a great deal.)

5. You know from talking to a woman in your class that she is being abused by her husband. He is a middle-class business executive, and she says he is really very nice and hits her only when he has been drinking. One day she comes to class with a broken arm and very bad bruises all over her body and tells you that her husband beat her up the night before. What advice would you give her? (She has three small children and no income of her own.)

6. Imagine that you are a spouse in a white working-class marriage. Describe your feelings about marriage, work, talking to your spouse, and raising your children. What are your plans for the evening and for a vacation this year? (If you are male, describe your feelings from the husband's point of view; if you are female, describe your feelings from the wife's point of view.)

7. One researcher has said, "The working class tends to cling to the concepts of masculinity and femininity as a way of being more normal. The individual tends to perceive others as being more successful (proving masculinity or femininity), and this perception reinforces the belief that the `system' is right and the individual is somehow deficient. It is difficult for the individual—especially the working-class man—to change perceptions because of the barriers of privacy. Therefore, rigid definitions of traditional masculinity and femininity tend to get reinforced." Does this apply to every group? If not, why does it apply more to the working class?

8. Imagine that you are a black working-class wife who has two young children. You work as a sales clerk while your mother takes care of the children. Your husband, who is an electrician's apprentice, is unemployed because of the recession. He wants to move to the sun belt, where he can find work. What kind of interaction would you have with your husband and family in making the decision about whether to go? Do you think you would decide to move?

NOTES

1. Jane F. Collier, Michelle Z. Rosaldo, and Sylvia Yanagisatko, "Is There a Family? New Anthropological Views," cited in Cynthia Epstein, *Deceptive Distinctions: Sex Gender and the Social Order* (New Haven, Conn.: Yale University Press, 1989), 192.
2. Margaret Paloma, Brian Pendelton, and T. Neal Garland, "Reconsidering the Dual-Career Marriage," *Journal of Family Issues* 2, no. 2 (1981):205–224.
3. *Ibid.*, pp. 214–215.

4. *Ibid.*, p. 217.

5. C. A. Hornung and B. C. McCullough, "Status Relationships in Dual-Employment Marriages: Consequences for Psychological Well-Being," *Journal of Marriage and the Family* 43 (1981):125–141.

6. Rosanna Hertz, *More Equal Than Others: Women and Men in Dual-Career Marriages* (Berkeley: University of California Press, 1986), p. 197.

7. *Ibid.*

8. Paloma et al., *op. cit.*, p. 206.

9. Joseph H. Pleck, "The Work-Family Role System," *Social Problems* 24 (1977): 417–427: Joseph H. Pleck, "Men's Family Work: Three Perspectives and Some New Data," *Family Coordinator* 28 (1979):481–488.

10. Lynda Lytle Holstrum, *The Two-Career Family* (Cambridge, Mass.: Schenkman. 1982), p. 17.

11. *Ibid.*, pp. 96–97.

12. H. Goldenberg, "Treating Contemporary Couples in Dual-Career Relationships," *Family Therapy Today* 1, no. 1 (1986):1–47.

13. Hertz, *op. cit.*

14. S. Scarr, *Mother Care/Other Care* (New York: Basic Books, 1984); Patricia Knaub, Deanna Eversoll, and Jaqueline Voss, "Is Parenthood a Desirable Adult Role?" *Sex Roles* 9 (1983):355–362.

15. Harry Stein, "The Case for Staying Home," in Ollie Pocs and Robert H. Walsh, eds., *Marriage and Family* (Guilford, Conn.: Dushkin Press, 1987), pp. 334–341.

16. Jaylan Mortimer and Gloria Sorensen, "Men, Women, Work and Family," in Kathryn M. Borman, Daisy Quarm, and Sarah Gideonse, eds., *Women in the Work-place: Effects on Families* (Norwood, N.J.: Ablex, 1984), pp. 220–227.

17. Kristin Moore and Sandra Hofferth, "Women and their Children," in Ralph E. Smith, ed., *The Subtle Revolution: Women at Work* (Washington, D.C.: Urban In-stitute, 1979), pp. 125–152.

18. *Ibid.*

19. Sally Bloom-Feshbach, Jonathan Bloom-Feshbach, and Kirby A. Heller, "Work, Family and Children's Perception of the World," in Sheila B. Kamerman and Cheryl S. Hayes, eds., *Families That Work: Children in a Changing World* (Wash-ington D.C.: National Academy Press, 1982).

20. *Ibid.*

21. C. Russell Hill and Frank Stafford, "Parental Care of Children: Time Diary Esti-mates of Quantity, Predictability and Variety," *Journal of Human Resources* 15 (1980):219–239.

22. Suzanne Model, "Housework by Husbands," *Journal of Family Issues* 2 (1981): 225–237; Karen D. Fox and Sharon Y. Nickols, "The Time Crunch: Wife's Em-ployment and Family Work," *Journal of Family Issues* 4 (1983):61–82.

23. Pleck, 1979, *op. cit.*

24. Shelley Coverman and Joseph F. Sheley, "Changes in Men's Housework and Child-Care Time, 1965–1975," *Journal of Marriage and the Family* 48 (1986):413–422.

25. Roas Shamir, "Unemployment and the Household Division of Labor," *Journal of Marriage and the Family* 48 (1986):195–206.

26. Hertz, *op. cit.*

27. L. M. Verbruge and J. H. Madans, "Women's Roles and Health," *Marriage and Di-vorce Today Newsletter* 10, no. 39 (1985):3–4.

28. James C. Coleman, *Intimate Relationships, Marriage and Family*, 2d ed. (New York: MacMillan, 1989), p. 287.

29. Lotte Bailyn, "Accommodation of Work to Family," in Arlene Skolnick and Jerome Skolnick, eds., *Family in Transition,* 3d ed. (Boston: Little, Brown, 1980), pp. 566–579.
30. *Ibid.*
31. Paloma et al., *op. cit.*
32. Bailyn, *op. cit.,* pp. 571–572.
33. Carol C. Nadelson and Theodore Nadelson, "Dual Career Marriages: Benefits and Costs," in Fran Pepitone-Rockwell, ed. *Dual-Career Couples* (Beverly Hills, Calif.: Sage, 1980), pp. 91–110.
34. Bailyn, *op. cit.*
35. Naomi Gerstel and Harriet Gross, *Commuter Marriage: A Study of Work and Family* (New York: Guilford Press, 1984).
36. *Ibid.*
37. Bam Dee Sharda and Barry Nangle, "Marital Effects on Occupational Attainment," *Journal of Family Issues* 2 (1981):148–163.
38. Paloma et al., *op. cit.*
39. Gary S. Becker, *A Treatise on the Family* (Cambridge, Mass.: Harvard University Press, 1981).
40. Glenna Spitze, "Women's Employment and Family Relations: A Review," *Journal of Marriage and the Family* 50 (1988):595–618; Carol C. Nadelson and Theodore Nadelson, "Dual Career Marriages: Benefits and Costs," in Pepitone-Rockwell, *op. cit.,* pp. 91–110.
41. Rhona Rapoport and Robert Rapoport, "Three Generations of Dual-Career Family Research," in Pepitone-Rockwell, *op. cit.,* pp. 23–48.
42. Holstrum, *op. cit.,* p. 44.
43. *Ibid.,* p. 137.
44. Nadelson and Nadelson, *op. cit.,* pp. 21–110; Holstrum, *op. cit.,* pp. 162–167; Bailyn, *op. cit.,* p. 568.
45. Paloma et al., *op. cit.*
46. Coleman, *op. cit.,* p. 379.
47. *Ibid.,* p. 49; Teresa Castro Martin and Larry L. Bumpass, "Recent Trends in Marital Disruption," *Demography* 26, no. 1 (1989):37–49.
48. Coleman, *op. cit.,* p. 379.
49. Robert Green and Patricia D. Crooks, "Family Member Adjustment and Family Dynamics in Established Single-Parent and Two-Parent Families," *Social Service Review* (December 1988):600–616.
50. U.S. Bureau of the Census, "Marital Status and Living Arrangements: March 1987," *Current Population Reports,* Series P-20, no. 271 (Washington, D.C.: U.S. Government Printing Office, 1988).
51. Arthur J. Norton and Paul G. Glick, "One-Parent Families: A Social and Economic Profile," *Family Relations* 35 (1986):9–12.
52. U.S. Bureau of the Census, "Consumer Income: Money Income and Poverty Status in the U.S.: 1987" (Advance data from the March 1988 *Current Population Reports*), Series P-60 (Washington, D.C.: U.S. Government Printing Office, 1988); A. J. Norton and J. E. Moorman, "Current Trends in Marriage and Divorce among American Women," *Journal of Marriage and the Family* 49 (1987): 3–14.
53. Lenore Weitzman, *The Divorce Revolution* (New York: Free Press, 1985): see also Terry J. Arendell, "Women and the Economics of Divorce in the Contemporary United States," *Signs* 13 (1987):121–136.

54. E. Mavis Hetherington, Martha Cox, and Roger Cox, "Stress and Coping in Divorce: A Focus on Women" (paper presented at the Michigan Council on Family Relations meetings, October 1978).
55. *Ibid.;* Marie Richmond-Abbott, "Sex Role Norms and Behaviors in Single-Parent Families" (paper presented at the National Council on Family Relations Conference, Portland, Oregon, October 1980).
56. J. K. Keshet "From Separation to Stepfamily: A Subsystem Analysis," *Journal of Family Issues* 1, no. 4 (1980):146–153.
57. V. George and P. Wilding, *Motherless Families* (London: Routledge-Kegan Paul, 1979).
58. Hetherington, et al., *op. cit.*
59. E. M. Hetherington, M. Cox, and R. Cox, "Long-Term Effects of Divorce and Remarriage on the Adjustment of Children," *Journal of the American Academy of Child Psychiatry* 24 (1985):518–530.
60. E. M. Hetherington, "Family Relations Six Years after Divorce,"in K. Pasley and M. Ihinger-Tailman, eds., *Remarriage and Step-Parenting: Current Research and Theory* (New York: Guilford Press, 1984), pp. 185–205.
61. *Ibid.*
62. Marie Richmond-Abbott, "Sex-Roles of Mothers and Children in Divorced, Single-Parent Families," *Journal of Divorce* 8 (1984):34–46; Green and Crooks, *op. cit.*, p. 609.
63. Helen R. Weingarten, "Marital Status and Well-Being: A National Study Comparing First-Married, Currently Divorced and Remarried Adults," *Journal of Marriage and the Family* 47 (1985):653–661.
64. Paul C. Glick, "Remarried Families, Stepfamilies and Stepchildren: A Brief Demographic Profile," *Family Relations* 38 (1989):24–27.
65. Keshet, *op. cit.*
66. P. Brown, L. Perry, E. Harburg "Sex Role Attitudes and Psychological Outcomes for Black and White Women Experiencing Marital Disillusion," *Journal of Marriage and the Family*, 39 (1977):549.
67. Richmond-Abbott, *op. cit.*, 1984.
68. *Ibid.*
69. Hetherington, *op. cit.*, p. 16.
70. E. M. Hetherington, R. Cox, and M. Cox, "The Development of Children in Mother-Headed Families" (paper presented at Conference on Families in Contemporary America, George Washington University, June 11, 1988), p. 18.
71. Eleanor E. Maccoby, Charlene E. Depner, and Robert H. Mnookin, "Coparenting in the Second Year after Divorce," *Journal of Marriage and the Family* 52 (1990): 141–156.
72. F. Frank Furstenberg, Jr., S. P. Morgan, and P. D. Allison, "Parental Participation and Children's Well-Being after Marital Dissolution," *American Sociological Review* 52 (1987):695–701.
73. E. Mavis Hetherington, M. Cox, and R. Cox, "Effects of Divorce on Parents and Children," pp. 233–285 in M. Lamb, ed., *Nontraditional Families* (Hillsdale, N.J.: Lawrence Erlbaum, 1982).
74. Carol R. Cowery, and S. A. Settle, "Effects of Divorce on Children: Differential Impact of Custody and Visitation Patterns," *Family Relations* 24 (1985):455–463.
75. Eleanor E. Maccoby, Charlene E. Depner, and Robert H. Mnookin, "Custody of Children Following Divorce," in E. M. Hetherington and J. Arasteh, eds., *The Impact of Divorce, Single-Parenting and Stepparenting on Children* (Hillsdale, N.J.: Lawrence Erlbaum, 1988).

76. Sara McLanahan and Karen Booth, "Mother Only Families: Problems and Prospects," *Journal of Marriage and the Family* 51 (1989):557–580; J. Wallenstein and J. B. Kelly, *Surviving the Breakup: How Children and Parents Cope with Divorce* (New York: Basic Books, 1980).

77. Hetherington, et al., *op. cit.,* 1982.

78. Richmond-Abbott, *op. cit.,* 1984.

79. A. J. Norton and J. E. Moorman, "Current Trends in Marriage and Divorce among American Women," *Journal of Marriage and the Family* 49 (1987):3–14.

80. A. Cherlin, *Marriage, Divorce and Remarriage: Social Trends in the United States* (Cambridge, Mass.: Harvard University Press, 1981).

81. Glick, *op. cit.*

82. William Goode, *After Divorce* (Glencoe, Ill.: The Free Press, 1956).

83. Andrew Cherlin and James McCarthy, "Remarried Couple Households: Data from the June 1980 Current Population Survey," *Journal of Marriage and the Family* 47 (1985):23–31.

84. Wallenstein and Kelly, *op. cit.;* F. F. Furstenberg and G. Spanier, *Recycling the Family: Remarriage after Divorce* (Beverly Hills, Calif.: Sage, 1984).

85. Norton and Moorman, *op. cit.;* Ellen Crawger, "Love and Marriage," *Detroit Free Press* (February 26, 1989):Li; Jean Giles-Sims and Margaret Crosbie-Burnett, "Stepfamily Research: Implications for Policy, Clinical Interventions, and Further Research," *Family Relations* 38 (1989):19–23; M. Coleman and L. Ganong, "Remarriage Myths: Implications for the Helping Professions," *Journal of Counseling and Development* 64 (1985):116–120.

86. L. White and A. Booth, "The Quality and Stability of Remarriages: The Role of Stepchildren," *American Sociological Review* (1985):689–698; G. Spanier and F. Furstenberg, "Remarriage after Divorce: A Longitudinal Analysis of Well-Being," *Journal of Marriage and the Family* 44 (1982):709–720.

87. H. Weingarten, "Remarriage and Well-Being," *Journal of Family Issues* 1 (1980): 553–559; Helen R. Weingarten, "Marital Status and Well-Being: A National Study Comparing First-Married, Currently Divorced and Remarried Adults," *Journal of Marriage and the Family* 47 (1985):653–661; Jean Giles-Sims, "Parental Role Sharing between Remarrieds and Ex-Spouses," *Youth and Society* 19 (1987): 34–150.

88. *Ibid.,* p. 553; Giles-Sims and Crosbie-Burnett, *op. cit.*

89. Glick, *op. cit.*

90. Laurel Richardson, *The Dynamics of Sex and Gender: A Sociological Perspective,* 3d ed. (New York: Harper & Row, 1988); Philip Blumstein and Pepper Schwartz, *American Couples: Money, Work, Sex* (New York: Morrow, 1983).

91. Richardson, *op. cit.,* pp. 219–226.

92. Blumstein and Schwartz, *op. cit.*

93. *Ibid.*

94. *Ibid.*

95. Alan P. Bell and Martin S. Weinberg, *Homosexualities: A Study of the Diversity among Men and Women* (New York: Simon & Schuster, 1978).

96. Frederick W. Bozett, "Gay Men as Fathers," in Shirley M. H. Hanson and Frederick W. Bozett, eds., *Dimensions of Fatherhood* (Beverly Hills, Calif.: Sage, 1985), pp. 141–153.

97. G. Dullea, "Gay Couples' Wish to Adopt Grows, along with Increasing Resistance," *New York Times* (February, 1988): 26.

98. Bell and Weinberg, *op. cit.*

99. Rebecca Nahas and Myra Turley, *The New Couple: Women and Gay Men* (New York: Seaview, 1980).

100. Claire M. Renzetti and Daniel J. Curran, *Women, Men, and Society: The Sociology of Gender* (Boston: Allyn & Bacon 1989).

101. L. K. Nicoloff and E. A. Stiglitz, "Lesbian Alcoholism: Etiology, Treatment and Recovery," in Boston Lesbian Psychologies Collective, eds., *Lesbian Psychologies* (Urbana: University of Illinois Press, 1987), pp. 283–293; L. Margolis, M. Becker, and K. Jackson-Brewer, "Internalized Homophobia: Identifying and Treating the Oppressor Within," in Boston Lesbian Psychologies Collective, *op. cit.*, pp. 229–241.

102. W. R. Greer, "Violence against Homosexuals Rising, Groups Seeking Wider Protection Say," *New York Times* (November, 23, 1986):36.

103. Adrienne Rich, "Compulsory Heterosexuality and Lesbian Existence," *Signs* 5 (1980):631–660.

104. Bell and Weinberg, *op. cit.*

105. *Ibid.*

106. Jean Seligmann, "Variations on a Theme," *Newsweek* (Special Edition: The 21st Century Family, Winter/Spring 1990):38–40, 44, 46.

107. Claire M. Renzetti, *op. cit.*, 348–349.

108. Seligmann, *op. cit.*

109. J. Ross Eshleman, *The Family: An Introduction*, 5th ed. (Boston: Allyn & Bacon, 1988).

110. Lee Rainwater, Richard Coleman, and Gerald Handel, *Workingman's Wife* (New York: Oceana, 1959); Myrra Komarovsky, *Blue-Collar Marriage* (New York: Random House, 1964); Lillian Rubin, *Worlds of Pain* (New York: Basic Books, 1976); Meg Luxton, *More Than a Labour of Love* (Toronto: Women's Educational Press, 1980); E. Rosen, *Bitter Choices* (Chicago: University of Chicago Press, 1987); Zavella, *Woman's Work and Chicano Families* (Ithaca, N.Y.: Cornell University Press, 1987).

111. Rubin, *op. cit.*, p. 38.

112. *Ibid.*, p. 26.

113. Komarovsky, *op. cit.*, p. 130.

114. Rubin, *op. cit.*, p. 60.

115. Luxton, *op. cit.*, p. 98.

116. Rubin, *op. cit.*, pp. 66–67.

117. *Ibid.*, p. 155.

118. Komarovsky, *op. cit.*, p. 100.

119. Rubin, *op. cit.*, p. 17.

120. Komarovsky, *op. cit.*, p. 100.

121. *Ibid.*, p. 44.

122. Rubin, *op. cit.*, p. 196.

123. Komarovsky, *op. cit.*, p. 127.

124. Rubin, *op. cit.*, p. 186.

125. *Ibid.*, p. 124.

126. *Ibid.*, p. 201.

127. *Ibid.*, p. 94.

128. *Ibid.*, p. 124.

129. Luxton, *op. cit.*, p. 52.

130. Jane C. Hood, *Becoming a Two-Job Family* (New York: Praeger, 1983), p. 73.

131. Lillian Rubin, "Blue-Collar Marriage and the Sexual Revolution," in Arlene Skolnick and Jerome Skolnick, eds., *The Family in Transition*, 3d ed. (Boston: Little, Brown, 1980), p. 160.
132. Luxton, *op. cit.*, p. 60.
133. *Ibid.*, p. 62.
134. *Ibid.*, p. 63.
135. Rubin, 1980, *op. cit.*
136. *Ibid.*, p. 165.
137. *Ibid.*, p. 166.
138. *Ibid.*
139. Rubin, 1976, *op. cit.*
140. *Ibid.*, p. 101.
141. Luxton, *op. cit.*, p. 45.
142. Rosen, *op. cit.*, pp. 97–99.
143. *Ibid.*, p. 102.
144. *Ibid.*, p. 105.
145. *Ibid.*, p. 108.
146. *Ibid.*
147. Hood, *op. cit.*, pp. 170–180.
148. Rubin, *op. cit.*, 1978 p. 104.
149. *Ibid.*, p. 97.
150. Myra Marx Feree, "The Confused American Housewife," *Psychology Today* (September 1976):87–93.; M. Feree, "Working Class Jobs: Housework and Paid Work as Sources of Satisfaction," *Social Problems* 23 (1975):431–441.
151. Rainwater et al., *op. cit.*, p. 72.
152. Hood, *op. cit.*, pp. 170–180.
153. Rainwater et al., *op. cit.*
154. Rubin, *op. cit.*, p. 126; Luxton, *op. cit.*
155. Franklin Fraiser, "Black Bourgeoisie," in Robert Staples, ed., *The Black Family: Essays and Studies* (Belmont, Calif.: Wadsworth, 1986), pp. 221–242.
156. R. J. Taylor, Bogart R. Leashere, and Susan Toliver, "An Assessment of the Provider Role as Perceived by Black Males," *Family Relations* 37 (1988):426–431.
157. Staples, *op. cit.*
158. U.S. Bureau of the Census, 1988, *op. cit.*
159. *Ibid.*
160. Norton and Moorman, *op. cit.*
161. *Ibid.*; Wilard L. Rodgers and Arland Thornton, "Changing Patterns of First Marriage in the United States," *Demography* 22 (1985):265–279.
162. Robert Staples, *Black Masculinity* (San Francisco: Black Scholar Press, 1982), p. 151.
163. Taylor, et al., *op. cit.*
164. M. Belinda Tucker and Robert Joseph Taylor, "Demographic Correlates of Relationship Status among Black Americans," *Journal of Marriage and the Family* 51 (1989):655–665.
165. Noel Cazenave, "Race, Socioeconomic Status and Age: The Social Context of American Masculinity," *Sex Roles* 11 (1984):639–656; Mark Testa, Nan Marie Astone, Marilyn Krough, and Kathryn M. Neckerman, "Employment and Marriage among Inner City Fathers," *Annals AAPSS* 501 (1989):79–90.
166. Elijah Anderson, "Sex Codes and Family Life among Poor Inner-City Youths," *Annals AAPSS* 501 (1989):59–78.

167. Staples, 1982, *op. cit.*
168. Noel Cazenave, "Middle-Income Fathers: An Analysis of the Provider Role," *The Family Coordinator* 28 (1978):583–593.
169. Cazenave, 1984, *op. cit.*
170. U.S. Bureau of the Census, 1988, *op. cit.*
171. Staples, 1982, *op. cit.*
172. Hariette Pipes McAdoo, "Factors Relating to Stability in Upwardly Mobile Black Families," *Journal of Marriage and the Family* 4, no. 4 (1978):762.
173. Staples, 1982, *op. cit.*, p. 15.
174. John Scanzoni, "Sex Roles, Economic Factors, and Marital Solidarity in Black and White Marriages," *Journal of Marriage and the Family* 37 (1975):130.
175. Jerome Heiss, *The Case of the Black Family* (New York: Columbia University Press, 1975).
176. *Ibid.*
177. C. L. Broman, "Household Work and Family Life Satisfaction of Blacks," *Journal of Marriage and the Family* 50 (1988):743–748.
178. J. E. Robinson, Wilfred Bailey, and John Smith, Jr., "Self-Perception of the Husband/Father in the Intact, Lower-Class Black Family," *Phylon* 46 (1985): 136–147.
179. Sharon Price-Bonham and Patsky Skeen, "A Comparison of Black and White Fathers with Implications for Parent Education," *The Family Coordinator* 28 (1979):53–59.
180. Cazenave, 1984, *op. cit.*
181. Heiss, *op. cit.*, p. 136.
182. *Ibid.*, p. 185, quoting Komarovsky's views on blue-collar marriage.
183. Richard E. Ball and Lynn Robbins, "Marital Status and Life Satisfaction among Black Americans," *Journal of Marriage and the Family* 48 (1986):389–394; Clifford Broman, "Satisfaction among Blacks: The Significance of Marriage and Parenthood," *Journal of Marriage and the Family* 50 (1988):45–51.
184. Richard E. Ball, "Marital Status, Household Structure and Life Satisfaction of Black Women," *Social Problems* 30 (1983):400–409.
185. Ann Zollar and J. Sherwood Williams, "The Contribution of Marriage to Life Satisfaction in Black Adults," *Journal of Marriage and the Family* 49 (1987):87–92.
186. Susan E. Crohan and Joseph Veroff, "Dimensions of Marital Well-Being among White and Black Newlyweds," *Journal of Marriage and the Family* 51 (1989):373–383.
187. Ball and Robbins, *op. cit.*
188. Alice F. Coner "Length of Marriage. Socioeconomic Status and Satisfaction among Black Married Couples" (paper presented at the annual meeting of the National Council on Family Relations, St. Paul, Minn., October 12–15, 1983).
189. Ball and Robbins, *op. cit.*; Broman, *op. cit.*
190. Staples, 1986, *op. cit.*
191. Crohan and Veroff, *op. cit.*
192. Scanzoni, *op. cit.*, p. 191.
193. Robert Staples, "Educating the Black Male for Marital Roles," in Staples, 1986, *op. cit.*, pp. 347–353.
194. Eugene Litwak, "Occupational Mobility and Extended Family Cohesion," *American Sociological Review* 25 (1960):9–21.
195. Elmer Martin and JoAnne Martin, *The Black Extended Family*, (Chicago: University of Chicago Press, 1978.)
196. Scanzoni, quoted in McAdoo, *op. cit.*, p. 762.

197. Carol Stack, *All Our Kin* (New York: Harper & Row, 1974).
198. Linda M. Chatters, Robert Joseph Taylor, and Harold W. Neighbors, "Size of Informal Helper Network Mobilized during a Serious Personal Problem among Black Americans," *Journal of Marriage and the Family* 51 (1989):667–676.
199. McAdoo, *op. cit.*, p. 763.
200. Albert McQueen, "Adaptations of Black Urban Families," quoting Robert Hill, "Strengths of Black Families," in David Reiss and Howard Hoffman, eds., *The American Family* (New York: Plenum, 1979), p. 84; Stack, *op. cit.*
201. Hill in Reiss, *op. cit.*
202. McAdoo, *op. cit.*, p. 775.
203. Chatters et al., *op. cit.*
204. L. E. Walker, *The Battered Woman* (New York: Harper & Row, 1979).
205. Murray A. Straus and Richard J. Gelles, "Changes in Family Violence from 1975 to 1985," *Journal of Marriage and the Family* 48, no. 3 (1986):465–480.
206. Richard Gelles, *Family Violence* (Beverly Hills, Calif.: Sage, 1987); Susan Steinmetz, "Family Violence: Past, Present and Future," in M. B. Sussman and S. K. Steinmetz, eds., *Handbook of Marriage and the Family* (New York: Plenum, 1987), pp. 125–176.
207. R. A. Berk, S. F. Berk, D. R. Loseke, and D. Rauma, "Mutual Combat and Other Family Violence Myths," in D. Finkelhor, R. J. Gelles, G. T. Hotaling, and M. A. Straus, eds., *The Dark Side of Families* (Beverly Hills, Calif.: Sage, 1983), pp. 197–212.
208. Angela Browne, "Family Homicide: When Victimized Women Kill," in Vincent B. Van Hasselt, Randall Morrison, Alan Bellack, and Michel Hersen, eds., *Handbook of Family Violence* (New York: Plenum, 1988), pp. 271–288.
209. Lenore E. Walker, "The Battered Woman Syndrome Study," in Finkelhor et al., *op. cit.*
210. *Ibid.*
211. *Ibid.*
212. Richard Gelles and C. P. Cornell, *Intimate Violence in Families* (Beverly Hills, Calif.: Sage, 1983).
213. Gelles, 1987, *op. cit.*
214. Kenneth E. Leonard and Theodore Jacob, "Alcohol, Alcoholism and Family Violence," in Van Hasselt et al., *op. cit.*, pp. 383–406.
215. J. Barling and A. Rosenbaum, "Work Stressors and Wife Abuse," *Journal of Applied Psychology* 71 (1986):346–348.
216. Walker, *op. cit.*
217. William J. Hauser, *Differences in Relative Resources, Familial Power and Spouse Abuse* (Palo Alto, Calif.: R&E. Research, 1982).
218. Walker, *op. cit.*
219. *Ibid.*
220. Attorney General's Task Force on Domestic Violence, 1984, cited in Gayla Margolin, Ginda Gorin Sibner, and Lisa Gleberman, "Wife Battering," in Van Hasselt et al., *op. cit.*, pp. 89–118.
221. Michael Strube and Linda Barbour, "Factors Relating to the Decision to Leave an Abusive Relationship," *Journal of Marriage and the Family* 46 (1984):837–844.
222. Walker, *op. cit.*
223. Anson Schupe, William A. Stacey, and Lonnie R. Hazlewood, *Violent Men, Violent Couples* (Lexington, Mass.: Lexington Books, 1987), p. 33.
224. Browne, *op. cit.*

225. Schupe et al., *op. cit.*
226. A. Rosenbaum and K. D. O'Leary, "Martial Violence: Characteristics of Abusive Couples," *Journal of Consulting and Clinical Psychology* 49 (1981):63–71.
227. Barling and Rosenbaum, *op. cit.*
228. F. J. Fitch and M. A. Papantonio, "Men Who Batter: Some Pertinent Characteristics," *Journal of Nervous and Mental Disease* 171 (1983):190–192.
229. D. Goldstein and A. Rosenbaum, "An Evaluation of the Self-Esteem of Maritally Violent Men," *Family Relations* 34 (1985):425–428.
230. Murray Straus and Richard J. Gelles, "Societal Change and Change in Family Violence from 1975 to 1985 as Revealed by Two National Surveys," *Journal of Marriage and the Family* 48 (1986):465–479.
231. L. Lerman and F. Livingston, "State Legislation on Domestic Violence," *Response to Violence in the Family and Sexual Assault* 6 (1983):1–27.
232. Jane O'Reilly, Barbara B. Dolan, and Elizabeth Taylor, "Wife Beating: The Silent Crime," *Time* (September 5, 1983):23–26.
233. "Police Role on Spouse-Beating," *New York Times* (July 7, 1986):C3.
234. Richard Berk and Phyllis J. Newton, "Does Arrest Really Deter Wife Battery? An Effort to Replicate the Findings of the Minneapolis Spouse Abuse Experiment," *American Sociological Review* 50 (1985):253–262.
235. *Ibid.*
236. Erin Pizzey, *Scream Quietly or the Neighbors Will Hear* (Baltimore: Hammondsworth, 1974).
237. L. Bowker and L. Maurer, "The Importance of Sheltering in the Lives of Battered Women," *Response to the Victimization of Women and Children* 8 (1985):2–8.
238. B. E. Aquirre, "Why Do They Return? Abused Wives in Shelters," *Social Work* 30 (1985):350–354; Andrea J. Sedlak, "Prevention of Wife Abuse," in Van Hasselt et al., *op. cit.*, pp. 319–358.
239. Z. Mettge, "Help for Men Who Batter: An Overview of Issues and Programs," *Response to Family Violence and Sexual Assault* 5 (1982):1–2, 7–8, 23.
240. A. R. Roberts, *Battered Women and Their Families: Intervention Strategies and Treatment Programs* (New York: Springer, 1984).
241. Rosenbaum and O'Leary, *op. cit.*
242. Domestic Violence Project, Inc., "Fact Sheet on Domestic Violence," Ann Arbor, Mich: Domestic Violence Project 1988.

Chapter 10

Religion and Science: Two Institutions That Enforce Stereotypes through Belief Systems

This chapter will look at two institutions that perpetuate and enforce stereotypes and scripts for gender roles. Organized religion is a societal institution that sends strong messages about gender roles and enforces its values in a variety of ways. We will also look at science and medicine as a knowledge base that tells us certain things about the nature of men and women.

RELIGION

The social control exerted by religion is particularly strong. As Laurel Richardson explains, the tenets of religion are usually learned at a very young age and constitute an important part of socialization that is incorporated into one's self-identity as well as one's feelings about the world. Religion provides support and reassurance about the nature of the world, and if one questions the part of the teaching that relates to gender roles, one may also have to question the parts that provide support and stability. Questioning religious doctrine may also entail the loss of a community of friends and neighbors and even ostracism or rejection. Thus, it is very difficult for many people who have a religious background to question the doctrines they hold. It is difficult even for less religious persons to question the churches because in doing so they are questioning a source of moral authority.[1]

People who have strong religious beliefs are likely to have more traditional attitudes about gender roles. One study looked at how depth of religious commitment, as measured by engaging in religious activities and having religious feelings, relates to gender roles and gender-role preference. In all five categories of gender roles, a strong religious commitment predicted preference for traditional gender roles. Religion was a stronger predictor of belief in traditional roles than were self-esteem, assertiveness, mother's education, and mother's employment.[2] Other studies have shown essentially the same thing.[3]

It is therefore very important to see what religion as an institution has had to say about gender roles in times past and present. The values of established religion have become the values of many people in every society in both historical and contemporary times.

We saw briefly in Chapter 2 that the Judeo-Christian tradition stereotyped women as being pure and virtuous (not interested in sexual matters and devoted to family and children above self) or as evil sexual temptresses. In either case they were seen as inferior to men, who were supposed to hold the major positions in the religion and to control society, including women and children. Religion buttressed its view of men as superior by asserting that only males were made in God's image and pointed to the scriptural assertion that women were made from men and for men. This view of women as tainted and/or inferior, however, was not prevalent in earlier times. When we look at the development of organized religion, we see a shift in views about the traits of women and men. These shifts often paralleled trends in the secular society.

Early Religious Ideology

Early religious ideology did not reflect dominance by either sex. Fisher says, "It seems likely that before the concept of a queen or king of heaven appeared, some few thousand years ago, the universe was viewed as a pantheistic collection of forces inherent in nature, forces that were female and male, animal and human, and combinations of both."[4] The early Mesopotamian pantheon of the fourth millennium B.C. included nature gods such as the mountain range, the sky, and the divine cow.

Reuther reports an early image of woman as a nature goddess in the myths of Babylonia and Canaan. These myths picture the cosmos as a world egg or womb that differentiates into sky and earth, which are male and female divinities. The earth mother and her daughter, the fertility goddess, are seen as powerful and autonomous figures.[5] The king is the son of the earth mother; he grows up to be her consort and produces a young king who takes his place. Reuther points out, however, that it is a son, not a daughter, whom the Great Mother puts on the throne. As time passes, sky and earth, which were once on the same level, become ranked in status hierarchy. Maleness (the sky) is identified with intellectuality and spirituality, and femaleness is identified with lower material nature.[6] Enki, the male god, takes center stage after about 2000 B.C. Myths have him ejaculating and filling the Tigris River with water; he comes to dominate the pantheon of other gods. Nannu, "she who gave birth to heaven and earth," becomes a housekeeper. Her daughter, the fertility goddess Inanna, remains, but judging from the change in ritual mating poses between the fourth millennium and 700 B.C., Inanna comes to be dominated by her consort. Another indication that male gods predominate is the fact that the last king to use a female goddess's name did so around 2000 B.C. During the second and first millennia, both kings and male commoners used only the names of gods.[7]

Judeo-Christian Religion and Male-Dominated Society

Some time in the thousand years preceding the birth of Christ men attempted to free themselves from dependence on nature. They raised domestic animals and bred them, tried irrigation, and in other ways attempted to assert mastery over nature. At the same time, they began to believe in a principle beyond the body, a higher being, a soul. Maleness became identified with intellectuality and spirituality. In the developing religious thought of this period, primarily in early Judaism, women remained linked to the subordinate and inferior natural world of the body. Older feelings about women's sexuality and its dangers were incorporated into new ideologies.

The religious beliefs of this time stressed that one could achieve divinity and spirituality by purging the evil of the earthly body and looking for the divine soul. As women were associated with the earthly body and its desires, they came to be associated with impurity and evil. We begin to find Greek tales such as that of Pandora's box, in which a women loosed all manner of evil upon the world. Later, in Christianity, Eve was pictured as the evil woman who tempted Adam out of the Garden of Eden, with the result that all humankind is supposedly cursed with original sin.[8] Intensified attempts were made to control women's sexuality and protect men from its influence. Early menstruation taboos were carried over to the major religions. In Judeo-Christian tradition, a menstruating woman was held to be unclean and a man who lay with her would become unclean.[9] There is an implication that if the couple had sexual relations during the menstrual period, they could be cut off from their people, although this was obviously difficult to enforce. In like fashion, a woman who gave birth was considered unclean, although not as much for a male child as for a female. Leviticus 12:2–5 tells us, "If a woman conceives and bears a male child, then she shall be unclean for seven days . . . but if she bears a female child, then she shall be unclean for two weeks." And another passage asks, "How can he be clean that was born of a woman?"

Women were also seen as being obsessed by sex and using their sexual nature to tempt and weaken men so that they could not complete their important work. This image of women as sexual temptresses who beguile and seduce men is seen in the Bible in the stories of Samson and Delilah, Bathsheba and David, and Jezebel and Ahab. The name Jezebel has become synonymous with one who deceives.

It was believed that women were so obsessed with sex that they had to be protected from their own base interests and that men had to be protected from them. Various methods of control over female sexuality show up in the written ideology and in the laws and customs of the time. Talmudic writers went so far as to prohibit a widow from keeping slaves or pet dogs for fear that she would use them to commit sexual indecencies.[10] Another way to control female sexuality was to make sure that women would not indulge in sex outside of marriage without great penalty. Virgins had to protect their honor at all costs. It was better to die than to be dishonored. A bride who was found not to be a virgin on her wedding night was sent home in disgrace, and the bride price was refunded. Adulteresses could be stoned to death and frequently were. In contrast, a man who strayed was ignored unless he damaged someone else's property. To keep women from enjoying sex—and thus, it was assumed, from straying—the process of **clitoridectomy** continued to be widespread. It was reasoned that if one removed the site of a woman's pleasure, she would have no reason to want to participate in sex.[11] Thus we see in biblical statements, in religious practices, in civil law, and in customs various attempts to control women's sexuality.

While abstinence and virginity were preferable, marriage was considered the saving grace that could direct sex to procreation and save man from his lustful nature. Women were thus married early and kept literally under wraps before marriage. This meant that they had little opportunity for education or participation in any but household affairs. A daily Orthodox Jewish prayer for men says, "I thank thee, O Lord, that thou hast not made me a woman."[12]

Much of the doctrine that developed about women in early Christianity seemed to be based on the Old Testament and earlier Jewish tradition as well as on interpretations by Christian religious leaders rather than on the teachings of Jesus.[13] Paul in particular regarded sexual intercourse and marriage only as concessions to the human condition and stated, "Now concerning the things whereof ye wrote unto me: It is good for a man not to touch a woman. . . . Nevertheless, to avoid fornication, let every man have his own wife, and let every woman have her own husband" (I Corinthians 7:1–2).

Religious doctrine also underlined the idea of women as secondary and inferior beings who were to submit themselves to men. Ephesians 5:22–23 states, "Wives, submit yourselves unto your husbands . . . for the husband is the head of the church," and Paul added, "Let the women learn in silence with all subjection . . . I suffer not a woman to usurp authority over men, but to be in the silence" (I Corinthians 14:34–35). The last phrase has often been used to justify keeping women out of positions of religious authority.

Ironically, the tradition of the mother goddess lingered in Judeo-Christian religion. As the people of the Old Testament try to drive Baal, the symbolic king of the nature religions, out of the conquered land, Yahweh, the new god, becomes the consort of the goddess mother. Myth says further that Israel becomes the bride of Yahweh. Later in Christian thought, the Church is seen as feminine and allied with God, the mediator between God and his children.[14] In the words of the old hymn:

The Church's one foundation is Jesus Christ the Lord,
She is his new creation by water and the word,
From heaven he came and sought *her*, to be his holy bride,
And with his blood he bought *her*, and for *her* sins he died.

The other obvious female symbol in the new religion is the figure of Mary, the mother of God. She becomes the maternal mediator between God and the faithful. There was little interest in Mary until around fourth century A.D., when strong prohibitions about sexual life were at their height. With the puritanical beliefs of this period, Mary became a symbol of the ideal of virginity. The virgin birth was stressed, and traditions about the natural earlier children of Mary and Joseph were suppressed.

Devotion to Mary developed rapidly in the fourth century, and in Egypt the idea that she ascended into heaven with Jesus developed and spread. Devotion to her, though, centered on the perception that she was the merciful and forgiving mother who could understand human inadequacies and intercede with her son so that sins could be forgiven.[15] Thus, we see in the ideology of Judeo-Christianity the development and elaboration of images of women that have remained with us since: Women have dual natures—virginal and pure or sexual and evil—and are subordinate and inferior to men.

Eastern Religions

Islam also established status differentiations between men and women. Islam rose about the seventh century A.D. with the birth of Mohammed in A.D. 570. Before that time the Arabs had been a male-centered tribal group that practiced polygyny. While Christianity regarded celibacy as the best state a person could maintain, under Islam marriage was seen as extremely important. All who could marry were urged to do so, and Mohammed suggested that men "marry of the women who seem good to you, two or three or four and if ye fear that ye cannot do justice to so many, then one. . . ."[16]

However, as Bullough points out, a positive attitude toward sex did not encourage a positive attitude toward women in Islamic countries. Women were seen as little more than the property of men, to be used for their enjoyment. While there were some laws protecting women, it was almost impossible for them to gain an education or have any kind of opportunity in the public sphere.

In these countries women were isolated, which kept them subjected. The ideal woman was to be virtuous and entirely devoted to her husband and family. As Bullough describes it,

> She speaks and laughs rarely and never without reason. She never leaves the house, even to see neighbors of her acquaintance. She has no women friends, gives her confidence to nobody, and her husband is her sole reliance. . . . She does not surrender herself to anybody but her husband, even if abstinence would kill her. If her husband shows his intention of performing the conjugal rite, she is agreeable to his desires and occasionally even provokes him.[17]

Interestingly, the seclusion and protection of women did lead to some opportunities for professional women in Islamic countries. As women were not supposed to be taught by male teachers or examined by male doctors, a group of professional women who devoted themselves exclusively to the service of women was allowed to develop.

More recently, in the Persian Gulf war of 1991, women exercised authority and even acted as resistance fighters in places such as Kuwait, where male leaders had left the country. As a result, they have been demanding more participation in society, and many of them would at least like the right to vote.

Buddhism, like Islam as interpreted in Moslem countries, kept women in their place. Early Buddhism, however, had the most positive view of women and stated that Nirvana was open to all. The availability of a religious life gave women opportunities beyond marriage and motherhood and more independence within marriage. However, more traditional views developed eventually. With beliefs similar to those of early Christianity, later Buddhism stated that the way to attain Nirvana was to give up worldly sexual desires. Women were viewed as "sexually ravenous, greedy, envious, stupid and generally repulsive." They were seen as sexually insatiable and as setting traps for men. "It was only by triumphing over the world of allure and senses in the world of women and withstanding their seduction that the Perfect One (The Buddha) entered into Nirvana and gained saving truth. . . ."[18]

In the Hindu religion, the duality of women's nature was also stressed. For example, Mother Earth was seen as the twin goddesses Nirrti and Prthvi. As Nirrti, she was decay, death, and destruction; as Prthvi, she mothered. These great goddesses—and mortal women—were seen as ineffective or dangerous if they did not have a male to control them. It was believed that "the male principle is necessary if the female principle is to be fertile and good. Alone the female principle tends to be evil and dangerous."[19]

Hinduism further defined the position of women in its belief about reincarnation. Hindu philosophy stressed that people are constantly reborn until they realize their oneness with the divine. The level of one's birth is determined by the quality of one's previous life, or karma. It was commonly believed that no woman could possibly gain salvation except in a future life when she was reborn as a man. Being born female was in itself indicative of having had a bad karma in a past life.

Women could advance their karma only by being good wives and exalting their husbands. The laws of Mana instructed women to be loyal even if their husbands were deformed, unfaithful, drunk, offensive, or debauched. To ritualize this attitude, the orthodox religion suggested that the wife adore the big toe of her husband's right foot morning and evening, bathing it, offering it incense, and waving lights before it. Because of women's lowered state, wifely duties were the only ones by which a woman could gain karma. Women were excluded from other prestigious forms of obtaining good karma, such as the study of the Vedas (religious works) and meditation.[20]

Later Development of Religious Doctrine

Thus, ideology that justified a lower position for women was developed and enforced by religions that worshiped male deities. These religions developed philosophies that defined women as inferior or evil and justified their isolation from the everyday affairs of education, trade, and politics and even from social contact. In practice, this meant that women lived in a world apart. They had no access to public power positions or to means of gaining power, such as trade or education. While some women exercised power informally at home or through women's groups, their isolation and seclusion made even this difficult in some areas. As the religions changed and developed, beliefs about women fluctuated in accordance with the economic situation and the philosophy that justified the economy.

We noted that as Christianity spread across Europe, religious ideology justified the curtailment of legal rights and set a pattern for women's subordinate position throughout the following periods. Women's rights were severely limited by law in the Middle Ages. However, women of the upper classes managed to control some land and had some political power, particularly when their husbands were absent. Before A.D. 800 women could be nuns and even had an important role in church administration. However, after the reorganization of the church under Charlemagne, clerics held government positions and women were not allowed to maintain church positions.[21]

During the Renaissance of the fourteenth through sixteenth centuries, a renewed interest in Greek and Roman antiquity revived the idea that women were sinful, sexual creatures and that abstinence and sexual chastity were the way to salvation. Although during these years wealthy women were allowed greater education, aristocratic women who in the past had run large estates and exercised political influence lost a great deal of their power as state power was consolidated.

The Protestant Reformation

The Protestant Reformation of the sixteenth century gave women access to sources of power that they had not had before. If, as Protestantism said, each person communicated personally with God and negotiated his or her own salvation according to faith, then women were on an equal footing with men and could be saved. This did not mean that they could get a position in the hierarchy of the church, but they could ascend into heaven. Protestants insisted that everyone should be able to read the scriptures and thus encouraged literacy among women.[22]

Protestantism also established the precedent that it was correct or even preferable to have romance in marriage and to be in love with one's spouse. This meant that women came to be viewed as something more than property and could even exercise power through their romantic attachments to their spouses. In addition, the new faith aided women as it sought to improve marriage by attacking wife beating and sexual double standards. The sexual natures of men and women were deemed to be more alike, and women were no longer viewed as wanton, unable to control their desires, and likely to lead men into sin.

A darker side of this period involved the difficulty of proving one's faith when ritual and hierarchy did not establish it. Any sign of rebellion or talking back in women could be construed as the work of the devil, and these women could be considered witches. Indeed, the word *feminus* was construed to mean "lacking in faith." Thousands of women died in witch-hunts in both Europe and America.[23] We see even in the relatively enlightened period of the Protestant Reformation the continuation of the theme that women are connected to evil and were the devil's work and that the way to prove one's "faith" for a woman was to be good and obedient.

Needless to say, with this philosophy, religious leadership was male and theology reflected the values and self-images of men. It was in most Western countries a primary cultural reinforcer of modern industrial patriarchy or male control. The all-pervasiveness of religious control over all aspects of political and cultural behavior, however, had diminished. By the time of the emergence of feminism in other contexts in the 1960s, religious institutions, at least in the United States, had become largely the guardian of family and home. "Church and home had become intertwined during the cult of domesticity in the nineteenth century; the home had become a religious sanctuary, and the church a second home and family. In contrast, whenever women demanded equal employment opportunities, help inside the home, and reproductive rights, they challenged not only gender roles but religious authority."[24] However, religion had little but moral sanctions to enforce its views. Religious domination of the state was over, although religious authority still was important in issues of marriage, family, and sexual morality. During the Reagan years, the opposition of the Roman Catholic Church to abortion was viewed by the administration as a major advantage in its antichoice campaign, yet the same administration hardly listened when the Catholic bishops criticized the government's position on welfare. As late as 1989, the Catholic Church attempted to use sanctions to support its views by threatening to excommunicate Catholic politicians who favored abortions.[25]

Feminism and Religion

Feminism has challenged religious authority not only in the larger society but also in the internal structure of many denominations. In particular, **feminists** have challenged organized religion by demanding ordination and other leadership roles, by asking churches and synagogues to adopt "inclusive language" which rejects generic male terms to denote human beings or God, and by resisting religious authority in areas outside the family.[26] How have they fared in these challenges?

There has been strong resistance to women moving into leadership roles in the Catholic Church. As recently as October 1988 the Pope restated his belief that women should not be priests. He based his statement on the fact that Jesus had only male disciples and added that women have a "nature" different from that of men that would make it difficult for them to be priests and to understand male parishioners.[27] Although resistance on the part of the Catholic Church has been hard to overcome, women have continued to move into the religious structure of Protestant denominations. In 1972, they accounted for only 4.7 percent of the enrollment in seminary programs, but by 1981 they constituted 14.7 percent of seminary enrollees.[28] They have also increased their representation on seminary faculties and in seminary administration. The number of women clergy is also increasing, and women now account for approximately 5 percent of all clergy.[29] Most of this growth occurred since 1970; before that time most denominations did not ordain women.

Reformed Judaism ordained women for the first time in 1972, the Lutheran church in 1970, and the Episcopal church in 1976, after a bitter struggle. In 1989, the first Episcopal woman bishop was consecrated. Women are still likely, however, to serve in subordinate positions as assistant pastors and are less likely to move upward in religious hierarchies.[30] The Conservative and Orthodox branches of Judaism still do not ordain females, nor do many Protestant churches.

In the fight for more inclusive language, the results have been mixed. Some churches have gone to great lengths to use nonsexist language in hymns and prayer books. A new version of the Bible has been written in much more gender-neutral language, yet there is a great deal of resistance to this language. In fundamentalist churches which literally believe in the words of the scriptures, this resistance is to be expected, but even in more liberal denominations, there is resistance based on a belief in keeping tradition intact.

Fighting the dictates of religious institutions on other fronts has been a more successful battle. As the majority of Catholic women use artificial contraception of some sort, the Catholic Church is not able to dictate to its adherents in this area.[31] In spite of the fact that many denominations glorify a wife and mother who stays at home and takes care of her children, the majority of women with young children work outside the home today.[32]

Another area where Catholics have evaded Church control of sexuality involves priests and nuns who have violated the Catholic insistence on celibacy for the clergy. There have always been rumors and some evidence that a certain percentage of the Catholic clergy have sexual liaisons. However, as recently as the 1970s, priests could leave the Church to get married without facing excommunication. Pope John Paul II, however, has granted far fewer dispensations for priests who wish to marry, and many seem to be sexually active without marriage. A survey of priests conducted between 1965 and 1980 estimates that about 20 percent are heterosexually active.[33] There is even a support group for women involved with priests. A majority of priests believe that celibacy should be optional for the clergy, but it is unlikely that the Catholic Church will change its policy in the near future.

Many religions have also attempted to dictate sexual preference, and feminists have decried this pressure. Homosexuality has been condemned by most organized religions for clergy, church members, and the population at large. The Catholic Church and conservative Protestant denominations have condemned homosexuality on the basis of several scriptures. They cite Leviticus 18:22, which says, "You shall not lie with a male as with a woman; it is an abomination." Gay men and lesbians have heard themselves called sinners and have suffered severe discrimination. Not only has this made it difficult for gays to have a relationship with a church or synagogue, but organized religion has also fostered homophobia among its members. A recent study of the relationship between religious orientation and antihomosexual feelings showed that those who are more religiously orthodox are likely to be prejudiced against both gay men and lesbians.[34]

Even in the more liberal Protestant denominations gay men and lesbians have had a difficult time being ordained. Only the United Church of Christ and the Unitarian Universalists had formally opened ordination to homosexuals before 1991. In that year, a lesbian was ordained as an Episcopal minister. In the 1970s discrimination against lesbians and gay men in Christian churches led to the foundation of the Metropolitan Community Church, which was primarily for gay males and lesbians. Within Judaism, separate gay synagogues have been established, and most Jewish homosexuals have been able to seek ordination and religious leadership within the religious mainstream as well.[35]

The question of gay men in the clergy is particularly pertinent today with the increasing fear about the spread of AIDS. Gay priests have been estimated to constitute between 20 and 40 percent of the 57,000 American Catholic priests. A survey utilizing 1,500 interviews of priests between 1960 and 1985 by the psychologist Richard Sipe, a former priest, estimates that about 20 percent of the priests are homosexual and that half of these gay men are sexually active. Other researchers say the figure is as high as 40 percent, and in the Episcopal church estimates run as high as 50 percent in urban dioceses such as San Francisco and New York. These priests keep their homosexuality secret because they fear rejection by their congregations. If they are found to be active homosexually, they are usually removed from pastoral duties, although in private the Catholic Church tends to protect those who fall from celibacy, often reassigning them to a different parish. Some Catholic seminaries accept homosexual candidates but require a pledge of celibacy. As late as 1987, the Catholic Church reaffirmed that a "natural inclination" toward homosexuality is an "objective disorder."[36] While some Protestant denominations ordain homosexuals, both gay and lesbian ministers are expected to be celibate.

Many lesbians have left their churches, and those who remain have little chance of being ordained as priests or pastors. Several lesbian theologians have been fired from seminaries and church-related colleges. However, a few are still active and have influenced feminism, if not church doctrine. Carter Heyward is on the faculty of the Episcopal Divinity School in Cambridge, Massachusetts, and has integrated her lesbian experience with her theological work.[37] Catholic lesbians such as Mary E. Hunt have argued that the Roman Catholic Church has been hostile to women but has provided settings in which women's friendships could flourish.[38] The fact that lesbians were a part of the Church's existence is reflected in books such as *Lesbian Nuns: Breaking Silence*.[39]

The New Feminist Theology

Since the 1960s there has been a tremendous growth in feminist theology. This theology criticizes not only the structure and positions of religion but also some of its male-based ideology. Those who are involved in the new theology tend to take one of two positions. *Reformists* believe that there can be a reinterpretation of scriptures and church history with gender-neutral language and a more female-oriented perspective. *Revolutionaries* believe that the cultural tradition that spawned the scriptures is so male-oriented that it is impossible to revise scripture and doctrine and emphasize the need for women to go beyond traditional religion and find their spirituality within their own experiences.

Reformists have been eager to reinterpret the Bible to show that it contains alternative views of women's and men's roles. While traditional scriptures emphasized the original sin of women and the need for submission by them, reformist feminists point out that there are contradictions in the Bible. Other scriptural passages can be read to contradict ones that have been used to condemn and subdue women. For example, the story of the Creation is told twice in the Bible. The first account, in Genesis 1:27–31, belongs to the traditional scriptures, but reformist feminists emphasize that it says that "God created man in his own image . . . male and female he created them." (Genesis 1:27) and point out that both men and women share in this creative image of God. They also emphasize that Genesis 3:18 states that "it is not good that man should be alone" and that God creates woman as his companion, not his slave or inferior. They point out that whereas the animals were modeled from clay, Eve was created of bone and flesh, as was Adam. Therefore, they state that if one reads with a slightly different perspective, the account in Genesis does not indicate the inferiority of women. They also point out that using a similar perspective, one can see that Adam and Eve shared equally in original sin.[40]

Reformist feminists point out that while the church fathers wrote about isolating women and keeping them submissive, Jesus's teachings were in sharp contrast to this. He teaches women even though his disciples are aghast at the prospect (John 4:7). He suggests that a woman's adultery should not be treated with greater severity than a man's (John 8:11), and he refuses men the right to divorce more easily than their wives (Matthew 19:10). He deals with women whether or not they are "polluted" by blood or unfavorable occupations; specifically, he judges them by their faith rather than by their ability to fulfill certain roles. He also sends women out to witness the resurrection (John 20:1).[41]

These feminists say that it was the church fathers who influenced our views on the place and worth of women. They believe this occurred because as orthodox Christianity developed into an established state religion, it was obliged to resist communities that were considered heretical. It thus became explicitly antifeminist. These views strengthened during the Middle Ages because the church fathers were held in such high esteem that their pronouncements were considered almost infallible, like those of the Pope.[42]

Revolutionary feminists say that there is little hope for women finding spiritual experiences in a male-dominated church and in male-dominated scriptures. Instead, they recommend that women find spirituality within their own experiences. Some have turned to goddess worship in the sense that the goddess is not divine but a symbol of the divinity in women. Judith Plaskow has emphasized that women's lives are a source of feminist spirituality; Carol Christ sees women's literature as a source of women's spiritual quest.[43] Radical feminist theologians include Mary Daly, whose book *The Church and the Second Sex* emphasizes the right of women to search for transcendence outside a male-dominated structure and whose more recent book, *Beyond God the Father*, sees inclusive language as a way to women's empowerment in churches.[44] The respected revolutionaries Elizabeth Schussler-Fiorenza (*In Memory of Her*) and Rosemary Reuther (*Sexism and Godtalk*) not only document misogyny in Western religion but also try to reconstruct theology around a feminine core and perspective.[45]

Thus, the role of religion in controlling the views of men and women is being changed by a changing society and by women who are challenging male-dominated scriptures, theology, and religious hierarchies. However, in spite of these changes, many of the traditional views about gender roles espoused by the churches continue to constrain our attitudes and behavior.

SCIENCE

The scientific establishment is another institution that has influenced views about men and women and controlled people's behavior. For the most part, science has been a male enterprise. Therefore, when we talk about science as an institution controlling men and women directly and through stereotypes, we are talking mainly about the control of women. Male-dominated science has been instrumental in shaping ideas about women's characteristics and abilities, although both traditionalists and those espousing equality for women have used scientific theories to support their arguments.

For example, biology was often used to buttress ideas about the proper roles of men and women. One controversy in the early scientific period was over brain size. Those opposed to higher education for women argued that women's smaller brains made it impossible for them to equal men in the intellectual realm so that it was futile to give them higher education.[46] Those who favored access to higher education for women argued that since the small size of women's brains resulted from their social inferiority, that inferiority should be changed so that women's brains could develop fully.[47]

Another "scientific" theory dealt with the proper roles of men and women in producing and caring for children. Darwin believed that there is a "selfish gene" and that each species and each individual within a species tries to maximize its reproductive potential. His followers claimed that as pregnant women invest so much in nurturing embryos, they can achieve the best reproductive success by continuing to invest time and effort in caring for children after they are born; by contrast, to maximize their reproductive possibilities, men should leave a child and mother after conception and go off to impregnate other females. Another argument said that women's hormones make them more receptive to infants and thus better suited to be mothers, while men's hormones make them more aggressive and thus better suited for the occupational world.[48]

In addition, science supported the view that women are delicate and need all their energies to attend to reproductive functions. Even Herbert Spencer argued in 1879 that because women bear children, they have little energy left over and their education should be restricted so that they do not become overly fatigued. Interestingly, neither in this case nor in the argument about brain size did scientific theory really change anything. The fact that women proved themselves capable when they were given access to higher education changed people's ideas about their ability.

Scientific thought also proposed that menstruation weakens women and that "raging hormones" make them unfit to work seriously at an occupation or participate in political life. Although a woman scientist, Leta Hollingsworth, showed that menstruation does not impair women physically or psychologically, researchers are still trying to prove such impairment.[49] In 1968, Broverman and colleagues argued that hormones affect the cognitive activity of women so that they can easily learn simple, repetitive tasks but have difficulty with more complex, creative endeavors.[50] The surgeon general of the United States claimed in 1977 that women's hormonal functioning affects their emotional stability and makes them unfit for high economic positions or government office.[51]

Scientists also cited women's supposedly different psychological traits as a reason to limit their participation in economic and political affairs. Darwin talked about limiting women's political rights because of their "instincts" to be kinder and more caring. Many scientists believed that such gentle instincts would be a liability in public office or even if women voted.[52] Others countered this position with the opposite view: If women are more naturally caring than men, they should do more in public life as this would help society. Again, future events supplied the answers about whether women might be different from men in the way they approach legal and political affairs. Women who voted or held public office did not ruin the country, as predicted, by spending too liberally on social welfare projects or dismantling defense structures. They were and are slightly more likely to care about educational and welfare issues and to be less hawkish about defense than men, but the differences in political behavior between men and women are small.

MEDICINE

The scientific speciality of medicine has been particularly important in defining and controlling the behavior of men and women. In particular, medical practitioners have affected views of gender roles in two important ways: the way in which they define illness and prescribe drugs and surgery differentially and the way in which they handle the reproductive functions of women.

Defining Illness

An example of the way in which the medical profession has differentially defined illness for women can be seen in its willingness to describe women's natural hormonal fluctuations as forms of disease while men's hormonal fluctuations are described as normal.

For years the medical profession ignored the complaints of women who had cramps, headaches, bloating, and mood changes before the menstrual period. These women were seen as complainers and hypochondriacs. More recent research proved the existence of many of these problems in a large number of women. The medical profession then did a complete reversal and defined premenstrual syndrome (PMS) as a disease. The American Psychological Association has even discussed the possibility of defining PMS as a mental disease.[53]

In a similar fashion, the medical profession has changed its beliefs about menopause. Originally menopause was seen as a natural transition of aging, and medical intervention was seldom deemed necessary. However, research on synthetic hormones gradually led to beliefs about menopause being a "deficiency disease." Once menopause was defined in this way, its treatment with estrogen was not only legitimate but became an obligation. While hormone replacement therapy for postmenopausal women has lessened the incidence of osteoporosis and helped preserve women's advantage over men in avoiding arteriosclerosis, it has also been implicated in increased rates of breast and uterine cancer. The prescription of artificial hormones to replace natural ones needs to be handled with careful thought about each individual case. Feminists point out that the "medicalization of menopause" strengthened the authority of medicine and created the implication that all postmenopausal women should seek medical help.

As a feminist researcher puts it, "The focus on biological changes acknowledged and explained the presence of menopausal symptoms in all women and the particularly uncomfortable experiences of some. It then provided a simple solution for relieving a woman's symptoms. Yet when used as the sole explanatory model of menopausal symptoms, it risked reducing the problems faced by aging women to biologically determined ones and reinforcing the traditional view of women as biologically different and inferior."[54]

Sometimes the medical profession has refused to recognize problems in women that it would have been quick to suspect in men. Data from 1990 show that heart attacks in women are much less likely to be suspected and diagnosed by physicians, with the result that more women die from an initial attack.[55]

The medical profession seems to vacillate between the view that women have more physical problems and thus legitimately need more medical help and the view that women are hypochondriacs who can be soothed with tranquilizers. Physicians tend to overprescribe drugs. It has been estimated that about 60 percent of the prescriptions drugs to which Americans are exposed have no therapeutic value. It has also been estimated that 30,000 Americans die annually as a result of adverse drug reactions; some studies have estimated the death toll to be as high as 100,000.[56]

Physicians tend to overprescribe particularly to women, often giving tranquilizers to "mildly anxious housewives." An example of both lack of protection and overprotection concerns thalidomide, a tranquilizer developed in the late 1950s by a European company and said to be safe even for pregnant women. This drug caused severe birth defects and other health problems, yet a male-oriented pharmaceutical industry kept it on the market in Europe, and only the willingness of one woman, Dr. Frances Kelsey, to resist the pressure of these companies kept it from being approved by the U.S. Food and Drug Administration (FDA) for use in this country. However, some American women obtained the drug and used it. After its side effects were made known, these women were often denied abortions in their own states and forced to go elsewhere for them.

Invasive Surgery

There is a greater tendency in the medical profession to use invasive surgery on women. While unnecessary surgery is performed on both sexes, one of the most blatant examples of its overuse is hysterectomy.

Hysterectomies are at an all-time high in the United States. It is the second most frequent surgical procedure. The U.S. rate per 100,000 population is twice that of England, and it rose an additional 25 percent between the mid-1960s and the 1970s.[57] By the age of 65, 35 percent of all women have had a hysterectomy, yet investigations have shown that a large proportion of these operations are unneeded.[58]

Some researchers have suggested that the high rate of hysterectomies can be traced to the fact that there is an oversupply of surgeons (an estimated 22,000 more than needed) in the United States, leading to insufficient patient caseloads for many, and that the fees for surgery are such that there is an incentive for profit which may increase the number of operations in marginal cases.[59] In trial programs in which second opinions were required, at least a fourth of the hysterectomies were found not to be needed.[60]

Hysterectomy can also be a subtle form of control when used for sterilization. Here the medical profession combines with the economic system to control women. In an infamous case, the American Cyanide Corporation, a chemical company that manufactured hazardous chemicals, required as a condition of employment that fertile women workers be sterilized. It did not want to risk lawsuits from women whose fetuses might be deformed.[61] Stellman and Henifin have documented other similar cases in the American workplace.[62]

Beliefs about Women's Sexuality and Reproductive Cycle

The medical profession is one of the primary sources of beliefs about women's sexuality and the nature of their reproductive cycle. These beliefs influence men and women alike and often initiate medical practices and even laws that affect and control women's reproductive cycle.

Defining Women's Sexuality. Obstetrics and gynecology textbooks have defined women's sexual feelings and responses largely from a male perspective.

In a fascinating summary done of the information in gynecology textbooks, Diana Scully and Pauline Bart discovered that most of the books contained incomplete, inaccurate, and male-biased information about female sexuality. In the period prior to the work of Kinsey and Masters and Johnson, they discovered that female sexuality was either omitted totally from the gynecology textbooks they surveyed (and they read almost everything published) or that the books had inaccurate and biased information. They quote one text published in 1943 as stating, "The fundamental biological factor in women is the urge of motherhood balanced by the fact that sexual pleasure is entirely secondary or even absent." Two books told gynecologists to instruct patients to fake orgasm.[63]

Even after the Kinsey study in the 1950s and the Masters and Johnson report in the 1960s showing that the seat of a woman's sexual pleasure is the clitoris, gynecology texts described the vaginal orgasm as the mature response and the clitoral orgasm as the immature and childish one. Some texts even stated that women who could not experience a vaginal orgasm were "frigid," and as late as 1965 gynecology texts talked about the vagina as the main source of a woman's pleasure. After the Masters and Johnson studies, there was some correction of inaccurate information in these texts, but even then, two-thirds of the books did not discuss the issue of vaginal versus clitoral orgasms. Eight continued to assert that the male sex drive is stronger (contrary to Masters and Johnson), two said that most women are frigid, and half protested that procreation is the major function of sex for the female.

These texts also seemed to prefer traditional gender roles, with males dominant and females passive. One text is quoted as saying, "An important feature of sex desire in the man is the urge to dominate the woman and subjugate her to his will; in the woman acquiescence to the masterful man takes a high place." Another text stated, "The traits that compose the core of the female personality are feminine narcissism, masochism, and passivity."[64]

Thus, obstetricians and gynecologists, who are supposed to be helpers of and advocates for women, were still being instructed with inaccurate myths about women's sexual nature and social role rather than with the more accurate scientific information that was available. We see the continuation of Victorian beliefs about the asexual wife who can be given only limited sexual pleasure, and then only by means of male penetration. In addition, we see the Freudian influence in views about women being interested only in procreation and suffering from penis envy. All these textbooks were written by men. One can only wonder at the damage that was wrought by passing on such inaccurate information about their "frigidity" and "immaturity" to women who desired sexual pleasure. One can also wonder why the available information about the nature of female and male sexual responses was not incorporated into later books. As late as 1970 one text stated, "The frequency of intercourse depends entirely upon the male sex drive. . . . The bride should be advised to allow her husband's sex drive to set their pace and she should attempt to gear hers satisfactorily to his. If she finds after several months or years that this is not possible, she is advised to consult her physician. . . ."[65] Popularized versions of gynecological information such as David Rubin's *All You Ever Wanted to Know about Sex* contain passages with similar kinds of inaccuracy and bias.

Thus, much past and recent scientific thought has portrayed women as passive, immature, asexual, and perhaps a little neurotic. The "scientific" portrayal of women has lagged far behind changing information about women's psychological and sexual nature, and the male bias in science has perpetuated a negative view of women. At the same time, the scientific community has perpetuated beliefs about the insatiable nature of the male's sexual appetite that have laid a heavy burden of performance upon men.

Regulating the Birth Process: The Medicalization of Childbirth

From the eleventh century until contemporary times men slowly appropriated women's traditional role of attending births, labeling their own "doctoring" as scientific while labeling midwifery as unsafe or even witchlike. When women were excluded from universities in the eleventh and twelfth centuries and later with the expansion of medicine in the eighteenth and nineteenth centuries, there was gender conflict over healing as well. In the fourteenth century, the Church decreed that a woman was a witch if she healed without formal education. Thousands of executions resulted from the ensuing hostility toward women healers in the fifteenth and sixteenth centuries. By early 1900 female healers and midwives had been displaced by male physicians.[66]

In contemporary times the birth process has been taken out of the hands of the family and midwives and medicalized so that it now usually takes place in the sterile atmosphere of a hospital with men in control and the woman unconscious or at least immobilized. Although a woman may have trained for natural childbirth and prefers little or no anesthetic, it is the doctor who makes the final decisions in these matters. While, technically, birth complications have been reduced or can be dealt with more easily in a hospital, the quality of the birthing experience and the feeling of closeness between mother and child have been reduced. There has been some recent realization of this loss, and attempts have been made to recreate "homey" labor rooms, include fathers, and have infants stay with their mothers after birth.

The improper use of drugs has also been thought to be a significant contributor to the high infant mortality rate in the world's most technologically advanced nation. For all its scientific knowledge, the United States has a high infant mortality rate; in fact, fifteen nations with populations of 2.5 million or more have better infant mortality rates than does the United States.[67] One big contributor to this high rate is the fact that 95 percent of American women get anesthesia when they give birth. Anesthesia depresses the fetal heart rate and respiration in most instances. Pearson and Clark quote a study by Guinther and state that they believe that by eliminating or limiting the use of drugs in delivery, a considerable amount of mental retardation may be prevented.[68]

In addition, more women are at risk from taking a variety of drugs during the first trimester of pregnancy. One study estimates that during the first trimester pregnant women take an average of three different drugs. It is not known how many of these medications affect the fetus either during the fetal period or long after birth. One researcher estimates that the escalation of medicines given to pregnant women means that we have reached a point where the fetus is potentially at greater risk from prescribed medications for the mother than from the hazards of pregnancy and childbirth.[69]

Another problem with the medicalization of childbirth is the tendency to use scientific advances in even routine deliveries. Despite the fact that nearly 90 percent of U.S. births are considered normal, physicians use forceps, induction of labor, and cesarean sections.[70] The last two practices are alleged by some people to be done largely for the convenience of physicians or to give residents an opportunity to practice techniques.[71]

The tendency of physicians to use invasive surgery rather than other possibilities should also be questioned. Cesarean rates increased from 5 percent of all deliveries in 1970 to 20 percent in 1983,[72] yet this is a serious abdominal surgery with the possibility of complications, long recovery times, and implications for a repeat in future deliveries.

Fertility and Birth Control

Fertility Stimulation.   At first glance, reproductive technologies that allow women to conceive via *in vitro* fertilization or bear babies via surrogate mothers appear to offer a positive solution for infertile women or couples. However, technology has changed our ideas about what it means to be pregnant. Gena Corea describes her research on the new technology in *The Mother Machine* and sees technology as transforming the experience of motherhood and placing it under the control of men. Men are the pioneering doctors; motherhood is divided up between genetic mothers, surrogate mothers, and mothers who raise the child. Thus, no one has a real claim to the child. The technology for increased fertility is also raising the question of the exploitation of women as "babytoriums."[73]

Other forms of reproductive technology that are usually associated with increased fertility, such as amniocentesis and ultrasound, also have their dangers. In particular, there are doubts about the safety of ultrasound. Women are often reassured to see the outline of the baby, watch it move, and hear its heartbeat, but the information given by scans is seldom 100 percent reliable, and there can be side effects. Animal studies have shown that ultrasound produces delayed neuromuscular development, altered emotional behavior, and fetal abnormalities in rats and blood changes, dilation of vessels, and corneal erosion in rabbits.[74]

Birth Control

We seem to have come a long way from Egyptian women who in 1850 B.C. used crocodile dung as a contraceptive, but some of the improvement may be illusory.[75] The surer forms of contraception today have serious and demonstrable side effects. The pill has been demonstrated to lead to blood clots as well as less serious but debilitating side effects such as severe headaches, depression, loss of libido, bloating, and weight gain. Some forms of the intrauterine device (IUD) have led to infections and even sterility. The new Depo-Provera three-month contraceptive shot which is widely used overseas is considered so unsafe that the FDA has not approved it.

Birth control is one scientific area that has lagged in our technologically advanced society. Since the birth control pill was approved by the FDA in 1960, almost no new contraceptive research has been initiated. While other countries have looked into five-year slow-release hormone capsules, long-lasting contraceptive shots, and even male contraceptives, almost no new innovations have taken place in the United States. (Only very recently were the slow-release progesterone capsules legalized for use here.) Pressure from far-right groups that oppose contraception and fear of lawsuits have kept many pharmaceutical companies from initiating research.

Abortion

The practice of abortion is not a recent phenomenon. Ancient societies relied on infanticide, abortion, and sexual taboos to control fertility. In ancient Greece and Rome, abortion was used as a form of birth control without criminal or social stigma.[76] Christian doctrine conflicted somewhat with this freedom but for many centuries followed Aristotle's view that the soul develops in three stages. The Church generally punished abortion only if it was performed after the soul became "animated," a time set at 40 days after conception for males and 80 days for females. In 1588 Pope Sextus V declared all abortion murder, but three years later Pope Gregory XIV revoked any Church penalties for abortion performed less than 40 days after conception. Under early Anglo-Saxon civil law in the thirteenth century, the legal beginning of fetal life was considered to be the quickening, or the beginning of fetal movement. Even after quickening, the act of destroying the fetus was considered different from murder and was punished less harshly.

The nineteenth century in the United States marked the beginning of repression of birth control and abortion. The evolution of public policy on abortion in the nineteenth century arose largely out of efforts by physicians to professionalize the practice of medicine. At this time medicine was so unregulated that two-thirds of the people who called themselves physicians in Philadelphia in 1800 were not graduates of a medical school. Trained physicians believed that the lack of abortion laws gave an unfair advantage to this untrained competition and began the first efforts to outlaw abortion.[77]

In 1821 the first law dealing with abortion was passed in Connecticut, although it dealt only with regulating the use of dangerous substances for that end. In 1830 New York law stated that abortions after fetal movement had started were criminal, although therapeutic exceptions were allowed. Between 1821 and 1841 ten states and one territory had enacted laws restricting abortions. These laws punished only the person performing the abortion, and therapeutic abortions were almost always exempted. As late as 1860 only three states had outlawed the right to abortion before quickening. During the next forty years, however, physicians increased their opposition to abortion, sometimes stating frankly that they were opposed to new social roles for women. By 1890 antiabortion laws existed in every state except Kentucky.[78]

By the early twentieth century the pendulum had swung back to an emphasis on choice. In the twentieth century, middle- and upper-class women could use better contraceptive techniques. Abortion was tapering off in this group, and the physicians' antiabortion campaign also lost momentum. There was also a change in attitudes about birth control information, and the World War I campaign against venereal disease included the distribution of condoms.

By 1932 there were approximately eighty birth-control clinics in the United States, and by 1938 two major legal decisions had upheld the right to distribute contraceptive literature without interference by the federal government. Physicians could prescribe contraceptives to patients in every state except Massachusetts and Connecticut.

With fear of overpopulation and changing lifestyles, public opinion became more favorable toward all aspects of birth control. The public was particularly concerned with the problem of deformed fetuses and the "quality of life." The publicity surrounding the case of Sherri Finkbine, who had to travel to Sweden to abort a fetus deformed by thalidomide, and the German measles epidemic in the 1960s broadened public support for legalized abortion.

Medical data showed that abortion competently performed during the first trimester is safer than a full-term pregnancy, and despite legal prohibitions, a substantial number of women continued to have abortions. A significant shift occurred in the attitudes of physicians. A 1967 survey showed that 87 percent of them favored more liberal abortion laws. By the late 1960s about one-third of the states allowed abortion for defects in the fetus, rape or incest, or danger to the physical or mental health of the mother. By 1970, four states—Alaska, Hawaii, New York, and Washington—had made first-trimester abortion legal.[79]

At the same time important U.S. Supreme Court cases began to change the legal situation surrounding birth control and abortion. Finally, in January 1973, in *Roe v. Wade*, the Court ruled that laws permitting abortion only to save the life of the mother were unconstitutional because they interfered with the right of privacy. In essence, *Roe v. Wade* said that a woman's right to privacy guarantees her the right to have an abortion.

In this decision the Court discussed several issues that are still the subject of a great deal of debate: (1) the physical and psychological harm pregnancy can cause to the mother, (2) when life begins, (3) whether the Fourteenth Amendment extends to the unborn, (4) at what point the state may regulate abortions, and (5) the essence of the constitutional right to privacy.

The Court did not deal with three issues that have since become focal points in the abortion controversy: public funding of abortions, spousal and/or parental consent or notification, and state-imposed restrictions on the performance of abortions. The Supreme Court held in 1977 that the states have no obligation to provide poor women with funding for nontherapeutic abortions, although it left open the question of whether laws can prohibit government funding of medically indicated abortions.[80]

The notification of the parents of minors using birth control or trying to obtaining an abortion has been a hotly debated issue. Public policy usually concedes the rights of minors to obtain confidential medical services for venereal disease and alcohol or drug abuse, realizing that withholding such care endangers the health of young people and of society. Cases are mixed on notification of parents if a minor wants an abortion. In a 1979 case the Court ruled that mature minors have a right to make this decision, but in a 1981 case the Court ruled that the state may require a physician to notify the parents of an immature and unemancipated minor whose "best interest" would be served by such notification.[81]

Opponents of legalized abortion have attempted since 1973 to change public policy in these matters. One week after *Roe v. Wade* was decided, the first human life constitutional amendment was introduced in Congress. Since then, two hundred similar antiabortion amendments have been sponsored. In addition to a constitutional amendment, right-to-life legislators propose human life bills that would require only a majority vote (rather than a two-thirds vote) in each house of Congress and the signature of the President to become law. Passage of any of these bills would force the Supreme Court to reconsider its decision in *Roe v. Wade* that a fetus is not entitled to constitutional protection and that the right of privacy extends to the decision to have an abortion. A question that these bills raise is whether it is possible to overturn a Supreme Court decision based on the Constitution through the passage of a federal statute. As these bills include stripping the lower federal courts of the right to hear abortion cases, there is also the question of the broader civil rights implications of Congress passing legislation that strips courts of their jurisdiction. Would Congress then be able to prevent federal court review of other civil rights–related cases?[82]

Right-to-life forces have pursued other alternatives to restrict access to abortion. During the conservative Reagan administration of the 1980s, the government proposed a swap in which the federal government would assume complete responsibility for Medicaid and food stamps while the states would take over Aid to Families with Dependent Children (AFDC). With complete federal control of the Medicaid program, states that currently use their own funds for Medicaid abortions would no longer have this option. While this option has not yet come to pass, it has been hotly pursued by antiabortion groups.

Right-to-life groups have proposed state legislation which would ban the use of state funds for abortion. They claim that the poor women involved will obtain the abortions anyway. In states where such legislation has been passed, the abortion rate has fallen. However, the number of women on welfare has risen commensurately. For example, in Michigan, one year after a law was passed limiting the use of state funds for abortion, abortions had declined 33 percent and welfare cases among young single mothers had risen 40 percent.[83]

What Is Happening Today?   The number of abortions as a ratio of live births has stayed relatively stable since 1980. In 1980, there were 426 abortions for every 1,000 live births; in 1984, 422; and in 1985, 425. Obviously, almost half the women who became pregnant in this country are choosing to end those pregnancies by means of abortion. The overwhelming majority of these abortions are obtained by unmarried women in their early twenties or younger.[84]

After a Supreme Court decision in 1989 that opened the way for states to regulate abortion, several states imposed abortion restrictions. Some of these laws were particularly restrictive and allowed no exemptions for rape or incest. These laws are currently being tested in the lower courts, and it is likely that these cases will eventually be heard by the Supreme Court because of their wide-ranging implications for the doctrine of privacy and for civil rights. In June of 1991, the Supreme Court decided that federally funded clinics could not mention the possibility of abortion to pregnant women. It is not possible for states to make laws that conflict with a federal law, and if *Roe v. Wade* is still in place when these cases come to the Supreme Court, it is likely the restrictive state laws will be found unconstitutional.[85] In the interim, Congress is attempting to pass legislation which will enable women to continue to be informed of all alternatives if they are pregnant. President Bush has threatened to veto this legislation.

However, there is some question about whether *Roe v. Wade* will still be in place when restrictive state laws are tested in the future. In the last decade the Supreme Court has changed its composition. It is no longer the liberal court that passed the *Roe v. Wade* decision. The Reagan administration appointed three conservative Supreme Court justices as well as half of all the lower court justices now sitting. As this book goes to press, two of the staunchest liberal justices left on the court, 83-year-old William Brennan and 85-year-old Thurgood Marshall, have resigned for health reasons. President Bush appointed a little-known judge, David Souter of New Hampshire, as Brennan's replacement and nominated a very conservative black judge, Clarence Thomas, to replace Marshall. Souter was the swing vote in the decision to not allow federally funded clinics to mention abortion to pregnant women. If Thomas is confirmed, his views are likely to be equally conservative. The Court may actually use one of the test cases to overturn *Roe v. Wade*.[86]

It is also feasible that in the new conservative climate a human rights bill or a constitutional amendment forbidding abortion could pass in Congress. Yet as late as 1988 an overwhelming majority of the American people said they opposed efforts to ban abortion under all circumstances. In fact, approximately 25 percent would not ban it under any circumstance.[87] Whether this choice remains depends largely on who has the power to make and enforce the laws.

A very recent technological phenomenon which is influencing the abortion debate is the invention of the pill called RU-486, which can induce abortion within the first few weeks of pregnancy. This pill has stirred up a major controversy in France, where it was taken off the market after antiabortion protesters threatened to boycott the drug company that sells it. After protests by gynecologists and obstetricians that the drug could help save thousands of women's lives which might otherwise be lost to botched abortions, the French health minister ordered the company to resume distribution of the drug in the interest of public health. While for the moment no U.S. company has plans to apply for FDA approval to market the drug here, the questions raised by the French controversy are at the heart of the abortion controversy. "It substantially affects the abortion debate if you no longer have to find a doctor to do surgery; you just have to take a drug," says Nancy Rhoden, professor of law and a bioethicist at the University of North Carolina, Chapel Hill. There is also the question of how far political pressures from antiabortion protesters should be allowed to influence medical decisions, especially when drugs such as RU-486 may have other medical uses.[88]

SUMMARY

We see in our discussion of the medical profession's role in regulating the birth process and fertility the tremendous control that this establishment has over women's reproductive lives. Because of the complex interweaving of reproduction with women's participation in the labor force and integration into other areas of society, this reproductive control has far-reaching consequences. In fact, control over women's reproductive lives is so important that it is part of the regulation of many institutions such as the legal and political establishments. We will look further at that in Chapter 11.

In addition, science and the allied field of medicine have attempted to define and control women and men throughout the centuries in many other ways. Their definitions and value systems have usually incorporated a status for women that is inferior to that for men. Scientific "fact" has become an ideology that is a conservative force for perpetuating stereotypes. Inaccurate portrayals of the nature of women and men have had a great influence because of the respect given to the scientific community, particularly in our technologically oriented society. This scientific "ideology" interacts with religion and other sources of norms and with the economic system to shape our perceptions of the proper gender roles for the sexes.

ESSAY QUESTIONS

1. Why is social control by religion particularly strong?
2. How did early Christianity view the nature of women?
3. How did Eastern religions view the nature and place of women? Was this different from the Judeo-Christian tradition?
4. How did the Protestant Reformation influence the position of women?
5. In what ways have feminists sought to change religious institutions? Name at least three ways.

6. How did early scientists and psychologists view women? Were their views supported by scientific evidence?
7. Name at least three ways in which the medical profession controls the views of men and women (for example, in defining illness).
8. Give at least two examples of invasive surgery used on women and show how at least one of them could be used for social control of women.
9. What view of women's sexuality have gynecology textbooks perpetuated? Is there any contradiction between this view and the religious view of women's sexuality?
10. In what ways has access to birth control and abortion been used to control women? (Cite historical and contemporary examples in your answer).

NOTES

1. Laurel Richardson, *The Dynamics of Sex and Gender: A Sociological Perspective*, 3d ed. (New York: Harper & Row, 1988).
2. Mary Morgan, "The Impact of Religion on Gender-Role Attitudes," *Psychology of Women Quarterly* 11 (1988):301–310.
3. Connecticut Mutual Life Company, The Connecticut Mutual Life Report on American Values in the 1980's, Hartford: Connecticut Mutual Life Company (1981); W. V. D'Antonio, "Family Life, Religion and Societal Values and Structures," in W. V. D'Antonio and J. Aldous, eds., *Families and Religions: Conflict and Change in Modern Society* (Beverly Hills, Calif.: Sage, 1983), pp. 333–351.
4. Elizabeth Fisher, *Women's Creation* (New York: McGraw-Hill, 1980), pp. 383–387.
5. Rosemary Reuther, *Sexism and Godtalk: Toward a Feminist Theology* (Boston: Beacon, 1983).
6. *Ibid.*
7. Fisher, *op. cit.*, pp. 286–297.
8. Vern Bullough, *The Subordinate Sex* (Baltimore: Penguin, 1974) p. 13.
9. Leviticus 15:2–4.
10. Bullough, *op. cit.*, pp. 18–19.
11. *Ibid.*
12. *Ibid.*, p. 34.
13. Reuther, *op. cit.*
14. *Ibid.*, pp. 40–46.
15. *Ibid.*, pp. 46–59.
16. Bullough, *op. cit.*, p. 138.
17. *Ibid.*, pp. 146–147.
18. Denise Lardner Carmody, *Women and World Religions* (New York: Parthenon, 1979), pp. 48–51.
19. *Ibid.*, p. 42.
20. *Ibid.*, pp. 6–7.
21. Daryl Hafter, "An Overview of Women's History," in Marie Richmond Abbott, ed., *The American Woman* (New York: Holt, Rinehart & Winston, 1979), p. 3.
22. Ruth H. Bloch, "Untangling the Roots of Modern Sex Roles: A Survey of Four Centuries of Change," *Signs* 4, no. 2 (1978):238.

23. Reuther, *op. cit.*, p. 103.

24. Sheila Briggs, "Women and Religion," in Beth Hess and Myra Marx Feree, eds., *Analyzing Gender* (Newberry Park, Calif.: Sage, 1987), p. 408.

25. Curtis Sitomer, "The Reagan Legacy and Abortion," *Christian Science Monitor,* (July 28, 1988):A–4.

26. Briggs, *op. cit.*, p. 417.

27. Papal Statement, October 1988.

28. Jackson W. Carroll, Barbara Hargrove, and Adair T. Lummis, *Women of the Cloth: A New Opportunity for Churches* (New York: Harper & Row, 1982).

29. Barbara J. MacHaffie, *Her Story: Women in Christian Tradition* (Philadelphia: Fortress Press, 1986).

30. Carroll et al., *op. cit.*, pp. 109–138.

31. James R. Kelley, "Residual or Prophetic? The Cultural Fate of Roman Catholic Sexual Ethics of Abortion and Contraception," *Social Thought* 12, no. 2 (Spring 1986):3–18.

32. Myra Marx Feree, "She Works Hard for a Living: Gender and Class on the Job," in Hess and Feree, *op. cit.*, pp. 322–347.

33. Gregory M. Herek, "Religious Orientation and Prejudice: A Comparison of Racial and Sexual Attitudes," *Personality and Social Psychology Bulletin* 13 no. 1 (1987): 34–44.

34. Mary Morgan, "The Impact of Religion on Gender-Role Attitudes," *Psychology of Women Quarterly* 11 (1987):301–310.

35. Briggs, *op. cit.*

36. *Ibid.*

37. C. Heyward, *The Redemption of God: A Theology of Mutual Relation* (Washington, D.C.: University Press of America, 1982).

38. Mary E. Hunt, "Lovingly Lesbian: Toward a Feminist Theology of Friendship," in R. Nugent, ed., *A Challenge to Love: Gay and Lesbian Catholics in the Church* (New York: Crossroad, 1983), pp. 27–36.

39. R. Curb and N. Manahan, eds., *Lesbian Nuns: Breaking Silence* (Tallahassee, Fla.: Naiad, 1985).

40. Briggs, *op. cit.*, p. 416.

41. Marie de Merode de Croy, "The Role of Women in the Old Testament," in Virgil Elizondo and Norbert Greinacher, *Women in a Man's Church* (New York: Seabury, 1980), pp. 162–178.

42. Ida Raming, "From the Freedom of the Gospel to the Petrified Men's Church," in Elizondo and Greinacher, *op. cit.*, pp. 3–13.

43. Carol P. Christ and Judith Plaskow, eds., *Womanspirit Rising: A Feminist Reader in Religion* (San Francisco: Harper & Row, 1979); Carol P. Christ, *Diving Deep and Surfacing: Women Writers on a Spiritual Quest* (Boston: Beacon, 1980).

44. Mary Daly, *The Church and the Second Sex* (Boston: Beacon, 1968); Mary Daly, *Beyond God the Father* (Boston: Beacon, 1973).

45. Elizabeth Schusler-Fiorenza, *In Memory of Her: A Feminist Theological Reconstruction of Christian Origins* (New York: Crossroad, 1984); Reuther, *op. cit.*

46. Janet Sayers, "Science, Sexual Difference and Feminism," in Hess and Feree, *op. cit.*, pp. 68–86.

47. W. L. Distant, "On the Mental Differences between the Sexes," *Journal of the Royal Anthropological Institute of Great Britain and Ireland* 4 (1984):78–87, quoted in Sayers, *op. cit.*, p. 78.

48. R. Dawkins, *The Selfish Gene* (New York: Oxford University Press, 1976).

49. C. Sherif, "Bias in Psychology," in J. A. Sherman and E. Beck, eds., *The Prism of Sex* (Madison: University of Wisconsin Press, 1979), pp. 223–241.
50. D. M. Broverman, E. L. Klaiber, Y. Kobayashi, and W. Vogel, "Roles of Activation and Inhibition in Sex Differences in Cognitive Abilities," *Psychological Review* 71, no. 1 (1968):23–50. S. A. Shields, "Functionalism, Darwinism and the Psychology of Women: A Study of Social Myth" *American Psychologist*, 30 (1975):739–754.
51. Shields, *op. cit.*, pp. 739–754; Broverman et al. *op. cit.*
52. Sayers, *op. cit.*
53. Emily Martin, *The Woman in the Body: A Cultural Analysis of Reproduction* (Boston: Beacon, 1987).
54. Susan E. Bell, "The Medicalization of Menopause," *Social Science Medicine* 24 (1987): 535–542.
55. Julie Rovner, "Senate Passes Bill Oking Women's Health Needs Research," *Congressional Quarterly Weekly Report* 48, no. 32 (August 4, 1990):2521–2522.
56. Willie Pearson, Jr., and Maxine L. Clark, "The Mal(e) Treatment of American Women in Gynecology and Obstetrics," *International Journal of Women's Studies* 5, no. 4 (1981):348–362.
57. Barbara Katz Rothman, "Reproduction," in Hess and Feree, *op. cit.*, pp. 154–170.
58. Duane Stroman, *The Quick Knife: Unnecessary Surgery in the U.S.A.* (Port Washington, New York: Kennikat, 1979), pp. 204–207.
59. John Guinther, *The Malpractitioners* (Garden City, N.Y.: Doubleday, 1978).
60. Stroman, *op. cit.*
61. *Ibid.*
62. Jeanne M. Stellman and Mary Sue Henifen, "No Fertile Women Need Apply: Employment Discrimination and Reporductive Hazards in the Workplace," in Ruth Hubard, Mary Sue Henifin, and Barbara Fried, eds., *Biological Woman: The Convenient Myths* (Cambridge, Mass.: Schenkman, 1982), pp. 262–274.
63. Diane Scully and Pauline Bart, "A Funny Thing Happened on the Way to the Orifice," in Joan Huber, ed., *Changing Women in a Changing Society* (Chicago: University of Chicago Press, 1973), pp. 283–288.
64. *Ibid.*
65. *Ibid.*
66. M. J. Gage, *Women, Church and State: The Original Exposé of Male Collaboration against the Female Sex* (Watertown, Mass.: Peresphone, 1980).
67. K. Osborne, "A Feminist Perspective on Women and Health," in A. Broome and L. Wallace, eds., *Psychology and Gynaecological Problems* (London: Tavistock, 1984), pp. 266–282.
68. Pearson and Clark, *op. cit.*, p. 349.
69. Gena Corea, *The Hidden Malpractice: How American Medicine Treats Women as Patients and Professionals* (New York: Morros, 1985).
70. Health Policy Advisory Center, "The Health Care Crisis," in John B. Williamson, Linda Evans, and Anne Munley, eds., *Social Problems: The Contemporary Debates*, 3d ed. (Boston: Little, Brown, 1981), pp. 371–384.
71. Corea, *op. cit.*
72. S. Taffel and P. Placek, "One-Fifth of 1983 U.S. Births by Caesarean Section," *American Journal of Public Health* 75 (1985):2.
73. Gena Corea, *The Mother Machine* (New York: Harper & Row, 1985).
74. R. Hubbard, "Research in Ultrasound Bioeffects," *Birth and the Family Journal* 7, no. 2 (1980):317–322.

75. League of Women Voters Education Fund, "Public Policy on Reproductive Choices," *Facts and Issues* (Washington, D.C.: Women Voters Education Fund, 1982), pp. 1–5.
76. *Ibid.*
77. *Ibid.*
78. Alfred Yonkover, "Legal Abortions," *American Journal of Public Health* 75 (1985): 714–715.
79. League of Women Voters Education Fund, *op. cit.*
80. *Ibid.*
81. *Ibid.*
82. Eloise Salholz et al., "The Future of Abortion," *Newsweek* (July 17, 1989):16ff.
83. Gary Blonston, "Taxpayers Pay More after Cutoff of Money," *Detroit Free Press* (February 5, 1989):C–1.
84. U.S. Bureau of the Census, Table 104, "Legal Abortions—Number, Rate per 1000 Women 15–44 Years Old, and Abortion/Live Birth Ratio by State of Occurrence: 1973–1985," *Vital Statistics* (Washington, D.C.: U.S. Government Printing Office, 1985):69.
85. Salholz et al., *op. cit.*
86. Tom Morganthau et al., "Popping the Question: Both Sides in the Abortion War Want Answers," *Newsweek* (August 6, 1990):17ff.
87. League of Women Voters Education Fund, *op. cit.*
88. Dolores Kong, "Abortion Debate Takes a Pill," *Detroit Free Press* (November 2, 1988):B1.

Chapter 11

The Marketplace: Men's and Women's Roles at Work

A Man's work gives him a secure place in a portion of reality, in the human community.[1]

The grievances and discontent of the young worker cannot be ignored. They affect the very basis of the system—productivity.[2]

Most of us, like the assembly-line worker, have jobs that are too small for our spirit. Jobs are not big enough for people.[3]

These quotes show the importance of work in a capitalistic, profit-oriented society. A man's life is defined by his work, his occupation. The first question a man is usually asked is, What do you do? People shape their perception of him in accordance with his answer. Increasingly, women are also working. Sixty-seven percent of women in the age range from 18 to 49 are currently employed.[4] More women expect to work outside the home, and their future spouses also expect them to do so. In 1988 the majority of mothers were in the work force.[5]

Yet the quotes that begin this chapter show an ambivalent attitude toward work in a changing society where achievement is equated with money rather than with making a creative product. While work is important, it may not be satisfying. However, whether it is satisfying or not, a man is expected to work, to be achievement-oriented, and to put other life goals, such as family interaction and fatherly care of children, in a secondary position. In the American culture, work is also important to a man because occupational success is associated with masculinity and thus with self-worth. While the rates of participation rates in the labor force among men and women are becoming more similar, their work experiences are still very different. Let us look at them separately.

MEN'S ROLES AT WORK: OCCUPATIONAL SUCCESS AND MASCULINITY

To understand the association between occupational success and masculinity in the American culture, we need to look at the relationship between achievement, occupational success, money, status, and masculinity. We must remember that American culture is a product of the **Protestant work ethic**—the belief that a man is shown whether he is "good" or "saved" (religiously) by the extent to which he prospers in the world. It was believed that God would punish sinners with poverty and illness and reward moral persons with health and wealth. This ethic was gradually expanded to mean that if one achieved success in the world, one was "good" or worthy as a person.[6]

In the American culture, the next step was to equate achievement with economic success. Success in frontier society was equated with the physical, the practical, the powerful, the big, and the new. This country did not, and does not now, particularly value intellectual success (witness the salaries of college professors versus those of business executives), nor have we traditionally valued the fine arts. While values are changing as the country ages and refines its tastes, the emphasis on physical prowess, youth, mobility, and tangible symbols of success such as money is still predominant.[7]

Thus economic success has not necessarily meant craftsmanship or producing goods of quality in the old sense of the word "achievement." As Myron Brenton points out, "truly creative jobs, those in which the individual feels a sense of autonomy, call for his best efforts, provide a solid sense of accomplishment, a real recognition of his particular service, and a knowledge that what he's doing is truly a worthwhile contribution to the world, are relatively few in number."[8] Rather, occupational success is measured by the fruits of labor: pay, prestige, and status.

In the next step, pay and status as measurements of occupational success become equated with worthiness as a man, with masculinity.[9] The adult male has had little alternative to this definition of success. Physical strength and sexual prowess are also symbols of masculinity, but the breadwinner role is primary if the adult male wishes to feel masculine. Even with the lessened commitment of young people to being family breadwinners, a man who is successful at work in terms of gaining money is successful in fulfilling the stereotyped masculine role. Money comes to be valued not only for itself and the goods it will buy but as symbolic evidence of success and thus personal worth.

Basing masculinity and success or even self-worth on earning money may be risky: Money can be lost overnight as it was during the stock market failures of the great depression; many men even committed suicide after losing their money.[10] Also, a man may feel anxiety if his wife decides to return to work and then makes a salary close to his; his marriage may be threatened because he is not the one providing all the money. Daniel Levinson describes a physician who wanted to do more research and work less in the private practice that provided his income. When the doctor's wife went to work and became successful at her career, he could have pursued his research. However, he was so threatened by the money she earned that he ended up working more hours in private practice so that he could make more income than she did.[11]

If one has certain traits that society has deemed masculine, such as aggressiveness, competitiveness, and unemotionality, monetary success is usually more readily achieved in our competitive, capitalistic society. Thus, success confirms the fact that one had masculine traits to begin with. In the honoring of these masculine traits, we see again the extension of the boyhood prescription to be tough, cool, and good at something.

Masculine stereotypes also limit job choice and may limit occupational satisfaction.[12] A man may say that his son is free to do anything he pleases, but he may get upset if his son decides to go into an occupation often designated for women, such as nursing, ballet dancing, or even teaching. The stigma connected with doing "women's work" and homophobia serve as a control mechanism that keeps many men from seeking creative jobs. A man may also get upset if his son takes less than a professional job when a profession may more readily guarantee occupational success.

In addition, occupational success usually carries with it all the burdens of the original masculine role prescription. It is wearing to always have to be competitive and tough. Having to be tough is worse when one cannot show any doubt, fear, or other emotion. One slip is enough to undo a career. The failure of Edmund Muskie to win the presidential nomination was attributed by many political observers to the fact that after a fatiguing and dirty campaign, tears came to his eyes at one point when his wife was criticized.

In today's automated world, work is often not very satisfying. Many people are such small cogs in the wheel of production that they feel divorced from the products they make. In the blue-collar world, the satisfaction of doing quality work on a craft job has been largely eliminated by the assembly line. The fear that automation will soon eliminate jobs is not far behind the loss of job satisfaction. The lyrics of Tom Lehrer's song "Automation" say it well: "They'll invent a little button that will push all the buttons and they won't need you and me."[13]

The corporate man's achievement may consist largely of personnel manipulation and shuffling papers.[14] A promotion may mean moving out of a job one enjoys to a job one dislikes, such as from sales or teaching to administration. In addition, high occupational achievement usually allows one little or no leisure. Men who are advancing through the corporate ranks must show commitment by working numerous overtime hours, and even blue-collar workers are often forced to work overtime or on weekends.

As success means continually moving upward—not staying in a job with which one is happy and comfortable—few workers get what they want in life or feel successful. A national poll showed that men are not philosophical about their lack of success; rather than blaming the system or bad luck, they blame themselves for failure. Eighty-two percent of the men polled believed that if one tries hard enough, one can usually get what one wants in life.[15] Thus, the great majority of men in this survey who did not succeed blamed themselves for not being "good enough." As a corollary to not being good enough, they did not feel masculine. These men often felt discouraged, beaten down, and alienated. However, they could not quit because they had families to support. They could not complain; complaining was not masculine. Yet they could not dismiss work; work was important to them even with its attendant dissatisfaction. Three out of four said they would work even if not guaranteed a good income.[16]

Job **alienation** is accelerated when men have fewer job choices. As the economy slows down, fewer new jobs are available and competition is intensified for the existing ones. Professors cannot find new academic situations easily as colleges contract; in a time of economic recession such as the early 1990s, businessmen may not be willing to risk changing jobs and giving up stock benefits and pension funds. Blue-collar workers are similarly tied to the company by seniority and pension plans. These workers cannot complain or change jobs; if they do, they may lose their retirement benefits and may not find another job.

The results of discouragement and alienation are clearly seen. Studs Terkel has documented the disaffection of men and women in all working groups:

> A stockbroker says, "I can't say what I'm doing has any value. This doesn't make me too happy. Oh, I'd like some morning to wake up and to go to work that gave me joy."[17]

> The president of a UAW local says, "The almighty dollar is not the only thing in my estimation. There's more to it—like how I'm treated. . . ."[18]

The Blue-Collar Worker

While the middle-class worker may dislike his job, power and privilege may make it palatable. He is sustaining the system and is closer to the rewards. However, the blue-collar worker has little hope for such power and privilege. He is forced to do monotonous jobs, and so his alienation is particularly intense. It is worst among young workers, who are last hired and first fired. Lack of seniority means the worst shifts or split shifts.[19] For young and old, there may be also the incredible authoritarianism and petty discipline of the factory.[20] The blue-collar worker is particularly alienated because he has no place to go: It is unlikely that he will be promoted, and the traditional way out of the factory—education—may not guarantee him a job anymore.[21] In addition, there is less respect for men who work with their hands.

To understand this alienation, let us look at another Terkel quote from an assembly-line worker:

> I don't like the pressure, the intimidation. How would you like to go up to someone and say, "I would like to go to the bathroom"? If the foreman doesn't like you, he'll make you hold it, just ignore you. Should I leave this job to go to the bathroom, I risk being fired. The line moves all the time. . . .
>
> You really begin to wonder. What price do they put on me? Look at the price they put on the machine. If that machine breaks down, there's someone to fix it right away. If I break down, I'm just pushed over to the side till another man takes my place. . . .

I don't eat lunch at work. I may grab a candy bar, that's enough. I wouldn't be able to hold it down. The tension your body is put under by the speed of the line. . . .[22]

The average working-class man is much closer to poverty than to affluence in spite of the highly touted salaries of assembly-line workers. The blue-collar worker must cope with frequent unemployment as well. Layoffs and unemployment have spread to the skilled crafts, to construction workers, and to more highly skilled autoworkers.

On the factory line, the alienation of the blue-collar worker shows up in absenteeism, drug use, alcoholism, sabotage, and hostility toward other workers, including women and blacks. At home, his alienation may be taken out on his family, sometimes in the form of wife and child abuse. As the probusiness government of the 1980s cut unemployment benefits and reduced safety standards, the working-class man became convinced that no one was going to help him; he became alienated from the total society and may in the future become radicalized as a voter.[23]

The Man in the Grey Flannel Suit

Although the middle-class worker has more hope of gaining power through the system, he too is alienated. Some middle-class workers drop out: Nearly 50 percent of the businessmen surveyed by the American Management Association had changed or considered changing occupational fields in the previous five years.[24] Yet most cannot drop out, and most would not want to. Terkel believes that Freud's statement about work was correct, that a man's "work at least gives him a secure place in a portion of reality, in the human community."[25] However, it is clear that "most of us, like the assembly-line worker, have jobs that are too small for our spirit. Jobs are not big enough for people."[26]

In *Men and Women of the Corporation,* Rosabeth Kanter has documented the alienation of even executives who have reached the highest rung of the corporate ladder. She points out that those who cannot climb to the top and are stuck in a job often become discouraged, dispirited, and cautious. They may turn their attention at work from achieving in occupational areas to achieving in social areas. Those who have been halted may also refuse to take risks and may develop a management style that is very controlling and conservative so that they can preserve what they have.[27]

Work and Family

In the climb up the career ladder or in the attempt to get more money, many men put the building of relationships with their wives and children second to their occupation. They may believe that they show their concern for their families by working long hours and bringing home a paycheck. They may seldom have chances to play with their children or to take vacations with their wives. They may also find it difficult to make the transition from the nonemotional, controlled world of the office or factory to a more expressive communication style at home. During this time of intense career involvement, families may grow apart, but a man may not be aware of the intimacy he is missing.[28]

In his discussion of the midlife transition that many men go through, Levinson states that "masculine" striving for career success in the middle class may be stymied by outside forces in middle age. This pause in a man's move up the career ladder may give him time to think about the things he is missing. Mentoring or helping protégés may take the place of a desperate climb to the top. A man's family may become a new source of intimacy and satisfaction; he may even explore his relationships with other men and attempt to free some of the feelings of brotherhood stifled by homophobia. However, in the period before such a transition or if such a transition does not occur, a man may sacrifice many intimate relationships because of his obsession with occupational success.[29]

Work and Health

Thus, for some men, alienation and occupational dissatisfaction may be reduced during the midlife transition. For others, the transition may add additional stress. The competitive, achievement-oriented male work style, combined with the repression of emotions demanded by the workplace and the male role, leaves men susceptible to a variety of health disorders. We see this stress most clearly in the middle years. We hear of a man of 40 who has had a heart attack and think, "He was so young."[30]

Addison Steele puts his finger on the problem:

> Climbing is so hard on the nervous system. I have known personally too many driving executives—mostly men in their late thirties and early forties—who have had crippling and sometimes fatal heart attacks. I have had lunches with too many colleagues who were nursing an ulcer or a spastic colon. And I have seen too much needless fear, as evidenced by hands trembling in a meeting, backs that suddenly go into spasm at the sight of a closed door, and voices that slide into the upper register . . . when the boss leaves a note on the desk saying, "Please drop by my office right away."[31]

Researchers point out that many more men than women have personality profiles that make them prone to stress and illness; they are hard-driving, competitive type A's.[32] While many working and nonworking women experience the same type of stress, they are more likely to relieve the stress by unburdening their feelings.[33] Goldberg has pointed out that men seldom talk to other men about their problems because they don't want to seem vulnerable. As a result, they may never become close to other men and will suffer from a lack of intimacy. They may also fear dependence on a woman, but when men do unburden themselves, it is usually to women.[34]

In addition, men are trained to ignore minor aches and pains and slight physical discomfort. Because they do not often listen to their bodies until their bodies rebel, many men miss the chance to avoid illness or catch it at an early stage.[35] Goldberg explains that a man is in a double bind if he does try to take care of himself. If he goes to bed not feeling well or otherwise pampers himself, he is considered hypochondriac, self-indulgent, and perhaps not quite masculine. If he pushes himself until forced to stop, he risks illness and early death.[36]

The problem of stress in the workplace is widely recognized today, and both individuals and businesses are more aware of the importance of fitness. Jogging has become the national pastime, running books and diet books consistently make the national best-seller list, and businesses encourage executives and other workers to stay fit by installing gyms and encouraging exercise. The emphasis on fitness does not really deal with the problem at its roots, however. Being physically fit is compatible with being masculine, but the competitive stress of the business environment and the repression of emotions accompanying that stress are also considered masculine.

Work and Leisure

The rapid expansion of leisure and sports activities may point out another stressful element of the American male role: the cultural—and particularly the male—emphasis on action. Europeans have commented for years that Americans never relax when they have free time from work, that they are always doing something, preferably something worthwhile. Thus, one sees a businessman practicing his golf putting, taking lessons for his tennis serve, waxing his car, fertilizing his lawn, or jogging to improve his health. There is also the prescription that one should be "good" at leisure pursuits, adding to the stress of the male role. An article entitled "Our Endless Pursuit of Happiness" states that the American male seldom has a real rest or change of pace. He carries the competitive stress of the work world into most of his leisure-time activities.[37]

Changing Norms?

There is an indication that for some people, particularly family men and women, the heavy stress on the work ethic and success is abating. Earlier studies documented the fact that the desire to achieve had declined among adolescents (Chapter 6), and we have all known a middle-aged career dropout who wants to "get away from it all." Another new trend involves corporation men who refuse promotions if such advances entail moves and family disruption.[38]

In fact, men seem to put family values at the top of their value structures. In a Harris Poll, the top four things that men valued were health, love, peace of mind, and family life, with 84 percent or more mentioning them as being "very important." Work came in a distant fifth, with only 65 percent mentioning it as one of the most important things in their lives. Thirty-five percent said they would like more leisure time and defined leisure as an opportunity to do things they enjoy with people who are close to them.[39]

There also seems to be more willingness to search for a job that fits one's personality even if the financial rewards are not high.[40] This trend may be leading to greater job satisfaction. In 1979, a Harris Poll of 2,000 men showed that 36 percent were very satisfied with their work, 37 percent were somewhat satisfied, and 21 percent were somewhat dissatisfied. In 1989, a Gallup Poll of 680 adults showed that 46 percent were very satisfied, 41 percent were somewhat satisfied, 8 percent were not too satisfied, and only 4 percent were very dissatisfied. However, in the age group from 18 to 29 only 36 percent were very satisfied, and the satisfaction of blue-collar workers was less than that of men in white-collar jobs.[41]

It is hard to reconcile these data with other reports of job alienation. Perhaps there is a new trend toward job selectivity and satisfaction. Perhaps people say they are at least somewhat satisfied because they see no alternatives.

It remains to be seen if the trend toward greater job selectivity, the decreasing emphasis on work, and the increasing emphasis on leisure and enjoyment will be sustained as economic times become more difficult. Some college professors have noted that the liberal arts majors of the 1970s gave way to a flood of business majors in the 1980s who were depending on a college degree to get a job.

In summary, we note some contradictory trends. The work ethic remains strong in American culture, and men are judged in terms of their occupational success. Yet few can really succeed, and many are alienated from and discouraged with their work. Their masculine self-image suffers as a result. They may retrench and emphasize other parts of the "masculine package," such as physical prowess and sexuality. However, they may be willing to try more varied routes to feelings of self-worth, such as a greater emphasis on fatherhood. This may go hand in hand with a deemphasis on work and greater job satisfaction.

WOMEN WAGE EARNERS

In this century in the United States women have moved in ever-increasing numbers into the labor force. Between 1900 and 1980, female participation in the labor force grew from 18 percent to 50 percent. (The number of women who worked for pay or were trying to find a job almost doubled between 1950 and 1974 alone.) By 1988, 56 percent of all women were in the work force. These rates of participation in the labor force are projected to continue to rise to the year 2000, but at a slower pace than in the last twenty years.[42] This movement into paid market activity has had profound consequences for women's lives and for the economics of our society. The reasons for the movement are varied and are closely connected with world events as well as with the economic scene in this country.

Historical Perspectives on Women's Work in This Country

The historical pattern of women's market work in the United States shows that women were heavily involved in economic production in our early history. In the agrarian society of early America, women had to plant and harvest crops, tend animals, and do other things that produced a money income as well as work in the household to produce cloth, make clothes, make butter and cheese, and preserve food. In addition, because of the short life expectancy, many women became widows and ran businesses or farms; other women worked as midwives, nurses, teachers, printers, laundresses, and innkeepers. Many middle-class women also worked invisibly by taking in boarders or sewing at home. In the early 1830s and 1840s women worked in textile mills and tobacco factories. By 1890, it has been estimated at least 1 million women were employed in factories, with others working in agricultural and domestic service.[43] Many of these women were immigrants. An 1887 U.S. Bureau of Labor study found that among 17,000 factory workers surveyed, 75 percent were of immigrant stock. Black women were also more likely to work; the 1900 census showed that 41 percent of all nonwhite women worked outside the home while only 17 percent of white women were employed. The great majority of white women did not work outside the home.[44] Their proper work was considered to be that of homemaker and mother.

Most of those who worked before the 1940s were young, single, or poor. They were segregated into occupations that were defined as work for women. Thirty percent were clerical workers, and many of the rest worked in textile or food-processing factories. Among the few women who were professionals, three out of four worked as elementary school teachers or nurses. As one historian of this era points out, there was a woman's place in the paid work force as well as at home.[45] Not only was certain work considered women's work, it was presumed that women should not be paid as much as men and that women should never be placed in a position competitive with or superior to that of men. There was almost no support for the employment of middle-class homemakers.

World War II marked the real turning point in women's employment in the United States. In 1940, 25.6 percent of all women worked; by 1945, that figure had risen to 36 percent as 6 million women entered the job market to take the place of men who had been called into military service.[46] These women did not fit the stereotype of young, single, or poor. Women who entered the labor market at this time were married and over 35. By the end of the war, it was just as likely for a wife over 40 to be employed as it was for a single woman under 25. At the end of the war quite a few of these working women quit to make room for the returning soldiers, but the boom in the economy enabled some women in service and clerical work to keep their jobs. In spite of the **feminine mystique**, which insisted that women should gain their greatest fulfillment as homemakers and mothers, many single and married women continued to work for pay outside the home.[47] During the 1950s the employment of women increased four times faster than that of men. By 1960, 37 percent of the women in this country were in the labor force, and 30 percent of these workers were married. By 1987, 56 percent of all women worked outside the home, including almost 56 percent of all married women, 61 percent of separated women, and 75 percent of women who were divorced.[48]

One of the striking trends in female employment during the 1960s and 1970s was the increasing number of mothers who were working. The fastest rise took place in the employment of mothers with preschool children. From 1959 to 1974 the employment rate for mothers with children under 3 more than doubled, from 15 to 31 percent. By 1987, 56 percent of mothers of children under 6 were in the labor force. While some of this increase was due to the need for greater family income, these young women also had more education and thus had greater job opportunities and more progressive sex-role attitudes.[49]

Although they were in conflict with the actual economic behavior of women, traditional attitudes about women's place persisted. Chafe has stated that this gap between traditional attitudes and actual behavior facilitated the expansion of the female labor force. As traditional values were given lipservice, women could enter the labor force "to help out" and were not resisted as crusaders who would change the status quo.[50]

Why Women Entered the Paid Labor Force

There were many reasons why women continued to enter the labor force after World War II. Real wages rose and job opportunities in the service sector expanded as the economy boomed. Women were also getting more education, and this made the working opportunities available to them more attractive. There was a slow change in gender-role attitudes as well, and by the mid-1960s the revival of feminism made it difficult to maintain the traditional view of women's place as being in the home. These changing attitudes influenced and combined with several demographic changes. Women began to marry later and were thus more likely to stay in the labor force longer. They also had fewer children, so that the last child was born sooner in their lives and they were freed from child care earlier to reenter the paid economy. As divorce rates rose, many more women were forced to rely on themselves for support.[51]

Other demographic and technical changes also helped women enter the labor market. The move from rural areas to cities made it easier for many women to find jobs. The development of labor-saving devices such as washing machines and frozen foods also meant that they could, at least theoretically, spend less time on housework and food preparation. In addition, the 1970s was a period of economic inflation in the United States. Families had gotten used to a higher standard of living, frequently maintaining a large home and two cars, sending their children to college, and enjoying expensive leisure-time activities. It was difficult to maintain this standard of living with inflation and as a result, there was more pressure for married women to enter the work force to provide a second income.

The Present Picture: Problems of Working Women

Salary Problems. However, in spite of women's increased employment, Supreme Court rulings, and affirmative action programs, women's salaries still lag far behind those of men. Among full-time workers, women still earn approximately 69 percent of what men earn. (White females earn approximately 67 percent of what white males earn; black females earn approximately 82 percent of what black males earn.)[52] In terms of earnings, men earn an average of $419 a week, and women earn $290.[53] Women are also more likely to work part-time, so their earnings are even lower than the figures above. In addition, they are more subject to layoffs during bad economic times and get fewer benefits such as health insurance.

These salary figures are also skewed by the fact that most of the improvement in women's salaries has come in professional and managerial occupations. Women have greatly increased their numbers in law, medicine, and a few other professional fields, and the pay that these few women receive makes the picture look far rosier than it is. Women who are college graduates but have no professional training get less pay than do men who have the same credentials, and the great majority of women (55 percent) are still clustered in clerical and service occupations where they receive low wages.[54]

While differences in pay between black and white men have declined and differences in wages between black and white women have been virtually eliminated, the difference in earnings between all women and white men has remained virtually the same over the last twenty years.[55]

Other Inequities.   In addition to low pay, women in the labor force have other problems. The National Commission on Working Women, a Washington-based arm of the National Manpower Institute, surveyed 150,000 women and discovered that although wages were a major difficulty for many, other problems were also severe. These women complained of differentials in fringe benefits, the lack of a chance to train for better jobs, increasing pay differentials as men were promoted, sexual harassment on the job, inadequate child-care facilities, the stress of the multiple roles of wife-worker-mother, and extremely limited leisure time. (Fifty-five percent of the professional women and 50 percent of the clerical, sales, and blue-collar workers surveyed said they had no leisure time.) These women wanted additional education but lacked the time and money to get it; they wanted job counseling but could not find it. Their husbands did not object to their working but provided almost no help with household chores. The women described themselves as frustrated, working in dead-end jobs with no chance for advancement or training. They felt underpaid and underutilized, with little or no respect for the work they contributed.[56] Let us look at these wage and nonwage problems.

Possible Reasons for Inequities

The National Research Council of the Academy of Sciences completed an assessment of job discrimination for the Equal Employment Opportunity Commission in 1983. In this assessment, they tried to pinpoint the reasons for the differential between men's wages and women's wages. The factors they found that affect wage rates and other benefits can be divided into measurable parts: human capital inequalities, institutional barriers, and discrimination.[57]

Human Capital Inequities.   According to human capital theory, some differences in earnings are due to inequalities in **human capital**, or characteristics of workers that enable them to produce more for a firm. These characteristics include education, experience, training, and commitment to work. Believers in this theory say that men usually have more human capital than women do and thus command higher wages.

There are many difficulties with this theory, including the fact that productivity is almost impossible to measure in some jobs, wages may not reflect the entire compensation for a job, and we do not have an open, competitive market for all jobs (remember the "old boy" network). Beyond the basic difficulties, however, statistics show that women get less return on investments in their own human capital than men do. For example, women with college educations get lower annual mean earnings than do men who are high school dropouts.[58]

In this theory, the major difference in the amount of wages is attributed to differences in work experience: overall work experience, on-the-job training, and the like. Women are less likely to get on-the-job training than men are because employers often believe that women are less committed workers and will not stay with the company. Women are also less likely to have continuous work experience. They may enter their careers after childbearing or interrupt them to raise children.[59] Women are the losers when they drop out of market. In a study that documented the gains from continuous work experience, the National Longitudinal Survey of the Work Experience of Mature Women, a national representative sample of 5,000 women aged 30 to 44 were interviewed eight times in the ten-year period 1967–1977. Women who worked continuously had real wage gains of about 20 percent, while those who entered and left employment were no better off in 1977 than they had been on average in 1967.[60] Even women with continuous experience, however, got less of a return on their experience than men did.[61]

Taking all these factors—education, on-the-job training, and continuous work experience—together, the National Research Council's report shows that only a relatively small percentage of the gap in salaries between men and women can be explained by human capital factors. Other studies have found that a slightly larger percentage of the wage differential can be accounted for by human capital, but current research indicates that it accounts for less than half the gap in earnings between men and women. We must look elsewhere to find out why women earn so much less than men.

Occupational Segregation and the Dual Labor Market.   Factors such as institutional barriers and job segregation seem to be more important than work experience in explaining the wage gap. One of the major reasons why women's earnings tend to be so low is that women are clustered in a narrow range of jobs. One-third work in clerical occupations, and one-quarter work in health care (not including physicians), education, domestic service, and food service.[62] Many of these jobs require higher than average educational levels (teacher, social worker, nurse) but pay low salaries. Few women have until very recently entered male-dominated professions, which are more highly paid. As of 1986, women accounted for only 17.6 percent of physicians, 4.4 percent of dentists, 18.1 percent of lawyers and judges, and 6 percent of engineers.[63]

Job segregation by sex seems to be an important factor in wage differentials. If we look at the twelve major occupational categories—professional and technical, managerial, sales, clerical, and so on—we do not see much difference in male and female salaries because the categories are so broad and job classifications differ markedly. When 479 job categories are used, however, studies show that job segregation accounts for a substantial amount of the gap in earnings.[64] In a study that used both human capital and job segregation variables, every additional percentage point of women in an occupation meant that workers in that job got an average of about $42 less in annual income.[65]

Fifty percent of employed women work in only twenty occupations.[66] Wage differentials occur with job segregation because by concentrating in only certain fields, women increase the supply of workers for those jobs and thus decrease their own wages. Economic theorists call this the **crowding theory**. In contrast, the short supply of engineers and physicians elevates wages in those male-dominated professions. Some of the jobs that have been designated for women are also contracting as a result of population trends and changes in technology. Low-level clerks and secretaries may be replaced as word processing becomes more automatic. Elementary school teachers are less needed as people have fewer children. However, women continue to enter jobs traditionally designated as female. As these fields become crowded, wages go down.

Are women restricted to these jobs? Socialization, training, and customs have made it difficult for women to enter male-dominated fields, although more women are doing so. While there are some indications of change (women entering law and medicine, for example), occupational segregation by sex is likely to continue. It has hardly decreased among whites for several decades, although it has decreased substantially among minorities.[67] Women seldom have the full information or mobility needed to choose jobs.[68] Employers seldom have access to all possible employees and are constrained by factors such as union contracts and agreements to promote from within.

Women are willing to take low pay and enter occupations with low status because most of these jobs fit well with the stereotype of being feminine. Many of the jobs with the highest percentage of female workers are nurturing in nature (teacher, social worker, nurse). In addition, some of these jobs have fairly flexible hours, which may aid a woman in combining them with domestic responsibilities. The professions traditionally designated for men, such as engineering, business management, and medicine, may require proficiency in mathematics or science, and women have been discouraged from taking courses in those areas. Thus, many women do not have the prerequisites to enter those professions.

The Dual-Burden Theory of Job Inequities.   The concept of the dual burden proposes that whatever jobs women pick, their family duties make it difficult for them to do the same work and reap the same rewards as men. A woman may have to choose between career and family responsibilities in a way that a man does not have to do. Women may be reluctant to work long hours or choose jobs that require travel because these things conflict with what they perceive as their responsibility to be the primary child rearer. Women may refuse promotions because of added burdens that conflict with home responsibilities or because of the fear of equaling or exceeding their husbands' salaries. Women who try to integrate their work lives with their family lives may find that employers are reluctant to grant maternity leave, resent time taken off to be with sick children, and generally believe that a woman's commitment to work is lessened if she becomes a mother. This perception may mean fewer promotions and lower salaries.

The plight of this dual burden has been summed up in Sylvia Hewlett's *The Lesser Life,* in which she compares the traditional American workplace with the more enlightened Swedish version.[69] It has also been the subject of a recent Diane Keaton movie, *Baby Boom,* in which a rising young female lawyer has to choose between a partnership in the firm and spending time with a baby.

Still more recently, the idea of the dual burden has been formalized by Felicia Schwartz. She discusses the problems that women executives have in combining work and family responsibilities and suggests that corporations officially recognize these difficulties with flexible, slower-paced jobs for women. Women without children could still be on the fast track with men. Feminists are horrified at the idea of establishing a formalized "mommy track" and singling out women with child-care responsibilities for less favorable treatment in the business world. Yet Schwartz has been willing to discuss a very real problem shared by many aspiring career women.[70]

While we discussed in some detail in Chapter 8 the problems of working women still doing the great majority of housework, it is instructive to give some other examples here to support the theory of the dual burden being part of the reason for the wage gap between men and women.

Hewlett points out that the family responsibilities borne by women exert a strong pull that leads to a woman receiving lower wages. Employment that is interrupted for childrearing, inability to put in overtime hours, and the decision not to travel for the company may make it difficult for a woman to get promotions. Hewlett shows that women who have never married have complete wage parity with never-married men while the wage gap between married men and married women is extremely large. For women to move up in the managerial ranks, they must frequently cut their family responsibilities, perhaps by deciding not to have children or even get married. More than 50 percent of managerial jobs are held by women who are childless and have continuous work histories. Hewlett believes that this dual burden of carrying family responsibilities in addition to a paid job affects women's salaries more than any other kind of discrimination does.[71]

She asserts that many highly educated professional women put their careers on hold, cut back to part-time work, or have various kinds of discontinuities in their work lives because of the problems of combining child raising and paid labor outside the home. She says that even for the superwomen who try to do it all, there is just not enough time and energy to equal those of male colleagues who are unencumbered with such tasks. She points out that in spite of the greatly increased number of women who work outside the home, recent studies show that American men still do less than 25 percent of all household tasks and that in the last twenty years the time spent by married men on housework has increased only 6 percent.[72] One study found that the workweek of American women is twenty-one hours longer than that of American men.[73]

Hewlett states that there is a Catch-22 in the dual-burden hypothesis. One of the reasons why men are unwilling to help more with housework is that their wives tend to make less money than they do. (Resources often determine the power one has to do work or have other people do it.) Obviously, if women continue to do the lion's share of housework and child raising, they will not be able to work in a way that will give them good salaries and family power.

The Residual Category of Discrimination.   When men and women work in the same fields, men still make more money. It is not just the nature of the job but the nature (sex) of the person that accounts for the difference in amount of pay. Thus, men who work in "women's" fields still earn $1,200 more annually than women in those fields do on the average, and in male-dominated occupations, men's salaries exceed those of women by an average of $2,400.[74]

Segregation within professions may also lead to different pay scales. Male computer specialists get $3,714 more than their female counterparts do. In retail sales, women and men are often in subcategories that pay differently. Men are more likely to sell big-ticket items such as appliances and furniture, which carry higher commissions.[75]

In addition, certain firms in the same occupational category are more likely to hire male workers while others are more likely to hire a greater percentage of female workers. Without exception, firms that are larger and more prestigious are more likely to hire men and pay them more money. This can be seen in law firms, accounting firms, and even restaurants (the more prestigious restaurants, where bills and tips are larger, hire only male table servers). More segregation occurs in this fashion than would be the case in a random hiring process. This difference among firms is believed to account for more of the wage gap than does the difference within any particular firm in terms of the jobs men and women take.[76]

Even within the same firm in an occupational category, men and women are likely to have different jobs. If they do not start in different categories, promotions may soon separate the sexes. A prime example of this occurred in an insurance company that was sued for sex discrimination. In this company, men were given "claims adjuster" jobs and women got jobs as "claims representatives." Each job required a college degree, yet not only were claims adjusters paid $2,500 more in wages than claims representatives who did the same work, but only the adjusters could obtain promotions.[77]

Thus, a differential exists between men's and women's wages that cannot be accounted for by human capital theory or job segregation. The reasons for this gap probably include various factors that we can combine under the categories of stereotypes and discrimination. The pay differential attributed to discrimination has been estimated to account for approximately one-third of the gap between female and male earnings.[78] When we talk about discrimination in this sense, we are not necessarily talking about an overt attempt to discriminate against women. We are also talking about the complex of customs, traditions, and understandings that lead to stereotyping and beliefs about who should do what work.

Myths That Justify Discrimination

Why do women in the labor force face discrimination? To answer this question, we need to look at some stereotypes about women workers. One of the first stereotypes is that a woman is a **secondary worker**, that her income is a second income for the household, and that she does not really need the money. This myth persists in spite of the facts that contradict it. The truth is that most women who work need money badly. (While all people who work need money as a basis of independence, a large percentage of working women need the money they earn for basic self-support.) Twenty-three percent of working women are single, and 19 percent are widowed, divorced, or separated and provide their families' main support. An additional 26 percent have husbands earning less than $10,000.[79] Of course, whether or not women really need the money should not be an issue: If they do equal work, they should get equal pay. Employers do not usually ask whether a man needs the money when it is time to adjust his salary or assess his qualifications for promotion.

Women are also seen as workers who are not serious about their work and are less committed and reliable than men. Employers expect them to be absent more than men and are reluctant to invest in them because they may quit. There seems to be no time when a woman worker is free of this stigma. When she is single, employers are afraid she will quit to get married. When she is married, they are afraid she will quit to have children or will follow her husband to a better job. If she already has had children, employers are afraid she will be absent a great deal because of child-care demands; if she is older and her children have left home, she may be considered too old and unattractive. The fact is that women are not absent from work any more than men; this is remarkable considering that many of them do have primary child-care responsibilities. Women and men are both absent an average of five and a half days a year.[80] While the overall quit rates of women are higher than those of men, women do not quit the same jobs more often than men do. The job attachment of anyone in a dead-end job is less than that of someone in a career that offers an opportunity for advancement. Men who are bank tellers quit as often as do women who are bank tellers; men who are physicians are no more or less committed to their work than are women who are physicians.[81]

Employers say that they do not promote women because people don't want to work for a woman boss and because women don't want the top jobs, can't handle responsibility, and are too emotional to be in management. The first two statements are probably true in many cases. Traditional gender-role stereotypes have dictated that women be dominated by men and not vice versa. Many people are uncomfortable when these stereotypes are reversed. Even women workers may accept the stereotype and not wish to be supervised by another woman. Sometimes they are accurate in their perception that "queen bees" who have reached the top are not eager to help other women up the ladder. In addition, women may not admit to wanting higher-echelon jobs because they know that the probability of their getting these jobs is low and that to accept such a job may entail accepting job responsibility that will conflict with home and family commitments.[82]

Rosabeth Kanter has pointed out that women managers may also be put in a position where it is difficult for them to help their subordinates advance. Some women may not want supervisory positions or promotions that entail additional responsibility, but in most cases this is the case because such a promotion means that they do not have enough time to handle family responsibilities or fear the difficulties that may come in exercising authority if coworkers resent them. Kanter also states that a great deal of the interchange in higher-echelon professional or business positions depends on common understanding and values. Men often prefer to work within a *homosocial* group (a group of people who are alike in race, sex, approximate age, and socioeconomic status) because they believe such a group will share their values. Men may fear that someone with a different status who does not share their background will make the working situation more difficult. In addition, many men are used to dealing with women only as secretaries or wives and may find it difficult to deal with a woman as an equal. Thus, for many reasons, women may not want to be managers and men may not want them in managerial positions.[83]

Sex as a Status Characteristic

As we examine the facts about women workers, we begin to see that sex is a status characteristic. It is used as a category to discriminate on the job and elsewhere in much the same way that race, religion, and age are used. The status of being female influences a woman's career aspirations, hiring possibilities, promotion chances, and salary as much as the personal qualifications she possesses or gains through education do.

When we think of **sex as status**, we see that discrimination against women is sometimes a matter of the upper-status group (men) retaining its power and privileges. As the work of men has always been more prestigious than that of women, men may consciously or unconsciously fear the dilution of their power and privileges if women join their ranks. The resistance of all-male groups such as the Harvard Club to opening their doors to women is a case in point. Men may feel their status, and thus their masculinity, threatened when women advance to parallel or supervisory positions in the work force.

To get around this difficulty, organizations consciously or unconsciously use various techniques to keep women out of the mainstream of advancement and decision making. Women's jobs may be reclassified to a lower category, or women may not be trained on the job to be eligible for promotion. Women may also be shifted into fields that do not lead to higher positions, such as personnel jobs. Personnel is usually considered an area that is a service function, and people who work in it are not on the upward track.[84]

In the blue-collar areas, unions have blatantly discriminated against women. Women were barred from craft unions for many years, and even today the requirements for membership may be difficult for women to meet. Union meetings may be held in halls or clubs where women feel uncomfortable or conducted after work or in the evening, when women have primary responsibilities at home. Harassment on blue-collar jobs may be overt and sexual; on white-collar jobs it may take the form of isolation, but the intent is the same: to show women that they should stay in their place.[85]

In a more radical description of the relationship between job segregation and discrimination, Hartmann suggests that as industrial society developed, men could not as easily maintain the control over women's work that they had had in the more personal preindustrial economic system. As jobs became more impersonal, control had to be institutionalized. She postulates that such control was continued by segregating industrial jobs by sex, with women making less money or unable to get work at all. Because of this segregation, women are partially or totally dependent on men for support and must perform domestic chores for their husbands. Thus men maintain control at home and are aided in their jobs by having domestic support. They also get higher wages because the labor supply is limited by women remaining home. Capitalism benefits because men are defined as the primary breadwinners and must work long hours to support their "idle" or partially employed wives.

Hartmann concludes that one cannot change women's position in the economic system without changing their household roles and that one cannot change household roles without changing job segregation in the economic system. As it is not to the benefit of those in power to change the system, it is unlikely that the system will be changed without conflict.[86]

Hartmann's inference that segregation of jobs by sex and discrimination against women are deliberate devices to enforce women's dependence may not be accepted by everyone. However, it is clear that occupational segregation by sex, in combination with conscious and unconscious discrimination, accounts for a great deal of the discrepancy between women's and men's wages and perpetuates women's secondary status as workers.

Women in Blue-Collar Jobs

While women in blue-collar jobs share certain kinds of discrimination with female white-collar workers, they also have unique problems of their own. In the late 1980s, women manual laborers who were employed in blue-collar industrial and service occupations constituted 38 percent of all employed women, or some 12.5 million women in all. Most of these women were white, but three of five black women worked in blue-collar jobs.[87]

While women went from 4 percent to 18 percent of the lawyers and even from 0.8 percent to 6.8 percent of the engineers between 1960 and 1985, the proportion of women carpenters rose only from 0.03 percent to 1.2 percent in that period.[88] There are several reasons for the difference. There are two and a half times as many carpenters as doctors, and the relative size of the crafts means that more women are needed to produce a similar proportion of female workers. There has been an expansion in the number of professional jobs, but the number of craft jobs has not grown substantially. Access to skilled craft jobs is provided by union apprenticeship, and entry is difficult for women because of union discrimination. Masculinity and work are interwoven in these blue-collar jobs, and women who work in them often face a great deal of resistance. They are often subjected to sexual and other forms of harassment and may be resegregated into jobs that are automated or due to be eliminated altogether.[89]

Occupational Segregation and the Dual Labor Market in Blue-Collar Jobs. As in white-collar organizations, blue-collar jobs are sex-segregated. Certain industries have traditionally hired women: garment factories, laundry establishments, small electrical equipment assemblers, communications industries, beauty salons, restaurants, hospitals, and domestic agencies. When both sexes are employed in the same industry, men hold the more prestigious and higher-paying jobs. In the apparel industry, for example, men are skilled cutters, pressers, and tailors, while women are sewing machine operators.[90]

The usual consequence of this segregation is lower pay for women. Women in industrial and service jobs earn about 60 percent of men's wages. In addition, many of the industries in which they work have poor fringe benefits, unstable employment, and exploitative part-time work. Many of the industries in which women work are not unionized. While unions have not treated men and women equally, the wages of women in unionized fields are somewhat better than the wages of those in nonunion areas.[91]

Women have not rushed to labor unions to relieve their problems.[92] Blue-collar unions have not generally been supportive of their female members. In particular, they have not supported wage equality for female employees, and during periods of high unemployment seniority and the desire to keep men on the job have taken precedence over demands for affirmative action.[93] There are few women in leadership positions who could change this situation. However, union membership among women workers is slowly increasing. Women have recognized that in most cases, unionization improves their wages.

Even women in unions who get good wages have many difficulties. They often face male coworkers' hostility and sexual advances. Men seldom help them learn their jobs, although they readily help other men. Yet it is estimated that as much as 80 percent of some kinds of work is learned informally from others on the job.[94] Manual jobs may entail changing shifts and forced overtime, which wreak havoc with a working mother's child-care arrangements and family obligations.[95]

Women have become aware that they must push their unions to work for benefits for female members. In 1974, 3,500 women formed the Coalition of Labor Union Women (CLUW) in an attempt to put more women into union leadership roles and work for affirmative action and legislation for women. One of their major actions is an attempt to reclassify women's jobs so that women can get into apprenticeship programs and receive higher wages. Many women's jobs are now erroneously classified at such low skill levels that not only do they pay poverty wages, but their classification keeps women from getting training to move into better-paid employment.[96]

Black Women in the Labor Force

Fifty-eight percent of all black women work, and they have traditionally been in the labor force in large numbers.[97] Only Asian-American women have proportionately more paid workers than blacks, although as white women have entered the labor force in greater numbers, their percentage has come close to that of black working women.

Striking changes have occurred in the jobs and earnings of black women in the last two decades. Traditionally, the median income among employed black women was very low, with a large proportion of them working in domestic service and the less-skilled manual trades. Early textile jobs were usually closed to black women, as were clerical and secretarial positions. During the 1980s, however, nearly one-fourth of black women changed jobs, moving into clerical occupations and the female-dominated professions.[98] The shift in occupation caused a marked improvement in their occupational prestige and earnings as they became nurses, teachers, and librarians, among other things.

Black women thus increased their earnings, and by 1987 they earned an average of 98 percent of what white women were making.[99] They must work harder and longer for the same pay, however. They are often still in jobs with lower occupational prestige and wages. They compensate by working longer hours and remaining in the labor force rather than interrupting employment for long periods while their children are small.[100]

There are many variations among black women workers. This fact is clearly seen in differences between age groups: Older black women are more likely to be in domestic work and other services, and the younger ones are more likely to be in the professions. As 54 percent of black women workers are also likely to be single heads of families or to have husbands who earn lower incomes, it is particularly necessary for them to work.

Differences also exist between black women and black men workers. In 1986 black women had a slightly higher educational attainment than black men, yet black women were earning only 62 percent of a black man's annual salary.[101] Sex segregation in occupations again tells the story. Black women, like their white counterparts, work in "feminine" and low-paid occupations. Black women account for 79 percent of black librarians, 97 percent of black nurses, and 78 percent of black noncollege teachers. They also constitute 46 percent of the professionals but only 7 percent of the engineers, 14 percent of the lawyers, and 24 percent of the physicians and dentists of their race.[102]

There is a disturbing trend toward the possible loss of jobs for many black women. Clerical work is the dominant occupation for young black women, who have been concentrated in routine jobs such as typing and filing, but many of these jobs are being eliminated because of automation.[103] Black clerical workers are also more likely to work for the government than for private employers and may lose jobs as a result of recent governmental budget cuts.[104]

However, sex discrimination rather than racial discrimination now seems to be the basic problem for black women workers. They approximate white women in labor force participation, occupational prestige, education, and earnings.

ISSUES OF EQUALITY FOR MEN AND WOMEN WORKERS

Legislation

The revival of the feminist movement and the increased numbers of working women have interacted to generate concern about the differential between women's and men's wages and about sex discrimination in the marketplace. A spate of laws and court interpretations have resulted from women's attempts to gain legal protection.

There are four basic measures that prohibit discrimination on the basis of sex. The Equal Pay Act of 1963 (Section 6d of the Fair Labor Standards Act of 1938, as amended) requires that employees receive equal wages for "equal work on jobs which are performed under similar working conditions."[105] This act does not prohibit discrimination in hiring or promotion, however. It was designed to aid women who were doing work equal to that done by men but were being paid less. In 1974, the Supreme Court interpreted the act to mean equal pay in all forms of remuneration from the employer, including fringe benefits such as medical insurance and pension plans. However, bona fide seniority and merit systems were exempted.[106]

Title VII of the Civil Rights Act of 1964 prohibits discrimination by race, color, religion, sex, or national origin in hiring, firing, promotion, training, seniority, retirement, and all other aspects of employment. The act also prohibits classification of employees in a way that deprives an individual of employment opportunities. It applies to employment agencies and unions as well as to businesses. Feminists lobbied strongly for the inclusion of sex as one of the categories of potential discrimination. While there was opposition to doing this, those opposed finally allowed sex to be included because they wanted to defeat the entire bill and thought that the inclusion of sex would cause that defeat. However, Title VII passed, and for the first time women were given a legal basis for insisting that they be allowed to compete with men for jobs and promotions. Even then, the Equal Employment Opportunity Commission (EEOC) refused for some time to enforce the sex provision and allowed employers to advertise "male jobs" and "female jobs."[107]

By 1966, pressure from feminist groups resulted in stricter enforcement of sex discrimination rules, and a 1972 amendment to Title VII (Title IX) expanded the law to include educational institutions and state and local governments as well as employers with fifteen or more employees. Since 1972, the EEOC has been able to bring suits against all those (except government agencies) who violate the act. Executive orders in 1965 and 1969 extended prohibitions against sex discrimination to federal contractors and to the federal government itself.[108]

Another important piece of legislation was the Age Discrimination Employment Act of 1967, which prohibited government, private employers, employment agencies, and unions from discriminating against persons between 40 and 65 years of age. As many women had not been hired or were fired for being "too old" or "old and unattractive," this was important for older women.[109]

There have been major tests of all these laws. Various groups and agencies have gone to court to see if the laws would be judged to be in line with the intent of the Constitution. The court which hears such a case uses a variety of legal "tests" to see if the law is indeed constitutional. For example, there is a provision in Title VII that sex can be used to discriminate in jobs when sex is a "bona fide occupational qualification reasonably necessary to the normal operation of that particular business or enterprise." The courts have narrowly interpreted this provision, however, and in most cases have held that being a certain sex is not a "bona fide occupational requirement" for hiring. An example was the decision that men as well as women have to be hired as flight attendants.

Pregnancy insurance and pension benefits have also been tested legally. For a time the courts ruled that pregnancy and childbirth disabilities should be covered by health insurance, but recently they have ruled that normal pregnancy expenses are not covered. The issue of pension benefits has never been resolved. Since women live longer than men on the average, insurance companies have regularly given them smaller monthly retirement sums, contending that the total sum paid equals out over the long run. Women have contested these smaller payments but have not yet won their suits.

A final area of concern has been the problem of seniority. The last-hired, first-fired policies that operate under seniority mean that those usually laid off are disproportionately minorities and women. Despite disagreement in the legal system, an appellate court ruled that under due process "if present hiring practices were nondiscriminatory, an employer's use of a long-established seniority system to establish the order of layoff and recall of employees was not a violation of Title VII."[110]

The 1980s and Affirmative Action

During the 1980s the Reagan administration deemphasized affirmative action. In fact, it followed the premise that affirmative action amounts to unlawful reverse discrimination against white males. Boris and Honey state that "the Office of Civil Rights within the Labor Department now deals with enforcement in the context of reducing Government spending and resulting paperwork."[111] Federal funds were cut, and Women's Bureau programs for displaced homemakers and new immigrants had to rely on the private sector.[112] Federal job creation programs were decimated. Three hundred thousand workers were cut from the job-training programs of CETA in 1981, and cutbacks in the Labor Department reduced the staff available for implementation of affirmative action and wage and hour regulations. Contract violations by businesses were simply not enforced.[113] Instead, the government urged voluntary compliance and eliminated the need for small contractors to adhere to affirmative action guidelines. "It appeared to civil rights and equal rights proponents that vigorous Federal affirmative action programs and public employment programs belonged to the past."[114]

It is noteworthy that the Supreme Court has not upheld the Reagan administration's philosophy. The Court has consistently upheld the affirmative action decisions of the lower courts provided that they did not unduly harm innocent white males. It has, however, prohibited preferential treatment for blacks during layoffs, preserving seniority rules in such cases. It has also forbidden the use of rigid, permanent quotas as a mechanism to achieve affirmative action.

In a recent decision which was hailed as a major victory for women and blacks, the Supreme Court stated that affirmative action violates neither the Constitution nor Title VII of the Civil Rights Act of 1964. In a case in Santa Clara County, California, in which a woman was promoted to the post of road dispatcher over a man who scored two points higher on a qualifying interview, the Court held that the agency had appropriately taken into account as one factor the sex of the applicants. Three justices dissented from the majority opinion: Byron White, William Rehnquist, and Antonin Scalia.

The dissent by Scalia included a provocative paragraph in which he blamed the victims, in this case women, for their own fate. He said it was "absurd to think" that road crew positions were "traditionally segregated" job categories because of a systematic exclusion of women "eager to shoulder pick and shovel." They have been male-dominated, he said, because they have "not been regarded by women themselves as desirable work."[115] This approach of blaming women for their own segregation in the labor force has been used frequently. In *EEOC v. Sears, Roebuck and Company,* the Court ruled in favor of Sears on the grounds that women have chosen their part-time and low-paying jobs as a way of balancing their home and family lives. Ironically, the female lawyer defending Sears used feminist scholarly works dealing with the segregated position of women in the labor force to make her case.[116] The path pursued by George Bush has not been very different from that of the Reagan administration. While he has not as actively attempted to dismantle affirmative action machinery, he has not pushed for enforcement of nondiscrimination.

Comparable Worth

Recently there has been an attempt to combat the segregation of women into low-paying jobs by applying the principle of *comparable worth*, that is, the idea of paying equally for jobs that demand the same level of skill, effort, responsibility, and working conditions even if they are not exactly the same jobs. Many people believe that men and women are unlikely to have exactly the same jobs and that without this technique, it will be difficult for women to ever earn equal pay. The idea of paying on the basis of job evaluation is not a new concept. Many jobs in our society, such as those in the federal government, now have pay determined by a job evaluation system. In a comparable worth job evaluation, the employer, employees, and union (when there is a collective bargaining agreement) select the criteria on which wages should be based and decide how much weight to assign to each factor. It is important to set the criteria without sex bias. Points are then assigned for every job in a company according to its evaluation system so that a job's total score represents its worth to the employer. Very different jobs may have similar scores. Each job may have salary ranges, and the actual salary for any worker falls into these ranges according to seniority and other qualifications without regard to sex or race. Some examples of jobs that have been ranked the same are listed in Table 1.

Several important court cases have tested the concept of comparable worth. In a San Jose, California, case in 1981, municipal workers struck to enforce a job evaluation study that showed that certain jobs dominated by women were underpaid. They received $1.5 million in pay adjustments. In another case, Westinghouse Corporation was sued for having a pay scale that placed women workers in the lowest pay categories. The corporation was forced to reevaluate its job categories and pay women commensurately. In 1983, women workers in the state of Washington won $800 million in back pay and wage increases on the basis of a comparable worth evaluation.[117]

Conservatives argue that comparable worth adjustments will be expensive and stress the difficulty of trying to rate jobs with disparate qualifications. Feminists state that there is no other sure way to cope with pay inequities as long as jobs remain largely segregated by sex. They point to the fact that the cost of implementing pay equity in the state of Minnesota came to less than 4 percent of the state's payroll budget.[118] They also state that pay equity will save tax dollars spent now on welfare for women and minorities whose wages are kept low by discrimination. They also emphasize that it will not lower any other workers' wages. Under the Equal Pay Act and Title VII, the courts have consistently held that an employer may not lower any employee's pay to eliminate wage discrimination.

Table 1   Job Evaluation

Employer	Occupation	Predominant Sex	Pay, $
Yale University	Administrative assistant	Female	13,000
	Truck driver	Male	18,000
State of Minnesota	Registered nurse	Female	20,676
	Vocational educator	Male	27,120
County of Los Angeles	Health technician	Minority	13,380
	Evidence and property custodian	White	16,812

SOURCE: Sociologists for Women in Society, *Facts about Pay Equity* (April 1986).

Let us look briefly at what the state of Minnesota did to get a better idea of how comparable worth can work. In Minnesota, beginning in 1970, studies showed that female workers were consistently being paid less than male workers. Social workers with more education and experience were paid less than painters; workers with the mentally retarded were paid less than workers in a zoo. There was no state evaluation system to allow for systematic compensation of jobs until 1979. At that time, a profile method developed earlier by Hay Associates called the Hay Guide Profile Method was used to rank jobs. With this method, points were awarded for (1) level of know-how, (2) problem solving, (3) accountability, and (4) working conditions.

In 1981, a state task force was established by the Commission on the Economic Status of Women to study the state's pay practices. It included members of the legislature, management, labor, and the general public and used the Hay scale to document pay disparities in jobs with equal point values. As an example of what they found, a land surveyor and a registered nurse had the same value points for their jobs, but there was a pay disparity of $250 a month in favor of the surveyor.

Legislators of both parties supported the state's Employees Pay Equity Act, which was passed in 1982. About 8,500 employees in 200 female-dominated classes received pay increases averaging about $2,200 annually; about 10 percent of these employees were men.

What did not happen after the pay adjustment is significant. No employees had their wages reduced or frozen. There were no strikes or lawsuits. There was no bureaucracy created to manage the program. Contrary to dire warnings that women would stay in all-female fields as pay increased, women still sought jobs in male areas. Collective bargaining was still very important, and morale was high.[119]

The concept of comparable worth was not supported by the Reagan administration in the 1980s. A Reagan appointee, Clarence Pendleton, chairman of the U.S. Civil Rights Commission, which is supposed to promote equality legislation, called the idea "the looniest idea since `Looney Tunes' came on the screen." William Reynolds, the assistant attorney general for civil rights, opposed the principle of comparable worth in court. By contrast, the Democratic leadership of the House of Representatives endorsed the idea of "equal pay for work of comparable social value."[120]

A different perspective on comparable worth is proposed by Ciancanelli and Berch. They posit that "employers are not the only opponents of comparable worth. Large numbers, perhaps even a `silent majority' of Americans, may be quite uncomfortable with women making as much money as men do as this would encroach on men's social power and disturb existing arrangements."[121]

Sexual Harassment

One of the most critical hidden aspects of women's work—sexual harassment—can be defined in a number of ways. What one person might call a flattering compliment, another person might call offensive. Marisa Manley says that "one person's offhand comment can be another's hostile environment."[122]

McGrath emphasizes that the key to the definition of sexual harassment is that it is "unwelcome."[123] A working definition by the Michigan Task Force on Sexual Harassment that encompasses many aspects of sexual harassment states that harassment

> includes continual or repeated verbal abuse of a sexual nature, including but not limited to graphic commentaries on the victim's body, sexually suggestive objects or pictures in the workplace, sexually degrading words used to describe the victim, or propositions of a sexual nature. Sexual harassment also includes the threat or insinuation that lack of sexual submission will adversely affect the victim's employment, wages, standing, or other conditions that affect the victim's livelihood.[124]

Sexual harassment has existed for as long as women have worked. In the nineteenth century young unmarried women who worked in the mills often became pregnant after "succumbing to male supervisors." Instead of action being taken against the perpetrator, the problem was confronted by questioning whether it was immoral for young girls to work alongside men. When it was decided that such contact was immoral, women were usually segregated into different jobs, often at lower pay.[125] In domestic work women were also victims of harassment. Louisa May Alcott in 1874 wrote about her experience with sexual harassment when she worked as a domestic for a married couple. After propositioning her many times, the husband ordered Alcott to do the hardest manual labor around the house and yard.[126]

One of the most pervasive early forms of sexual harassment was that endured by black women slaves. There is clear documentation that slave women were consistent victims of sexual abuse at the hands of white masters.[127] Minority women are still among the most severely exploited today. As Catherine MacKinnon puts it, sexual harassment in this case can be a "sexist way to express racism or a racist way to express sexism."[128]

Types of Harassment. According to the legal definition, sexual harassment usually falls into two categories: "quid pro quo" and "hostile environment."[129] The former basically means one thing in return for another (for example, a raise for sex), and the latter is anything that is perceived to be an expression of hostility by the person receiving it.

Peggy Crull states that certain kinds of behaviors usually happen to women according to their field of work. Quid pro quo behavior usually is directed at women in traditional fields of work, places where women are expected to be working. Hostile environment behavior usually happens to women with jobs typically held by men.[130]

Crull believes that the hostile environment is more likely to occur on nontraditional jobs because the perpetrator is likely to be a coworker who does not necessarily have the power to offer a quid pro quo. To this coworker, the woman may symbolize the power on the job which he is losing.[131] In the traditional job, Crull says, harassment is more likely to be provoked by what she calls "sex role spillover,"[132] in which the roles of the two genders on the job are similar to the roles of a patriarchal family and the boss is acting toward the woman as he would if she were his wife. A woman in a traditional job steps out of her role when she refuses the boss's sexual requests—a threat to patriarchy. Crull points out that sexual harassment is "only the tip of the iceberg and what lies beneath is a whole system of assumptions, practices and structures through which sexuality negatively affects the woman's position in the marketplace."[133]

Paul Engel sees sexual harassment as the culmination of "41,000 years of habit" resulting from "societal sex role conditioning,"[134] while Lin Farley focuses on job segregation by sex and men's need to control women's work.[135] Catherine MacKinnon points out how behavior in the home carries over to the workplace. To her, sexual harassment in the workplace is just another example of "normal relations between the sexes . . . that express unequal social power."[136]

Rulings against both quid pro quo and hostile environment types of sexual harassment have been upheld by the Supreme Court. In June 1986, in *Meritor Savings Bank v. Michelle Vinson,* an opinion by William Rehnquist stated, "Without question, when a supervisor sexually harasses a subordinate because of a subordinate's sex, that supervisor discriminates on the basis of sex."[137] This ruling paved the way for the treatment of sexual harassment as sex discrimination under Title VII of the Civil Rights Act of 1964.

In spite of this landmark ruling, questions about many areas of sexual harassment have not been answered. These questions center on employer liability, definitions of "unwelcome," and situations in which there was previous consensual sexual activity.[138] Because of the uniqueness of each case, the Court has been deciding each question on a case by case basis.

Extent. In the late 1980s several studies were conducted to determine the extent of sexual harassment in the workplace. Between 1985 and 1987 the U.S. Merit Systems Protection Board surveyed over 23,000 federal employees about their experiences. The study found that 42 percent of women federal workers had been sexually harassed. A survey of 160 companies done by *Working Women* magazine asked about the incidence of specific behaviors and found that 42 percent of the women had experienced teasing sexual comments, 26 percent had experienced touching or cornering, 17 percent had experienced pressure for sexual favors, and 12 percent had experienced pressure for dates.[139] Such harassment had happened to a diverse group of women ranging from coal miners, factory workers, and police officers to nurses, secretaries, lawyers, and professors. MacKinnon states that the diversity of occupations supports the hypothesis that harassment occurs because of the groups' common characteristic—sex.[140]

One commonly asked question about harassment is, Doesn't it happen to men, too? Approximately one-tenth of the harassment incidents reported are those in which men are victims or harassment occurs between two people of the same sex: men harassed by men or women harassed by women.[141] Few women are in positions of authority over men in the workplace; they simply do not have the societal power to harass men sexually.

Effects on Women. In many ways women respond to sexual harassment in the same way they respond to rape. Women may feel a variety of things emotionally, such as embarrassment, intimidation, fear, despair, guilt, shame, and anger. Physiologically, they may experience stomachaches, headaches, loss of appetite, bouts of crying, and insomnia.[142] They may begin to question their own integrity and ask themselves what they are doing to provoke this behavior. Most women fear repercussions or retaliation in terms of their jobs. Many quit their jobs.

Although black women experience the same emotional and physical reactions that nonminority victims do, their actions in response to harassment may differ. A number of white women will leave their jobs; black women are more likely to take legal action. They have taken such action in disproportionate numbers. MacKinnon hypothesizes that they have no choice but to act legally because of their "least advantaged position in the economy."[143]

Responding to Sexual Harassment.   Clearly, both the workplace and women have a stake in ending this unwanted behavior. Businesses cannot afford to have situations that cause emotional and physical stress for employees, and there is always the potential for a lawsuit if an organization does not address the situation.

Many experts suggest that confronting the harasser is important and may even end the situation. According to some studies, when a woman ignores harassment, it intensifies 75 percent of the time.[144] Responding with "I'm not receptive to this" or "Please don't" may be all it takes, says Saltzman.[145] If confrontation does not work, telling someone is the next step.[146] Several experts suggest keeping records of the incidents for reporting purposes as well as for a possible lawsuit. Some companies have ombudsmen or employee assistance plans which provide confidential assistance. Another suggestion for company behavior to end sexual harassment is to have open discussions. People need to know exactly what constitutes such behavior and be aware that it is a violation of civil rights under federal law. Having a formal written company policy stating that sexual harassment is inappropriate and not acceptable to the organization is also important.[147] Procedures should be set up to handle any incidents and should include prompt investigation and corrective action.

While there is certainly more awareness of this issue today and while some corrective action has been taken by companies and the courts, sexual harassment is still commonplace and widespread. It is an integral part of women's experience in the work force. Catherine MacKinnon sums up the insidious nature of harassment when she says, "Sexual harassment undercuts women's potential for social equality in two ways: it uses employment to coerce her sexually and it uses her sexual position to coerce her economically."[148]

Other Important Work Issues

Family Leave and Maternity Health Coverage.   One of the problems that working women who want children have had to face is lack of parental leaves and maternity health coverage. The United States is the only industrialized country that has no statutory maternity leave as such. Over a hundred industrialized nations have family leave policies, most of which include paid leave.[149]

Some corporations offer their own maternity policies, and the best of these are to be found in the large corporations. A 1981 survey of 250 large corporations found 88 percent offering some type of maternity leave, usually six weeks paid and six weeks unpaid. However, only about 25 percent of all working women have jobs in these large corporations.[150] For the great majority, maternity leave with some financial benefits is only a dream.

Hewlett points out that fewer than 40 percent of working women in the United States have maternity coverage.[151] Much of this coverage is provided under an amendment to Title VII of the Civil Rights Act which states that an employer can no longer fire a worker solely because she is pregnant.[152] Women are also eligible for the same fringe benefits that workers with other disabilities get. This seems to indicate the right to use temporary disability insurance for pregnancy, but the catch is that the federal government does not require employers to provide disability insurance. Only five states (California, Hawaii, New Jersey, New York, and Rhode Island) require such coverage. Even this coverage usually amounts to only six to ten weeks at partial wages.[153]

We will see in Chapter 12 that attempts have been made to pass family and medical leave legislation. However, these attempts have been thwarted by big business, which balks at the cost.

Child Care for Working Parents.   Child care is another important issue for working women. Providing adequate child care and subsidies for such care is another way to deal with the dual burden. Hewlett points out that the United States is far behind other industrialized nations in providing such care. Public day care centers in the United States provide approximately 10 percent of the child care used by working mothers. About half of these centers cater to poor families and are publicly subsidized. However, the Reagan budget cuts have lowered the funding for these centers 21 percent since 1980.[154]

The other half are private day care centers that can cost from $80 to $200 a week per child. While they have to make a profit to exist, many of these centers seem more interested in making money than in giving quality care. Low salaries for their staffs may keep the centers open but often causes a lack of qualified, consistent workers. By contrast, many other nations spend considerable amounts to provide child care for working mothers because they consider it a good investment in raising children who will be future citizens. France, for example, spends more than 4 percent of its gross national product on subsidies to preschool children.[155] However, in the United States there is decreasing public support for children. "Since 1980, an additional 3 million children have fallen into poverty. Seven hundred thousand poor children have been struck from the Medicaid rolls and 200,000 have lost their day-care subsidies."[156]

Bills have been introduced at the federal level to correct this situation, such as the Act for Better Child Care (ABC) sponsored by Dale Kildee, a Michigan congressman. This bill provides new funds to make child care more affordable for low- and moderate-income families through partnerships between private persons and groups and at the state or federal level. Another bill known as the Latchkey Bill has similar provisions. We will look at their fate in Chapter 12.

Other Laws.   Other government laws also affect those in the labor force, especially women. Tax and Social Security laws that penalize two-worker families may make it less rewarding for a woman to work, and veterans' benefits may mean that it is more difficult for a woman to get some jobs or that she may not get the same benefits a man would.

SUMMARY

Women in the job market have lower wages and lower job status than men do for a number of reasons. As a matter of choice or discrimination, they may not make the investment in human capital that gives them access to more prestigious and high-paying jobs. They are likely to enter jobs that are segregated and pay less and in which there may be a glut in the near future. They are also discriminated against for a variety of reasons, which include myths and the weight of cultural tradition. As unequal pay per se is illegal, the means for this discrimination is usually to place women in jobs with secondary status. Laws and government policies add to the low status of women workers. Thus, conscious or unconscious institutional discrimination against women means that they retain their status as secondary workers with unequal wages and low job status.

THE FUTURE: WOMEN, MEN, AND WORK

Gail Lapidus sums up the problems for the future as follows:

> A political culture which treats freedom, equality, and achievement as supreme and universal norms collides with pervasive cultural assumptions about the need for a sexual division of labor, for differentiation . . . between male and female roles. . . . The primacy assigned to the homemaking and maternal roles of women encourages the treatment of their participation in the workforce as secondary and residual.
> These cultural norms are reinforced by patterns of socialization which receive formal expression in educational institutions. Differential expectations for boys and girls are embedded in educational curricula . . . and, of course, differential expectations elicit differences in behavior. . . .
> Finally, these values are mirrored and reinforced by public policy . . . ranging from taxation measures to the provision of social services. . . . [157]

This summary of the condition of work in this country itemizes clearly the points that we have tried to make in our discussion of the marketplace. First, cultural assumptions about a sexual division of labor mean that men and women are expected to do different jobs. Women are expected to work at home while men engage in paid labor outside the home, but if this cannot be accomplished, then women are considered "secondary workers" in the paid labor force and go into appropriately female occupations. These attitudes toward women doing paid work are changing, but the basic cultural assumptions about women as secondary workers remain strong and mean that women are segregated into certain fields that have low status and are low paying.

The second point made by Lapidus is that these cultural assumptions are enforced by cultural institutions from the curricula of educational institutions to the kinds of job advertising employers do. Finally, these institutional policies and cultural assumptions are mirrored and reinforced by public policy: tax laws, credit laws, and lack of child care and family and maternal leave. If we accept Hartmann's theory that the perpetuation of job segregation is a deliberate controlling of women so that they will be dependent on men and be willing to perform domestic chores for them, we will be pessimistic about change in the future.[158] Even if we are not willing to accept that radical a view, we may be pessimistic because men who have traditionally held positions of privilege and power may be reluctant to relinquish them.

However, there are also important forces for change. It is likely that women will keep working in greater numbers, pushed into the work force by the demands of inflationary prices and pulled by their own educational attainment, need for self-support, and need for personal satisfaction. The U.S. Bureau of the Census estimates that women will account for 61 percent of the labor force by the year 2000.[159]

Women are also entering jobs that have traditionally been held by men and have been increasingly socialized to value these higher-paying jobs and train for them. While men may be threatened by the movement of women into their traditional strongholds, they may not be able to stem the tide. The necessity of having two wage earners in a family may also provide a rationale that will allow men to accept women's participation in the paid work force. Men may actually welcome some relief from the burdens of being in the role of the sole provider. With the increasing emphasis on the health problems of achievement-oriented men, they may be willing to relinquish one measure of masculinity in order to lessen stress and have more time with their families.

Whether men are willing to relinquish the provider role may depend on many other factors, including the nature of the political and economic system in this country. The demands of a profit-oriented capitalistic system may push us back into old molds (unless women are willing to substitute woman-hours for man-hours). Our economic system is also not growing as in the past; fewer jobs are being created, and automation is eliminating many entry-level jobs. These difficult economic times may make it hard for women to get jobs or for men to leave them. We will look at some factors influencing the political system in Chapter 12.

ESSAY QUESTIONS

1. How is occupational success defined in the American culture? How does a man show this success, and how is such success related to masculinity?
2. How does the average middle-aged man in the American culture feel about his occupational success? If he has achieved prominence in his line of work and is happy with what he does, is this enough to make him comfortable? If not, why not?
3. Why is the blue-collar worker particularly alienated?
4. Discuss the reasons why women have been entering the labor force in greater numbers since World War II.
5. What is the present situation of women workers in terms of how their salaries and fringe benefits compare to those of men? What specific problems do women workers cite when asked about their occupations?
6. Discuss why or why not human capital theory explains the difference between women's wages and men's wages.
7. How does occupational segregation contribute to wage differentials between men and women? Discuss segregation within occupational fields as well as between types of occupations. Why do women go into certain types of jobs, and why do these jobs pay less?
8. What part have labor unions played in helping women achieve better wages? How are unions handling the conflict between affirmative action and seniority?
9. Describe the concept of comparable worth and discuss how well it has or has not worked where it has been introduced.
10. How much do women suffer from sexual harassment at work, and what are some of the remedies available to them?
11. How will an economic recession or an economy that is not growing affect women's chances to improve their employment situation?

EXERCISES

1. Have you ever worked in a factory or on an assembly line? If so, discuss how you felt about your work. If you have never done that type of work, how do you imagine you would feel? Have you ever heard blue-collar workers talk about their jobs?
2. Pretend you are a woman being interviewed for a beginning management position. The company does not really want to hire a woman but is being forced to interview women to comply with affirmative action requirements. What kinds of questions might be asked? How could you reply to loaded questions without giving in to sexism?
3. Assume you are a husband whose wife has just decided to go back to work full-time. You are not pleased about losing your support system at

home or having your breadwinner role challenged. What kinds of things might you say to your wife that would convince her that a job outside the home would not be in the family's best interest?

4. Pretend you are the president of an autoworkers union. You are being asked by women members of your union to press for affirmative action, but you are really concerned with keeping jobs for all the union members. What would you tell the women members, and what would you do?

5. If you are a woman, pretend you are a man and discuss why it is important for you to succeed at your chosen occupation. If you are a man, discuss your feelings about this subject.

NOTES

1. Calvin Hall, *A Primer of Freudian Psychology* (New York: World, 1954).
2. Andrew Levinson, "The Rebellion of Blue-Collar Youth," in *Annual Editions: Readings in Social Problems* (New York: Dushkin, 1987), pp. 43–48.
3. Studs Terkel, *Working* (New York: Avon, 1972), pp. 446–447.
4. "Working Women: More Than You Think," *Supermarket Business* 43 (September 1988):40–43.
5. Susan E. Shank, "Women and the Labor Market: The Link Grows Stronger," *Monthly Labor Review* 11 (March 1988):3–8.
6. Jesse Bernard, "The Good-Provider Role: Its Rise and Fall," in Arlene Skolnick and Jerome Skolnick, eds., *Family in Transition,* 6th ed. (Boston: Scott, Foresman, 1989), pp. 143–162.
7. Michael Kimmel, "The Cult of Masculinity: American Social Character and the Legacy of the Cowboy," in Michael Kaufman, ed., *Beyond Patriarchy* (New York: Oxford University Press, 1987), pp. 235–249.
8. Myron Brenton, "The Breadwinner," in Deborah David and Robert Brannon, eds., *The Forty-nine Percent Majority: The Male Sex Role* (Reading, Mass.: Addison-Wesley, 1976), pp. 113–118.
9. Robert Gould, "Measuring Masculinity by the Size of a Paycheck," in David and Brannon, *op. cit.,* pp. 113–118.
10. *Ibid.*
11. Daniel Levinson with Charolette Darrow, Edward Klein, Marcia Levinson, and Braxton McKee, *The Seasons of a Man's Life* (New York: Ballantine, 1978), pp. 247–248.
12. Brenton, *op. cit.,* p. 95.
13. Tom Lehrer, "Automation," in *That Was the Year That Was* (album R6179 from Reprise Records, July 1965).
14. Rosabeth Kanter, *Men and Women of the Corporation* (New York: Basic Books, 1977).
15. Louis Harris and Associates, "The Playboy Report on American Men: A Study of the Values, Attitudes, and Goals of U.S. Males 18–49 Years Old" (survey conducted by Playboy Enterprises, 1979).
16. *Ibid.,* p. 39.
17. Terkel, *op. cit.,* pp. 446–447.
18. Terkel, *op. cit.,* pp. 256–265.

19. Harris, *op. cit.*, pp. 35–36, 38.
20. A. Levinson, *op. cit.*
21. Stan Gray, "Sharing the Shop Floor," in Kaufman, *op. cit.*, pp. 216–234.
22. Terkel, *op. cit.*, pp. 223ff.
23. Tim Carrigan, Bob Connell, and John Lee, "Hard and Heavy: Toward a New Sociology of Masculinity," in Kaufman, *op. cit.*, pp. 139–194.
24. Elaine Wethington, Jane D. McLeod, and Ronald C. Kessler, "The Importance of Life Events for Explaining Sex Differences in Psychological Distress," in Rosalind Barnett, Losi Biener, and Grace K. Baruch, eds., *Gender and Stress* (New York: The Free Press, 1987), pp. 144–158.
25. Terkel, *op. cit.*, p. xx.
26. *Ibid*, p. xxix.
27. Rosabeth Kanter, *op. cit.*
28. Brenton, *op. cit.*, p. 96.
29. D. Levinson et al., *op. cit.*, pp. 197–244.
30. Andrea Z. LaCroix and Suzane G. Haynes, "Gender Differences in the Health Effects of Workplace Roles," in Barnett et al., *op. cit.*, pp. 96–121.
31. Addison Steele, quoted in James Doyle, *The Male Experience* (Dubuque, Iowa: W. C. Brown, 1983), p. 178.
32. Paul D. Cleary, "Gender Differences in Stress-Related Disorders," in Barnett et al., *op. cit.*, pp. 39–74.
33. Deborah Belle, "Gender Differences in the Social Moderators of Stress," in Barnett et al., *op. cit.*, pp. 257–277.
34. Herbert Goldberg, *The Hazards of Being Male* (New York: New American Library, 1976), p. 126.
35. Carol S. Aneshensel and Leonard I. Pearlin, "Structural Contexts of Sex Differences in Stress," in Barnett et al., *op. cit.*, pp. 75–95.
36. Goldberg, *op. cit.*, p. 95.
37. "Our Endless Pursuit of Happiness," *U.S. News and World Report* (August 10, 1981):35.
38. Lotte Bailyn, "Accommodation of Work to Career," in Skolnick and Skolnick, *op. cit.*, p. 568.
39. Harris, *op. cit.*
40. Shawn Hartley Hancock, "For Love, Not Money," *Executive Female* (May–June 1987):36–37.
41. Harris, *op. cit.*; Gallup Poll quoted in "Facts and Figures," *Training* 26 (1989):74.
42. Shank, *op. cit.*
43. William H. Chafe, "Looking Backward in Order to Look Forward," in Juanite Kreps, ed., *Women and the American Economy* (Englewood Cliffs, N.J.: Prentice-Hall, 1976), p. 9.
44. *Ibid.*
45. *Ibid.*, pp. 15–16.
46. Ralph Smith, "The Movement of Women into the Labor Force," in Ralph Smith, ed., *The Subtle Revolution: Women at Work* (Washington, D.C.: The Urban Institute, 1979), p. 3.
47. *Ibid.*, p. 8.
48. U.S. Bureau of the Census, Bureau of Labor Statistics, *Current Population Reports,* Series P-50, Bulletin 2096 (Washington, D.C.: U.S. Government Printing Office, 1987).

49. Hancock, *op. cit.;* Myra Marx Feree, "She Works Hard for a Living: Gender and Class on the Job," in Beth Hess and Myra Marx Feree, eds., *Analyzing Gender: A Handbook of Social Science Research* (Beverly Hills, Calif.: Sage, 1987), p. 324.

50. Chafe, *op. cit.,* p. 25.

51. Smith, *op. cit.,* p. 8.

52. U.S. Department of Labor, Bureau of Labor Statistics, "Number of Workers with Earnings and Median Earnings, by Occupation of Longest Job Held and Sex," Table 653, *Statistical Abstract of the United States* (Washington, D.C.: U.S. Government Printing Office, January 1988).

53. U.S. Department of Labor, Bureau of Labor Statistics, "Full-Time Wage and Salary Workers; Number and Median Weekly Earnings by Selected Characteristics, 1983–1987," Table 651, in *Statistical Abstract of the United States, op. cit.*

54. Nancy S. Barret, "Women in the Job Market: Occupations, Earnings and Career Opportunities," in Smith, *op. cit.,* p. 32.

55. Elizabeth Almquist and Juanita Wehrle-Einhorn, "The Doubly Disadvantaged: Minority Women in the Labor Force," in A. Stromberg and S. Harkness, eds., *Women Working: Theories and Facts in Perspective* (Palo Alto, Calif.: Mayfield, 1978), pp. 63–88.

56. Cynthia Costello, "Women's Work in the Office," *Social Science Journal* 21 (1984):116–119.

57. Donald J. Treiman and Patricia A. Roos, "Sex and Earnings in Industrial Society: A Nine-Nation Comparison," *American Journal of Sociology* 89, no. 3 (1983):612–650.

58. Paula England and Lori McCreary, "Gender Inequality in Paid Employment," in Hess and Feree, *op. cit.,* pp. 286–321.

59. Penelope Ciancanelli and Bettina Berch, "Gender and the GNP," in Hess and Feree, *op. cit.,* pp. 244–266.

60. Marianne Ferber and Joe Spaeth, "Work Characteristics and the Male-Female Earnings Gap," *American Economic Review Proceedings* 74 (May 1984):260–264.

61. *Ibid.;* Jacob Mincer and Ofek Haim, "Interrupted Work Careers: Depreciation and Restoration of Human Capital," *Journal of Human Resources* 17 (1983):3–24.; Joe L. Spaeth, "Job Power and Earnings," *American Sociological Review* 50 (1985):603–617.

62. Spaeth, *op. cit.*

63. U.S. Department of Labor, Bureau of Labor Statistics, "Employed Persons by Sex, Race and Occupation: 1986," Table 627, in *Statistical Abstract of the United States, op. cit.*

64. National Research Council, "Women, Work, and Wages: Equal Pay for Jobs of Equal Value" (Washington, D.C.: National Academy Press, 1981), p. 33.

65. *Ibid.,* pp. 54–56.

66. England and McCreary, *op. cit.*

67. National Research Council, *op. cit.,* p. 45.

68. *Ibid.,* pp. 56–58.

69. Sylvia Ann Hewlett, *A Lesser Life: The Myth of Women's Liberation in America* (New York: Warner, 1986).

70. Felicia Schwartz, quoted in Martha Moore and David Proctor, "USA Firms Facing 'New Facts of Life,'" *USA Today* (March 11, 1989):1A

71. Hewlett, *op. cit.,* p. 83.

72. *Ibid.,* p. 89.

73. Heidi Hartmann, "The Family as the Locus of Gender, Class and Political Struggle," *Signs* (Spring 1981):366–394.

74. National Research Council, *op. cit.,* p. 27.

75. Francine D. Blau, *Equal Pay in the Office* (Lexington, Mass.: Lexington Books, 1987), quoted in National Research Council, *op. cit.,* p. 39.

76. National Research Council, *op. cit.,* p. 56–58.

77. England and McCreary, *op. cit.*

78. U.S. Department of Labor, Women's Bureau, "Why Women Work," chart reproduced in Kay Scholzman, "Women and Unemployment: Assessing the Biggest Myths," in Jo Freeman, *Women: A Feminist Perspective,* 2d ed. (Palo Alto, Calif.: Mayfield), pp. 290–312.

79. *Ibid.*

80. *Ibid.*

81. Smith, *op. cit.,* p. 39.

82. Kanter, *op. cit.,* chaps. 6 and 7; Martha S. Hill, "Authority at Work: How Men and Women Differ," in Greg J. Duncan and James N. Morgan, eds., *Five Thousand American Families: Patterns of Economic Progress* (Ann Arbor, Mich.: Institute for Social Research, 1980), pp. 175–188.

83. Kanter, *op. cit.,* p. 99.

84. Sally H. Baker, "Women in Blue-Collar and Service Occupations," in Stromberg and Harkness, *op. cit.,* pp. 352–355.

85. *Ibid.*

86. Heidi Hartmann, "Capitalism, Patriarcy and Job Segregation by Sex," *Signs* 1, no. 2 (1976):137–169.

87. Baker, *op. cit.,* p. 348.

88. U.S. Bureau of the Census, U.S. Department of Labor, "Percentages in Occupations by Sex and Race, 1986," *Statistical Abstract of the United States, 1988* (Washington D.C.: U.S. Government Printing Office, 1988), p. 20.

89. Feree, *op. cit.,* p. 334.

91. Barbara Wertheimer, "Union Is Power: Sketches from Women's Labor History," in Freeman, *op. cit.,* p. 339.

92. *Ibid.*

93. Baker, *op. cit.,* p. 351.

94. Wertheimer, *op. cit.,* p. 339.

95. L. Lamphere, "Bringing the Family to Work; Women's Culture on the Shop Floor," *Feminist Studies,* 11, no. 3, 519–540.

96. Baker, *op. cit.,* p. 368.

97. *Statistical Abstract of the United States, op. cit.*

98. *Ibid.*

99. *Ibid.*

100. Feree, *op. cit.,* p. 329.

101. *Ibid.*

102. *Ibid.*

103. Reynolds Farley, "Trends in Racial Inequalities: Have the Gains of the 1960's Disappeared in the 1970's?" *American Sociological Review* 42 (1977):422–430, adapted in E. Almquist and Juanita Wehrle-Einhorn, "The Doubly Disadvantaged: Minority Women in the Labor Force," in Stromberg and Harkness, *op. cit.,* pp. 439–454.

104. *Ibid.*

105. Mary Eastwood, "Legal Protection against Sex Discrimination," in Stromberg and Harkness, *op. cit.,* p. 109.

106. *Ibid.;* Phyllis A. Wallace, "Legal Protection against Sex Discrimination," in Stromberg and Harkness, *op. cit.,* p. 125.
107. Wallace, *op. cit.;* Eastwood, *op. cit.,* pp. 109–112.
108. Eastwood, *op. cit.*
109. *Ibid.*
110. Wallace, *op. cit.,* p. 135.
111. Eileen Boris and Michael Honey, "Gender, Race and the Policies of the Labor Department, *Monthly Labor Review* III (February 1978):26–36.
112. Women's Bureau, *Thirty-fourth Annual Report of the Secretary of Labor* (Washington, D.C.: U.S. Government Printing Office, 1946).
113. Boris and Honey, *op. cit.,* p. 34.
114. *Ibid.*
115. *Congressional Quarterly* (March 28, 1987):582.
116. Jacquelyn Dowd Hall, "Women's History Goes to Trial," *Signs,* 11, no. 4 (1986):332–347.
117. Donald E. Klingner, "Comparable Worth and Public Personnel Values," *Review of Public Personnel Administration* 9, no. 1 (Fall 1988):45–60; Donald Treiman and Heide Hartmann, eds., *Women, Work and Wages: Equal Pay for Jobs of Equal Value* (Washington, D.C.: National Academy Press, 1981).
118. Nina Rothchild and Bonnie Watkins, "Pay Equity in Minnesota: The Facts Are In," *Review of Public Personnel Administration* 7 (Summer 1987):16–28.
119. *Ibid.*
120. Hewlett, *op. cit.,* p. 77.
121. Ciancanelli and Berch, *op. cit.*
122. Marisa Manley, "Dealing with Sexual Harassment," *Inc.* (May 1987):145–146.
123. Ann McGrath, "The Touchy Issue of Sexual Harassment," *Savvy* (April 1987): 18–19.
124. Patricia Stover and Yvone Gillies, "Sexual Harassment in the Workplace," (Conference report, October 27, 1987, Detroit, Michigan, sponsored by the Michigan Task Force on Sexual Harassment).
125. Peggy Crull, "Hidden Aspects of Women's Work," in Christine Bose and Roslyn Feldberg, eds., *Hidden Aspects of Women's Work* (New York: Praeger, 1987).
126. Tamar Lewin, "The Grueling Struggle for Equality," *New York Times* (November 9, 1986):F12–13.
127. Catherine MacKinnon, *Sexual Harassment of Working Women* (New Haven, Conn.: Yale University Press, 1979).
128. *Ibid.*
129. Crull, *op. cit.*
130. *Ibid.*
131. *Ibid.*
132. *Ibid.,* p. 233.
133. *Ibid.,* p. 227.
134. Paul Engel, "Sexual Harassment: Victims Talk, Management Listens," *Industry Week* (June 24, 1985):57–58.
135. Lin Farley, *Sexual Shakedown: The Sexual Harassment of Women on the Job* (New York: Praeger, 1988).
136. MacKinnon, *op. cit.,* p. 220.
137. Susan Omilian, *Sexual Harassment in Employment* (Wilmette, Ill.: Callaghan, 1987), p. 3.

138. *Ibid.*
139. Associated Press, "Survey Finds That Sexual Harassment Is Widespread," *Detroit Free Press* (November 23, 1988).
140. MacKinnon, *op. cit.*
141. *Ibid.*
142. *Ibid.*, p. 47.
143. *Ibid.*, p. 53.
144. *Ibid.*, p. 55.
145. Amy Saltzman, "Hands Off at the Office," *U.S. News and World Report* (August 1, 1988):56–58.
146. McGrath, *op. cit.*
147. Saltzman, *op. cit.;* Manley, *op. cit.*
148. MacKinnon, *op. cit.*, p. 220.
149. Hewlett, *op. cit.*, p. 93.
150. *Ibid.*, p. 91.
151. *Ibid.*, p. 119.
152. *Ibid.*, p. 129.
153. *Ibid.*
154. Michigan Women's Commission, *Women's Political Issues* (Lansing: Michigan Department of Management and Budget, 1988).
155. *Ibid.*
156. *Ibid.*
157. Gail Lapidus, "Occupational Segregation and Public Policy: A Comparative Analysis of American and Soviet Patterns," in Martha Blaxall and Barbara Regan, eds., *Women and the Workplace* (Chicago: University of Chicago Press, 1976), p. 121.
158. Hartmann 1976, *op. cit.*
159. U.S. Bureau of the Census, "Percentages of Occupations," *op. cit.*

Chapter 12

The Polling Place: Law, the Women's and Men's Movements, Political Elites, and Bloc Voting

The legal and political institutions of this country have been fortresses of tradition. Because laws are made by politicians and few women have been able to exercise power, the political and legal systems have historically resisted changes that would give women and minorities more rights. The laws of the land have usually discriminated against both. Only recently, for example, have women gained legal protection guaranteeing them things such as credit and equal employment opportunity, but these new laws are only as good as their enforcement.

The women's movement has attempted to change the position of women by making people aware that women are treated as second-class citizens and by aiming for a wide variety of social changes based on changes in values. People in the movement have also attempted to initiate legal change through various kinds of political action. Yet women have not joined political elites in large numbers and are still divided on the issues of concern and solutions to their problems; a strong voting bloc has not yet emerged. Men have responded to the concerns of women and to changing laws with their own movement.

In this chapter we will examine the positions of men and women under the law, the history and current status of the women's and men's movements, and the role of men and women in the political process.

WOMEN, MEN, AND THE LAW

We have examined many of the specific laws dealing with women's issues in previous chapters. In this section we will summarize legal changes in many of these disparate areas in the sense that these changes have been initiated by changes in views of women. We will also examine how these laws have influenced legal theory as it deals with male-female differences. We will deal more with women than with men because laws affecting gender-role behavior have usually limited the behavior of women. However, when unequal treatment under the law seems to exist or when men's behavior seems to be affected, we will point this out as well.

Women's legal status in the United States has been strongly influenced by the English common law doctrine of *coverture.* Under this doctrine, a married woman lost a separate legal identity. According to the legal thought of the time, "the wife and husband are one and that one is the husband." Among other things, the wife lost legal title to her own property and the ability to execute contracts. As most women were assumed to marry and in fact 95 percent did, the doctrine of coverture effectively removed the legal identity of most women in the United States. In addition, under coverture, a husband had the right to restrain, punish, and rape his wife. Wives had little opportunity to divorce, and husbands usually got guardianship of the children.[1]

The enactment of the Married Women's Property Act in 1873 removed many of these restrictions. However, in many researchers' opinion, this legislation did not really increase women's control over property or improve their legal status.[2]

Commonly held beliefs about the separate spheres of men and women furnished the justification for many of the sex-based laws that followed. For example, in *Bradwell v. Illinois* (1873) the Supreme Court held that admission to the legal profession could be restricted for women because "civil law as well as nature herself has always recognized a wide difference in the respective spheres and destinies of man and women."[3] Yet the private sphere, the family, was seen as a place where the law did not intrude. Marriage was not viewed in the same way as other contracts, and husbands had spousal immunity from criminal and civil law in most cases.[4]

Family Law

Many vestiges of coverture remained in the common law assumptions that underlaid laws that dealt with the family in the American legal system. As we saw above, until recently a number of states restricted women's right to make contracts or engage in business without their husbands' consent. The assumption was that the husband was the head of the household. As such, he was supposed to furnish support to his wife, but he could determine the level of support. The wife was expected to give him her company and her service. A married woman had to take as her legal domicile that of her husband (this was important in property and tuition cases). Although she no longer has to take her husband's name (except in Hawaii), many state laws are based on the presumption that she will, and if, for example, she wishes to have a driver's license in her maiden name, she may have to go through a legal name change.

The ability to obtain divorce was limited for women in the early days of the country. They were expected to stay married even when their husbands were cruel or deserted them. Gradually, however, divorce laws were reformed, and by 1970 most states had some version of a no-fault divorce law. Such laws allow a marriage to be declared "irretrievably broken," and neither spouse is considered officially guilty. However, the desire for equal treat-ment in divorce has often worked to women's disadvantage. Lenore Weitzman documents the fact that women's income falls 73 percent after divorce while that of men rises 41 percent.[5] Alimony, if it is awarded at all, is usually limited to a few years of rehabilitation, and child support is often inadequate and seldom paid in full. In a similar fashion, child custody is more often awarded to fathers than it was before and women are also liable for child support payments.[6]

Laws Dealing with Sexuality and Sexual Violence

As we have seen in looking at reproductive and abortion laws, the legal sys-tem regulates female sexuality and reproduction in accordance with ideology about gender and sexuality. Many laws that apply differentially to men and women relate to the image of women as frail and theoretically sexually pure. Thus, many states have laws that prohibit using obscene language in the pres-ence of women, and two states make it a crime to impugn the chastity of a woman.[7] Some states require only the man to get a venereal disease test for a marriage license.[8] Statutory rape laws make it a crime for an adult male to have sexual intercourse with a female under a certain age; however, no such law applies to an adult female and an underage male.

Many people believe that opposition to legal abortion is also based on the good-bad female dichotomy. The fact that state laws prohibiting legal abortion have often been linked to state laws prohibiting the dissemination of informa-tion about contraception seems to show a punitive intent rather than a concern for the fetus: "Be good, or else!" It has also been pointed out that many people who believe that the fetus is a person at conception and that abortion is thus murder are still willing to permit abortion for rape or incest. Feminists state that this inconsistency seems to say that if a good girl gets into trouble by force, abortion (murder?) is acceptable, but if a bad girl gets pregnant willing-ly, the rules should be strictly enforced. The attempt to cut off money for Medicaid abortions for poor women also, some say, shows not only a class bias but a feeling that poor women are "bad" and thus should not be able to get an abortion. Obviously, these are extreme views and many people oppose abortion for religious or philosophical reasons, but it is interesting to look at these views and the way they reflect gender-role stereotypes in our culture.

The same good girl–bad girl ideology and mixed feelings about female sex-uality have influenced legal views about rape. As one feminist says, the sys-tem "assumed female passivity, victimization and masochism."[9] Women were and often still are assumed to want to be raped and to lie about being raped. Most states in the past required a witness or proof of strong resistance (injuries) to establish that a rape had occurred. Any evidence of a past sexual history could discredit a woman's claim of having been raped. It was impossi-ble to claim rape by a spouse.

With the advent of the women's movement and heightened awareness about the underlying assumptions in rape trials, many states passed new rape legislation. Between 1976 and 1979 thirty-two states changed their sex offense laws. Some of the changes were minor, but some were major structural changes. An important change was "rape shield laws" that kept the victim's past sexual history out of deliberations on a case. Other important changes were defining rape in sex-neutral terms, including acts other than intercourse; allowing husbands to be charged; and mandatory counseling for rapists.[10]

In wife abuse cases, similar feelings about women's passivity and masochism seem to have existed along with the Western cultural tradition that a man should enjoy privacy in his home and should dominate his wife and children. Remember that early U.S. law condoned beating a wife with a stick as long as the stick was no thicker than a man's thumb. Laypersons and legal officials were always reluctant to intervene in family disputes, and witnesses were necessary to make assault charges stick.[11]

The women's movement exposed many of these assumptions, and many states and localities have reformed their laws. One of the most promising trends is to put the abuser immediately in jail. In localities where this has become the practice, repeat domestic violence calls have dropped significantly.

Work Laws and Protective Legislation

We have already reviewed the equal employment opportunity laws (Chapter 11). Here we will deal more with the general theory underlying the approaches to equal opportunity in the workplace.

For many years courts used the belief that women's place is in the home to deny women access to various occupations. In 1873 the Supreme Court denied the right of Myra Bradwell to practice law in Illinois, saying,

> The natural and proper timidity and delicacy which belongs to the female sex evidently unfits it for many of the occupations of civil life. The constitution of the family organization, which is founded to the divine ordinance, as well as in the nature of things indicates the domestic sphere as that which properly belongs to the domain and functions of womanhood. . . . It is true that many women are unmarried . . . but these are exceptions to the general rule. The paramount destiny and mission of woman are to fulfill the noble and benign offices of wife and mother.[12]

As part of the rationale for identifying women as a special group with a defined social role, the courts did pass special legislation to protect them in the workplace. Some of this legislation was an ill-disguised attempt to keep women out of specific occupations, but other laws did seem to be in women's interests at the time. Such legislation usually restricted the number of hours they could work and the amount of weight they could lift and sometimes provided for special rest periods. One case in particular, *Mueller v. Oregon*, restricted women's employment to ten hours a day in "factories, laundries or other `mechanical establishments' " and was used as a precedent to support the idea that sex is a valid reason for differences in treatment. It was cited in such diverse instances as excluding women from juries and state-supported colleges and from getting licenses for certain occupations.[13]

Feminists hoped to use the Fourteenth Amendment, which extended equal treatment under the law, to all citizens to support their contention that they should not be deprived of their civil rights by being treated differently. However, the Supreme Court held that only race had been in the minds of the legislators when the Fourteenth Amendment was passed and that differential treatment for women was still permissible. Laws and issues dealing with racial issues were subject to "strict scrutiny," while those dealing with women were subject to the lesser standard of scrutiny on a "rational basis."[14] This difference was very important. Cases subject to strict scrutiny were automatically and carefully reviewed by the courts. It was much more likely in these instances that the courts would find that discrimination had occurred.

The constitutionality of protective laws was not questioned until the passage of the Equal Pay Act of 1963 and the Civil Rights Act (Title VII) of 1964 (Chapter 11). The real turning point in views about women as a class came in 1971, when the Court held in *Reed v. Reed* that Idaho could not show preference to males in the appointment of administrators of estates. In a case two years later, eight members of the Supreme Court found unconstitutional a law that provided dependent allowances for men in the armed services with no proof of the economic dependence of their wives but permitted such allowances for women soldiers only if they could show that their husbands were dependent on them for support. Four of the justices applied the doctrine of strict scrutiny and said:

> There can be no doubt that our Nation has had a long and unfortunate history of sex discrimination. Traditionally, such discrimination was rationalized by an attitude of "romantic paternalism" which in practical effect, put women not on a pedestal, but in a cage. . . .
>
> Moreover, since sex like race and national origin, is an immutable characteristic determined solely by the accident of birth, the imposition of special disabilities upon members of a particular sex because of their sex would seem to violate the basic concept of our system that legal burdens should bear some relationship to individual responsibilities. . . .[15]

In subsequent cases the Court applied a "strict rational basis" standard, and in 1976 it said it would apply stricter "intermediate scrutiny" to cases involving women. The ideology also shifted to a view that family responsibilities were no longer a reason to treat women differently under the law, particularly when such differential treatment enforced economic dependence.

Gender Neutrality or Special Circumstances: A Theoretical Debate

Feminists have been divided about whether the legal position of "special circumstances" aided women more than did laws which were simply gender-neutral. In 1974, the Supreme Court took the position that when women are not "similarly situated" and if the difference in situation is to their disadvantage, they should be given special protection under the law. In 1974, in *Schlesinger v. Ballard*, the Court allowed female naval officers more time to attain promotion before mandatory discharge on the grounds that women were not allowed in combat and most sea duty so that it would take them longer to compile favorable service records. Therefore they were not "similarly situated."[16] To some degree this was a return to the days of protective legislation, but some feminists believed these special circumstances laws aided women.

Other feminists pressed for only gender-neutral laws, believing they would win more support for legal change with this strategy. Under gender neutrality, women gained equal access to benefits under military, Social Security, welfare, and worker's compensation programs. However, cases involving gender neutrality violations or sex discrimination began to be dominated by males and were focused on male rights. Women lost many of the benefits they had gained under protective legislation.[17]

A landmark case in sex discrimination was the celebrated case in which Allan Bakke, a 38-year-old white engineer, sued the University of California's medical school at Davis, charging reverse discrimination and saying that less-well-qualified minority persons were admitted as students when he was not. The Supreme Court decision in that case was assumed to have great significance, as it was the first time the Court had attempted to define the limits of affirmative action for minorities or women. The decision was somewhat ambiguous. The Court held that "quotas" (setting aside places for a certain number of minorities) were unacceptable but found in a five-to-four vote that race may be considered as one factor in a university's admission policy. Bakke was granted admission to the medical school.

Minorities and women were pleased with the decision that it is illegal to use quotas in the process of admission, as these quotas are often used to limit rather than encourage admission. However, the other parts of the decision were not as favorable to affirmative action. The fact that the decision was based on Title VI of the Civil Rights Act of 1964 rather than on the Constitution was also seen to dilute the decision, and the Court was careful to make its decision applicable only to universities, not to businesses. Future cases will decide the real impact of the Bakke decision and determine whether the Court's rather tenuous commitment to affirmative action will extend to sex discrimination and to business.[18]

Because of decisions like this, most feminists began disagreeing with the gender-neutral approach and said that the "equal employment cases in the 1970's simply required the Court to treat women like men. Now the legal system must deal with the `hard issues'—that is, the cases in which women are not like men."[19] They had reproductive and biological issues in mind, but also areas such as comparable worth.[20]

Feminists are still split about whether the equal treatment with gender neutrality approach or the special situation approach to the law is the correct one. In addition, they are split about whether to fight for consolidation of the gains they have made and ward off right-wing erosion of legal gains in the areas of affirmative action and reproduction or whether to concentrate on fighting in even more difficult areas such as comparable worth legislation. Some feminists even wonder whether it is worth trying to use the law to obtain change; they believe it is too steeped in male bias and that other avenues of social change might provide better results.

The Proposed Equal Rights Amendment

While we get ahead of our story to some degree by discussing the Equal Rights Amendment before talking about the women's movement itself, it is important to see the Equal Rights Amendment in the context of other legislation.

Many states have adopted equal rights laws, but because of the remaining inequalities, various discrepancies in state laws, and the possibility of existing legislation being reversed, women have pushed for an Equal Rights Amendment (ERA) to the Constitution that will guarantee all groups their rights. Although there has been a lot of misunderstanding about what the ERA actually says, the proposed amendment simply reads, "Equality of rights under the law shall not be denied or abridged by the United States or any State on account of sex."[21]

The ERA was needed to equalize laws throughout the country and to put the rights of women in constitutional form. In 1979, for example, there were still eight states where a woman did not have clear title to property in her name.[22] The push for repeal of prochoice legislation and affirmative action laws in the conservative 1980s showed even more clearly how fragile the legislation protecting women was and how much women needed a constitutional amendment to ensure their rights.

Although the Equal Rights Amendment was introduced in Congress in 1923, it did not pass both houses until March 22, 1972. After that it faced the long fight to be ratified in three-fifths of the states. Polls in 1975 showed that the majority of men and women were in favor of the amendment, and ratification looked relatively assured in 1978, when all but three of the states needed had ratified. The amendment's ratification had failed by only two to three votes in several states, and it was hoped that it would pass in the next session of their legislatures. However, opponents of the ERA lobbied heavily against it and took advantage of the legislative process to bottle it up in committee in several states.[23]

Far-right groups took advantage of the confusion about the amendment to claim that it would destroy the family, encourage homosexuality (no discrimination by "sex"), cause women to be drafted, and give rise to coed bathrooms. All these claims were totally false or greatly exaggerated. The right to privacy protects separate male and female bathrooms and dressing facilities, women can be drafted now if the President chooses, and homosexuality has nothing to do with equal protection by sex under the law. Married women would lose some special privileges, such as automatic preference in child custody and

support cases, but they would gain other benefits in the sense that their contribution to a marriage as a homemaker would be recognized in a divorce settle-
ment. Men would also gain, as protective laws that really *do* protect would be
extended to them. Of course, this amendment would apply to state and federal situations. Nothing in the private realm would be affected.[24] The real effect
of the law would be to codify existing legislation and remove inequalities
between the states; any impact it had would be subject to the way it was
enforced.

As the political climate of the country changed with the resurgence of far-
right groups and the election of Ronald Reagan as President, prospects for the
passage of the ERA grew dim. Reagan ran on a conservative platform that dis-
avowed support for the ERA and promised support for profamily legislation
and antiabortion laws. In the election many liberal members of Congress lost
their seats. Most feminists felt that there was little chance of getting the ERA
ratified even after the time limit was extended to June 1982. The National
Organization for Women (NOW) continued to concentrate its efforts on passing the amendment, however, and held a "Last March for the ERA" in
Washington in the fall of 1981 in a last-ditch effort to get it passed before the
deadline. The amendment was still three states short of ratification when the
deadline expired. The irony was that a June 1981 *Time* magazine poll reported
that 61 percent of the population was in favor of the ERA. A Washington-ABC
poll at about the same time confirmed that finding.[25]

Current Issues of Concern to Women

Child Care.   One of the most important political issues for the 1990s is child
care. In a Michigan Women's Commission survey of working women which
asked them to prioritize twenty-six different issues of concern, child care was
overwhelmingly the number one concern.[26] Approximately 10 million
American children under age 6 have employed mothers, but there are only
900,000 center-based slots for these children and there is a shrinking supply of
informal child-care providers. The quality and cost of available child care is
also a concern. It costs an average of $3,000 a year for one child's full-time
care, and many working parents, especially single mothers, cannot afford that.

The problem of inadequate child care will continue. In 1990, 65 percent of
all workers entering the work force were women and 85 percent of them were
of childbearing age. Business has done little to alleviate the child-care problem. In 1986, out of 6 million U.S. businesses of all sizes, only 3,000 supported
the child-care needs of their employees in any way. Government has also been
unresponsive to the need, in spite of a recent Harris Poll in which 73 percent
of the respondents indicated that they would be willing to increase their taxes
to pay for child care.[27]

Several bills were introduced in 1989 which dealt with various aspects of
the child-care problem. Each took a slightly different approach. The Act for
Better Child Care (ABC) wanted to establish federal-state-private partnerships
which essentially would provide new funds to make child care more afford-

able. It also had provisions regulating the quality of care. The Latchkey Bill would have allowed federal funds to be used for the start-up and operational expenses of programs as well as for information and referral.[28] However, Congress adjourned before the end of 1989 without passing either one. This is one of the few industrialized nations not to realize the importance of quality child care. Almost all European nations have state-subsidized and regulated systems of care for preschoolers as well as after-school care.

Family Leave.   Another issue important to women is family and medical leave. As we have seen above, the United States is the only industrialized nation without a policy on such leave. Over a hundred industrialized nations have family leave policies, most of which offer paid leave. France, for example, just passed legislation mandating fourteen weeks paid maternity leave. While some businesses in the United States offer leave for childbirth, most do not do so for adoption or care of a seriously ill child or parent.[29]

A 1989 bill introduced into the House of Representatives, the Family and Medical Leave Act, required all employers with fifty or more employees to offer ten weeks of family leave over a two-year period for birth or adoption or the care of an ill child or parent. The employee would have to have been employed at least one year, twenty hours or more a week, to take advantage of such a leave. The bill also provided up to fifteen weeks of medical leave for an employee's own disabling health condition. All leaves would be unpaid, but jobs would be guaranteed.[30] In July 1990, President Bush vetoed this bill, saying that the costs to business would be too high.

Divorce Laws.   Another major issue which will have to be addressed is reform in divorce settlements. As we have seen, no-fault divorce laws work in favor of men. With the dramatic reduction in income after divorce, almost 50 percent of divorced women have to go on welfare and many are able to support their families only at a level slightly above the poverty line.[31] The recognition of women's contribution to the family and unequal potential earnings is important in future laws. Collecting allocated child support is also an essential part of reform in this area. Many states have passed statutes mandating collection of support by attaching the delinquent father's paycheck. Some sort of federal statute is badly needed so that fathers cannot simply move to states without such laws to escape their obligations.

Welfare Reform.   In 1989 two bills were introduced dealing with welfare reform. The first, House Bill 1720, would replace the existing AFDC program with a family support plan. It would create or amend programs for work and training, child care, transportation and other work-related expenses, and health care. One program specifically addresses teen parents and their needs.[32] House Bill 5304 is known as the Work Incentive Welfare Reduction Act. It attempts to give work incentives to welfare recipients by providing forty months of medical assistance through Medicaid to those who find employment but would not get benefits and child-care subsidies for up to forty months.[33] As this book goes to press, these bills are still being debated.

Other Issues.   Other issues of concern to women are raising the federal minimum wage and pay equity programs such as comparable worth legislation, which was discussed in Chapter 11.

One of the major holding actions for women involves abortion. As we saw in Chapter 10 and in the section on judicial decisions in this chapter, attempts are being made to outlaw abortion by a constitutional amendment, by legislation, and by overturning the *Roe v. Wade* decision which made it legal nationwide. In 1989, a Supreme Court decision gave the states limited rights to restrict abortion, and several states immediately restricted the use of public funds or public facilities. Other pending Supreme Court cases focus on state laws requiring that one or both parents be notified before a minor gets an abortion. A recent Louisiana law prohibits abortion except under conditions of the pregnancy resulting from rape or incest and these are strictly defined. As several of these laws are extremely restrictive and controversial, and they are likely to be heard by an increasingly conservative Supreme Court in the near future, there were many threats to women's access to legal abortion at the beginning of the 1990s.

THE WOMEN'S MOVEMENT

Over the years many of my students in gender-role classes have told me that they do not know how the women's movement originated, what its aims were, and how it has developed and changed. Because that knowledge is so important to an understanding of gender-related political movements, I have included here a brief review of the historical events leading up to the current women's movement.

The real beginning of the feminist movement probably coincided with the growing emphasis on individual rights and democratic philosophy in the 1800s. While women were not specifically included in the ideal of human rights for men (males), the whole principle of individual dignity and freedom encouraged women's desire to free themselves from laws that made them little more than property and left them subject to men's control. Whether they fought for reform of the marriage laws, fought for equal educational facilities, or emphasized the importance of suffrage as a means and expression of equality, the trend of thought behind the shades of feminist opinion was the democratic ideology.[34]

The general social reform movement of the early 1800s led women to fight for more education. In 1833, Oberlin College became the first college in the United States to admit both men and women; others followed suit, and all-women's colleges were also founded. However, the abolition movement of the 1830s was the real birthplace of the political aspect of the women's movement. Women such as the Grimkés and Lucy Stone, who fought for abolition, found that they were attacked for speaking in public and were excluded from many men's abolitionist groups. As the abolitionist movement expanded, it included women such as Lucretia Mott and Elizabeth Cady Stanton, who were delegates to a world antislavery convention in London in 1840. Their exclusion from real participation in that convention convinced these women that it was important to achieve women's rights as well as black rights.

They continued to work for women's property and family rights after returning from London, and in 1848 they advertised that a Woman's Rights Convention would be held in Seneca, New York. Three hundred women and men attended this first meeting, and the conference developed a list of twelve resolutions that were very similar in some parts to the Declaration of Independence, including a resolution that women should secure to themselves "their sacred right to the elective franchise." However, at that time most of the delegates were more interested in gaining the right to control their own property and wages and getting custody of their children when they divorced. After 1848 and until the beginning of the Civil War, women's rights conventions were held every year.

When the Civil War began, women's rights supporters were urged to give up their struggle, support the war effort, and continue to push for the abolition of slavery. They did so, assuming that they would be included in the Fourteenth and Fifteenth amendments, which secured the rights, privileges, and immunities of citizens for black men. However, many businessmen who wanted the black vote because they believed it would ensure Republican victories in the South saw no gain in giving women the vote. In fact, they were afraid that adding women's rights to the Constitution would jeopardize these amendments. Thus, as the Fourteenth and Fifteenth amendments to the Constitution were interpreted, they guaranteed only the civil rights of men.

Women were disappointed and disillusioned, but in 1869 they formed the Women's American Suffrage Association, which attempted to push for women's right to vote. This association eschewed other women's issues in an attempt to make its activities respectable. At approximately the same time Susan B. Anthony and Elizabeth Cady Stanton organized the National Women's Suffrage Association, which pushed for all kinds of women's rights and saw the vote only as a means of achieving those rights. During this period the temperance movement also attracted large numbers of women, including suffragists, who believed that restricting alcohol would improve their status vis-à-vis drunken or deserting husbands. Although the two suffrage organizations and the temperance movement coexisted for twenty years, the American Suffrage Association, with its limited aim of working only for the vote, began to attract more people. In 1890 the two suffrage organizations merged to form the National American Women's Suffrage Association (NAWSA), with the single aim of gaining the vote for women.

Around 1900 a new generation of suffragists became the leaders of the organization, including Carrie Chapman Catt, who succeeded Susan Anthony as president. Gradual progress was made as a few Western states gave the vote to women, but the major impetus to the campaign for suffrage came when Alice Paul, a young militant, formed the Congressional Union, a small radical group, to campaign for federal women's suffrage. This group organized parades and hunger strikes to call attention to its cause, and many of its members were vilified and even jailed for their efforts.[35]

Before women got the vote in 1920, they had organized 56 referendum campaigns, 480 campaigns at state constitutional conventions for suffrage, 277 campaigns to include suffrage in state party programs, 30 campaigns to get women's suffrage into national party programs, and 19 campaigns to get the Nineteenth Amendment through Congress.[36] The **Nineteenth Amendment**, or Women's Suffrage Amendment (also known as the Anthony Amendment), was introduced into every session of Congress from 1878 on and was finally ratified on August 2, 1920.

Unfortunately, so much energy had gone into winning the vote that the women's movement had little energy left for other issues. During the 1920s, the country was involved in enjoying itself as the war came to an end; in the 1930s, it was occupied with getting out of the great depression; and by the 1940s, it was in another war. After the war, women were urged to return to home and hearth.

As a result of their work experience during World War II, women briefly renewed the fight for equal rights during the Progressive party campaign of 1948, but they were overcome by the conservative advocates of a "return to normalcy."[37] However, by 1960, 36 percent of all women were in the work force and were concerned about their wages and treatment. It took the civil rights movements of the early 1960s to show them that they, as well as blacks, needed to fight for their rights. Many women gained political experience in the civil rights movement and the antiwar movement that followed in the mid-1960s and were thus better equipped to advance the feminist cause. Women began to vote in greater numbers from the 1960s on, and they were voting at roughly the same rates as men by 1976. The voting record of black women was almost equal to that of black men in the presidential elections of 1964, 1968, and 1972.[38]

The Current Movement

In 1963 Betty Friedan published *The Feminine Mystique,* an indictment of the "happy homemaker" role. This book gave voice to women's discontent, and many people feel that its publication marked the beginning of the contemporary women's movement.[39] Betty Friedan, Martha Griffiths, and others organized the National Organization for Women (NOW) in 1966. The early organizers of NOW tended to be older, white, middle-class, college-educated women. While NOW was seen as radical, its style was actually somewhat conservative, and it stressed working through established legislative channels to achieve rights for women. Other women's groups formed that also emphasized working through the establishment to achieve change. Groups such as the National Women's Political Caucus, the Women's Equity Action League, Federally Employed Women, and many different organizations of professional women were active. All these groups had formal organizations with elected officers.[40]

At the same time another branch of the women's movement was forming among younger women. As early as 1964 Rudy Robinson presented to a Student Non-Violent Coordinating Committee (SNCC) conference a paper in which she protested the inferior status accorded women within that organization. These younger, more radical women had become politicized in the civil rights and antiwar movements and in student demonstrations. In all these new left movements, women's liberation had taken hold and women objected to being used only as envelope stuffers and sexual partners while the men made major decisions and dominated meetings. Stokely Carmichael added fuel to their discontent with his infamous statement, "The only position for women in SNCC is prone."[41]

Women in the new left attempted to incorporate feminist ideas into the programs of their various organizations, but their task was not easy. Women who demanded at the 1966 Students for a Democratic Society (SDS) national convention that the organization adopt a plank supporting women's rights were pelted with tomatoes and expelled from the convention. In other new left organizations, women were manipulated into giving up their stand for women's rights.[42]

Eventually, women in the new left splintered into two major factions: **politicos**, who believed that the political issues of their groups should come before women's rights, and **feminists**, who favored an independent women's movement.[43] The feminists grew more discontented with the position of the new left on women's issues, and the antagonism between the two groups came to a head in January 1969 at the counterinaugural demonstration in Washington organized by Mobilization for Peace. Men in the audience responded to a very mild feminist speech by booing the speaker and yelling remarks such as, "Take her off the stage and fuck her." The women in the audience were outraged, and many who had been hesitating about their political affiliation were convinced that they needed an independent women's movement.[44]

Although the new left men included some women's rights issues in later platforms, many feminist women left the male-dominated movement to form loosely structured independent women's groups. These groups were different in nature and intent from the older, strictly organized NOW. Their membership not only was younger but generally espoused a much more radical philosophy.

Liberal versus Radical Feminism

The earlier feminists who were concentrated in NOW and similar organizations perceived sexism as being "based on a `society' or the `system' which created `sex role stereotypes' oppressing both men and women equally."[45] **Radical feminists** disliked this approach because they believed that it had three major weaknesses: (1) It did not stress the fact men were the true political enemy, (2) it made it look as though women were brainwashed ("socialized") into an inferior position rather than forced into it by the superior power—that is, it stressed the stereotypes created by institutions rather than domination by men, and (3) it was **ethnocentric** and applied mainly to middle- and upper-class women.

The radical feminists believed in addition that women's issues were part of a general revolutionary struggle, that one could not change the system within the established economic and political system and its institutions. Women had to exclude men from their movement, they thought, because they gained nothing by cooperation with their oppressors.

Yet these women did not have a specific program for changing society. They believed that they could effect radical change on an individual grass roots basis by forming small, personal "rap groups" for "consciousness raising." Women would be drawn into these groups on the basis of their personal experiences with sexism and would transform those experiences into a political awareness of sexism. "The revolutionary transformation of society would follow as more and more women had their consciousness raised and rejected the ideological and institutional bases of sexism."[46] The radical feminists used other techniques as well: street theater, new language, demonstrations (the famous "bra burnings," where uncomfortable clothes were rejected and thrown into trash cans before the Miss America pageant of 1968), and an emphasis on political lesbianism.

However, this younger branch of the movement had tough going. At first the media ridiculed it, and then some of its issues were incorporated in more mainstream liberal feminist philosophy. The more conservative organizations became the voice of the women's liberation movement to the outside world.[47]

The new left further isolated the radical feminists by excluding them (or they excluded themselves) from the general leftist movement or by attempting to use radical feminist groups for its own ends. At one point, the Young Socialist Alliance tried to infiltrate the radical feminist movement with the idea of making socialist converts. While they were expelled after a bitter conflict, the confrontation further weakened the radical feminists.[48]

Another major crisis occurred over the role of lesbians in the movement. Lesbians within the movement espoused the idea that lesbianism is the feminist ideal. They believed that lesbian women typify the independence needed by all women, as they provide their own support, take care of their own affairs, and do not depend on men in any way. The extreme of this view was that one was not really a feminist unless one was a lesbian.

Straight women were not eager to be identified with lesbianism and felt that lesbian rhetoric added a difficult and unacceptable value system to the women's rights philosophy. Many straight women dropped out of these radical groups, and many joined NOW or rejoined the new left. Eventually, gay women predominated in the rap groups by about four to one, and the focus changed from recruiting new members to building a women's culture for those who remained.[49]

The National Organization for Women

In the meantime, the movement of many of these radical women into NOW and the pressure from the rap groups caused NOW to move in a more radical direction in the mid-1970s.[50] Eventually the ideology of NOW focused on a single issue: the passage of the proposed Equal Rights Amendment. As rightist groups arose that fought abortion, busing, and gay rights along with the

ERA, the amendment became symbolic of the continuation of the movement for equal rights for women. When the potential amendment still lacked three states for ratification a year after the March 22, 1979, deadline, NOW decided to concentrate its efforts on the passage of the ERA. Freeman and Carden have pointed out that with this decision NOW became an interest group rather than a social movement. It had developed a single-issue focus, as had the early suffrage movement, that would make it difficult to consider other issues in the future.[51]

When the ERA deadline expired in July 1982 three states short of ratification, the women's groups which had pushed so hard for it turned to the ballot box to unseat ERA opponents and gain other goals of the women's movement. The gender gap in voting seemed to offer an opportunity to appeal to women voters who would elect progressive candidates.[52]

Feminists believed that to obtain the goals of the women's movement, new voters had to be registered, especially women who might be sympathetic to women candidates and women's economic issues. NOW was joined by groups such as the American Association of University Women, the League of Women Voters, and the national Federation of Business and Professional Women's Clubs in the attempt to register voters.[53] Among other strategies, these organizations agreed on a national get-out-the-vote day the last Saturday before the 1982 elections. Their motto was "It's a man's world unless women vote!"[54] The gender gap which resulted in the 1982 elections showed the power of the women's vote.

In June 1983 the League of Women Voters Education Fund established the Women's Vote Project in order to use their local affiliates to register their own members and others who had not previously voted. They set a goal of registering 1.5 million new women voters by the 1984 election, especially minorities, single heads of households, the poor, and younger women. Added to the old motto was a new one: "Register today and take charge of tomorrow."

By the election date, seventy-six organizations were participating and the project had exceeded by 300,000 its goal of registering 1.5 million. Women also broke all records for casting ballots in 1984.[55]

Johanna Mendelson, who has researched the Women's Vote Project, points out that it was important because of its timing. The project unified women's groups at a time when divisive issues were fragmenting them. Voter registration was an issue upon which women of all persuasions could agree. There was some evidence that the coalition of women's organizations would continue to operate and exercise influence. As late as the winter of 1986, the Women's Roundtable, which orchestrated the vote project, continued to hold regular meetings that were well attended.[56]

The International Scene

On the international scene, the United Nations had condemned sex discrimination worldwide and had called 1975 the International Women's Year (IWY). One hundred thirty-three countries sent a total of 1,300 delegates to the IWY conference in Mexico City. The aim was to develop a ten-year plan of action to begin a movement for total reform of society's laws and attitudes to enable women to become equal with men.

It was clear from the beginning of the IWY conference that the delegates were not going to listen to the dictates and platform of white, affluent nations. In a confrontation between Chicanas, blacks, and Betty Friedan, it was made clear that while delegates from other nations respected the older leaders of the feminist movement, they wanted to speak for themselves. In spite of many disagreements, a ten-year plan was developed, and the delegates recommended holding another conference in five years to check on its progress.[57]

In the United States, a National Commission on the Observance of Women's Year, with thirty-five private and four congressional members as well as dozens of committees on the state level, developed proposals to implement the plan in this country. Two of the major accomplishments of this commission were an amendment to foreign aid bills by Charles Percy which required that the impact on women be considered when training programs in overseas countries were instituted and an agreement by the Census Bureau that it would target women who had been divorced five years or more to ask about problems involving alimony and child support. The commission also worked toward convening a national conference the following year.[58]

The National Women's Conference was convened at Houston in November 1977. The conference and its proposed program for women's rights came under heavy attack from rightist groups spearheaded by Phyllis Schlafly and 15,000 antiabortion demonstrators. Although these groups were unable to disrupt the feminist gathering as they had hoped, the feminists had other problems. There was increasing concern about the need to deal with the problems of black and working-class women, particularly with issues such as day care and conditions of employment. It was also necessary to deal with the explosive and disruptive issue of lesbian rights. Dealing with these issues was particularly difficult because the incorporation of the demands of blacks and gays into the platform of the feminist movement added fuel to the attack from the right. However, the conference adopted a platform endorsing lesbian rights and a commitment to press for day care and improved conditions of employment, among other concerns of black and working-class women.[59]

There was a world assembly of women at Copenhagen in 1980 and another at Nairobi in 1985. In Nairobi, nearly 17,000 women from 159 nations came together and, according to Betty Friedan, were able to put aside some of the issues that divided them to talk about concrete ways of surviving and earning a living in a man's world. They adopted a resolution endorsing a program of strategies to advance women to equality and called on the U.N. to implement these points and report back to another world assembly of women before the year 2000.[60]

Black Feminism

Black women have not been in the forefront of the current women's movement, and a number of reasons have been advanced to explain their lack of interest and participation. The women's movement arose at the same time that the civil rights and black power movements were gaining prominence. Many black intellectuals and spokespersons believed that sexism would be a racially divisive issue and were concerned about keeping the focus on the liberation of black men. In particular, because black women were often able to find jobs when black men could not and because the myth of black matriarchy was so prevalent, many black leaders believed that push toward liberation by black women would further emasculate black men.[61]

An editorial in *Ebony* paid tribute to the black woman's accomplishments but reminded readers that the "past is behind us, the immediate goal of the Negro woman today should be the establishment of a strong family unit in which the father is the dominant person." The black woman should follow the example of the Jewish mother, "who pushed her husband to success, educated her male children first, and engineered good marriages for her daughters."[62] Many divisions of the black power movement, such as the Black Muslims, emphasized the submission of black women, and black churches stressed biblical teachings about the importance of patriarchy.[63]

Racism among white women was also an issue. Many black women saw all whites—men and women—as sharing the same values and were reluctant to identify with anything affecting the white female.[64] In addition, the early women's liberation movement did not concern itself with many of the issues that were of greatest concern to black women: unemployment and underemployment, poor education in the schools, child care, a minimum wage for service workers, and increased wages at all levels. Willa Mae Hemmons points out that while white women were attempting to enter the labor force in greater numbers, many black women would have been happy to give up their jobs if only they could have counted on the economic support of a black man.[65]

The women's liberation movement made little attempt to recruit blacks until very recent years. After the International Women's Year meeting in Mexico City in 1975, issues of concern to nonwhite women in this country and in the third world were more clearly seen, and many issues such as child care and a minimum wage for domestic service were made priorities at the Houston National Women's Conference. However, NOW's absorption with the passage of the ERA at that time diluted the concern with those issues.

At the same time, black women were coming to see that any women's power movement is important to them. Various female black intellectuals pointed out the necessity of combating sexism as well as racism. Michelle Wallace urged other black women to stop being superwomen and to push for their own aspirations.[66] Shirley Chisholm, one of the first black women legislators, described how she had suffered more discrimination from being a woman than from being a black.[67] Pauline Stone summed up many of the reasons why black women should be involved in eradicating sexism:

1. It would enable black women and men to attain a more accurate and deeper level of understanding. . . . Such problems as the black male unemployment rate, the absence of the black male in the family, the large representation of

black women on welfare, and the high black illegitimacy rate are just a few of the many social problems afflicting blacks that are, in part at least, attributable to the operation of sexism in our society.

2. Elimination of sexism on the interpersonal level within black culture would result in . . . increasing the general pool of black abilities.

3. A feminist consciousness in ridding black males and females of their socially conditioned anxieties concerning masculinity and femininity would foster greater psychological well-being. . . .[68]

Whether black women will actually become more involved in the organized women's liberation movement will, however, depend a great deal on the direction the movement takes in the future and on whether it addresses the concerns of the black community.

The Future

The conservative mood of the country showed in the election of the very conservative Ronald Reagan in 1980 and 1984 and the continuation of conservatism under George Bush in 1988. Betty Friedan, founding mother of the women's movement, points out that the 1980s were difficult for women. She mentions their impotence in confronting the well-financed fundamentalist backlash, their failure to mobilize a younger generation, and their preoccupation with issues that do not affect all women's lives. She states that 90 percent of the world's governments have national bodies for the advancement of women while that of the United States has been dismantled.[69] She agrees with Sylvia Hewlett that in spite of young people's beliefs to the contrary, women in the United States have far fewer advantages than do most women in other industrialized countries.[70]

Friedan says that the women's movement has become fragmented and concerned with minor issues. Young women have become complacent about economic and social rights and do not realize that they are just one Supreme Court justice's vote away from losing the right to choose an abortion. She offers a list of ten strategies for getting the women's movement moving again. They include (1) beginning a new round of consciousness raising for the new generation, (2) mobilizing the new professional networks and the old volunteer organizations to save women's rights, (3) facing up to the problem of poverty among women, especially in the situation of divorce, (4) reaffirming abortion as the choice of women and not letting antiabortion groups choose the terminology or dictate the arguments, (5) concentrating on helping older women, (6) affirming the differences between men and women but bringing the men into the fight for women's rights, and (7) fighting for real political power and not getting hung up on single issues.[71]

Women's groups have also been concerned about keeping on the books the important legislation for which the movement was largely responsible. Such legislation has come under attack by a number of conservative groups. Groups such as the National Association for Abortion Rights Legislation (NAARL) are determined to keep the right to choose abortion that was guaranteed by the Supreme Court in 1973. Planned Parenthood has battled Reagan and Bush administration proposals to institute squeal rules and turn back the clock in terms of contraception. Other groups are working to keep the focus on affirmative action and prevent the federal government from cutting funds for day care. The difficulty of their task was pointed out by Phyllis Shlafly, spokesperson for the conservatives, who vowed that she and her followers would fight against sex education, nonsexist textbooks, and even the nuclear freeze.[72]

In the fight to consolidate and extend rights, the women's movement has been able to count on few allies. Liberal senators were targeted for defeat and indeed were defeated in recent elections. Unions have been preoccupied with keeping jobs for their members rather than with affirmative action. The poorer groups associated with the movement have been occupied with survival in a recessionary economy. The media have given the movement little publicity. There is also dissension among different factions of the movement and disagreement about which goals to emphasize.

One rallying issue is abortion. In March 1988, 500,000 women and men descended on Washington to make their voices heard for choice. They represented all age, class, and sexual preference groups and most ethnic groups and political parties.[73] The outpouring of support by women who wanted to keep abortion legal showed that there were common issues on which women of many different groups could agree. Another march in the fall of 1989, just before crucial Supreme Court decisions and pending legislation in Congress, was attended by another large number of prochoice supporters.[74] Women's groups that had gained political sophistication in the long battle for the ERA said they would fight with the ballot box to keep legalized abortion.

THE MEN'S MOVEMENT

One of the accompaniments to women's liberation was a similar movement for men. As women recognized the oppression of gender roles, many men realized that they too were oppressed. As women strove for equal rights in court, many men realized that they felt cheated in court decisions such as custody cases in which a mother was likely to have more clout than a father. Out of these beginning realizations came a budding men's movement. This movement had two focuses. One was promen without necessarily being prowomen or feminist; the other was promen and prowomen at the same time.

Kathleen Gerson sums up the reasons for the differences between the two groups:

> Whether a man supports or opposes nontraditional demands from women will depend largely on what he stands to lose or gain from social change. Many men will vigorously oppose the mounting assaults on male power and privilege; others may find unexpected benefits in sharing the burdens of breadwinning and the pleasures of parenthood.[75]

Joseph Pleck has said that "patriarchy is a dual system: a system in which men oppress women, themselves and each other."[76] He believes that one of the most important questions raised by the women's movement is, Why do men oppress women? This has forced many men to confront the fact that they do oppress women and to look inside themselves as well as at the structures of society to see why.

Part of the answer to this question, Pleck believes, is that men want to keep the benefits and privileges that power over women provide them. However, he believes that there must be more to it than this if men's power over women includes violence, rape, wife beating, and child abuse. It is more than just keeping superior power; it seems to be dominance based on fear—perhaps, Pleck says, the fear that women actually exercise dominance over men in many ways.

One way in which women have power over men is that they usually control child rearing. In fact, Pleck points out that there is an irony in the female control of that realm. Because women's power is restricted in most other areas of life, women are allowed to control child rearing. Yet because of this control, young boys feel powerless and dominated and grow up feeling that they want to restrict women's power.

Pleck believes that there are other ways in which women have power over men. Women have expressive power, and men have come to rely on women to express their emotions for them. Women also validate masculinity. If women are "feminine," then men can feel "masculine"; that is, if women are passive, then men can feel aggressive. (Thus, he feels, men's groups put so much emphasis on expressing emotions and on validating each other.) He believes that when men can emphasize being fathers and not feel dominated by women in these other ways, part of the reason they oppress women will disappear.[77]

Pleck also points out that patriarchy and rigid definitions of masculinity lead men to oppress other men. Men create hierarchies among themselves according to the criteria of masculinity. They compete with each other in success, toughness, and the like. As definitions of masculinity are associated with heterosexuality, one way to compete is to be more sexual—that is, more heterosexual—than the next man. Conversely, not to be heterosexual is to lose in the competition. Straight men put down gay men.[78]

Men's power over women is related to this power of men over men. Women are used as success symbols. If a man can get a beautiful, sexy woman, he is seen as successful. He may believe that women enter into male competition in the sense that they reduce it or make it bearable. They provide men a refuge from the male competitive world. They also get men together and "provide the social lubrication" for men to relate to one another; finally, they reduce the stress of male competition by serving as an underclass. As long as women remain an underclass, men can feel superior to some group.[79]

The third part of the devil's triangle of patriarchy is men's power in relation to themselves and their own life definitions. On one level, their social identity is defined by the power they have over women and some other men; at another level, they have very little power in their own lives and patriarchy confines them as well.

In particular, Pleck believes that men are trained to play a rigid role in the economic sphere and that this role severely restricts their self-satisfaction and options. As work becomes less satisfying, masculinity is equated with money rather than with satisfaction at work. (In the past, the equation of money with masculinity was also linked to the breadwinner role; thus, women could not be allowed to supersede males in the workplace. A man's family ties also had to be minimized so that he would fulfill his commitments at work.)[80]

However, Ehrenreich points out that "today's middle-class or upwardly mobile male is less terrified about moving down the slope toward genderlessness than he is about simply moving down the scale." The new middle-class male may show all the signs, at least outwardly, of androgyny. He may cook, decorate his bachelor apartment, and express his sensitivity. He is now status-conscious rather than gender-conscious. However, Ehrenreich raises the question, Is this really the new man the feminists wanted? Are these role changes any more than superficial? Isn't the real oppression of roles and classes still present?[81]

Corrigan and colleagues criticize the new male who has changed his roles. Indeed, they criticize the emphasis of the male liberation movement. They point out that early gender-role literature had very little conception of power. Today we still speak of gender roles, although we mean societal training rather than biologically linked traits. However, we do not use terms like "race roles" and "class roles." Our terminology and view of gender roles play down power relationships.[82]

Thus, the early discussions of roles deemphasized men's power over women, but it particularly played down men's power over other men. It talked of changes in men coming from changes within the individual or changes in roles rather than from a change in power relationships. Recent discussions about men's liberation are more likely to talk about a dialectic of gender relations and how men are changing in response to changes in women and in the power structure. If one can be openly gay, for example, and not suffer legal discrimination, this changes the power relationship of gay men to straight men. If masculinity is no longer defined in relation to a breadwinner role (and may even be defined in conjunction with a fathering role), this changes men's relationship with women.

The power structure that is not changing is that of class. It is probably no accident that some of the worst oppression of and violence against women is found in the working class. This group of men still needs to feel superior to someone.

Thus, to return to Gerson's quote, the men's movement contains two types of men: men who want "their" rights and men who are also willing to support changes for women. The latter are probably not as threatened by changing gender roles, and while they are still oppressed by the power structure, they have more resources to lead a satisfactory life.

Franklin argues that in response to women's definition of themselves as a group, men sharpened their group consciousness as well. He describes several recently formed men's organizations, especially the National Organization for Changing Men (NOCM). He describes NOCM as a liberal group of men who are "supportive of such men's issues as improved fathering, lessening homophobia, improved men's mental health and gay rights and of a variety of other issues like ending violence against women, ending sexual harassment, improving equity in the workplace."[83]

On the other end of the continuum are men's organizations which are politically conservative about gender issues. One such organization is Men's Rights, which focuses on the problem's of men's roles. Another is the National Congress for Men, which, according to Franklin, "devotes its attention to correcting what it calls the callous and unfair treatment of men."[84] The men in these organizations are angry about men's static roles and women's changing ones. They are angry at being vilified by women and do not want their legal rights eroded. Organizations on both ends of the political continuum are concerned about men's sexuality and particularly about the rights of gay men.[85]

Men's Studies

One of the elements of the new men's movement has been a growing interest in men's studies spurred by the growth in women's studies programs around the country. Harry Brod defends men's studies courses as not just a repetition of male scholarship of the past but as offering a new male perspective not found in women's studies. Men's studies focus on issues of concern to women, such as men's violence against women, and also on issues more primarily focused on men, such as men's health concerns, homophobia, and expression of emotions.[86]

Both the women's movement and the men's movement have led to some changes in societal institutions. In the past our societal institutions were supportive of traditional masculinity. In particular, the economic system and the Protestant work ethic supported the breadwinner role. The inexpressive, noncomplaining, tough hardworking man was an asset for the economic system whether he was a manual worker or wore a white collar. Politicians until recently were free to wheel and deal and womanize without repurcussions. Yet these institutions are having to change in reaction to perceptions of what masculinity should be. Overt womanizing by politicians is no longer condoned or overlooked by the media. Many men are no longer willing to sacrifice time with their families and growing children to prove their commitment to the corporation. The media have told us that a real man can use hairspray and hand lotion. There is, indeed, a dialectic of the kind Corrigan and colleagues envisioned. Institutions are changing in response to role change and are in turn creating more change. All the theorists, both men and women, agree, however, that power structures have changed very little.

WOMEN AND MEN IN POLITICAL ELITES

Women have seldom been found in large numbers in political elites. Politics has always been seen as a dirty and smoke-filled arena reserved for men.

Women have also been few in numbers in the occupations that have led to political office. More than half the members of Congress have always been lawyers, and men have traditionally dominated the political parties. Another difficulty for women seeking political office is an inability to raise funds. Women are not likely to have the business connections and credit that men have; nor are they likely to be considered winning candidates and thus be financed. Most of the early women in Congress were widows of congressmen.

As of the 1990 election, there are three women state governors: Dixie Ray in Oregon, Kay Orr in Nebraska, and Anne Richards in Texas. There are thirty-one women members of Congress, twenty-nine in the House and two in the Senate, or approximately 7 percent of the seats. While they have increased their numbers by five since the last election, they have few positions of influence. No woman chairs a committee in either chamber.[87]

By contrast, there are twenty-four black members of the House and twelve Hispanic and seven Asian and Pacific Islander members of Congress. While all these groups remain underrepresented in Congress compared with their share of the total population, they have a great deal of clout. Since most of these representatives are elected from safe seats, they have been able to use seniority to get leadership positions. For example, although blacks make up only 5 percent of the House membership, they chair 25 percent of the standing and select committees.[88]

There are signs that things are changing. In 1965, 4 percent of all law students were women, but by 1985, 43 percent were.[89] Women represented approximately 16 percent of the lawyers. However, this may not make a difference. Although the number of women lawyers has increased, women are often lost in the bureaucracy. They are likely to be in the less prestigious areas of law and are less likely to have their voices heard against "the backdrop of patriarchal legal traditions, institution, processes and statutes."[90] In addition, women inside and outside the legal system are facing courts that are becoming more conservative in their philosophy.

Women's record in attaining high administrative or appointed posts has been very limited. There have only been a few female cabinet members. President Reagan appointed only a small number of women and almost none to administrative policy-making positions, except Elizabeth Dole as secretary of transportation. However, he mollified women with the appointment of a conservative woman juror, Sandra O'Connor, as the first woman on the U.S. Supreme Court. Bush appointed one woman to his cabinet, Elizabeth Dole, as secretary of labor; after her resignation in 1990, he appointed another woman, Lynn Martin.[91]

Another problem for women in getting their voices heard on social issues in the future may be posed by the population shift to the Southern states. States that have traditionally been Democratic are losing population, and the South, which has recently gone staunchly Republican, is gaining population and seats in the Electoral College. If the Republicans gain these votes and the Democrats continue to be the party that best represents women's issues, women may have a hard time influencing policy.[92]

In spite of the lack of power of women at present, most researchers see them slowly increasing their numbers in political elites as more women lawyers and judges move into the system and more women stand for political office. The proportion of women in legislatures, however, is influenced not only by the extent to which new women candidates come forward but by the extent to which women stay in office. As qualified women move up through the system, they leave vacancies which may be filled by men.

In 1985 women had only 7 percent of the judgeships. One study points out that three conditions have to be met for the number of women judges to increase. There has to be an increase in the number of women eligible, the total number of judicial positions, and the number of gatekeepers who will give women fair consideration for the posts. The last factor—lack of a positive attitude toward women judges by gatekeepers (those who select candidates for law jobs)—is probably the most important factor keeping the number of women in judicial positions low.[93]

It is also true that women are either barred from or find it difficult to obtain some of the opportunities which lead to the higher courts. The Rhodes scholarship, the U.S. Supreme Court clerkship, the U.S. Department of Justice office, and the elite law firm partnership[94] all help individuals get to higher judicial posts, but these routes have often been closed, at least informally, to women.

Thus, the impact of women in political elites is mixed. Their numbers are increasing only slowly, and they are facing conservative resistance in getting positions and having an impact on legislation.

THE COURTS TODAY

President Reagan's judicial legacy to the country was 3 Supreme Court appointments and 357 other judicial appointments, including nearly half of all full-time appeals court judges. He has also appointed almost *50 percent* of the district court judges who serve full-time. Reagan was determined to stock the courts with conservative judges, and according to people who study such appointments, he succeeded.[95]

Reagan appointed several women, blacks, and Hispanics to the federal bench, but his numbers were much lower than Carter's. In the court of appeals, six appointees are women; in the district courts, twenty-four are. Even fewer of the appointments were black in spite of the fact that the NAACP developed a talent bank and urged the President to appoint minorities to these posts.[96]

It will take years to realize the total impact of these appointments, but some trends can already be seen. In the Midwestern 7th Circuit Court, a civil rights lawyer who has been practicing in the circuit for a decade says that his work has become more difficult. He states, "We are beginning to have an uphill struggle in cases involving individual rights." The director of the regional office in Atlanta for the American Civil Liberties Union states that he can now see how fragile the state of civil rights really is.[97]

The impact of the three justices Reagan appointed to the Supreme Court is most likely to be felt. One of Reagan's cherished hopes was to overturn the *Roe v. Wade* decision that established a woman's right to have a legal abortion. George Bush has already asked his new attorney general, Richard Thornburgh, to continue the fight to overturn *Roe v. Wade*.[98] In addition, Bush has had an opportunity to fill the Supreme Court vacancy created by William Brennan's resignation in early 1990. Bush appointed David Souter, an obscure Republican judge from New Hampshire, to fill the vacancy. While Souter's views are not widely known, it can be assumed that he is far more conservative than the staunchly liberal Brennan. Shortly thereafter Thurgood Marshall, one of the leading liberal justices, resigned. Bush has nominated a black conservative, Clarence Thomas, as his replacement. If confirmed, he will increase the conservative majority on the Court. All of these new justices are young and their decisions on reproductive issues and affirmative action will affect laws for many years to come.

MEN AND WOMEN AS VOTERS

The Growing Women's Vote

What are the chances that women can form an effective voting bloc to push their interests or increase their numbers in political elites?

Although women did not vote in great numbers right after they achieved the franchise, their political participation began to improve at about the time of the New Deal. Lansing suggests that in the late 1940s and 1950s women voted less than men because they did not feel that they could influence anything by their vote. Recent changes in the level of women voting are closely associated with women's increasing level of education and participation in the work force.[99] Younger women, who are among the best educated, participate most fully in the political process.

What is the relationship of feminism to women's participation in the political process? A study published in March 1981 shows that strength of general personal attitudes (liberal or conservative) is probably more likely than feminism is to cause greater political participation by women. Feminist attitudes are related to political participation, but this is noticeably true only for minority women, who, when they do not hold such values, normally participate less than white women do in campaign activity, voting, local political participation, and protest participation.[100]

Feelings of efficacy or control are also important for women if they are to participate in the political process. Fulkenwilder says that after the high point of the passage of the ERA in Congress with overwhelming votes in 1972, women's sense of political efficacy has declined. She notes that by 1976 strong opposition to the ERA was evident in right-wing groups, the pay gap between men and women had actually widened, and feminist demands such as day care and homemaker rights were being evaded by politicians. By 1976, more feminists than other women were likely to say that they did not feel they could influence or control government. Minority women were particularly likely to say that they did not feel they had control of government, as they saw the dismantling of many antipoverty programs and the loss of benefits.[101]

When women do vote, their stand on issues such as abortion and the ERA is not very different from that of men.[102] In fact, early voting data described women as more conservative than men, but in three of the last four elections women have voted more heavily for Democratic presidential candidates. Polls conducted by Harris and Gallup show that women do vote differently on some issues. They are less likely to seek military solutions to international problems, for example.[103]

The Gender Gap

During the 1980 presidential election, women voters came into their own with the development of the gender gap. Only 46 percent of women compared with 54 percent of men voted for the successful candidate, Ronald Reagan. It was felt that this was largely because of Reagan's hawkish stance on war and the fact that Carter had promoted health, education, and welfare issues.[104]

In spite of the fact that the term "gender gap" was coined in the 1980 election, 1980 was not the first presidential election in which there were sex differences in support for presidential candidates. In 1956, women favored Eisenhower by 62 percent compared to the men's vote of 56 percent—another 6 percent gap. In 1960, 53 percent of women voted for Richard Nixon compared to 48 percent of men. Yet 1980 was the first time the gender gap was really noticed and publicized as such. In the 1982 off-year elections for Congress, an activist warned that "any politician who does not heed the implications of the gender gap is walking on thin ice."[105] This was particularly appropriate advice because the 1982 election was the first in which a number of national women's organizations endorsed candidates and contributed significant amounts of money to their campaigns.

In the 1982 off-year Congressional elections women gave Democratic candidates 57 percent of their vote, 6 percent more than men did. Republicans became concerned enough about the threat to hire a "gender gap specialist" to divide women into groups, track each group, and target them for particular appeals.[106]

Yet in 1984 Reagan won forty-nine states in spite of Geraldine Ferraro being the vice-presidential candidate for the Democrats. The continuing differences in voting patterns were buried in the landslide, and Transportation Secretary Elizabeth Dole said, "I think we can declare the gender gap closed."[107]

However, in spite of the Reagan landslide, exit polls showed that there was still remarkable continuity in the size of the gender spread between 1980 and 1984. Fifty-six percent of the women had voted for Reagan versus 62 percent of the men—a continuing gender gap of 6 percentage points. Reagan had won over enough women to win, but their level of support still differed from that of men.[108]

Why were more women willing to vote for Reagan in 1984? Many analysts suggested that just before the election he tried to tone down his saber rattling. His new noninterventionism enhanced his standing among women, but economic issues continued to create a gender gap. Ethnic women, younger women, single women, and women who worked outside the home were less likely to vote Republican. The congressional races that year reflected even more of a gender gap, with women voting Democratic in the House races at a rate 10 percent higher than that of men.[109]

Pollsters had a field day trying to assess the impact of the Ferraro factor in the election. Some speculated that having Geraldine Ferraro as the vice-presidential candidate might have cost the Democrats votes, but most polls suggested that she helped a weak ticket. Women in particular turned out in larger numbers (61 percent compared to 59 percent of men) to vote. It is hard to know what effect Ferraro's candidacy had on the women's vote. Forty-five percent of women supported the Mondale-Ferraro ticket compared to only 38 percent of men, yet among women 14 percent said that Ferraro's candidacy made them *less* likely to vote Democratic and only 19 percent said that it made them more likely to vote for Mondale and Ferraro.[110]

The gender gap was compounded by age and race factors. Young women voted Democratic by 48 to 43 percent, while men under 30 voted Republican by 53 to 37 percent, for a 10 percent gender gap in this age group. Ethnic women were particularly likely to vote for Mondale. Ninety-three percent of black women, 73 percent of Jewish women, and 65 percent of Hispanic women voted Democratic.[111]

Analyses of the youth and ethnic vote showed where the real source of the gender gap lay in this election. Even after Reagan had stepped back from his militaristic posturing, economic issues were very important. The movement of "women into the labor market fueled the gender gap by fostering increased political participation and the liberalization of attitudes."[112] Working women discovered the dollar gender gap, and poor women and ethnic women felt threatened by cutbacks in federal social programs. In the 1982 congressional elections, which came after sharp Reagan budget cuts, AFDC recipients and jobless persons registered in the "greatest turnout increases and sharpest shift away from Reagan-backed candidates of any group in the electorate."[113]

The gender gap continued in the 1988 election. Fifty-eight percent of men voted for Bush, but only 49 percent of women did. Forty percent of men voted for Dukakis, but 50 percent of women did so. The change was that women voted for the Republican and Democratic candidates in almost equal numbers. This can be seen more clearly in Table 1, which compares the 1984 and 1988 elections:

Table 1   **Changes in Voting Patterns**

| | 1984 | | 1988 | | |
Voters	*Republican, %*	*Democratic, %*	*Republican, %*	*Democratic, %*	*Change, %*
All (100%)	59	41	54	45	−5
Men (50%)	63	37	58	40	−5
Women (50%)	56	44	49	50	−7
Whites (85%)	67	33	57	41	−10
Blacks (8%)	9	91	11	86	+2
Hispanics (4%)	47	53	38	61	−9

SOURCE: Cable News Network: *Los Angeles Times* exit polls, in "Explaining Their Vote, *National Journal* (November 12, 1988):2853–2858.

One can see that both women and men were more likely to vote Democratic in 1988 than in 1984. The defection from the Republicans can be attributed to Bush's lack of Reagan's personal popularity. Women increased their Democratic vote even more than men did, and so the gender gap continued. If Dukakis had run a smarter campaign, he might have capitalized on defense spending, child care, and welfare and gotten even more of the women's vote. Certainly early polls showed the gender gap as being much greater. But Bush was able to neutralize many of the traditional Democratic issues with his hard-hitting negative campaign, and Dukakis did not respond in time to save more of the women's vote.

One can also see from looking at the table that blacks and Hispanics were the largest Democratic supporters, mainly for economic reasons. Hispanics are slightly less likely than blacks to support the Democrats because Cuban Hispanics are very hawkish about defense and Republicans have traditionally emphasized a strong defense. Blacks supported the Democratic candidate slightly less than they did in 1984, probably because of their disappointment about not having Jesse Jackson as a presidential or vice-presidential candidate.

As the *National Journal* pointed out, "the gender gap represents one of the great ironies of the 1988 election. The gap between men and women was slightly wider this year (10 points) than it had been in 1980 (6 points) and 1984 (7 points). In 1980 and 1984, however, the gender gap didn't make any difference to the outcome. Both men and women voted for Reagan." However, in 1988 the gender gap was one which spotlighted the votes of men. While women split their votes almost evenly between the Democrats and the Republicans, men gave Bush a margin of 18 points. "The gender gap controlled the outcome of the 1988 election but not in the way that feminists had predicted. *Men elected Bush.*"[114]

The large gap in men's' preference for the Republicans over the Democrats was not offset by a woman's vote in the opposite direction. While the Democrats actually picked up votes from both men and women, they did not pick up as many from women as they expected. In this election Bush was careful to do things that would appeal to the women's vote. He announced that he was in favor of a child-care initiative before Dukakis had a chance to do so. His attacks on Dukakis forced the Democratic candidate to extremes such as having his picture taken in a tank and saying that he was not in favor of cutting *all* defense spending. Using carefully planned spots with his large family and his grandchildren, Bush usurped the family issue as well. Thus, Bush neutralized the traditional Democratic issues of children and family and also managed to come across as strong and decisive about defense, though not as much as a hawk as Reagan had been or as liberal and pacifistic as he made Dukakis out to be. An important lesson from this election and that of 1984 was that the Republicans took women's voting patterns seriously and the Democrats did not.[115]

Will the Gender Gap Continue in the Future?

It seems likely from what we have seen that the sexes will continue to vote differentially. Whether the women's vote will be an effective force in the future will depend on whether traditional Democratic issues such as peace initiatives, health, education, and welfare can be usurped again by the Republicans. It also depends on whether women can overcome class and race differences to see themselves as a voting bloc in favor of certain things.

How likely are women to develop this group consciousness? Wolfinger's description of factors necessary for ethnic group voting also applies to women. The first factor he cites as being necessary for such bloc voting is intensity of identity with the group. The second factor is the level of relevance of issues in a particular election to the group. The third is identification with group members running for office.[116] Given those three factors, research disagrees as to whether a woman's bloc vote will continue to develop.

Gurin points out that women are becoming more strongly identified with their group in a way that groups such as blacks and the elderly have been. When presented with a list of more than a dozen groups (such as liberals, conservatives, Southerners, blacks, whites, and farmers), women have increasingly chosen women as the group to which they feel the most similar in ideas, interests, and feelings.[117] Labor force participation, increased education, and political activism are all forces which increased that group consciousness, while religious activism deterred it and marital status did not seem to matter.[118] As women are getting more education and moving in greater numbers into the labor force as well as becoming more politically active, the factors increasing group consciousness will continue.

However, Gurin believes that another factor intervenes in the development of group consciousness: lack of discontent with the in-group's power. When asked about their own groups' power and influence in American life and politics, blacks and older people have increasingly said they have too little power. By contrast, women are far less concerned. Gurin says,

> Nearly everyone acknowledges that women earn less than men, that women have fewer opportunities and lower-status jobs, and that there are not many women in

power or leadership roles. But for gender consciousness to develop, women must question the legitimacy of these disparities . . . because a subordinate group is not going to organize unless it feels that the disparities are unfair.[119]

Gurin uses the same reasons that Lipman-Blumen has given for why the powerless don't revolt: Women are isolated from one another, and no other oppressed group has such an intimate relationship with the dominant group."[120]

When we examine the third factor in women supporting women candidates, the messages are mixed. Groups such as NOW have given their support not to women candidates per se but to candidates, male or female, who support women's issues. On abortion, for example, a male prochoice candidate would get NOW's endorsement while a female right-to-life candidate would not. Women were also as likely to say that Ferraro's presence on the ticket would make them less likely to vote Democratic as they were to say that it would make them more likely to vote for the Democrats.[121] Therefore, women seem willing to give their support to women's issues but not necessarily to women candidates just because they are women. The split in views about issues such as abortion and the ERA means that women do not have a united front even on women's issues.

In summary, we can say that women are developing a group consciousness and that demographic trends will probably accelerate this trend. However, women's isolation and ties to the dominant group mean that they are not willing to perceive inequities as unjust. Further, they may see issues like abortion in very different ways. Thus, they are not speaking with a united voice on issues and are not willing to support women candidates on the basis of sex alone. A true voting bloc is likely to be very slow in coming if it develops at all. However, voting patterns different from those of men will probably persist.

Anne Costain, who has researched the gender gap, says that the most effective strategy for the women's movement seems to be some combination of being a special interest group and pushing for things which relate to all women (child care, family leave) and having women's organizations such as the National Abortion Rights Action League push for separate agendas.[122]

THE FUTURE

Pat Reuss, WEAL lobbyist, said in 1984,

Women's issues are no longer just ERA and abortion, the economy and pocketbook concerns are the issues today. We tell members of Congress "You cannot forget women when you are working on social security. You have to think of women when you do a jobs bill." Economic bills must look at their impact on women since so many are now in the work force.[123]

In looking at the future, we need to assess the overall role of the state in promoting the interests of women. (We assume that the state has always advanced the interests of most men.) Many feminists have questioned whether the state, the courts, or the legislature can advance women's interests. They see government as too male-dominated, at least for the present, and only another form of social control. Others have argued that the welfare state is an important place to empower women.[124] Women's economic and political subordination could be changed radically if the state were willing to advance their interests.

The political process is an important part of change. In these changing times, the laws and protections that have enabled change to occur can easily be eliminated. The extent to which women participate in the political process may determine the future course of legal changes that affect sex roles. It is necessary for women to consolidate their votes if they wish to influence candidates to support women's issues. Women must be active in fund-raising and political organizing if they wish to elect women candidates. Although the current political climate is not promising in terms of women's rights, women are more likely to have the means to enter the political arena and to gain political power as women's socialization and occupational roles change. As a result, women are more likely to be able to influence and enact legislation that will help them in the future.

ESSAY QUESTIONS

1. Describe the "double standard of the law" as it applies to men and women. Be sure to include laws dealing with sexual attitudes and behavior, economics, and employment in your answer.
2. What is the text of the Equal Rights Amendment as proposed? Why have feminists pushed for its passage, and what would it actually do in terms of alleged changes like coed bathrooms if passed?
3. Discuss the statement "Although women have had the vote for only sixty years, they are not participating equally in politics with men, both in voting behavior and participation in political elites." How accurate is this statement?
4. Discuss the possibilities of women developing a bloc vote in the future according to the information you have gained about their historical participation in politics. Do you believe that feminism will influence and accelerate the development of such a bloc vote?

EXERCISES

1. Discuss your feelings about laws that protect women, such as laws putting weight limits on what they can lift at work and laws that keep them from taking "unsavory" work. Do you feel that such laws should be continued?

2. Do you believe that the situation of women and minorities has been improved with the equal opportunity employment laws? Why or why not?
3. How do you feel about the proposed Equal Rights Amendment and the possibility that women will lose privileges such as preference in child custody cases? What do you feel should be the relationship between rights and responsibilities as the law changes? Discuss these issues.
4. If women had access to public sources of funding for campaign funds, do you believe that they would be better represented in political elites? Discuss why you think so or not.
5. Pretend you are a woman who would like to run for President of the United States. What particular issues would you emphasize in your campaign to appeal to the "women's vote"?
6. Do you believe that a woman would make as good a President as a man would? Discuss your feelings about this issue. Do the women differ from the men in the class in their views?

NOTES

1. Ava Baron, "Feminist Legal Strategies: The Powers of Difference," in Beth B. Hess and Myra Marx Feree, *Analyzing Gender: A Handbook of Social Science Research* (New York: Sage, 1987), pp. 474–503.
2. Lenore J. Weitzman, "Legal Definition of Marriage: Tradition and Change," *California Law Review* 62 (July–September 1974):1169 1228.
3. N. Taub and E. Schneider, "Perspectives on Women's Subordination and the Role of Law," in D. Kairys, ed., *The Politics of Law* (New York: Pantheon, 1982), pp. 117–139.
4. Joan Hoff-Wilson, "The Unfinished Revolution: Changing Legal Status of U.S. Women," *Signs* 13 (1987):7–36.
5. Lenore J. Weitzman, *The Divorce Revolution* (New York: The Free Press, 1985).
6. *Ibid.*
7. Barbara Deckhard, *The Women's Movement* (New York: Harper & Row, 1979), p. 157.
8. *Ibid.*, p. 151.
9. Baron, *op. cit.*, p. 481.
10. *Ibid.*
11. Laura L. Crites, "Wife Abuse: The Judicial Record," in Laura L. Crites and Winifred L. Hepperle, eds., *Women, the Courts and Equality* (New York: Sage, 1987), pp. 38–53.
12. Jo Freeman, "Women, Law and Public Policy," in Jo Freeman, ed., *Women: A Feminist Perspective*, 3d ed. (Palo Alto, Calif.: Mayfield, 1984), pp. 381–401.
13. *Ibid.*
14. *Ibid.*
15. *Ibid.*, p. 386.
16. Freeman discussing *Schlesinger v. Ballard*, in Freeman, *op. cit.*, p. 390.
17. Baron, *op. cit.*, p. 488.
18. Jerrold K. Footlick with Diane Camper and Lucy Howard, "The Landmark Bakke

Ruling," *Newsweek* (July 10, 1978), reprinted in *Annual Editions, Social Problems, 1979–80* (Guilford, Conn.: Dushkin, 1979), pp. 27–31.

19. Baron, *op. cit.,* p. 491.
20. Jo Freeman, "The Women's Liberation Movement: Its Origins, Structure, Activities, and Ideas," in Freeman, *op. cit.,* pp. 343–557.
21. Marjorie Lansing, "Women in American Politics," in Marie Richmond-Abbott, ed., *The American Woman* (New York: Holt, Rinehart & Winston, 1978), p. 239.
22. *Ibid.,* pp. 239–241; Deckhard, *op. cit.,* pp. 85–89.
23. Sara Medina, "Twilight of the ERA," *Time* (July 13, 1981):17; Ann Beck, M. Shiels, and L. Donosky, "Last Hurrah for the ERA?" *Newsweek* (June 13, 1981):24.
24. Deckhard, *op. cit.,* pp. 185–189.
25. *Ibid.,* pp. 280–300; Lansing, *op. cit.,* pp. 228–229.
26. Michigan Women's Commission, *Women's Political Issues, 1988* (Lansing, Mich.: Department of Management and Budget, 1988).
27. *Ibid.,* p. 2.
28. *Ibid.*
29. *Ibid.,* p. 3; Sylvia Hewlett, *A Lesser Life* (New York: Warner, 1986).
30. Michigan Women's Commission, *op. cit.,* p. 3
31. Weitzman, *op. cit.,* 1985.
32. Michigan Women's Commission, *op. cit.,* p. 5.
33. *Ibid.*
34. Viola Klein, "Feminism: The Historical Background," in Freeman, *op. cit.,*
35. Judith Hole and Ellen Levine, "The First Feminists," in Freeman, *op. cit.,* pp. 533–542.
36. Carrie Chapman Catt and Nettie Rogers Shuler, *Woman Suffrage and Politics* (New York, 1923), p. 107, quoted in Hole and Levine, *op. cit.,* p. 554.
37. Deckhard, *op. cit.,* pp. 342–343.
38. John Stucker, "Women as Voters," in Marianne Githens and Jewel Prestage, eds., *A Portrait of Marginality* (New York, McKay, 1977), p. 276; Patricia Collins, "Learning from the Outsider: The Social Significance of Black Feminist Thought," *Social Problems* 33 (1986):514–532.
39. Freeman, "The Women's Liberation Movement, *op. cit.*
40. Hole and Levine, *op. cit.*
41. *Ibid.*
42. Freeman, "The Women's Liberation Movement," *op. cit.*
43. *Ibid.*
44. *Ibid.*
45. David Bouchier, "The Deradicalization of Feminism: Ideology and Utopia in Action," *Sociology* 13 (1979):387–402.
46. *Ibid.,* p. 389.
47. *Ibid.,* p. 394.
48. Freeman, "The Women's Liberation Movement," *op. cit.*
49. Bouchier, *op. cit.*
50. Freeman, "The Women's Liberation Movement," *op. cit.*
51. Jane J. Mansbridge, *Why We Lost the ERA* (Chicago: University of Chicago Press, 1986).
52. Lansing, *op. cit.,* pp. 232–234.
53. Johanna S. R. Mendelson, "The Ballot Box Revolution: The Drive to Register Women," in Carol M. Mueller, ed., *The Politics of the Gender Gap: The Social Construction of Political Influence* (New York: Sage, 1988), pp. 61–80.

54. *Ibid.*, p. 69.

55. *Ibid*, p. 75.

56. *Ibid*, p. 78.

57. Klein, *op. cit.*

58. *Ibid.*

59. M. Sheilds, L. Donosky, L. Howard, E. Sciolino, and H. Bruno, "A Woman's Agenda: National Women's Conference in Houston," *Newsweek* (November 28, 1977):57–58; A. T. Fleming, "That Week in Houston: National Women's Conference," *New York Times Magazine* (December 25, 1977):10–13.

60. Betty Friedan, "How to Get the Women's Movement Moving Again," *New York Times Magazine* (November 3, 1985):26, 28, 66, 67, 84, 85.

61. Pauline Terrelonge Stone, "Feminist Consciousness and Black Women," in Freeman, *op. cit.*, pp. 557–567; Robyn Rowland, "Women Who Do and Women Who Don't Join the Women's Movement: Issues for Conflict and Collaboration," *Sex Roles* 14 (1986):679–692.

62. Stone, *op. cit.*

63. *Ibid.*, p. 575.

64. *Ibid.*, p. 583.

65. Willa Mae Hemmons, "The Women's Liberation Movement: Understanding Black Women's Attitudes," in La Frances Rodgers-Rose, ed., *The Black Woman* (Beverly Hills, Calif.: Sage, 1980), pp. 285–300.

66. Michelle Wallace, *Black Macho and the Myth of the Superwoman* (New York: Dial, 1978).

67. Shirley Chisholm, "Women Must Rebel," in Stone, *op. cit.*, pp. 207–216.

68. Stone, *op. cit.*, p. 583.

69. Friedan, *op. cit.*

70. Hewlett, *op. cit.*

71. Friedan, *op. cit.*

72. *Ibid.*

73. Charles J. Gans, "Two Cases Could Mean More Changes in Abortion Law," *Ann Arbor News* (November 24, 1989):C–1.

74. Ellen Goodman, "Abortion Issue Puts Bush on Spot," *Ann Arbor News* (November 28, 1989):C–6.

75. Kathleen Gerson, "What Do Women Want from Men? Men's Influence on Women's Work and Family Choices," in Michael S. Kimmel, ed., *Changing Men: New Directions in Research on Men and Masculinity* (Beverly Hills, Calif.: Sage, 1987), pp. 115–130.

76. Joseph Pleck, "Men's Power with Women, Other Men and Society: A Men's Movement Analysis," in Michael S. Kimmel and Michael A. Messner, eds., *Men's Lives* (New York: MacMillan, 1989), pp. 21–29.

77. *Ibid.*

78. *Ibid.*

79. Mavis Klein, "Time for Men's Liberation," *Women and Therapy* 4 (1985):23–28; Paul Schurmann, "Male Liberation," *Pastoral Psychology* 35 (1987):189–199.

80. Pleck, *op. cit.*

81. Barbara Ehrenreich, "A Feminist's View of the New Man," in Kimmel and Messner, *op. cit.*, p. 37.

82. Tim Corrigan, Bob Connell, and John Lee, "Hard and Heavy: Toward a New Sociology of Masculinity," in Michael Kaufman, ed., *Beyond Patriarchy: Essays by*

Men on Pleasure, Power and Change (New York: Oxford University Press, 1987), pp. 139–192.

83. Klein, *op. cit.*
84. Clyde W. Franklin II, *Men and Society* (Chicago: Nelson Hall, 1988).
85. Franklin, *op. cit.,* p. 129.
86. Harry Brod, "A Case for Men's Studies," in Kimmel, *op. cit.,* pp. 263–277.
87. Mike Mills, "Voters Elect Record Number of Women, Blacks." *Congressional Quarterly Weekly Report* 48, no. 45 (November 12, 1990):3222–3225.
88. R. Darey and James R. Choike, "A Formal Analysis of Legislative Turnover: Women Candidates and Legislative Representation," *American Journal of Political Science* 30 (1986):237–255.
89. U.S. Department of Labor, Bureau of Labor Statistics, "Employed Persons by Sex, Race and Occupation," Table 627, *Statistical Abstract of the United States* (Washington, D.C.: U.S. Government Printing Office, 1988).
90. C. Epstein, *Women and the Law* (New York: Basic Books, 1981), pp. 4–5.
91. Nadine Cohodas, "Bush on Judiciary: The Signals are Mixed," *Congressional Quarterly Weekly Report* 46 no. 48 (November 26, 1988):3395.
92. James A. Barnes, "Election '88, Republican Tilt," *National Journal* (November 12, 1988):2845–2848.
93. Beverly Blair Cook, "Women Judges in the Opportunity Structure," in Crites and Hepperle, *op. cit.,* pp. 143–174.
94. *Ibid.*
95. Nadine Cohodas, "Reagan's Legacy is Not Only on the Bench," *Congressional Quarterly Weekly Report* 46, no. 48 (November 26, 1988):3392–3396.
96. *Ibid.*
97. *Ibid.,* p. 3395
98. *Ibid.*
99. Lansing, *op. cit,* p. 236.
100. Claire Knoche Fulkenwilder, "Feminist Ideology and the Political Attitudes and Participation of White and Minority Women," *Western Political Quarterly* 34 (1981):25.
101. *Ibid.,* p. 23.
102. Lansing, *op. cit.,* p. 230; John Soule and Wilma McGraths, "A Comparative Study of Male-Female Political Attitudes at Citizen and Elite Levels," in Githens and Prestage, *op. cit.,* p. 185.
103. *Ibid.*
104. Linda L. M. Bennett, "The Gender Gap: When an Opinion Gap Is Not a Voting Bloc," *Social Science Quarterly* 67 (1986):613–625.
105. *Ibid.,* p. 613.
106. Mendelson, *op. cit.*
107. Evans Witt, "What the Republicans Have Learned about Women," *Public Opinion* (October–November 1985):49–52.
108. Harold Brackman and Steven P. Erie, "The Future of the Gender Gap," *Social Policy* 16 (1986):5–11.
109. *Ibid.*
110. Daniel Wirls, "Reinterpreting the Gender Gap," *Public Opinion Quarterly* 50 (1986):316–330.
111. Bennett, *op. cit.,* p. 622.
112. Brackman and Erie, *op. cit.*

113. *Ibid.*
114. Cable News Network: *Los Angeles Times* exit polls, in "Explaining Their Vote," *National Journal* (November 12, 1988):2853–2858.
115. Witt, *op. cit.*
116. Wolfinger, discussed in Bennett, *op. cit.*
117. Patricia Gurin, "Group Consciousness," *Institute for Social Research Newsletter,* University of Michigan (Spring–Summer 1982):2.
118. *Ibid.*
119. *Ibid.* p. 4.
120. *Ibid.;* Jean Lipman-Blumen, *Gender Roles and Power* (Englewood Cliffs, N.J.: Prentice-Hall, 1984).
121. Kathleen A. Frankovic, "The Ferraro Factor: The Women's Movement, the Polls, and the Press," in C. Mueller, *The Politics of the Gender Gap* (Newbury Park, Calif.:Sage, 1987), pp. 102–123.
122. Quoted on p. 169 of Anne N. Costain, "Women's Claims as a Special Interest," in Mueller, *op. cit.,* pp. 150–172.
123. *Ibid.*
124. Baron, *op. cit.*

Eric Kroll/Omni-Photo Communications, Inc.

Chapter 13

Gender Roles over the Life Cycle: What Does the Future Hold?

We have come full circle from our discussion of sex, status, and gender roles in Chapter 1. We have seen that male-dominated institutions cause and perpetuate the differential status of the sexes. We have also seen how gender limits people's socialization and assignment to social roles. Aside from the power structure, socialization and the cultural assignment of social roles are the major elements that affect the development of individual traits and behaviors.

We also realize just how much sex is a stimulus variable. We have seen that our culture believes that different behavior patterns are appropriate for each sex and that people react differently to the same behavior from a man or a woman. Not only are behavioral expectations different for each sex, but they have status rankings: Masculine traits and behaviors are preferred in the great majority of situations by most people. Thus, one's gender becomes a status that limits one's behavior and affects one's chances for success in the world in the same way that race and age each constitute a status. The limits on behavior are carefully taught through gender-role socialization and are enforced by institutional arrangements. Let us review some of the socialization and institutional arrangements that operate over the life cycle.

Socialization into gender roles in our culture varies over the life cycle. It begins at a very young age, and a child learns gradually to reproduce behavior stereotyped as appropriate for her or his sex. The cultural messages that tell the child what kind of behavior is appropriate and reinforce the proper action are very strong. From the unspoken expectations and modeling of parents to the heavy-handed depictions on television and in schoolbooks, cultural messages about appropriate behavior are impossible to escape. Once the child reaches school age and leaves the parental home for several hours a day, control over gender-stereotyped messages may be impossible even for parents who are determined to raise their children in a nonstereotyped way. The norms of the peer group become particularly important in adolescence, and it is difficult for young men and women to deviate from prescriptions for traditional gender roles. It is hard enough for adolescents to develop a firm identity within the confines of traditional roles, and few will risk the uncertainty of moving into uncharted territory. However, there are pressures for change in peer group norms as more young women play sports and train for nontraditional occupations and as fewer young men are willing to sacrifice everything for achievement and success.

There are also pressures for change that stem from the years of singlehood that may follow school. As women get more education, make investments in careers, and stay single longer to pursue those careers, they are more likely to develop a resource base as well as nontraditional interests and behaviors. There is also evidence that marriages may become more equal as women enter them with greater power. Women are older when they marry and are more likely to have an education that approximates that of their husbands. Far more married women are working and are gaining power by contributing resources to the marriage, and many fewer lose power by being tied down by having a large number of children. However, women still have the primary responsibility for domestic chores and child care, and this dual burden may limit a woman's career achievement. Where norms allow a woman to hold onto the power she gains, as in the black family, there is more equality in decision making if not in the sharing of domestic chores; where norms hold a woman back from using her earned power, as in the working-class white family, traditional family relationships are likely to continue. Gay couples, single-parent families, and even remarried families are less traditional and may even be considered the vanguard of change. Fathers who are more interested in parenting contribute to such family change.

As the years pass, the gender-role behavior of men and women may change. Many women today are through with their child-rearing years by their early forties and reenter the job market or more actively pursue exciting careers. These women may develop assertive, achievement-oriented, and competent behaviors that they might not have been able to develop in earlier years. In contrast, a man's career may have peaked by his middle forties, and with the stimulus of a midlife crisis, he may reevaluate what he wants to do with the rest of his life. He may turn away from achievement-oriented behavior and toward more nurturant and generative activities either with his own children or with protégés at work. He is also more likely to be aware of the stress engendered by inexpressiveness and to want to get in touch with his feelings during this period. Family power relationships may be realigned as women without children and with a career gain power and men who are close to retirement or retired lose the provider role. The later years probably reflect for both sexes more behaviors, activities, and interests in common and more of the same kinds of androgynous behavior that we find in early childhood.

Thus, there is a curvilinear development of gender roles over the life cycle, from relatively undifferentiated roles in early childhood, through the strictly polarized roles of adolescence and early adulthood, to the more undifferentiated roles of middle and old age. Some researchers have suggested that this curvilinear process of development can be accelerated and accentuated, that there is a possibility for transcending gender roles at all times during the life span.[1]

POSSIBILITIES FOR THE FUTURE

A Theoretical Model of Possibilities for Sex Roles

While working on a model for transcending sex roles, Hefner and colleagues developed a model of the various possibilities that exist for the relationship between the power positions of the sexes. The model is an extension of one that suggests the possibilities of various relationships between the races. In pictorial form it would look like the following:

Genocide (of men)	Separatism	Assimilation	Androgyny (melting pot)	Cultural pluralism	Assimilation	Segregation	Genocide (of women)

On the far right, one has the extreme position of **genocide**, in which men have life-and-death power over women. This situation existed in ancient Greece and Rome and may exist in various parts of the Islamic world today. In this situation, male values are supreme; women are seen as inferior and allowed to exist only to propagate the species.

The next alternative, **segregation**, is similar but less extreme. In this situation, men seldom have the power to kill women, but they have control over them. Men's sphere of influence (the public domain) is valued and separate from the domestic sphere of women, which is considered inferior.

The next alternative is **assimilation**. In this situation, male values are still supreme and the male sphere of influence is still predominant, but women are allowed to enter the male arena (to have careers in business, for example) if they adopt the male system of values.

The next possibility is **cultural pluralism**. Under this system, masculine and feminine traits and behavior are equally valued. Women and men are distinct in their roles, but neither masculine nor feminine traits and pursuits have greater acceptability.[2]

The middle ground of **androgyny**, or the melting pot style, has been discussed before. Under this system, there is a blending of both traits and roles. Both men and women have masculine and feminine traits of behavior and have similar roles.

Moving to the left of androgyny, we see the possibility of *assimilation* again, but this time with feminine values being predominant. Under this system, such feminine values as nurturance and cooperation are the norm for the society and maternal roles have great value. Men attempt to adopt the values of women and are allowed to partake in feminine roles to a limited degree. Margaret Mead's description of Arapesh society in *Sex and Temperament* is close to this type of society.[3]

Farther to the left, we see the possibility of **separatism**. Under this system, the roles of men and women are separate as they are under segregation, but in this case the feminine role has greater value. Women choose to be separate from men and do not interact with them. Radical lesbian groups and organizations such as SCUM (Society for the Cutting Up of Men) represent this point of view.

Finally, on the far left side is the possibility of *genocide,* this time with women having life-and-death power over men. In this extreme situation, men are used as sperm banks but have little role in society.

While this example depicts all the possible extremes, the actual possibilities for gender roles probably will be limited to the spectrum from assimilation on the right to androgyny on the left. The current cultural situation is probably an intermediate form of assimilation, with vestiges of segregation still occurring in some areas and possibilities of cultural pluralism and androgyny opening up in others.

However, Rebecca and associates have suggested another possibility that in a sense represents an ultimate form of androgyny. They expand upon an earlier interpretation of androgyny made by Bem, who said about androgyny:

> If there is a moral to the concept of psychological androgyny, it is that behavior should have no gender. . . . But there is an irony here, for the concept of androgyny contains an inner contradiction and hence the seeds of its own destruction. . . . The concept of androgyny necessarily presupposes that the concepts of masculinity and femininity themselves have distinct and substantive content. But *to the extent that the androgynous message is absorbed by the culture, the concepts of masculinity and femininity will cease to have such content, and the distinctions to which they refer will blur into invisibility.*[4] [Italics added.]

As Rebecca and associates see it, individuals go through three stages of gender-role development. Stage 1 is a stage of undifferentiated sex roles. A child is unaware of culturally imposed restrictions on behavior that are based on biological sex. As the child grows older, he or she become aware of parental and societal values about gender roles and gradually moves into stage 2, which is a stage of polarized gender roles. The child may be able to perform the behavior of both sexes but is aware of which behavior is appropriate for his or her gender and therefore adheres more or less strictly to the feminine or masculine role. Rebecca and associates see stage 3 as a moving back toward undifferentiated roles. In the full development of stage 3, a person has transcended gender roles. As they put it, "choice of behavioral and emotional expression is not determined by rigid adherence to `appropriate' sex-related characteristics. Individuals feel free to express their human qualities without fear of retribution for violating gender-role norms. This is a transcending of the stereotypes and a reorganization of the possibilities learned in stage 2 into a more personally relevant frame."

Therefore, in an ideal society, gender-role development would reach its full potential in stage 3—an undifferentiated stage in which gender roles have been transcended and, as Bem has said, masculinity and femininity have lost their meaning.[5] But Rebecca and associates believe that individuals and institutions in our society are stuck at an intermediate and incomplete stage of gender-role development. It is difficult for an individual to move to stage 3 because there is no institutional or cultural support for this.

A Theoretical Model of Levels of Change

Two analyses have been made of the attempt to liberalize gender roles in American society. Giele uses Smelser's theoretical model of how innovations are selected and utilized in a society to suggest how gender roles may change in the American culture.[6] Polk's analysis can, with only a little distortion, be fitted into the same framework. Their combined analysis shows how branches of the women's movement have concentrated their efforts for gender-role change on certain levels of the society but also point out that a combined thrust at every level is necessary to effect a useful transition.

The first level of change Smelser identified is that of the individual personality and role characteristics of individuals. Giele and Polk point out that the earliest efforts at changing the relative status of the sexes were directed at the individual or personality level. This included the concept of gender-role socialization. Some of the major ideas of this level are that gender roles are systematically taught to individuals from birth and are reinforced by cultural rewards. These gender roles are particularly difficult to unlearn because they are connected with concepts of sexuality. Gender roles are basic roles and modify expectations for behavior in almost all other roles. The male role also has higher status, which is directly rewarding and gives males access to further status and rewards.[7] The emphasis on this level implies that if individuals could be "resocialized" and if women could learn behaviors that would give them access to the system, the problem of sex discrimination would be solved without further changes.[8]

Smelser sees the second level of change as that of organizing characteristics of collectives such as schools and places of work. These organizing characteristics not only are structural in nature but include definitions of appropriate masculine and feminine values and behavior. Masculine behavior includes competitiveness, aggressiveness, independence, and rationality. Feminine behavior includes cooperativeness, passivity, dependence, and emotionality.[9] Men usually learn only their own values and behavior, which have higher status and lead to societal success, but women learn both behavior systems because they must survive as females and live in the culture. Women are, however, devalued if they use the alternative male values and behavior system (a woman at work is seen as pushy, not forceful; rigid, not firm). Although some feminists believe that masculine values have led to destructive behavior in our society, it is difficult for women to enter work organizations where male values and behavior predominate because feminine values and behavior are not compatible with the organization as it is structured and because women are devalued when they use masculine ways of doing things.[10] In a similar fashion, men may have difficulty using feminine values or behavior in interacting with their children or helping with housework because these behaviors are defined as inappropriate for a man.[11]

The third level is that of change in major societal complexes such as the economic system and the government. This level is particularly important because changes in institutions must occur if individual and cultural or value (second-stage) change is to be achieved. If the government does not support nondiscrimination in education and opportunities for the disadvantaged to enter the system, there is little possibility for ultimate change in spite of change on an individual level. Ideas about what is appropriately masculine or feminine are equally unlikely to change without the leading function of the law or without changing economic institutions.[12] Yet legal and economic institutions are controlled by men who gain power and privilege through that control. Polk states that at this level men "occupy and exclude women from positions of economic and political power; male roles have greater behavioral and economic options, including the option of oppressing women . . . and marriage is an institution of personal and sexual slavery for women."[13] It is unlikely that men will give up power and privilege at the institutional level unless they are forced to do so or convinced that it is in their best interest. Therefore, the third level of change may be slow in coming.

The fourth level of change Smelser identifies is the institutional value system, which dominates all governmental policies as well as the cultural norms that influence individual behavioral. Our general values are those which support democracy and capitalism, though not necessarily in that order. Some feminists believe that to institute any gender-role change, we must institute changes in basic values and thus in the economic and political systems. They believe that the oppression of women (and to some extent that of men in poorer classes) stems from the structure of capitalism. They reason that (1) the development of private property gave men resources with which to dominate women, (2) women were defined as property under capitalism because of their capacity to reproduce and give the society new workers, (3) because of the domestic labor of women, society gets two workers for the price of one— "surplus value" is produced, and the worker gets no benefit, and (4) the existence of a reserve army of cheap female labor suppresses wages for all workers.[14]

POSSIBILITIES FOR THE FUTURE: IDEAL AND REAL

We now have a theoretical model for various levels of possible change in traditional gender roles. We are also aware of demographic and other changes that have taken place in our society that may influence any move toward more liberalized roles. Let us now use these models to assess the possibilities and probabilities of change.

The Ideal: One Person's Conception of a Better Future

If gender-role change is to occur at the individual level, men and women will have to socialize their children in a different manner. They will have to be aware of their own expectations and their behavior toward their children, and they will have to monitor the environment in which their children grow and play so that it is nonsexist. Both sexes will get all types of toys and equal chances to participate in sports and passive activities. Language, books, television, and school will change to reflect the different non-sex-typed options open to men and women. In the home environment provided for these children, men and women will share child care and employment in whatever ratio they choose. This option contains great possibilities for more marital and family satisfaction if we can judge from the reports of androgynous parents that their marital satisfaction stays high and does not experience the usual decline as time passes.[15]

On a more theoretical level, what kind of liberalized gender roles would we have if socialization changed in this fashion? Androgyny is only one possibility. It seems likely that there would be a multistage transition with a different kind of liberalized gender-role operation at each stage. Bernard has suggested various possible futures.[16] One possibility is a world not too different from the one we have now except that women would have more power. We suggest that this would be a first stage of transition to liberalized roles and might include two substages. In the first substage, women would be likely to assimilate the male value system. However, as they gained more power, they would insist on an equal recognition of what have been known as feminine values, such as cooperation and nonviolence. Thus, the second substage of liberalized gender roles would be one of cultural pluralism in which both masculine and feminine values were given equal status.

As liberalized gender roles were more widely accepted, a second stage might develop that would be a unisex or melting pot system. This might occur in conjunction with a steady-state, technological, highly developed society. Finally, in the third stage, androgyny might come into being and gender roles would be transcended. As Bem said, "If androgyny comes to exist in the culture, the concepts of masculinity and femininity will cease to have such content and the distinction to which they refer will blur into invisibility."[17] Gender roles would be transcended, or to put it another way, sex would simply no longer be a requisite characteristic for the occupancy of social positions or the performance of social roles.[18]

On the organization level, family roles would reflect the commitment to equality in other ways. Men as well as women would be free to choose not to work, and the definition of work would include domestic chores.[19] More women and men might choose to stay single or not to have children. Fewer women and men who chose to work would have to be "supermoms" or "superdads" because institutional hours would be more flexible and day care would be available. Men and women would choose their occupations according to their unique talents and predispositions, not their gender. Education and periodic job retraining would be a available to all. There would be national health care of some sort and probably a minimum wage so that everyone could live in a decent manner. Women would have the right to control their bodies by having access to contraception and abortion.

On the institutional or societal level, there would be a real commitment to liberalized roles. Women—and some men—would form a political bloc vote that could elect representatives who would institute new laws and speed the expansion of change. There would be changes in the income tax and Social Security laws so that they did not discriminate against the poor and women; there would be enforcement of equal opportunity for employment legislation. The government would actively ensure that adequate income, health care, education, and occupational training were obtainable by all citizens. There would also be a link between these changes and the world situation of growing population and limited food and energy resources. In this best of all possible worlds there would be a commitment to setting limits to growth, establishing population control, and living in harmony with the environment so that these other goals could be achieved.[20] It is possible, though not probable given our political history, that a new form of government or economy may arise that is not based on profit-oriented capitalism.

The values that would institute and sustain all these possible changes would have to be equalitarian and democratic in the best sense of the word. Such values might even include feminine norms about not using violent solutions to problems.

The Reality

Obviously, this best of all possible worlds is unlikely to come about at once and would be difficult to bring about even piecemeal. What kinds of changes can we realistically expect?

Biologically, it is likely that most men will continue to be larger and stronger than most women. This means that when physical power is important and there are no "equalizers," men are likely to dominate women. However, this strength advantage is likely to become less important as our society continues to refine its technology and be more oriented toward services.

Individual Changes.   Women will continue to bear children, but the burdens of pregnancy and child care will probably be lightened. More women are using contraceptives and planning smaller families. There is also a possibility of surrogate mothers for women who do not want to take time out from occupations. Of course, infants will still remain in a state of prolonged helplessness and will have to be raised by someone. If men do not participate more in child care or if institutional arrangements are not found for such care, many women may opt not to have children.

If there are any slight differences between the sexes in cognition or in predisposition toward aggressive behavior, they will probably disappear as different kinds of experience and training are made available to both sexes. We have already seen differences lessening; as more women have taken math and engaged in sports, their spatial perception has become very similar to that of men. Educators are already discussing ways of training boys in verbal abilities such as reading that will tap into their slightly different cognitive style.

Value Changes.   There also seem to be some changes on the value level. While men still agree that prescriptions for being tough and nonfeminine and having status exist as part of male role **norms**, they do not necessarily endorse these prescriptions.[21] Women also prefer a more androgynous model for themselves and the men in their lives.[22] Unfortunately, many men still prefer feminine women as the women in their lives,[23] although they are willing to endorse more equal roles in the larger society.

Pleck has pointed out the pleasures of men being able to express their emotions and get close to other men, to women, and to their children.[24] They are also enjoying relief from being the main breadwinner. However, he states that the domestic workload has changed little even in homes with androgynous parents. The mother does three-quarters of the household tasks and is getting madder about this division of labor.

There may also be more resistance to certain kinds of androgynous behavior in women. Kahn found that a male or female who cried and a male who became angry in a frustrating situation were seen sympathetically. However, women who got angry were not seen sympathetically, especially by men.[26] Other research shows that the woman who is seen as most successfully adopting male roles is the one who retains an element of womanliness.[27]

Goode has pointed out that men believe they are burdened more than advantaged; as individuals, they do not feel they are part of a conspiracy to dominate women. They are hurt that their "gifts of support" are being spurned by their wives and children, and they feel threatened. Goode believes that they will adjust when they can no longer dominate the system. He explains that many men are not living up to the stereotypes and are getting away with it. He also emphasizes that there is a worldwide demand for equality (of which women's equality is only a part) and that it is stronger and more persistent than it was in any previous epoch. He believes men as a sex are different from a dominating class, as they share few collective goals and women *can* enter the system. However, he also believes that men will resist the change to different roles.[28] They are unlikely to give up behaviors that are esteemed and lead to cultural success.

Lipman-Blumen has shown how the isolation of women from one another and their physical closeness to certain men keep them from developing the group consciousness that enables the powerless to revolt.[29] Epstein adds that the symbolic and actual segregation of women reduces their visibility and supports the belief that they do not perform adequately in male areas.[30]

We must also realize that while there may be ideological acceptance of change at an intellectual level, many people are not willing to institute changes in their own lives. For some a change away from traditional roles means a change toward uncharted territory and ways of behaving. A change in power relations may put some people at a disadvantage. We tend to fear change whether institutions serve us well or ill.

Unger warns that it is important not to confuse personality change with social change. "Because people become more androgynous does not necessarily indicate that they will be more tolerant of the androgyny of others."[31] Helmreich and colleagues have shown that there is little relationship between a person's score on an androgyny scale and that person's attitude about gender roles.[32] With all this possible personal change, what can we expect on the institutional level?

Institutional Change

The Economic System.   The values of profit-oriented capitalism underlie the other values (competitiveness, aggressiveness, achievement orientation) and structures of our system. Socialist feminists say that the oppression of women (and other poorer groups) stems directly from the structure of capitalism; many of them would also say that the oppression of women is only one aspect of the problems of an oppressive economic system.

What are the chances that the basic values of the economic system in this country will change? One writer suggests that the Republican dismantling of the welfare state in the 1980s may cause an electoral reaction that *could* produce a laborite or socialist alternative to the government if the Democrats cannot come up with an attractive alternative.[33] However, the political structure of the American government has given little chance to third parties, nor does it look as though there is mandate for overthrowing the government by force. In the near future, we will continue to live with the value system of profit-oriented capitalism, although the system may be modified somewhat by certain forces that are now at work.

American business has been built on a "bigger is better" foundation, on a belief that the growth of individual business as well as the growth of the economy is important. This tradition is strong, and institutions are slow to change even though the trend toward a steady-state economy without growth has been well established. If the economy does contract in the future, the switch to more conservation-minded, "small is beautiful" policies may stimulate change.[34] This stagnant economy will hurt minorities and women at first. In a period of less than full employment, women (the last hired) will be the first ones laid off or will be unable to find work.

As the economy contracts or stabilizes at a no-growth level and switches toward more service industries, other changes may take place. Fewer men will succeed because there will be less room at the top, and men may have to look for alternative ways to demonstrate masculinity. There is also a possibility that couples will be less achievement-oriented and have more leisure as the work is spread around. These trends are already evident and may lead to more androgynous roles.

The current period is still one of a heavy emphasis on the right of business to make a profit at almost any cost. Indeed, the rich are getting richer while the poor are getting poorer, and there is little the poor, including women, have been able to do about it. One sees clearly the influence of male-dominated economic institutions and the fact that those who have power and affluence will not willingly share it. Yet changes in the environment and the global economy may eventually modify the system.

The Family.   Other institutions are heavily intertwined with the economy. Socialist feminists state that women's domestic labor is an important source of value to the capitalist system. The ability to draw women from the home into the paid labor force when they are needed and to shunt them back to the home when they are not is also important for the economic system. It is no coincidence that the contracting economy has given rise to calls from rightist groups for the reestablishment of "family values." These values imply that a woman's place is in the home and that she should not take a job from a man who needs it. The outcry against sex education, abortion, and contraception can also be seen in this perspective. Women who have no access to sex education or contraception are likely to have larger families and may need to stay home and take care of them.

If these conservative values predominate, family roles are likely to remain traditional. A woman without an income is dependent and not equal. A man who is the sole breadwinner is not likely to share tasks and child care. A woman with several children and no income is unlikely to have the wherewithal to leave an unhappy marriage.

At the same time, we must remember that contraception is available and that women are opting to remain single longer, to have fewer or no children, and to pursue careers. Because of these factors, women have more leverage to gain equality in family roles. Thus, there are forces for and against change at the family level.

Religion.   Intertwined with family values is the position of religion. Conservatives buttress their arguments about women's place by referring to biblical passages and religious dogma. We noted before that religion is an important influence in black women's rejection of feminism. The fundamentalists claim that religious values prohibit interference with bringing forth life and that contraception and abortion are sins. They also claim that any form of sexuality—such as homosexuality—that does not result in procreation is a sin. Some denominations are allowing women to be ordained as ministers and are attempting to get rid of sexist language in the prayer books and hymnals, while others are helping conservative values gain ascendancy.

Education.   The expansion of education has advanced role change. Highly educated men are more likely to at least give lip service to equality for the sexes; highly educated women are more likely to be employed, to have fewer children, and to insist on equality in their families. Expansion of education has also entailed the creation of opportunities for women and minorities to get training and enter the system.

The conservative "get the government out of education" mood of the 1980s led to a cutting back of educational opportunities. Fewer student loans meant that fewer minority and female students were able to go to school. This combined with the economic climate to make college a place to learn a job, not a philosophy of life. However, more people are getting college degrees, and higher education usually correlates positively with liberal values.

The Legal and Political Systems.   The last two decades have seen a tremendous improvement in women's legal status in this country. Legislation has prohibited discrimination in everything from hiring and pay to the granting of credit. At the same time, much of this legislation is only as good as its enforcement and is also under attack. Protective laws still bar women from certain work, the ERA did not get ratified, and comprehensive child-care, family leave, and welfare reform legislation has not passed Congress. Poor women and blue-collar women in particular have been hurt by changes in welfare requirements and cutbacks in job retraining programs. While some reform legislation is being considered in Congress, there is unlikely to be a major initiative in favor of affirmative action or civil rights. In fact, women will be lucky to keep the gains of the last few decades. One hope is that as women are increasing their membership in occupations leading to political elites, they may have an opportunity to institute legal and political changes. They are unlikely, however, to constitute a voting bloc.

SUMMARY

As we assess the situation at all four levels of change, the institutional picture is gloomy. Individual awareness of the limitations of gender-role stereotypes has taken place in many areas and some attempts are being made to change individual behavior, but many of these attempts are stymied because the institutional structure perpetuates a different value system. Some of the institutions not only inhibit individual change but actively seek to restrict change and reverse the changes which have taken place. Perhaps after a period of retrenchment there will again be steps in a more liberated direction.

With all the inherent problems, women and men have a great stake in liberalizing gender roles so that they can reach their full human potential. People need not only to change on an individual level but also to ensure that institutional changes give birth to a coherent program for social change that will enable everyone to realize the great variety of human options. To do this, we must try to change in small, individual ways and then work up to attacking the societal Goliath with slingshots and arrows. We must, in Chessler's prescription for change, "withdraw energy and loyalty from interactions and institutions that are not supportive of . . . [our] best."[35] In this way, both women and men can realize their full potential not as members of a particular sex but as human beings.

ESSAY QUESTIONS

1. Discuss the ways in which traditional gender roles affect the physical and mental health of men and women and affect the flexibility of their behavior.
2. What is meant by the concept of androgyny? What are some of the problems in defining it? What are the possibilities for moving beyond it?
3. Discuss possible patterns of interaction between the sexes and patterns of valuation of the traits that societies can choose (for example, genocide, separatism, and cultural pluralism). What groups are likely to support each of these patterns?
4. Discuss what biology and past socialization predict in terms of change on an individual level in the future.
5. Discuss what the various institutions of society tell us we can expect in terms of future changes in individuals and institutions. (The institutions you should include are the economy, the family, religion, education, and the political system.)

EXERCISES

1. Imagine a particular situation and discuss how you would act in an androgynous fashion in that situation.
2. Imagine a society in which transcendence of gender roles has occurred. Describe what it is like.
3. Discuss your conception of the best of all possible worlds in terms of gender roles. Do you think it can be achieved?
4. Discuss what you see as the barriers to the achievement of such a utopia.
5. Draw up a five-year plan for yourself in which you discuss changes you would like to make in your social gender role. If you don't want to make any changes, discuss why not.

NOTES

1. Meda Rebecca, Robert Hefner, and Barbara Oleshansky, "A Model of Sex-Role Transcendence," in Alexandra Kaplan and Joan Bean, eds., *Beyond Sex-Role Stereotypes: Readings toward a Psychology of Androgyny* (Boston: Little, Brown, 1976), pp. 89–97.

2. Robert Hefner, Meda Rebecca, Barbara Oleshansky, and Virginia Norden, "Sex-Role Transcendence Study" (final Report under Contract NIE-C-74-0144 between the National Institute of Education and the University of Michigan, 1976); Rebecca et al. *op. cit.*

3. Margaret Mead, *Sex and Temperament* (1935; reprint ed., New York: Morrow, 1963).

4. Sandra Bem, "Probing the Promise of Androgyny," in Kaplan and Bean, *op. cit.* p. 59; Sandra Bem, "Gender Schema Theory and Its Implications for Child Development," in Mary Walsh, ed., *Psychology of Women: Ongoing Debates* (New Haven, Conn.: Yale University Press, 1987, pp. 226–244.)

5. Rebecca et al., *op. cit.*, p. 95; Hefner et al., *op. cit.*

6. Janet Giele, *Women and the Future* (New York, The Free Press, 1978), pp. 4–5.

7. Barbara Bounee Polk, "Male Power and the Woman's Movement," in Jo Freeman, ed., *Women: A Feminist Perspective* (Palo Alto, Calif.: Mayfield, 1984), pp. 589–606.

8. Giele, *op. cit.*, pp. 86ff.

9. Polk, *op. cit.*, p. 592.

10. *Ibid.*, pp. 592–593.

11. Giele, *op. cit.*, pp. 86ff.

12. *Ibid.*, p. 31.

13. Polk, *op. cit.*, p. 594.

14. *Ibid.*, p. 595.

15. John de Frain, "Androgynous Parents Tell Us Who They Are and What They Need," *Family Coordinator* 28 (1979):237–242.

16. Jessie Bernard, "Sex Differences: An Overview," in Kaplan and Bean, *op. cit.*, pp. 19–20.

17. Bem, "Probing the Promise of Androgyny," *op. cit.*, p. 59.

18. J. T. Spence, and L. Sawin, "Images of Masculine and Feminine: A Reconceptualization," in V. O. Leary, R. Unger, and B. Wallston, eds., *Women, Gender and Social Psychology* (Hillsdale, N.J.: Lawrence Erlhaum, 1985), pp. 35–66.

19. Kay Shaffer, *Sex Roles and Human Behavior* (Cambridge, Mass.: Winthrop, 1981).

20. Giele, *op. cit.*

21. Edward H. Thompson, Jr., and Joseph H. Pleck, "The Structure of Male Role Norms," *American Behavioral Scientist* 29 (1986):31–43.

22. J. D. Duke, "Sex Differences in Self-Perceptions among a Sample of College Students," *Psychological Reports* 62 (1988):993–994.

23. *Ibid.*

24. Joseph Pleck, *The Myth or Masculinity* (Cambridge, Mass.: MIT Press, 1981), pp. 131–134.

25. de Frain, *op. cit.*

26. A. Kahn, "Latitudes of Emotional Expressions in Women and Men" (paper presented at meeting of the American Psychological Association, New York City, September 1979), quoted in Rhoda Unger, *Female and Male Psychological Perspectives* (New York: Harper & Row, 1979), p. 433.

27. G. Tunnell, "Sex Role and Cognitive Schemata: Personal Perception of Feminine and Androgynous Women," *Journal of Personality and Social Psychology* 40 (1981): 1126–1136.

28. William Goode, "Why Men Resist," *Dissent* 27 (1980):181–193.

29. Jean Lipman-Blumen, *Gender Roles and Power* (Englewood Cliffs, N.J.: Prentice-Hall, 1984).

30. Cynthia Epstein, *Deceptive Distinctions: Sex, Gender and the Social Order* (New Haven, Conn.: Yale University Press, 1988).

31. Unger, *op. cit.*
32. Robert Helmreich, Janet Spence, and Carole Holahan, "Psychological Androgyny and Sex-Role Flexibility: A Test of Two Hypotheses," *Journal of Personality and Social Psychology* 37 (1979):1634.
33. Walter Dean Burnhan, "American Politics in the 1980s," *Sociological Focus* 14 (1981):149–160.
34. Giele, *op. cit.*
35. Phyllis Chessler, "Psychotherapy and Women" (paper presented at the American Psychological Association, 1970), quoted in Judith Laws, *The Second `X'* (New York: Elsevier, 1979), p. 375.

Glossary

Accommodation   A dual-career marriage style in which one spouse has the primary work responsibility and lesser home responsibility, while the other has the reverse.

Achieved Status   Social position achieved through one's own efforts.

Alienation   The feeling of being isolated from and unable to influence a particular area of life, such as one's job or the political scene.

Androgyny   A person's ability to function by using both "masculine" and "feminine" stereotyped behavior; also one of the categories on the Bem Sex Role inventory in which persons have high masculinity and high femininity scores.

Ascribed Status   Social position resulting from such inherited characteristics as family background, social class, race, and sex.

Assimilation   A stage of sex-role development in which the minority is incorporated partially or totally into the majority society on the dominant group's terms.

Attractive Alternative   An opportunity to do something as attractive as what you are now doing. (For example, a career may be an attractive alternative to marriage for some people.)

Biological Theories of Sex Roles   Theories assuming that behavioral differences between men and women are based on biologically inherited traits.

Clitoridectomy   The cutting out of the clitoris, the group of nerve endings that are the seat of a woman's sexual pleasure.

Cognitive Developmental Theory   A theory, developed by Kohlberg and others, holding that children progress at individual rates through mental stages, develop a belief that they are of a particular gender, and then want to do the behaviors that are appropriate for that gender.

Cohabitation   Situation in which two or more unmarried people of different sexes live together.

Conjugal   Pertaining to the nuclear family, as in the relationship between husband and wife.

Couvade   A custom in which the father takes to his bed when his child is born, pretends to have labor pains, and simulates fatigue after "giving birth."

Crowding Theory   The economic premise that an excess of workers in an occupation causes wages to fall because employers have many workers to choose from.

Cultural Context   The social culture in which an action or situation occurs. (The culture in which resources are gained may determine whether having resources leads to having power.)

Cultural Pluralism   A state in which many points of view, value systems, or orientations coexist and are equally valued in a culture.

Demographics   The study of population trends, including rates of mobility, fertility, death, and illness.

Equal Sharing   A form of division of labor tried by dual-career couples in which both husband and wife share work and family roles even though both may emphasize work roles more than family roles, or vice versa.

Ethnocentrism   The belief that one's own culture is the foremost and best of all cultures. (Thus one views other cultures through one's own cultural lens.)

Fear of Success   Women's fear of being successful in a masculine area arising from perceived negative consequences of success such as isolation, stigma, and possibly losing a chance to marry.

Feminine Mystique   The concept, identified by Betty Friedan and prevalent in the 1950s, that women are ultimately feminine if they stay home and raise numerous children.

Femininity   A set of role prescriptions in the U.S. culture that has included being passive, nurturing, and self-sacrificing; also a category on the Bem Sex Role Inventory in which persons have a high femininity score and a low masculinity score.

Feminists   Branch of the early women's movement that favored independence from any political organization. Informally used to refer to women who are in favor of equal rights for women.

Field Independence   Ability to distinguish a figure from a background, such as "finding the lion in the trees."

Formal Power   Power exercised through specific offices, institutions, or any legitimate authority like "head of household" or "leader."

Freudian Theory   Freud's theory of the development of sexual identity, which includes the child's progression through successive physical stages (oral, anal, phallic, latency, and adolescence), attraction to a parent of the opposite sex, and resolution of this attraction/conflict by identification with the parent of the same sex.

Gender Identity (also Sex Identity)   The sex (gender) one believes oneself to be.

Gender Role   Behavior, "masculine" or "feminine," prescribed by the culture for a particular sex in addition to the personality traits expected of that sex.

Genocide   The killing or attempted killing of all members of a particular group.

Homophobia   Excessive fear of homosexuality.

Human Capital   The investment in education, job training, and work experience that workers bring to a job.

Ideology   A set of beliefs that incorporates the norms and values of a particular culture.

Informal Power   Power exercised in nonofficial ways, perhaps by manipulation.

Latency   In Freudian theory, the period from about five years of age to the onset of puberty.

Lateralization   The ability of the brain to transfer information from one side to the other.

Marriage Gradient   Jesse Bernard's depiction of men's tendency to marry down to wives with lower social status and education.

Marriage Penalty   The extra taxes a married couple pays when both spouses work. (Their combined tax is greater than that of two single people making the same wages.)

Marriage Squeeze   Condition caused by the baby boom of the 1950s, when more women were born than men were born in the 1940s: if women marry older men, there will not be enough men for all the women to marry.

Masculinity   A set of role prescriptions for males in the U.S. culture which includes behaviors such as being a breadwinner and traits such as being unemotional, competitive, and aggressive; also a category on the Bem Sex Role Inventory in which persons have a high masculinity score and a low femininity score.

Matriarchy   Dominance by the women in a cultural system.

Menarche   The first menstrual period or beginning of puberty.

Modeling   Demonstrating a particular behavior or serving as a model for someone to imitate. (For example, a father models masculine behavior for his son.)

Nineteenth Amendment   Amendment to the U.S. Constitution, passed in 1920, that gives female citizens the right to vote.

Norms   The values and rules by which a society operates. They may be formally stated (as in laws) or unspoken but commonly understood.

Occupational Segregation Theory   A theory stating that the segregation of the sexes in different occupations or groups within occupations leads to a salary differential between men and women.

Politicos   A group of women who, in the early years of the women's movement, felt that their allegiance was primarily to political groups such as the Socialist party and only secondarily to women's interests.

Power   Ability to influence the actions of others so that they behave in ways that one desires.

Preference and Process   The idea that the process of achieving a certain behavior may lag behind the preference for that behavior, and vice versa.

Private Sphere   The household or domestic arena, which is set aside from the public arena of paid work.

Protestant Work Ethic   The belief that work and related success demonstrate one's moral worth (based on the early Protestant idea that God would show the faithful that they were "saved" by allowing them to be successful).

Public Sphere   Social, economic, and political interaction outside the household or domestic arena.

Radical Feminists   A group in the women's movement that believes women's issues are part of a general revolutionary struggle.

Resource Theory   The theory, developed by Blood and Wolfe, that those who bring resources to the family will gain power in the family.

Rites of Passage   Various rituals or special occasions that mark the transition from one status in life to another, as from child to adult.

Role Homophily   The theory, proposed by Simpson and England, postulating that similar marital roles (such as both spouses combining work and family commitments) build marital solidarity.

Secondary Workers   Workers (mostly women) who are not considered primary, full-time workers and who are often shunted out of the market when there are not enough jobs to go around.

Segregation   Separation of groups by race, sex, or class in one or many areas, such as housing and occupations.

Separatism   The stage in a model of possible sex roles in which the sexes are segregated but feminine values dominate in the culture.

Sex as Status   The idea that sex is a status, like race or class, that determines one's occupational choices and life opportunities.

Sex Role   Behavior connected with physical sex, such as ejaculation or menstruation.

Sexual Scripts   Behavior that society deems appropriate for each sex, including occupational choice, parenting, and the like.

Social Learning Theory   A theory of sexual identity formation, developed by Mischel, Bandura, and others, according to which a child learns sex-role behavior by imitation and later identification with same-sex models.

Social Position   Position or status in society that results from one's sex and can determine one's social role and opportunities.

Social Role   The behavior that goes along with certain social positions in society. (For example, the social role of husband encompasses certain behaviors, such as being a breadwinner.)

Socialization   The process of learning the values and behavior expected by a particular culture.

Sociobiological Theories   Theories that link human social behavior to the biological development of early humankind.

Stages of Development   The stages a country or culture goes through as it evolves from a hunting-and-gathering or other type of subsistence economy to an industrial economy.

Stereotypes   Generalized and exaggerated descriptions of a group.

Stratification   Differential ranking of people, values, and groups.

Subsistence   The minimum food or shelter necessary to support life. A subsistence economy is one in which only a bare minimum of food is available.

Suspect Group   A group that the legal system assumes may be discriminated against and whose cases are therefore automatically reviewed.

Transcendence of Sex Roles   Moving beyond stereotyped sex-role behavior so that the concepts of "masculine" and "feminine" lose their meaning.

Undifferentiated   One of the categories on the Bem Sex Role Inventory in which both masculinity and femininity scores are below the median for the sample.

Indexes

Name Index

Subject Index

Abortion, 161, 293–297, 345
Abuse, wife, 256–261
Accommodation, patterns of, 230–231
Achievement orientation, 54–56
Act for Better Child Care (ABC), 331, 350
Adolescence, 119–121, 153–154
   dating in, 155–159
   friendship in, 154–155
   homosexuality in, 169–172
   sexuality in, 160–172
   socialization in, 119–143
Advertising, gender roles in, 102–104
Affirmative action, 324–325
Age Discrimination Employment Act of 1967, 324
Aggression, 7–8, 52–53, 79
Aging, double standard of, 209
AIDS, 169, 241, 242
American culture, 26–28
American family (see Family)
Anal stage, 77
Analytic ability, 48–49
Androgen insensitivity, 40
Androgenital syndrome, 39–40
Androgens, 40, 42
Androgyny, 7, 10–11, 383, 384
   elderly and, 212–213
Anorexia nervosa, 132–133
Anxiety, 55
Appearance, improving, 75
Assimilation, 383

Attractiveness, physical, 122, 131–133

Beauty, 8, 132–133
Behavior, cross-cultural differences in, 56–58
Behavioral sex differences, 52–54
Bem Sex Role Inventory, 10–11
Biological differences, 4
Birth control, 292–293
Birth process, regulating, 291–292
Birth rates, declining, 204
Black families, 250–256
Black feminism, 358–360
Black marriage, 254
Black matriarchy, 253
Blacks:
   division of labor of, 253–254
   extended family in, 255–256
   fear of success by, 140
   marital satisfaction in, 254–255
   in school, 110–111
   in sports, 125
   on television, 100
   women:
      in labor force, 322–323
      situation of, 252–253
Blue-collar families, 242–250
Blue-collar jobs, women in, 320–322
Blue-collar workers, 306–307
Body build, 122
Body language, 96–98
Books for children, 104–107